NAPOLEON'S AMERICAN PRISONERS

NAPOLEON'S AMERICAN PRISONERS

Anne Morddel

THE BOYDELL PRESS

© Anne Morddel 2025

All Rights Reserved. Except as permitted under current legislation
no part of this work may be photocopied, stored in a retrieval system,
published, performed in public, adapted, broadcast,
transmitted, recorded or reproduced in any form or by any means,
without the prior permission of the copyright owner

The right of Anne Morddel to be identified as the author of this work has been
asserted in accordance with sections 77 and 78 of the
Copyright, Designs and Patents Act 1988

First published 2025
The Boydell Press, Woodbridge

ISBN 978 1 83765 116 0

The Boydell Press is an imprint of Boydell & Brewer Ltd
PO Box 9, Woodbridge, Suffolk IP12 3DF, UK
and of Boydell & Brewer Inc.
668 Mt Hope Avenue, Rochester, NY 14620-2731, USA
website: www.boydellandbrewer.com

Our Authorised Representative for product safety in the EU is Easy Access
System Europe – Mustamäe tee 50, 10621 Tallinn, Estonia,
gpsr.requests@easproject.com

A CIP catalogue record for this book is available
from the British Library

The publisher has no responsibility for the continued existence or accuracy
of URLs for external or third-party internet websites referred to in this book,
and does not guarantee that any content on such websites is,
or will remain, accurate or appropriate

*To my children,
To my nephews,
and
in memory of
Reuben Hathaway,
an American merchant seaman from Boston
who died in a French prison in 1809*

CONTENTS

Acknowledgements	viii
Introduction	1
PART ONE – FROM MERCHANT SEAMAN TO PRISONER OF WAR	
1. The Early Republic Merchant Seaman	11
2. Sailing into Europe's Wars	29
3. Captives	44
PART TWO – TRAPPED IN A THORNY MAZE	
4. The French in Control	77
5. The American Diplomats in France	97
6. A Seaman's Citizenship	125
PART THREE – ÉLARGISSEMENT – RELEASE	
7. "Bad prizes", Passengers and Compassion	152
8. Trading Information for Freedom	165
9. Fighting for the French	175
10. Negotiated Releases	188
Conclusion	211
Epilogue	214
Appendix A – American Prisoners Who Were Released	218
Appendix B – American Prisoners Who Escaped	224
Appendix C – American Prisoners Who Died in France	227
Bibliographic Essay	230
Primary Sources	246
Bibliography	267
Index	276

ACKNOWLEDGEMENTS

So many people contributed to the research for this work: archivists, librarians, friends, family. Much of the research for this book was done during the lockdowns of the pandemic in 2020, when no travel was possible. Prior to that, though I visited many archives in France and some in Britain, it was not possible to travel to all of the countries where the archives, libraries and institutes that hold the documents used for this research are located. The Internet, postal services and the kindness of many more than sufficed. At each facility contacted, the staff shared their expertise and time and were enormously generous and helpful in sending copies. Where large amounts of copies were needed, more than even the most generous staff could provide, far-flung friends and family took days off work to go to unfamiliar locations to film documents and registers of little interest to them. Without all of their help, the pieces of the story this book tells never would have come together. Naming them here is the best that one can do by way of expressing my gratitude.

Madame Son Bernard at the *Service Historique de la Défense*, Valerie de Wolf, Christèle Tabusse, Thierry Pin, Isabelle Geoffroy, Karim Korchi, Nadia Bouzid, Gilles Poizat at the *Archives nationales*, Kim Y. Mckeithan, Nathaniel Wiltzen, Kirsten Carter, Cathleen Brennan, Sondra Duplantis and Damani Davis at the National Archives, A. Cronin, Ms. Cook and Sabina Beauchard at the Massachusetts Historical Society, Mr. Groom at the Staffordshire Record Office, Mallory Herberger and Ms. Westwood at the Maryland Center for History and Culture, Emily at the Houghton Library, Harvard University, T. Kiter at the New York Historical Society, Adam Minakowski at the Nimitz Library, C. Murphy and T. Link at the Maine Historical Society, Elizabeth Oldham at the Nantucket Historical Association Research Library, T. Potter at the Philadelphia Maritime Museum, Deana Preston at New York State Parks, Marybeth Quinlan at Mystic Seaport Museum , Holly Snyder at the John Hay Library, Brown University, Ms. Thayer in Special Collections at the University of Vermont.

Researchers, readers, translators and legal advisors, friends and family: S.D.C. Poupel, H.S.K. Poupel, Tyler Dodge, Nicola Scott-Francis, Joseph Allegro, Diane Boumenot, H.S. Robinson, John Morris, Isabelle Sonntag, Polina Khomenko, Iryna Balytska, Rebekah Finch, and Brian Cooper.

INTRODUCTION

From 1803 to 1814, more than 1500 Americans were held as prisoners of war in France. Nearly all of them were merchant seamen.[1] They were taken prisoner when the vessels on which they were working were captured at sea by French privateers or were shipwrecked on French shores. They were taken in to French ports, held in local jails, then marched to prison camps, or depots, in the interior, where they were held with and as if they were British prisoners of war, *les prisonniers de guerre anglais*.

France (like Britain) followed the custom of, when a vessel flying the flag of an enemy country was captured in time of war, the crew were to be treated as if they had the same nationality as the vessel's flag. Thus, these American seamen went to prisoner of war depots because they had taken work on a British merchant vessel which was then captured by the French. Additionally, during part of this time, Napoleon issued decrees targeting American shipping specifically, seizing American vessels in French ports or encouraging French privateers to capture them at sea. As France had no prison depot designated for Americans, the crews of those vessels were also sent to the depots used for British prisoners of war.

For the entirety of the period, the American Minister Plenipotentiary and consuls in France struggled to obtain their countrymen's release, on the grounds that the United States was neutral in Europe's wars and so, American citizens could not justifiably be held as prisoners of war. They had one large and a few smaller successes when Napoleon allowed some Americans to be released and sent home. Towards the end of the Napoleonic Wars, in June 1812, the United States declared war on Britain, and the latter became the shared enemy of both France and the United States. This should have brought about the release of all of the American prisoners, as the American diplomats argued and, initially, Napoleon agreed. However, through the chicanery of some Americans, the majority were held until the end of the European wars in 1814, when there was a general release of prisoners of war of all nationalities.

---

[1] Included among them were fewer than a dozen people who were not mariners: some passengers, a supercargo, a family with children.

This book tells the story of these American seamen prisoners in France, often in their own words, for they wrote many letters. It also describes the officials and the laws that ruled their lives at work on ships and on shore in order to explain how they came to be in prison and the success or failure of the efforts made to free them. It straddles a number of subject areas, particularly those of prisoners of war and maritime social history, but it also touches on developing concepts of nationality and citizenship, the nascent consular corps of the United States in France, ministerial administration in Napoleonic France, privateering, the Napoleonic Wars and the War of 1812. As such, it approaches this telling from both the tradition of history from below (or "history from the bottom up"), in detailing the lives of people who worked in a labour force that was usually treated as a mass of nameless, inarticulate and illiterate unknowns,[2] and, at the same time, from the more familiar tradition of history that describes the laws, decrees, actions and decisions emanating from the rulers, politicians and government bodies that affected events and lives.

The research began with the seamen prisoners, with collecting their names from prison lists held in the military archives of the *Service Historique de la Défense*, in Vincennes, then adding to each man's file any bits of information about him found in numerous archives and libraries in France, the United States and Great Britain: prisoner of war lists, shipping records, naval records, crew

---

[2] My interest in "history from below" stems from an inherent sense of practicality, from a desire to understand what grand statements about sweeping historical events mean in practical reality, e.g., how did these events happen and who were the people who actually performed the many actions that comprised these events? Moreover, this book does not come from digging deeper into a historical period to find the people at the "bottom", but from finding them first and placing them within history. For giving me more form and discipline to this approach, I am indebted to the works of a number of historians, initially those of the Annales School; later, as I concentrated on seamen: *The Many-Headed Hydra: Sailors, Slaves, Commoners, and the Hidden History of the Revolutionary Atlantic*, by Peter Linebaugh and Marcus Rediker. Gibraltar: Beacon Press, 2000; "Jack Tar in the Streets: Merchant Seamen in the Politics of Revolutionary America", by Jesse Lemisch, in *The William and Mary Quarterly*, 25:3 (July 1968). However, these works are, by definition, not truly "history from below" because they are observations and analyses of the writings of the "marginalised" by those of the very sex, race and profession that, in previous generations, marginalised them. I am even more indebted, therefore, to the seamen and sea captains who wrote their stories and, especially to the publishers who printed those stories, or the archivists who preserved them. The most important of these is surely Richard Henry Dana, Jr.'s *Two Years Before the Mast*. Harper & Brothers, 1840, though he was only briefly a seaman, and James Durand's *The Life and Adventures of James R. Durand: During a Period of Fifteen Years, from 1801 to 1816: in which times he was impressed on board the British fleet and held in detestable bondage for more than seven years*. Chapman Billies, 1995.

lists, muster books, pay books, seamen's letters, captains' reports, financial records relating to privateers, prize cases, ministerial correspondence and ministers' reports to Napoleon, consular correspondence, post-war memoirs. A seaman's name can crop up in any of them, as a witness, as a crew member, as a victim. Further sources could be accessed thanks to a field of research that is still scorned by historians, genealogy, which has been the driver of the availability online of a mass of sources, many of them archival, that can be used to research ordinary individuals: death, marriage and birth records, historic newspapers of both large and very small towns, census returns, tax records, family histories (which so often show the families' merchant seamen as simply "lost at sea", vanished) and, most importantly, Seaman's Protection Certificate application affidavits.

Paul A. Gilje wrote that, because of his "willingness to sail under almost any flag", their youth and lack of property, a seaman was "exactly the kind of person most difficult to trace."[3] His meaning is that records about the seaman's work on a vessel could be in the shipping and customs archives of any country under the flag of which he sailed, he was too young to have married and appeared in civil registrations, and, not owning property, he cannot be traced through land and tax records.

In reality, thanks to archives' digitizing their records and finding aids and putting them online, seamen are not quite so difficult to research as they once were, but traces of details about them are spread across many types of sources, making them difficult to study as a group or a tribe. Merchant seamen do not often appear as a group in a single record type, such as in Ira Dye's study of the Philadelphia Seaman's Protection Certificate Applications and the General Entry Books for American Prisoners of War of British prison depots.[4] Single sources permit the gathering of the same information about a group of individuals, in largely the same format, which can be mined for statistics, but which provide little insight into the individuals. This book's research gradually revealed the lives of individual seamen during this period based on many sources that varied in the kind of information gathered and the way that it was written. As more and more information was gathered about him, each man's individuality became evident; at the same time, it was their commonalities that have made possible the telling of the overall story.

---

[3] Paul A. Gilje. "The Elusive Jack Tar", *Pirates, Jack Tar, and memory: new directions in American maritime history*, eds Paul A. Gilje and William Pencak. Mystic: Mystic Seaport Museum, 2007, p1.

[4] See Ira Dye. "Early American Merchant Seafarers", *Proceedings of the American Philosophical Society*, Vol. 120, No. 5 (1976); and "Physical and Social Profiles of Early American Seafarers, 1812–1815", *Jack Tar in History: essays in the history of maritime life and labour*, eds Colin D. Howell and Richard J. Twomey. Fredericton: Acadiensis, 1991, pp220–235.

However, the variety of sources used here, each with different data elements and in different formats, makes for a statistician's nightmare. No tidy database can be constructed from the data or accommodate the biographical material accumulated. What statistical extrapolation has been possible demonstrates that this group of American merchant seamen held as prisoners of war in Napoleonic France has slipped through the net of most of the historiography of the subject areas mentioned above. Consular histories make almost no mention of the efforts of American consuls in France to help seamen in distress.[5] In discussion of emerging concepts of citizenship as relates to seamen, the English-language historiography concentrates on the tension between Britain and America and the problem of impressment, with the creation of the identity document, the Seaman's Protection Certificate; none looks at American seamen in French prisons in the same period. The historians of naval battles write of the vessels and their actions and fates but make little mention of their crewmen taken prisoner and sent to France. Historians of prisoners of war do indeed discuss the prisoners of the Napoleonic Wars, especially those from Britain and Spain, but not the Americans. While much has been written about the American prisoners of war at Dartmoor in Britain during the War of 1812,[6] again, nothing about the Americans in France during the Napoleonic Wars.[7] But for Le Goff, most of those writing about French privateers, make no mention of the more than 220 American seamen prisoners who were on the

---

[5] See Silvia Marzagalli. « Le réseau consulaire des États-Unis en Méditerranée, 1790–1815: logiques étatiques, logiques marchandes ? », Arnaud Bartolomei et al., *De l'utilité commerciale des consuls. L'institution consulaire et les marchands dans le monde méditerranéen (XVIIe–XXe siècle)* École française de Rome (2017), which examines the commercial activities of the consuls but not at all their efforts to help seamen. For studies of the earliest and one of the most important diplomatic efforts to aid American seamen, that for the mariners held prisoners by the Dey of Algiers, see Richard B. Parker, *Uncle Sam in Barbary: a Diplomatic History.* Gainesville: University Press of Florida, 2004; and Frederick C. Leiner. *Prisoners of the Bashaw.* Yardley: Westholme, 2022.

[6] Amongst the many works on the subject, see especially Alan Taylor, *The Civil War of 1812: American Citizens, British Subjects, Irish Rebels & Indian Allies.* Vantage Books, 2010 for a balanced explanation of Britain's treatment of American prisoners of war and the "Dartmoor Massacre".

[7] An exception is Nathan Perl-Rosenthal, *Citizen Sailors: Becoming American in the Age of Revolution.* Cambridge: Belknap Press, 2015, who discusses briefly a single case of a man held in France, Benjamin Sanborn, Jr., of the *Neptune*, a ship seized by the French in 1808. Perl-Rosenthal cites the "Miscellaneous Correspondence Regarding Impressed Seamen" (Record Group 59) in NARA, which could contain information on a few more of the men held in France, and which it was not possible for me to access.

crews.[8] (Specific historiographies are discussed in more detail in the chapters that follow.)

This absence of discussion of the French-held American seamen in the historiography is reasonable, if the numbers are considered. Only about thirty-five of the seamen who were prisoners in France also ended up as War of 1812 prisoners at Dartmoor and many of them were held as French, not American, prisoners, because they had been captured while on French privateers, making them prisoners of a different war. The amount of time and paper that Napoleon dedicated to these American prisoners was so little that they appear as no more than a passing mention in the truly vast amount (more than 60,000 books) written about him and about the First Empire. Looking at the historiography of the War of 1812 and the enthusiasm for it of the American community in France, discussion of that community's exploitation of the American prisoners held in France is negligible.[9] As fewer than eighty of the American seamen prisoners in France also had been impressed by Britain's Royal Navy, though the enormous canon of works on the Royal

---

[8] T.J.A. Le Goff. "The Labour Market for Sailors in France", *Merchant Organization and Maritime Trade in the North Atlantic, 1660–1815*, Research in Maritime History, No. 15, Olaf Uwe Janzen ed., International Maritime Economic History Association (1998). The early historians of French privateers list such details as their captures, home ports, owners and captains, the last often with some biographical notes. See M. Napoléon Gallois. *Les Corsaires français de la République et l'Empire.* Julien, Lanier, 1847 ; Maistre. *Les corsaires de la Manche sous la République et l'Empire*, unpublished thesis, Ecole de Guerre Navale, 1923; Henri Malo. *Les Corsaires: Mémoires et Documents Inédits.* (Société du Mercure de France, 1908); C.B. Norman. *The Corsairs of France.* Sampson, Low, Marston, Searle & Rivington, 1887; F. Robidou. *Les Derniers Corsaires Malouins: La Course sous la République et l'Empire, 1793–1814* (1910). For more modern works, which also ignore the foreigners on the crews, see Alain Demerliac. *La Marine du Consulat et du Premier Empire: Nomenclature des Navires français de 1800 à 1815.* Editions A.N.C.R.E., 2003; Patrick Villiers. *Les Corsaires.* Editions Jean-Paul Gisserot, 2007; Jean-Pierre Hirrien. *Corsaires! Guerre de course en Léon, 1689–1815.* Editions Skol Vreizh, 2004; F.L. Russell. *The French Corsairs.* London: Robert Hale, 1970; René Guillemin. *Corsaires de la République et de l'Empire.* Editions France-Empire, 1982; Gilbert Buti and Philippe Hrodej. *Dictionnaire des corsaires et des pirates.* CNRS, 2013. Additionally, scattered across the internet, on the websites of French archival facilities, can be found excellent and very useful introductory essays to finding aids, which do, on occasion mention the crews of the privateers.

[9] All of the many nineteenth-century works on the American privateers of the War of 1812 are filled with inaccuracies; even so, they continue as the oft-cited sources for most later works on the subject. Only one, by Edgar Stanton Maclay, *A History of American Privateers.* D. Appleton, 1899 mentions that the *True-Blooded Yankee* was manned by prisoners, though the details he gives are incorrect. See the Bibliographic Essay.

Navy and impressment includes works about Americans who were impressed as well as works about the British sailors held prisoner in France, they do not mention the few impressed Americans held with the British prisoners in France.[10] In each of these subject areas, Americans at Dartmoor, Napoleonic administration, the War of 1812 and American privateers, the Royal Navy, British prisoners of war in France, the number of Americans who were held prisoner in France and who were also included in the groups they discuss were quite few. Yet, as a group defined in its own terms, that of American merchant seamen held as prisoners of war in Napoleonic France, 1500 is not an insignificant number. Though they are small in number in those larger stories, here they are many and they form the central story.

James Monroe, when Secretary of State, in presenting a report on impressed seamen, in early 1812, added a comment concerning merchant seamen held prisoner in France:

> It is equally impossible from the want of precise returns, to make an accurate report of the names or number of citizens of the United States who have been compelled to enter into the French service, or are held in captivity under the authority of that government, ... the names of a few only, greatly below the number believed to be so detained, being within the knowledge of this department.[11]

This study aims to address that lacuna in the knowledge concerning the American seamen held as prisoners in France during the Napoleonic Wars.

The structure of the book is chronological, while going from the general to the specific. Part One explains how an American merchant seaman became a prisoner of war in France. It begins with an explanation of the work and place in society of merchant seamen of the American Early Republic, then looks at the maritime and navigational laws and European wartime regulations that impinged on the seamen and how that caused them to become prisoners of war and, lastly, examines in depth their capture, the prison depots, the seamen's long, brutal march and their life in the French fortress prisons. Part Two describes the complexity of the captive seaman's position. It explains the powers and the personalities of the officials, both French and American, who fought over or used them diplomatically, and how the seamen's citizenship

---

[10] See the many articles by Elodie Duché, most importantly her thesis, "A passage to imprisonment: The British prisoners of war in Verdun under the First French Empire". University of Warwick, 2014.

[11] James Fulton Zimmerman. *Impressment of American Seamen*. Port Washington: Kennikat Press, 1966, pp273–274, quoting the "Message from the President of the United States transmitting a report of the Secretary of State on the subject of impressment", which he notes is to be "found in a miscellaneous collection of executive documents of the Twelfth Congress".

was defined within that context. Part Three is about getting out. In illustrative vignettes, it details the different situations in which some seamen were released, and reveals how most of them were betrayed by the greed of their own countrymen.

A Note on Terminology

Firstly, most authors writing on the subject today have to decide whether or not to use the word "seaman", apparently for fear of the puerile titters of those who cannot spell. In the letters written by the seamen themselves and in the diplomatic correspondence about them, the word is used almost interchangeably with "sailor", with a slight preference for "seaman". Here, I use "seaman" to indicate a man working in the merchant marine, and "sailor" to indicate a man in a nation's navy.

Secondly, traditionally, ships have been referred to using the female gender pronouns, unnecessary since English, unlike Latin languages, has a gender-neutral pronoun. This is in the process of change. Lloyd's Register of Shipping and the Scottish Maritime Museum now refer to ships with the pronoun "it", as is advised by the more recent editions of the *Chicago Manual of Style* and the Style Manuals of the Government of Australia and of Associated Press. The Royal Navy continues to use "she". Here, I have opted for "it".

Thirdly, in the documentation produced by officials in early nineteenth century France, the United States and Britain, seamen who were Black and/or of African birth or descent were identified as such. (Some of the reasons for this are described in more detail in the paragraphs under the heading Sources on African-American Seamen Prisoners in the Bibliographic Essay at the end of this book.) While their motives for doing this may have been reprehensible, for the modern researcher, these identifications provide an opportunity to add to the knowledge of the careers of African-American seamen of the period.[12]

However, it must be noted that the records and archival material used in this work contain outdated, racist and discriminatory language. The documents cited show the historical racism of Britain, the United States and Napoleonic France, with the terms in them that describe Black, African or African-American seamen being offensive and inappropriate to modern readers. These words have been included only where necessary for illustrative purposes and are denoted with inverted commas (quotation marks). Additionally, while

---

[12] The most important works on this subject are: W. Jeffrey Bolster. *Black Jacks: African American Seamen in the Age of Sail.* Cambridge: Harvard University Press, 1997; Martha S. Putney. *Black Sailors: Afro-American Merchant Seamen and Whalemen Prior to the Civil War.* Evesham: Greenwood Press, 1987; Charles R. Foy. "Eighteenth Century French Black Seamen" (*Lumières*, No. 35, 2020); James Barker Farr. *Black Odyssey: The Seafaring Traditions of Afro-Americans.* Peter Lang, 1989.

the original creators of most of those sources were clearly thinking of race when they referred to a seaman as Black, its use here would be incorrect and obliquely perpetuating their racism. Because all but one (a Native American) of the seamen in this study who were referred to as "*noir*" were either born in Africa or were the descendants of Africans transported to North America, they are identified here as either African or African-American.

Lastly, I find the word "tar" or the pseudo-affectionate term "Jack Tar" to be pejorative. Its origin is British and refers to men of the lowest ranks in the Royal Navy because, it is thought, they wore hats and other clothing coated in tar, as so much was on ships, to make them waterproof.[13] This book is about American seamen who worked on merchant vessels and of whose headgear little is known. "Seaman", "sailor", "mariner", etc. are professions; "Jack Tar" is a caricature and a stereotype, and is both generalizing and demeaning. In spite of the fact that the term "Jack Tar" has been widely accepted and used by maritime historians to refer to any mariners of the Atlantic world, there are no "tars" in this book.

---

[13] William Little et al. *The Shorter Oxford English Dictionary On Historical Principles*. Oxford: Clarendon Press, 1973, Vol. 2, p2245.

PART ONE

FROM MERCHANT SEAMAN TO PRISONER OF WAR

1

THE EARLY REPUBLIC MERCHANT SEAMAN

This chapter looks at one generation of American merchant seamen in the larger context of maritime social history. The maritime social history is a fairly new field in historical study. Beginning with Harold D. Langley's *Social Reform in the United States Navy, 1798–1862*, which came out in 1967, and Jesse Lemisch's "Jack Tar in the Streets: Merchant Seamen in the Politics of Revolutionary America", which was published the following year, labour, or working-class, historical studies were applied to American mariners. Writing such histories was an uphill battle, as many historians wrote, against the overly romantic view of a seaman's life wandering the world's oceans. Another difficulty, and one that affects this work particularly, has been the effort to separate the study of the merchant seaman from that of the naval sailor. In *Between the Devil and the Deep Blue Sea: Merchant Seamen, Pirates, and the Anglo-American Maritime World, 1700–1750*, Marcus Rediker, writing about an era before the United States and thus, American seamen, existed, that "It is impossible to separate the work experiences and the cultural life of the merchant service and the Royal Navy in the seventeenth and eighteenth centuries."[1] There then were then a number of writings about every aspect of the lives of seamen and sailors of previous centuries, from their wages to their tattoos to their friendships to their masculinity.[2] With each decade, the research into who the merchant seamen were goes deeper, always hampered by the inevitable conflation with naval sailors.[3]

---

[1] Marcus Rediker. *Between the Devil and the Deep Blue Sea.* Cambridge: Cambridge University Press, 1987, p154.
[2] See Howell and Twomey, *Jack Tar in History;* and Gilje and Pencak, *Pirates, Jack Tar, and memory.*
[3] For more of this burgeoning historiography, see as well: Daniel Vickers. *Farmers & Fishermen: Two Centuries of Work in Essex County, Massachusetts, 1630–1850.* Omohundro Institute and University of North Carolina Press, 1994; Myra C. Glenn. *Jack Tar's Story: The Autobiographies and Memoirs of Sailors in Antebellum America.* Cambridge: Cambridge University Press, 2010; and Helen Watt with Anne Hawkins. *Letters of Seamen in the Wars with France, 1793–1815.* Woodbridge: Boydell Press, 2016. More recently, the two volumes of Cheryl Fury's *Social History of English*

Descriptions of merchant seamen are consistently generalizations and often derive from contemporary, highly prejudicial sources that describe them as both oddly dressed, slovenly, rowdy drunks on shore and death-defying, mightily agile heroes at sea. There are not enough descriptions of themselves from the seamen but it is hoped that, with more studies of their letters and memoirs, some of their thoughts and feelings can be learned.[4] The brief description that may reveal the most comes not from a historian or from a seaman, but from a mariner, a lieutenant commander in the United States Naval Reserve, writing in 1932, with all of the prejudices that are unpalatable today, in an effort to explain merchant seamen to naval sailors (by then, the two were quite distinct from one another). Summarized, his points are firstly that, because, sooner or later, every merchant seaman will have to make decisions concerning the lives of all aboard completely on his own, he will have a somewhat steely, unromantic clarity of thought; secondly, that the constant, close contact with shipmates, and the attendant lack of privacy combined with, at the same time, insulation from the rest of human society for long periods produce an extreme taciturnity; and, finally, that "man for man, gauging them by the yardstick of ability, the merchant seaman is the poorest paid worker in the world".[5]

There were just twenty years between the end of the American Revolution in 1783, and, on the other side of the Atlantic Ocean, the beginning of the Napoleonic Wars in 1803. During that period, a generation of merchant seamen reached maturity. Who were these men, the first generation of seamen born as Americans? How did they differ from their parents, who had experienced the American Revolution, and their grandparents, who had been British colonists? Most of these men were born during or just after the American Revolution and could not have served in the Continental Navy (America's first navy). That navy was disbanded in 1785. The United States had no navy again until the Naval Act of 1794 authorized its creation, with the construction of six frigates. It was another four years before the first of those frigates was launched. Thus, from 1785 to 1798, any Early Republic seaman was a merchant seaman, any seafaring family was not a naval family but a family of merchant mariners and shippers. Business was booming and these young seamen were needed to sail the ships laden with goods.

The majority of them had been reared in port cities, surrounded by the evidence of the recent war for independence. Every young seaman in New York City, for example, would have seen the exposed bones of the Americans who had died on the British prisoner of war ship in that harbour, the *Jersey*.

Seamen. Woodbridge: Boydell Press, 2012, though still primarily about English naval sailors, contains much on merchant seamen.

[4] The recent works by Watt and Hawkins and of Glenn (see the previous note) do just that with English, not American, seamen.

[5] Felix Reisenberg. "Merchant Seamen", *Proceedings*, Vol. 58, No. 5. (May 1932).

For many years after the end of the war, the sandy beaches of Wallabout Bay remained littered with the bones of men who died in the prison ships – one resident of the area described skulls lying about as thick as pumpkins in an autumn cornfield – while the abandoned black hulk of the *Jersey* slowly broke up out in the mud flats beyond.[6]

In Stonington and New London, Connecticut, a young seaman would have walked daily past the buildings and wharves shattered by the British attacks on those towns. Older people would have been talking about the war over the heads of the children; stories of battles would have been familiar to them.

The war and winning it had also altered old trade relationships with Britain and her other colonies but merchants up and down the eastern seaboard were energetically seeking and creating new relationships and finding new trade routes. Independence brought a certain insecurity and the young country needed to create on its own what had previously been given from the "mother country." The new governments, both state and federal, did all that they could to help American merchants and shipping with tax exemptions and commercial incentives.[7]

During the early years of the United States, the individual states were quarrelsome with one another. Cohesion was not an easy thing to achieve. If the states' representatives in Congress saw their home states as individual powers, so their inhabitants may have thought of themselves as citizens of a state or even of a town more than of a country. The new generation of seamen would have been coming to manhood in the midst of feverish rebuilding, of the both local and national patriotisms that competed against one another, and of an intensive increase in merchant shipping. Going to sea, for many young men, would have been the natural and obvious thing for a New Londoner or a New Yorker or a Virginian to do. They would also have had an awareness of, if not personal experience of, war and of the privations and cruelty endured by prisoners of war.

In the first decade of the nineteenth century, much as young seamen were required, for both the merchant marine and the new navy, they were also disparaged and distrusted. When the United States Navy was established, in 1794, it initially followed the structure and style of the British Royal Navy, in which

> ...every warship was like a little kingdom that was ruled with a firm hand by the captain, assisted by junior officers who were analogous

---

[6] Edwin G. Burrows. *Forgotten Patriots: the Untold Story of American Prisoners During the Revolutionary War*. New York: Basic Books, 2008, pp209–210.

[7] Glenn Stine Gordinier. *Versatility in Crisis: The Merchants of New London Customs District Respond to the Embargo of 1807–1809*. Doctoral thesis, University of Connecticut, 2001, pp17–18.

to nobles. At the bottom of this social structure were the seamen, who were characterized as serfs, peasants, or unruly rabble, but seldom as freemen...[8]

The disdain for ordinary merchant seamen was not unique to the English-speaking nations. The French considered their merchant seamen to be "blasphemers, thieves, mutinous, violent or querulous, lazy, refusing to obey orders unless punished."[9]

At the same time as having this very low opinion of sailors, the new United States Navy wanted only the best young men. They rejected anyone of "suspicious character" and they had so much distrust of those of whom they might approve that they required a recommendation from a "responsible citizen".[10] The incongruity of demanding the best of men but treating them as the worst meant that the new navy suffered a chronic shortage of sailors.

Since the Navy as an employment option was negligible, a seaman's remaining options were whaling vessels, fishing vessels, coastal traders, slavers, or deep-sea merchant vessels. These last went on voyages to the West Indies, to Europe, to Africa and, later, to China. The average seaman on these voyages, in his twenties or thirties, without the education to be a shipmaster, or the training to be a ship's carpenter or sailmaker, or the experience to be a mate, was hired, a voyage at a time, at the basic seaman's wage of about fourteen dollars a month.[11] The United States Navy was paying an able seaman from ten to twelve dollars per month.[12] Ordinary or common seamen received

---

[8] Harold D. Langley. *Social Reform in the United States Navy, 1798–1862*. Urbana: University of Illinois Press, 1967, p. viii.

[9] Christian Borde. *Les Consuls de France et le repatriement des marins du commerce et de la pêche: entre répression et humanitarisme (1804–1891)*. Consuls et services consulaires au XIXe siècle. Jörg Ulbert and Lukian Prijac, eds, Hamburg: DOBU Verlag, 2010, pp62–63. Translation by the author.

[10] Langley, *Social Reform in the United States Navy*, p74.

[11] Paul A. Gilje. "On the Waterfront: Maritime Workers in New York City in the Early Republic, 1800 –1850". *New York History*, Vol. 77, No. 4 (October 1996), pp395–426. Fenimore Art Museum, https://www.jstor.org/stable/23182552. [Accessed: 22 March 2019] 422. After demonstrations in the streets of New York in 1802, fourteen dollars became the agreed wage.

[12] With just a few frigates, the United States Navy did not, in its early days, require large numbers of men and so there was no form of conscription (termed the Selective Service) or impressment. Historically, the U.S. Navy has found its personnel through volunteers and did not employ conscription until the Second World War. See L.W. Hesselman, "Some Selective Service Aspects Of Interest To The Navy", *Proceedings* (Vol. 68, December 1942) and *American Selective Service: a Brief Account of Its Historical Background and Its Probable Future Form*, prepared under the supervision of the Joint Army and Navy Selective Service Committee (October 1939). The latter may explain why the Navy insisted on "only the best men", in its description of the consequences of the resistance of the states to anything federal: "Even when bounties

about two dollars less, or eight to ten dollars per month.[13] The salary alone should have inclined many seamen, as well as many unskilled men, to sign on to merchant vessels.[14] Hiring the unskilled, as Benjamin Homans had to do, could lose a ship, which happened to his in a storm. One of the passengers, the American consul to Bordeaux, William Lee, described the inexperience of the crew when the vessel ran aground and broke up:

> The sailors are much alarmed. None of them are good seamen, an unfortunate thing for us, for had we had a good crew, the Captain is of the opinion that we would have made our passage in fifteen or eighteen days. Not one of the men can steer the ship when it blows hard. The great demand for American seamen, with the high wages given, has induced many to take to this element for a livelihood that would do better to plough the earth than the seas. They now take anything that looks like a sailor, and many suffer for it.[15]

The merchant seaman found his work on a vessel in different ways. He could get a good position through friends and family, if they were in the shipping business, and many of the seamen from the smaller coastal cities did take their first voyages as boys on family-owned vessels.[16] If he were not in a shipping family but a young, urban man in New York City or Charleston or Boston, he may have gone to the offices of shipping firms or even just walked along the docks and asked at each vessel for work. Conversely, "captains and recruiters came to [seamen's] boarding houses looking for extra hands when a ship needed a full roster of men on deck before leaving port."[17] An experienced seaman who had been on shore for a while and needed work was probably staying in such a waterfront boarding house, and the boarding house

---

were offered, the volunteer system broke down. Conscription for the National Army was then proposed [in 1812], but the old prejudice in favor of the State militia was too strong, and it was decided to rely on it again." The recruits were "undisciplined mobs under untrained officers…[who] fled at the first shot" (p8).

[13] Langley, *Social Reform in the United States Navy*, p78.

[14] See especially Jesse Lemisch. "Jack Tar in the Streets: Merchant Seamen in the Politics of Revolutionary America". *The William and Mary Quarterly*, Vol. 25, No. 3 (July 1968), pp371–407. Omohundro Institute of Early American History and Culture, https://www.jstor.org/stable/1921773 [Accessed 28 March 2019], for more on the possible motives a young man might have had for going to sea.

[15] William Lee. Edited by Mary Lee Mann. *A Yankee Jeffersonian: Selections from the Diary and Letters of William Lee of Massachusetts, Written from 1796 to 1840*. Cambridge: Belknap Press, 1958, p5.

[16] Nathan Perl-Rosenthal. *Citizen Sailors: Becoming American in the Age of Revolution.* Cambridge: Belknap Press, 2015, p28.

[17] Jonathan Thayer. "Mapping New York City's Sailortown", *Seamen's Church Institute*. 1 August 2016. https://seamenschurch.org/article/mapping-new-york-citys-sailortown [Accessed 17 April 2019].

keeper might offer his or her services in finding him a place on a vessel.[18] A man may not even have wanted to go to sea but once he had fallen prey to a crimp (who may also have been one and the same as the boarding house keeper) he had no choice.

Langley describes how these parasitic crimps took advantage of seamen. Knowing that seamen received an advance and sometimes a bonus when they signed on to a vessel, the crimp operated by accompanying a man when he signed on and then taking his advance, usually as payment for extortionate debts run up in the boarding house. The ploy worked best if a man were already in debt but the crimp could lure him into debt quickly. Then, often by either drugging him or getting him drunk, the crimp got the seaman on board the vessel and in receipt of his advance, then presented him with a bill that was equal to or more than the advance. The seaman was trapped. Not permitted to leave the vessel, inebriated, and perhaps naïve, he gave all his money to the crimp, who strolled away to find his next victim.[19] It cannot be said that men who became merchant seamen through the entrapment of crimps truly chose their profession. Langley writes that the crimp was often compared to the pimp and the exploitative activity of the two is, indeed, comparable.

It would appear that another avenue of seeking employment, and much more, was Freemasonry. Membership in a Masonic lodge may have been instrumental in helping an American seaman find work, especially in a foreign port. There was at least one Masonic lodge specifically for mariners, as the lodge names often indicated, in nearly every port around the Atlantic Ocean. As well as having the wealthy and educated merchants, shippers, and captains as members, many also allowed common seamen to join.

As early as 1768, the lodge in Portsmouth, Rhode Island reported that so many of its members were at sea that a meeting could not be held.[20] The "Marine Lodge" of Falmouth, Massachusetts was founded in 1798 by a "Doctor and a few Sea Captains",[21] and the "Merchants' Lodge" of Liverpool in England had among its founders in 1780 "a ship's painter, a ship-owner, a ship's captain (who was also a privateer), a merchant who was also a ship-owner."[22] Twenty-five years later, Liverpool was the busiest port in Britain

---

[18] Gilje, "On the Waterfront", p399.

[19] Langley, *Social Reform in the United States Navy*, p76.

[20] Alain Doré. "*Histoire des Loges Maritimes, Première Partie*". *Triple-Point*, 18 April 2008, http://triple-point.xooit.com/t2322-Les-loges-maritimes-18e-19e-s.htm [Accessed 3 April 2019].

[21] Robert A. Greenfield. "A Brief History of Marine Lodge", Marine Lodge AF&AM. https://www.marinelodge.org/about-the-lodge/a-brief-history-of-marine-lodge/ [Accessed 28 March 2019].

[22] "Our History". Merchants' Lodge of Liverpool. http://www.merchantslodge.co.uk/our-history.html [Accessed 28 March 2019].

during the Napoleonic Wars and the members of the lodge then included "master mariners and ships' officers and ordinary seamen" as well as "Swedish sailors, merchants from New Orleans and a Spaniard".[23]

Every port in France had Masonic lodges, recently reopened after having been closed and banned during the Revolution.[24] The French mariners' lodges, *les loges maritimes*, were many. At the end of the eighteenth century, Marseilles had sixteen mariners' lodges, with the *Choix des Hommes Libres* composed of merchants and seamen; Brest had fourteen lodges, Bordeaux had twenty, Nantes and Toulon had thirteen each.[25] Naval hero of the American Revolution, John Paul Jones, had been a member of the lodge *Neuf Soeurs* in Paris before his death there in 1792.[26] By the time the Napoleonic Wars began, the American seaman who was a Mason could find a lodge in ports on both sides of the Atlantic, in the West Indies and in the ports around the Mediterranean, including those of the Ottoman Empire.[27]

Freemasons were issued with a certificate of membership, sometimes called a "Masonic passport", which would grant them entry to any lodge, anywhere in the world.[28] They also had various secret signs and handshakes by which they recognized one another. Some American merchant seamen boldly flaunted their affiliation by having Masonic symbols tattooed on their bodies, such as Masonic coats of arms or an "All Seeing Eye".[29] Once he had entered and been welcomed as a "travelling brother", a seaman who was a Mason may have found a lodge to have been a place for sober gatherings of camaraderie for those times when he was not of a mood to carouse or if he were a man who could not stomach alcohol. Though boarding houses "were the social, cultural and to some extent economic epicentre of the mariner's world while he was in the port…",[30] they also, as has been explained, threatened his

---

[23] "Our History". Merchants' Lodge of Liverpool.

[24] Philippe Henwood and Edmond Monange. *Brest un Port en Révolution, 1789–1799*. Rennes: Editions Ouest–France, 1989, p206.

[25] Alain Le Bihan and Alain Doré. "*Histoire des Loges Maritimes, Quatrième Partie*". *Triple–Point*, 18 April 2008, http://triple-point.xooit.com/t2322-Les-loges-maritimes-18e-19e-s.htm [Accessed 3 April 2019].

[26] Samuel Eliot Morison. *John Paul Jones: A Sailor's Biography*. Boston: Little, Brown, 1959, p394.

[27] Jan C. Jansen. "In Search of Atlantic Sociability: Freemasons, Empires, and Atlantic History", *Bulletin of the GHI* [German Historical Institute], No. 57, 2015, Fall issue, pp75–99, https://www.academia.edu/23329099/In_Search_of_Atlantic_Sociability_Freemasons_Empires_and_Atlantic_History [Accessed 3 April 2019] p86.

[28] Roger Burt. "'Wherever Dispersed': The Travelling Mason in the Nineteenth Century", Prestonian Lecture 2015. Exeter: privately printed, 2015, p13.

[29] Simon Newman. "Reading the Bodies of Early American Seafarers". *William and Mary Quarterly*, Vol. 55, No. 1, January 1998, pp59–82, p70.

[30] Thayer, "Mapping New York City's Sailortown".

financial security, for "once a sailor set foot inside such a place it was only a matter of time before he was broke and in debt to the landlord."[31] That seaman who had been fleeced by a crimping boarding house keeper once too often may have sought an alternative, for the daytime hours at least, in the local Masonic lodge. It may have been the only such place for him before the American Seaman's Friend Society, with its teetotal boarding houses, was founded in 1826, though that organization was not global and its superior and paternalistic view of the seaman as an infantile drunk needing to be saved would have contrasted rather sharply with the more egalitarian brotherhood of a Masonic lodge.[32]

The atmosphere within the lodges was reputed to have been quite democratic, with a fraternity where men called one another "brothers", and that allowed conversation across social barriers that would not have been acceptable in public.[33] This welcome would have extended to the African-American seaman who was a Freemason for, though some American lodges barred "men of colour", not all did so. Many other lodges around the world welcomed free "men of colour" who had Masonic passports.[34] At a time when American diplomacy was in its infancy and there were many foreign ports without an American consul or even commercial agent, this global network may have provided a sense of community or security to a seaman when far from home, the possibility of encountering other American mariner Masons, and perhaps even aid in times of need. In at least one case, Freemasons arranged the release of a prisoner.[35] Almost certainly, for a seaman who was also a Freemason, lodges filled with ship owners, masters, captains, merchants and other seamen could also have been places to learn of the next vessel out, even though all discussion of business was banned inside the lodges.

At the end of each voyage, in whatever port around the world, the seaman was unemployed again and again looking for a ship. In truth, he was, for all of his skills, a temporary worker. If he had been hired for a return voyage, he would be looking for employment in his home port. Alternatively, he could have found himself looking for work in a foreign port. This could have come about if he had been hired for the outgoing voyage only, or if he were abandoned, or if the owner-captain sold the ship on arrival at the destination

---

[31] Langley. *Social Reform in the United States Navy,* p61. He was speaking of naval sailors here but it was also true for merchant seamen.

[32] Margaret Creighton. "Fraternity in the American Forecastle, 1830–1870", *The New England Quarterly*, Vol. 63, No. 4 (December 1990), pp531–537. The New England Quarterly, Inc., https://www.jstor.org/stable/365917 [Accessed: 22 March 2019] p553.

[33] Jansen, "In Search of Atlantic Sociability", pp79–80.

[34] Jansen, "In Search of Atlantic Sociability", p97.

[35] Stephen Clubb, of whom much more below, was British and claimed, incorrectly, that his marriage to an American gave him citizenship of the United States.

port, a common practice at the time,[36] and left the crew to find their own way home. This last was the case with John Hale or Hail of Philadelphia. He had sailed on the *Boston* under Captain John Williams, who sold the vessel in Livorno (Leghorn) in May 1804. After some wandering and getting into a fight, Hale ended up in prison in France.[37] Some men, perhaps not able or wishing to spend all of their pay in an inn, signed on to the first possible vessel, whatever the nationality, languages spoken on board, or destination.

In Europe or the West Indies, if money were his object and he had no fear of danger, a seaman's vessel of choice might have been a privateer, the most lucrative, and also the most dangerous type of work, short of outright piracy. Before the War of 1812, America's neutrality meant that no American privateers were supposed to be at sea, but Americans turn up on the crew lists of privateers under the flags of both Britain and France during this period (as do Portuguese, Swedish, Danish and Prussian seamen). The crew list of the English privateer, *Hearn*, 16 cannons, captured by the French privateer *Brestois*, in 1810, as an example, had a first mate from New York and two American seamen on the crew.[38] A book of payments to the crews of French privateers out of Dieppe from 1805 to 1809 shows close to eighty American seamen on the crew lists of twenty-eight privateer cruises.[39] It is clear from the multi-national crew lists that seamen of all nationalities moved freely from one vessel to another, regardless of its registration or flag, and that the captains had no objections to hiring them.[40]

On board, the merchant seaman was under the absolute authority of the captain or master (who could also have been the owner, solely or in part), of the vessel, in a way that was not very different from on a naval vessel. The phrase for the captain's or master's power, that he came "next after God", seems to have been coined at least a century later, but it aptly states the complete and total power that the shipmaster had on his vessel; every rule and every law was his and his alone to make.[41] While both popular literature, and contemporary accounts have many stories of the Royal Navy captain, with a full complement of marines on board to enforce his rule, ordering

---

[36] Patrick Crowhurst. *The French War on Trade: Privateering 1793–1815.* Aldershot: Scolar Press, 1989, p59.

[37] *Guerre et Armée de Terre, Prisonniers de guerre français et étrangers* (1792–1874). SHDV. Yj19.

[38] *Archives de la Marine, Affaires maritimes, Quartier de Saint-Malo, 1689–1890.* SHDB. 1P10.

[39] "*Armements en Corse: règlement et répartition de parts de prises, an XII–1811*", *Tribunal de Commerce de Dieppe, AD Seine-Maritime,* 6 U 1/246.

[40] The only restriction seems to have been enemy nationalities. In this research, no French seamen have been found on British privateers or British seamen on French privateers after 1803.

[41] Memorial University of Newfoundland. "More Than a List of Crew". https://www.mun.ca/mha/mlc/articles/shipmasters/ [Accessed 10 April 2019].

punishments (usually flogging but at times more sadistic)[42] of any men who defied his authority, a merchant captain had no such military support.[43] He and the mate had to maintain authority over the crew with the promise of good pay, with charm and reason if they possessed them, or otherwise with their own brute force, if they possessed that.[44] Writing of unscrupulous captains, William H. Crawford, Minister Plenipotentiary for the United States in France, wrote to the Secretary of State that "Several complaints have been made to me by different vessels, that American Captains treat individuals belonging to their crews with great inhumanity..."[45]

If he could not enforce his rule over a particular seaman, or if the seaman were ill, a bad captain would rid himself of the man simply by abandoning him. Such an abandonment happened to John Clarke of Boston, who said he had "served on the [United States Navy's] *Constellation* under Commodore Truxton when it captured the *Insurgente*".[46] Clarke was on the crew of a merchant vessel in 1805 when he got into a quarrel with the captain, a man named Kennedy, who put him ashore at Blaye, near Bordeaux, where he was arrested by the local police.[47] Abandonment of crew in foreign ports was such a problem that the consul general in Paris, writing in 1802, said that shipmasters should be required to submit their crew lists to the consul on entering a port. The consul would then use the list to ensure that the master either hired the same seamen for the return voyage or ensured their voyage home.[48]

The 1804 case of a master, George Haley, of the *Brutus*, refusing to pay both wages and compensation after abandonning his mate, Benjamin Franklin Seaver, took a vicious twist, and is fully documented by the outraged consul

---

[42] Jean Choate, ed. *At Sea Under Impressment: Accounts of Involuntary Service Aboard Navy and Pirate Vessels, 1700–1820*. Jefferson: McFarland, 2010. There are numerous first-hand accounts of brutal punishments.

[43] Langley, *Social Reform in the United States Navy*, p6.

[44] Charles Tyng. *Before the Wind: The Memoire of an American Sea Captain, 1808–1833*. New York: Penguin Books, 1999, p89. Tyng, then the mate, tells of knocking down two mutinous seamen with a capstan bar, a long, heavy piece of wood used for turning the capstan.

[45] Crawford to Monroe. 20 September 1813. United States. Department of State. *Despatches from United States Ministers to France, 1789–1906*. Vol. 14. Microfilm copy.

[46] Thus, Clarke had been a naval sailor. The battle between the *Constellation* and the French *Insurgente*, took place in February 1799, off the Leeward Islands.

[47] *Guerre et Armée de Terre, Prisonniers de guerre français et étrangers* (1792–1874) Yj19, Yj29, and *Prisonniers de guerre anglais*, series Yj34–81, SHDV. Also: Clarke to Skipwith. 14 January 1807. Causten-Pickett Papers (1765–1916), Fulwar Skipwith Papers, Correspondence, LOC. MSS15420. Additionally: The Massachusetts Circuit and District Court Cases both contain a number of suits by seamen who were abandoned in foreign ports.

[48] Skipwith to Madison. 8 December 1802. United States. Department of State. *Despatches from United States Consuls in Paris, 1790–1906*. Vol. 1. Microfilm copy.

at Bordeaux, William Lee. Seaver had taken his complaint to the consul, who arranged an adjudication overseen by himself and two impartial captains. Both Seaver and Haley gave statements; the decision made was in favour of Seaver, requiring Haley to pay him close to 400 dollars, which he did not do. Seaver wrote a letter to Haley filled with insults and an ultimatum. Haley, now aided by his brother, the privateer Nathan Haley (of whom more below), who was living in France, denounced Seaver to the French police as a British spy.[49] This was an offense punishable by death. Poor Seaver was arrested and jailed.[50]

A particularly wicked case of abandonment was that of Benjamin Bean, an eleven-year-old orphaned boy from New York. In 1813, he was discovered alone, in rags and without money in London by J. Stoffers, who was probably Dutch, master of the *Calina*. The child had arrived in England on the *Flora*, which was sold there by the master, one Harkins, who simply "took no more notice of" young Bean. The War of 1812 was raging, so Stoffers "interceded that he should not be made prisoner as American born". He clothed and fed the boy and took him across the Channel to comparative safety at Dunkirk. There, he left him with the acting vice-consul for the United States, writing in his statement "I thought I could not behave more generously with a boy 11 years of age who buried both father and mother."[51]

A seaman's working life on board a sailing vessel was extremely hard physically, requiring strength, agility, dexterity, and stamina. He had to be able to climb masts and lines of great height, to furl heavy, wet sails in high winds while precariously balanced at that height, to remain alert on watches with little or broken sleep, to lift heavy loads of cargo into and out of boats and holds. Dangers were considerable: maiming or death by falling from a mast or spar, drowning after falling overboard or when a ship sank, being crushed by cargo or a broken mast, by fighting, by disease, by exhaustion. In just one of hundreds of cases of seamen being hurt or lost:

> ...a man overboard, who luckily recovered by a rope, though not without being much hurt by the rubbish that went overboard with him. His legs are considerably bruised, his face cut, and his eye dangerously wounded.[52]

It was not work for those who were clumsy or unwell or slow to react. Living conditions were unpleasant, crowded and the air below decks foul, smoky

---

[49] Lee to Madison. 6 October to 17 November 1804. United States. Department of State. *Despatches from United States Consuls in Bordeaux, 1783–1906.* Vol. 2. Microfilm copy.

[50] Seaver was released and went on to have a rather exciting career, dying a naval hero of Argentina in the Battle of Martin Garcia.

[51] Letter from J. Stoffers. 11 September 1813. *Correspondance Politique États-unis.* Arch. dip. 39CP/70. Microfilm copy.

[52] Lee, *A Yankee Jeffersonian*, p6.

and fusty. Food on a merchant vessel may not have been as bad as that on a Royal Navy vessel but, after a week or so at sea, became what today (and perhaps then as well) would be considered vile and inedible. Even the best of vessels would have had rats and the diseases that they and the parasites on them carried.[53]

Given that the state of public health in the early nineteenth century was quite low by modern standards, especially in the crowded conditions of a vessel or a seamen's boarding house, and that the average seaman's lifestyle and diet were not the best for promoting good health, he may not have been an entirely well man. Surely, before adulthood, he might have survived at least a couple of such deathly childhood diseases as scarlet fever, rheumatic fever, diphtheria, rubella and measles, any one of which could have damaged or weakened his body in some way. As port communities were "the first to experience the ravages of infectious epidemic diseases",[54] there was a good chance that he may also have had pneumonia, smallpox (which would have left him pock-marked), cholera, yellow fever (particularly if he visited Philadelphia, Washington, D.C. or Charleston) and, with increasing likelihood, tuberculosis. If he had been a seaman for long enough, he almost certainly had a sexually transmitted disease, bad teeth, and lice. If he had been impressed, his back might have been crisscrossed with the scars of floggings. After a few months of the work, he would have become muscular, or "stout" and, presumably, he would have been quite strong but, if he drank as much as he was reputed to have done, cirrhosis of his liver would have eventually weakened him. That and the bad food might have made him feel somewhat nauseous all of the time.[55] As so few

---

[53] A number of writers and historians have asked, with some incredulity, why. Would anyone choose such work, one that was so difficult, lonely, unhealthy and poorly paid? The very posing of the question reveals the economic, social and cultural privilege of the writer, as does their usual conclusion that it was for "adventure" (perhaps partly based on the fact that most seamen's, sailors' and soldiers' memoirs of the period include the word in their title). No one does the vile work of this world for adventure; they do it because they need the money to survive. For someone with nothing and in debt, the arrangement for seamen was particularly attractive; one could pay debts and have some fun on the advance pay, then have some weeks of free food and shelter, with the added benefit of being out of reach of any other creditors. See Linebaugh and Rediker, *The Many-Headed Hydra*...

[54] Gerald N. Grob. *The Deadly Truth: a History of Disease in America.* Cambridge: Harvard University Press, 2002, p72.

[55] Other than some documents, such as Seaman's Protection Certificate Applications and British prisoner of war entry lists, which state when men had smallpox scars, there is no systematic health data on early American seamen. Paul Gilje, in "On the Waterfront", and Ira Dye, in "Early American Merchant Seafarers", both discuss height, longevity and general health. For diseases prevalent in late eighteenth and early nineteenth century in America, see Grob's *The Deadly Truth*, noted above.

personal accounts exist, the state of his mental health can only be imagined, but seamen were also known to have a tendency toward violence, and to be prone to rampages and rioting in packs at little provocation,[56] which would, today, be examined in an individual as a mental health issue.

In 1813, David Bailie Warden, the consul in Paris, citing classical history, wrote:

> The debts and disputes of seamen, when in port, required frequent and prompt attention. Accustomed to privations and to slavish treatment, this brave and generous, though turbulent race of men, were guilty of gross excesses. Among the earliest commercial nations, undisciplined seamen were the same as in the present times…'An incorrigible race, whose fury is more difficult to quench than a violent conflagration. Hardened by crimes, they consider him as wicked who has not been guilty of some marked atrocity.'[57]

On shore in a foreign port, the seaman was not necessarily much better off than he had been in his home port. If, while at home, a seaman might have been unsophisticated and illiterate, and thus vulnerable, especially after drinking, to abuse, deceit and manipulation, how much more he would be so if he did not speak the local language. If, in American ports, flush with his pay after a voyage, he stepped onto the dock and into a crowd of boarding house keepers and brothel owners who "competed with each other in promising liquor and/or women to the sailors who would put up at their establishments",[58] he surely encountered the same in British or French or Spanish ports. Yet, just as some at home managed to avoid temptation and escape death to settle down and live a quieter life, so in foreign ports some found a place or person enough to their liking that they stayed, married and remained for the rest of their lives. The marriage registers of French port cities contain the names of quite a few American seamen, like that of Robert Johnson, of North Carolina, who married in Roscoff in the summer of 1809.[59]

The dangers a seaman faced when he signed on to a vessel were the result of his more or less freely made choice to do so, but this was not the case when he was impressed. For the seaman, being on any vessel that was stopped at sea by a Royal Navy ship brought the dreaded risk of impressment.[60] A

---

[56] Lemisch, "Jack Tar in the Streets". p399.

[57] David Bailie Warden. *On the Origin, Nature, Progress and Influence of Consular Establishments*. Paris, 1813, p18.

[58] Langley, *Social Reform in the United States Navy*, p61.

[59] Roscoff. *Registre des mariages, an XI–1812* (Johnson-Bian Marriage) 24 July 1809. *AD Finistère*, http://www.archives-finistere.fr/ [Accessed 20 March 2020].

[60] For discussions of impressment generally, see Denver Brunsman. *The Evil Necessity British Naval Impressment in the Eighteenth-century Atlantic World*.

British naval officer would board and take by force, essentially kidnap, the strongest and most skilled seamen. All men on board the victim vessel were hunted out by British officers and lined up, their names checked against the crew list; there was no point in a man attempting to hide. With years of experience in the Navy, the officer would have been expert at judging a man's health and strength at a glance, at spotting intelligence, or the lack of it, in a man's eyes, at recognizing a carpenter's or sailmaker's hands. They stripped away the best of the crew, whether they captured the vessel or not, leaving merchant vessels under-manned and less able to cope with a disastrous storm or to outsail a privateer.

On shore, it was the same. In ports around the Atlantic and Caribbean, the press gangs from Royal Navy vessels snapped up American seamen where they found them. In London, Kingston, Lisbon, Cadiz, Liverpool and elsewhere, American seamen were kidnapped and forced to serve an expanding British Navy perpetually in need of men. (There was no shortage of British males; the Navy simply did not want to pay them a fair wage. The inadequate pay and brutal treatment of seamen had already caused mutinies in the 1790s). Somewhere between 8000 and 15,000 American seamen were impressed by the Royal Navy. The high number of American seamen impressed by the British meant that the newly seized men often encountered other impressed

---

(Charlottesville: University of Virginia Press, 2013), which also covers impressment of Americans before and after the American Revolution; the most important work on the impressment of American seamen, almost all of them merchant seamen, remains James Fulton Zimmerman's *Impressment of American Seamen.* Port Washington: Kennikat Press, 1925. Nathan Perl-Rosenthal's *Citizen Sailors: Becoming American in the Age of Revolution* (Cambridge: Belknap Press, 2015) is based largely on the documentation of the impressment of thousands of Americans by the Royal Navy. Sara Caputo's excellent *Foreign Jack Tars: The British Navy and Transnational Seafarers during the Revolutionary and Napoleonic Wars* clearly states that her focus is on "continental European seamen in the British Navy" (p8) which clearly does not include American seamen. J. Ross Dancy's controversial The *Myth of the Press Gang: Volunteers, Impressment and the Naval Manpower Problem in the Late Eighteenth Century* (Woodbridge: Boydell Press, 2015) skirts the issue of impressed Americans almost completely: most American seamen who were impressed, according to Brunsman, were seized in and near the West Indies; Dancy's study concerns only the Channel Fleet, not any of the foreign stations; the majority of Americans were impressed at sea; Dancy does not discuss sea impressments as those were not done by press gangs; most historians of the subject agree that impressment increased dramatically from the beginning of Britain's wars with France, in 1793, and lasting until the fall of the French First Empire in 1814; Dancy deals only with a selection of Royal Navy ships commissioned between 1793 and 1801, the French Revolutionary Wars. Lastly, as Perl-Rosenthal has shown, the best sources on impressed American seamen are their letters, their documents of justification and the diplomatic correspondence between the Admiralty and American consuls; Dancy's sole source for details of seamen is the collection of muster books for the ships he studied which, as will be seen below, often disguised Americans.

American seamen on board the vessel. They met and spoke, received or gave advice on how to survive the dreadful situation. James Durand, of New Haven, Connecticut, wrote of such an encounter on the occasion of his impressment by the frigate, *Narcissus*, off Plymouth:

> They boarded our brig and they came below where I was asleep. With much abuse, they hauled me out of bed, not suffering me to even put on or take anything except my trousers.
>
> In this miserable condition, I was taken on board their ship……I refused [to work] telling him I was an American…..
>
> "If you will not work I'll flog you until you're glad to set about it," said the Captain. "Go below, for I won't hear another word out of you."
>
> Below decks, I found twelve more Americans who had been previously impressed. One of them told me that, when he refused to obey an order, the Captain had given him four dozen lashes. "Therefore," he said to me, "I advise you to do as you are bid."[61]

The brutality of impressment had life-shattering and lifelong consequences, if a man survived.[62] During the eighteenth and early nineteenth centuries, in addition to not paying seamen, the Royal Navy also did not want to spend the money to feed them properly or to care for them, causing the deaths through disease of approximately 5000 crewmen each year, enough men to man two

---

[61] James Durand. *The Life and Adventures of James R. Durand: During a Period of Fifteen Years, from 1801 to 1816: in which times he was impressed on board the British fleet and held in detestable bondage for more than seven years*. Sandwich: Chapman Billies, 1995, pp49–50.

[62] N.A.M. Rodger's fascinating *The Wooden World: an Anatomy of the Georgian Navy* (Fontana, 1988) changed the way people imagined life in the Royal Navy in the eighteenth century. He describes the Royal Navy fifty years before the period covered by this book, during the Seven Years' War, ending his study at about the time that the American Revolution began. The picture he and others, such as James Davey and J. Ross Dancy, paint is of life on a Royal Navy vessel that is more pleasant and less brutal than what I give here. These things are relative. There are contemporary accounts that describe a hellish life and those that describe one that is not so bad (none makes it sound a paradise). Comparisons of a sailor's life with that of a starving street urchin or a destitute, unskilled labourer are favourable; comparisons of that same sailor's life with that of a man who had a home and family, grew wholesome vegetables and had his own dairy cow are not quite so favourable. From the point of view of an impressed American merchant seaman, forced labour for a foreign power is an injustice, the measure of brutality notwithstanding. See also James Davey. *In Nelson's Wake: How the Royal Navy Ruled the Waves After Trafalgar*. New Haven: Yale University Press, 2015; and Dorothy Denneen Volo and James M. Volo, *Daily Life in the Age of Sail*. Evesham: Greenwood, 2002.

and a half ships of the line per year.⁶³ Those on long voyages or who were on vessels that sat in the blockade of France for months at a time, died of scurvy, typhus and other diseases of filth and malnutrition. Ships did return to British ports for fresh food but not often enough. The Royal Navy, long after the navies of other nations, in 1796, finally ordered the inclusion of lime juice (for the prevention of scurvy) in the crew's diet, but these orders were not always followed. As to typhus and the body lice that spread it, when there was an outbreak on board, the commander might order a thorough scrubbing of the vessel but not of the men. If surgeons and officers did not understand the spread of the disease, it would appear that many sailors did. Friedenberg describes a case in which a surgeon was astonished when a sick man's "shipmates had washed his clothing, blankets and hammock and transferred him to another area on the deck…'because he was lousy'."⁶⁴

In addition to disease and battles, shipwrecks, and the many types of accidents on board, the most common form of discipline, flogging, could cripple, madden or kill a man. If he survived, he might be:

> …a seaman hospitalized because of brutal lacerations and festering sores at the draining sites of whiplash wounds on his back and buttocks.
>
> Such whipped patients were so psychologically disturbed that they frequently went into fits of hysteria, weeping, and delirium, while the other men in the wards silently looked on and wept in sympathy…⁶⁵

Needless to say, under these circumstances, sailors deserted in droves. Life on board was so dreadful that they considered a wreck and imprisonment something to celebrate. The *Shannon* was wrecked off the coast of France in December 1803.⁶⁶ The people at Valognes in France were shocked to witness the surviving crew, now prisoners of war, on the march to the prison depots:

> …so gay, singing, dancing as if at a wedding. When asked about this phenomenal behaviour, they replied that, having been kidnapped by press gangs, and serving on board only because they were impressed, they were very happy to have been wrecked and freed …⁶⁷

---

⁶³ Zachary B. Friedenberg. *Medicine Under Sail*. Annapolis: Naval Institute Press, 2002. p99.

⁶⁴ Friedenberg. *Medicine Under Sail*, p77.

⁶⁵ Friedenberg. *Medicine Under Sail*, p31.

⁶⁶ Rif Winfield. *British Warships in the Age of Sail 1793–1817: Design, Construction, Careers and Fates.* Barnsley, South Yorkshire: Seaforth Publishing, 2008, p158.

⁶⁷ *La Gazette nationale ou le Moniteur universel,* 22 December 1803 pl. *RetroNews, le site de presse de la BnF.* https://www.retronews.fr/ [Accessed 25 March 2023].

Putting it more simply, Caster Mitchell of New York, impressed from the *Samuel & Jane*, wrote to Skipwith, "It is very hard to suffer for another country against my will."[68]

The risks of a merchant seaman's life were many. Beyond the dangers of seafaring that often threatened life and limb, of abandonment in a foreign land, and of impressment, seamen faced the risk of being attacked by privateers who would steal or burn the ship, take the cargo, the crew's money and papers, and sometimes even their very clothes. In the Caribbean, they risked encountering one or another of the innumerable pirates in those waters, who might force them into piracy, abandon them on an empty island or simply kill them. For more than a century, in the Mediterranean, North African privateers had been known to capture merchant vessels from New England. Their states held some passengers as hostages until ransoms were paid, and enslaved many of the crew. At slave markets in Algiers, "the captives were paraded before potential buyers, physically inspected for strengths and weaknesses, and closely questioned regarding their experience and skills."[69] More recently, many seamen would have read or had read to them Royall Tyler's harrowing, though fictional, memoir, *The Algerine Captive: the Life and Adventures of Doctor Updike Underhill: Six Years a Prisoner among the Algerines*, published in 1797.[70] Only a year earlier, the United States government had paid the ransom for over one hundred captive American seamen held as slaves in Algiers.[71] They were in a pitiable state.

> Several of them are probably rendered incapable of gaining a living: one is in a state of total blindness, another is reduced nearly to the same condition, two or three carry the marks of unmerciful treatment

[68] Mitchell to Skipwith. 27 November 1806. Fulwar Skipwith Papers. The impressed American merchant seaman who had also been a sailor in the Continental Navy, James Durand, voiced similar feelings: "only lately I had quitted the service of the U. States after enduring everything. The thought of serving with the British fleet touched every nerve with distress and almost deprived me of reason." See John B. Hattendorf. "Changing American Perceptions of the Royal Navy Since 1775", *International Journal of Naval History* (2014).

[69] Beth Bower. "'Captivity with ye Barbarous Turks': Seventeenth-Century New Englanders Held Hostage". *American Ancestors: New England, New York, and Beyond*. Vol. 13, No. 2, Spring 2012. New England Historic Genealogical Society, p18.

[70] Royall Tyler. *The Algerine Captive: the Life and Adventures of Doctor Updike Underhill: Six Years a Prisoner among the Algerines*. New York: Cosimo Classics, 2009.

[71] See James Leander Cathcart's personal account of such captivity in *The Captives, by James Leander Cathcart, eleven years a prisoner in Algiers*. Compiled by his daughter, J.B. Newkirk. Herald Prin, 1899; and Frederick C. Leiner. *Prisoners of the Bashaw: the Nineteen Month Captivity of American Sailors in Tripoli*. Yardley: Westholme, 2022.

in ruptures produced by hard labor, others have had their constitutions injured by the plague.[72]

It is important here to differentiate between the two types of shipboard life described above, that on a merchant vessel and that on a Royal Navy vessel. Most of the historiography about shipboard life describes the latter. Naval sailors and merchant seamen of the early nineteenth century would have shared an understanding of the sea, the principles of sailing and familiarity with certain ports, and little else. The sailor was in the military, whether as a volunteer or impressed, and his training was to engage in war, the merchant seaman was a civilian who had taken work on a merchant vessel by choice (though, to be sure, that choice may have been very limited by economic and other constraints) transporting goods to be traded. The sailor might find himself on a massive ship, a frigate or a ship of the line, with crews in the hundreds, and with a complicated hierarchical structure of authority, while the merchant seaman would have been on a much smaller vessel, a brig or a schooner or a sloop, that could have a crew of as few as eight, rarely more than twelve, and he answered only to the shipmaster and the mate. The Royal Navy sailor's voyages could take months, but the merchant seaman's transtlantic voyages took only a few weeks. The sailor could not leave his ship at the end of the voyage, while the merchant seaman usually did so. The differences are many and important for they inform the discussion of the American merchant seamen who were prisoners of war when their country was neutral, who could hope for release before the end of the war, who could join a French privateer and, by doing so, enter the war on their own without fear of being accused of treason, none of which was true for the Royal Navy sailor.

In conclusion, the benefits to a young man of taking work on a merchant vessel were that, because of the labour shortage, it was easy to get, even if one had no skills, it gave advance pay (which most low-level jobs did not), and (with a careful selection of the voyage) it could be over soon. At the same time, a merchant seaman's life was both physically and psychologically very hard, poorly paid, with high risks of sickness, injury, being kidnapped and forced to work on a foreign naval ship, and death. Increasingly, seamen also faced the risk of ending up as a prisoner of war in France.

---

[72] Charles Burr Todd. *Life and Letters of Joel Barlow, LL.D. Poet, Statesman, Philosopher....* New York: Putnam's Sons, 1886, p136.

2

SAILING INTO EUROPE'S WARS

Looking briefly at the shipping and navigation laws of the different nations relevant to this study, the United States, France and Britain, is necessary in order to show how American merchant seamen's lives, work and, in some cases, freedom were affected by them.[1] It is not possible, in this chapter, to describe all of the three countries' maritime laws and treaties, nor would it be particularly helpful in understanding the plight of the American prisoners of war in France. However, a basic survey will help to demonstrate that laws on shipping and commerce affected not only merchants and shipowners but the seamen who operated the vessels and transported the merchandise.

Laws that applied to the vessel also applied to the men. If a vessel were operating illegally, for example with false papers, the crew were all considered to be criminals. On a pirate ship, all men, whether forced onto the crew or not, were considered pirates. Whatever his place of birth, a seaman was treated initially as if he were of the same nationality as that of the vessel. Thus, a seaman on a Royal Navy vessel was considered British, even if he were of a different nationality and had been forced onto the vessel. By the same reasoning, all seamen captured on French vessels by the British were treated as if they were French. When wars broke out, vessels of a nationality that may have traded on friendly terms suddenly could have become enemy vessels and their crew enemy seamen. News of changes in laws and even of war travelled slowly and voyages at sea could be long. A seaman's status could change without his knowing it until he found himself imprisoned. Given that some were illiterate, they must have been confused and angry at the circumstances in which they found themselves when that happened. The

---

[1] Aside from the published laws, now available to read online, see the contemporary review of English law in John Reeves. *A History of the Law of Shipping and Navigation* (1792) and in John Irving Maxwell. *The Spirit of Marine Law*…(1808) Later, and again British law, see James Reddie. *An Historical View of the Law of Maritime Commerce* (Blackwood, 1841). For American laws relating specifically to seamen, see Richard Henry Dana, Jr. *A seaman's Friend*…, Thomas Groom, 1851; Walter MacArthur, *The Seaman's Contract, 1790–1918*…, Walter MacArthur, 1919; and the invaluable *American Maritime Documents, 1776–1860* by Douglas L. Stein. Mystic: Mystic Seaport Museum, 1992.

precariousness of a seaman's status was worsened by the fact that some of the laws were designed specifically to eliminate his usefulness to an enemy by taking him out of service. As ever, he was treated as a work animal and not quite fully a person.

Prior to the American Revolution, the shipping of the British colonies was covered by the British Navigation Acts. These had been protecting trade with and between British colonies since the seventeenth century by prohibiting foreign ships from trading with British colonies. They also prohibited a foreign ship from transporting goods into Britain that were of a nationality different from that of the ship.[2] After the American Revolution, American merchants were no longer citizens of Britain and were no longer able to trade with Britain and her colonies with the same freedoms and inclusive protections as prior to independence. More seriously, American vessels were no longer able to sail in the convoys protected by Royal Navy escorts. In the late 1790s, there were hardly any American naval vessels available to protect American shipping in the Caribbean. Most of the American merchant vessels crossing the Atlantic sailed alone or in small groups and were very vulnerable.

France's Revolution had begun in 1789 and the subsequent Revolutionary Wars and civil wars, especially the War in the Vendée, brought hardship and trade limitations. From 1798 to 1800, French naval and privateering vessels captured the vulnerable American merchant ships, seizing them at sea and taking them to France. They sold the ships and cargos, but did not imprison the crew for long and never held them as prisoners of war. At the same time, the Royal Navy was stopping American ships at sea and impressing their crews and British privateers were capturing American vessels and taking them to Britain.[3] Each of the European powers justified their aggression with their own maritime laws while the United States, relatively powerless, joined this legal chess game with new protective laws of its own.

In France, the civil wars ended and those who had opposed the Revolution lost. Napoleon came to power in 1799 as First Consul. In Europe, the Revolutionary Wars ended with the Treaty of Amiens in 1802. It brought a peace that did not last long. War broke out again in May 1803. A year later, in May 1804, the First Empire was declared in France, and Napoleon crowned himself emperor that December. It was now to be Napoleon personally, instead

---

[2] "October 1651: An Act for increase of Shipping, and Encouragement of the Navigation of this Nation", in *Acts and Ordinances of the Interregnum, 1642–1660*, eds C.H. Firth and R.S. Rait (London, 1911), pp559–562. *British History Online* http://www.british-history.ac.uk/no-series/acts-ordinances-interregnum/pp559-562 [Accessed 27 March 2019].

[3] Ulane Bonnel. *La France, les États-Unis et la guerre de course (1797–1813)*. Paris: Nouvelles Éditions Latines, 1961, pp48–114, chapter on the Quasi-War.

of the Directory or the Consulate, who issued decrees concerning French maritime activity.

French armies were conquering much of Europe on land while, at sea, Britain's Royal Navy outnumbered France's Navy, the Marine. The French Navy had been seriously reduced by the losses in the sea battle of 1 June 1794.[4] Then, in the 1805 Battle of Trafalgar, the combined French and Spanish navies were destroyed, leaving Britain's Royal Navy the major sea power of the three and well able to maintain a blockade of French ports that lasted to the end of the wars.[5] The United States was determined to remain neutral in Europe's wars. It was that neutrality that enabled American merchants to take advantage of the wars in Europe to make huge profits. A neutral vessel was supposed to be able to sail the oceans without being molested, stopped or seized by any of the warring powers. A merchant of neutral nationality could trade with all of the belligerents who, being at war, did not trade with one another but who still needed markets for their goods and sources for the goods they required.

From 1806, the passing of laws and decrees concerning commerce increased on all sides. In April of that year, the United States passed the Non-Importation Act, prohibiting the importation of certain British goods into America.[6] The next month, a British Order of Council declared a blockade of all ports from Brest in France to the Elbe River and the port of Hamburg in what is now Germany, attempting to cut off all trade with this part of the French Empire.[7] In November, Napoleon issued the Berlin Decree, which prohibited the importation into the French Empire (which, at that point, included large parts of Europe) of any raw or manufactured goods from Britain or any of her colonies, hoping in this way to starve British commerce by blocking all trade between Britain and Continental Europe.[8] The following year, Britain issued more Orders of Council, extending the blockade of France's ports and those of her allies and extending the trade restrictions to include neutral countries

---

[4] William S. Cormack. *Revolution and Political Conflict in the French Navy,* Cambridge: Cambridge University Press, 1995. pp287–285.

[5] David G. Chandler. *Dictionary of the Napoleonic Wars*. London: Arms and Armour Press, 1979, pp448–451.

[6] "An Act to prohibit the importation of certain goods, wares and merchandise." *United States Statutes at Large*, Vol. 2, 9th Congress, 1st Session, Chapter 29, 18 April 1806.

[7] *The Orders of Council, and Instructions for Imposing the Restrictions of Blockade; and for Regulating The Navigation of the Sea....* London: N. Shury, 1808.

[8] "Décret du Blocus Continental du 21 novembre 1806". *Histoire des Deux Empires. Le Site d'Histoire de la Fondation Napoléon.* Napoleon.org. https://www.napoleon.org/histoire-des-2-empires/articles/decret-du-blocus-continental-du-21-novembre-1806/ [Accessed 27 March 2019] Quoting *Le Moniteur*, 4 December 1806.

as well. Napoleon countered by restricting neutral trade with Britain in the Milan Decrees in November and December, which declared that any vessel that traded with Britain or with her colonies at all was no longer neutral but had become an enemy vessel, in essence, a collaborator.[9] The United States passed the Embargo Act in December, preventing American ships from receiving permission to voyage to those dangerous foreign ports, following the reasoning that the best way to avoid being seized was never to sail at all.[10]

The Embargo Act of 1807, restraining American vessels from sailing to belligerent ports, was extremely unpopular with the American merchants who concentrated on that wartime trade. Napoleon's response to it was the Bayonne Decree, authorizing the capture of any American vessels entering French ports. Napoleon's reasoning behind the Bayonne Decree was that since, by its own Embargo Act, America's vessels could not leave their ports for foreign ports, any American vessel entering a port of the French Empire must have come from Britain and would be, therefore, liable to seizure as a vessel no longer neutral.[11] In March 1809, the United States lifted the Embargo Act, allowing American merchants to voyage to foreign ports again, but the Non-Intercourse Act, passed in the same month, prohibited them from going to belligerent French or British ports.[12] American merchants, however, were more interested in profit, even with the risk of loss and capture, than with safety. They continued to send their vessels to France and Britain.[13]

---

[9] "2ème décret de Milan, 17 décembre 1807". *Histoire des Deux Empires. Le Site d'Histoire de la Fondation Napoléon.* Napoleon.org. https://www.napoleon.org/histoire-des-2-empires/articles/2eme-decret-de-milan-17-decembre-1807/ [Accessed 27 March 2019].

[10] "An Act laying an Embargo on all ships and vessels in the ports and harbors of the United States." *United States Statutes at Large*, Vol. 2, 10th Congress, 1st Session, Chapter 5, 22 December 1807.

[11] Bonnel, *La France, les États-Unis et la guerre de course.* pp234–235.

[12] "An Act to interdict the commercial intercourse between the United States and Great Britain and France, and their dependencies; and for other purposes." *United States Statutes at Large*, Vol. 2, 10th Congress, 1st Session, Chapter 24, March 1 1809.

[13] It is not possible to discuss at length here Napoleon's maritime strategy. From 1805, after the French losses at Trafalgar, he needed time to rebuild the French fleet. The Continental Blockade, by causing the Royal Navy to use many more vessels to defend convoys and access to ports and so, distract it, was intended to buy him that time. If it also disrupted British trade, so much the better. Nudging America into war with Britain would further spread and drain the Royal Navy's resources. See Tony Corn. "Global Napoléon" (2021); Kenneth Johnson. "1804–1814: 'Harassing the British with expenses & fatigue'—Napoleon's Naval Strategy" (2023); Silvia Marzagalli. "The Continental System: A view from the sea"; Johan Joor and Katherine Aaslestad, eds, *Revisiting Napoleon's Continental System: Local, Regional, and European*

The French ruled that an American vessel that had British cargo or had called at a British port or even simply been stopped at sea by the Royal Navy, had served the enemy's cause and was liable to capture. The captures of American vessels voyaging to or from Britain by French privateers from this period are reflected in the increase of the numbers of American seamen in prison in France. In 1809, more than 300 men were captured. Had American merchants heeded the Bayonne Decree and the Non-Intercourse Act, it is likely that many of their seamen would not have suffered the fate of French imprisonment.

At this point, the United States was the only one of the three nations to have revoked one of its acts. The French Berlin and Milan Decrees and the British Orders of Council remained in force as the wars continued. The Royal Navy blockade of French ports and the seizures of vessels that attempted to enter them, including American vessels, continued. In March 1810, Napoleon issued the Rambouillet Decree, citing the United States Non-Intercourse Act, to order that, from 20 May the *previous* year, all vessels under the American flag and/or owned or even partly owned by American citizens which had entered any of the ports of the French Empire, of its colonies or of the countries it controlled, that had been seized would not be returned and their cargo would be sold. Napoleon was attempting to force the Americans into the war on commerce, preferably on France's side. In being retroactive, this decree allowed the seizure of all American vessels already in French ports and of their seamen who, consequently, became prisoners of war. At least two American vessels, the *Holland Trader* and the *Neptune*, were seized by reason of the Rambouillet Decree and their crews sent to prisons.

Two months later, the United States passed an act that was a clumsy attempt to manipulate the belligerents into recognizing American vessels' neutrality in their wars and to allow them to trade with all nations. Briefly, it said that whichever country, France or Britain, was first to stop attacking American vessels and to recognize their neutrality would receive the reward of America ending all trade with the other.[14] Quick to respond, Napoleon instructed his Minister for External Relations,[15] Jean-Baptiste de Nompère de Champagny, the Duke of Cadore, to write a letter (which became known as the Cadore

---

Experiences, Basingstoke: Palgrave, 2014; Roger Knight. *Convoys: the British Struggle Against Napoleonic Europe and America.* New Haven: Yale University Press, 2022.

[14] "An Act concerning the commercial intercourse between the United States and Great Britain and France, and their dependencies, and for other purposes." *United States Statutes at Large*, Vol. 2, 11th Congress, 2nd Session, Chapter 39, 1 May 1810.

[15] From 1794 to 1814, this ministry was known firstly as the *Commissaire des Relations extérieurs*, then as the *Ministère des Relations extérieurs*. Before and after that period, it was known as the *Ministère des Affairs étrangères*, the Ministry of Foreign Relations. See the fuller description below.

Letter) saying that he would take this offered plum and revoke the Berlin and Milan Decrees, but only if Britain ended the blockade of France's ports; if not, then the United States would have to undertake, as stated in their act, to terminate trade with Britain, which President Madison did.[16] As Henry Adams pointed out, for all of their intelligence, American officials were no match for Napoleon at political manipulation.[17] He had successfully manoeuvred them closer to war with Britain and the Cadore Letter is considered one of the key events leading up to that war. In June 1812, the United States declared war against Britain, becoming if not an ally of France, at least at war with a common enemy.

The question and determination of neutrality was increasingly disputed. The United States was determined to be allowed by both France and Britain to trade with both at the same time. To succeed in this, the United States had to insist on its neutrality in the European wars and to insist that the belligerents accept that American vessels were neutral vessels and their cargo, whatever its origin, was, by virtue of being on a neutral vessel, neutral cargo. Britain and France, however, each wanting the United States to trade solely with it and not the other, allowed that only those American vessels that traded exclusively with one of them were neutral and asserted that those that traded with the enemy were not.

Whenever a merchant vessel was stopped, its papers were examined closely. Vessel registration papers, issued by a nation's maritime authority, were proof of the vessel's nationality. In the United States, these registration papers gave the name and nationality of the owner, the name and the home port of the vessel, and the name of the shipmaster or captain. A detailed description of the vessel's type and dimensions was also given.[18] A crew list was required for all vessels, giving the name, place of birth, age and position of each man. The crew list was used to help to determine a vessel's nationality. At least seventy-five percent of the crew had to be of the same nationality as the vessel's flag.[19] France, with the Cadore Letter, added the requirement that, from 1 November 1810, American vessels leaving French ports would have to carry a license, signed by Napoleon, confirming that they had not been "denationalized" and

---

[16] Donald R. Hickey. *The War of 1812: a Forgotten Conflict, Bicentennial Edition.* Urbana: University of Illinois Press, 2012, p21.

[17] Henry Adams. *History of the United States of America During the Administrations of James Madison.* New York: Literary Classics of the United States, 1986, pp180–181.

[18] For vessel registration examples, see Record Group 41, "Bureau of Marine Inspection & Navigation – Certificates of Registration, 1789–1894", NARA, Washington, D.C.

[19] The rules on the nationality of the crew were regularly flouted and, during wartime, often relaxed, yet failure to comply was still used as a reason for the condemnation of a prize in France.

lost their neutrality by complying with any British regulations or failing to comply with any French regulations.[20]

Not having the correct papers automatically exposed a vessel to seizure, and Prize Courts used the slightest inconsistency or fault in a vessel's papers to condemn the vessel as a good, or legitimate, prize. (Yet, by 1810, desperate for grain, the French government threw reason to the wind and authorized the use of false flags. In August of that year, the Minister of Marine, Decrès, had issued a secret order to the effect that special licenses, valid for one year, could be issued to vessels registered as French, *falsely or not*, to import foreign goods, and authorizing French seamen working on those vessels to use false names.[21] American merchants based in France took full advantage of this opportunity.)

The issue of defining a cargo's neutrality was also regularly disputed, with the belligerents asserting that the place of origin determined the nationality of the cargo and the Americans that it was determined by the nationality of the vessel carrying it. Neutral ships made neutral cargoes, the Americans claimed; whatever the origin of the cargo, once it was on an American vessel, its origin became American. Thus, French wine in a neutral American vessel would be deemed French and enemy cargo, and liable to seizure by the British, while to the United States, in claiming that the neutrality of its vessels applied also to the vessels' contents, the wine would be deemed to be American, thus neutral cargo, and not liable to British seizure. In order to combat this, the French began, with the Berlin Decree, to require additional cargo documentation. They now required the cargo to have a certificate of origin from the French consul in the American port of the vessel's departure.[22]

This meant that every American vessel sailing the Atlantic had to have documents to prove neutrality and to comply with the laws of either Britain or France but also not to have on board any documents revealing visits to or compliance with the laws of one or the other if it were stopped. A vessel captain wanted to be able to show to the British that he was not violating the Orders of Council by going into or out of a blockaded French port, or trading with France, her colonies or her allies. He also wanted to be able to prove to the Americans that he was not violating the Non-Importation Act and carried no British cargo into American ports and that his was a wholly American-owned vessel so that only the lowest tonnage tax might be charged. At the

---

[20] Bonnel, *La France, les États-Unis et la guerre de course*, p270.

[21] Edouard Delobette. *Ces "Messieurs du Havre". Négociants, Commissionaires et Armateurs de 1680 à 1830. Thèse de doctorat de IIIe cycle préparée sous la direction de Monsieur le Professeur André ZYSBERG, soutenue à l'Université de Caen le samedi 26 novembre* 2005, p886, note.

[22] Silvia Marzagalli, "The Continental System: A view from the sea", p86; Gordinier, *Versatility in Crisis*, p21 and p25.

same time, he might want to be able to prove to the French that he had not visited a British port and was not carrying British goods into France, which would have been a violation of the Berlin Decree. After 1807, he wanted to show that he had not been to a British port, which would have violated the Milan Decree and later, that he was not violating the Bayonne Decree in an American vessel that had sailed to a foreign port in violation of his own country's Embargo Act.

Yet, quite a lot of money was to be made in selling grains, cotton, and British colonial goods to France, in selling French textiles and luxury goods to America, in selling French wine to Britain and in selling British manufactured goods to America. The greatest profits were made (and the greatest risks taken) in selling French goods to Britain and British goods to France. A very large number of American merchants and the captains of their vessels made no effort to comply with the laws but every effort to evade them, using time-honoured ruses to transport illegal goods and developing new ones as the trade laws changed.

The methods that they used involved false flags, multiple versions of ships' papers and false cargo papers. The *Rolla*, for example, was an American vessel from New York that was captured by the French privateer, *Intrépide*, as it was sailing from Sardinia to Sweden with a legal cargo of oil, salt and lemons, and with the illegal cargo of colonial products of sugar and tobacco. A full search of the vessel found 149 different documents hidden all around that revealed the illegal goods were being transported for an English merchant.[23] As Crowhurst pointed out, "The availability of false documents is one of the features of the age, when printing was widely available but means of verification absent."[24]

To evade the contradictory laws of France and Britain, the Americans also used broken voyages and re-exporting. A broken voyage was an indirect voyage, with a stop at another port, changing the vessel's and cargo's nationality along the way. An American vessel taking a French cargo directly from France to Britain was violating both belligerent countries' trade laws. The same vessel, carrying the same cargo, going from France to New York, where the cargo was offloaded, then reloaded onto the same vessel, which then went on to Britain, where the goods were sold as American, was not trading directly between the two that were at war and was not violating their trade laws. The return voyage would take British goods to sell in America or elsewhere. The same was done with sugar from the French or British colonies. It was transported to America, offloaded, reloaded and sold in Europe as American sugar. Begun as early as 1793, these broken voyages became the substance of American trade during the Napoleonic Wars.[25] For a fee, Americans also

---

[23] Bonnel, *La France, les États-Unis et la guerre de course*, p275.
[24] Crowhurst, *The French War on Trade*, p35.
[25] Gordinier, *Versatility in Crisis*, p26.

handled French merchants' exports, taking them beyond the British blockade in their neutral, American ships. As Silvia Marzagalli has pointed out, during this period, American merchants were using their home ports as warehouses for the European and Caribbean goods that they were re-exporting. Countless American vessels, re-exporting in broken voyages, are what constituted the so-called trade boom in America during this period.[26]

Re-exporting doubled the number of voyages and, consequently, the employment opportunities for the seaman. This, and the increased risk of capture occasioned by all of the trade laws, may have contributed to the rise in the American seaman's average monthly wage to twenty and even thirty dollars by 1807. (As prices and the cost of living also rose, however, the value of his real wages did not go up.)[27] The voyages crossing the Atlantic to Britain and Europe were short, compared to those of whalers going to the South Atlantic or merchant vessels going to the Far East, which could last years. Depending upon the weather, currents and route chosen, the average voyage from New York to Liverpool was roughly three to four weeks. A seaman who worked the Atlantic routes was therefore making numerous crossings per year and was at risk of capture or impressment on every one of them.

Every vessel, as it entered belligerent nations' waters, faced the risk of being stopped, searched and possibly seized. Both France and Britain pursued this activity avidly, Britain with its navy and France with privateers. The Royal Navy patrolled the sea, escorted convoys of British merchant ships, and maintained its blockade of France's Atlantic coast. This blockade used large and small vessels to try to keep French ships from being able to leave harbours and go to sea. In the early years of the wars, when France threatened to invade Britain and Napoleon was amassing an invasion fleet at Boulogne-sur-Mer, the blockade was for defensive purposes, to keep that fleet from sailing, which it never did. As the wars progressed, the blockade of France became more offensive. Smaller, faster, light vessels patrolled the French coast as closely as possible, investigating activity, capturing vessels, and occasionally bombing a town or firing on a fortress. Further out to sea, but still within signal range, were the inshore squadrons, groups of six ships, mostly frigates. They patrolled the sea and were quick to sail in for an attack or engagement on a signal from the light vessels. Still further out, and within signal distance of the inshore squadron, would be ships of the line, the great warships of from seventy-four to more than a hundred guns, patrolling the sea lanes that approached France.

---

[26] Marzagalli, "The Continental System: A view from the sea"; Donald R, Adams, Jr. "American Neutrality and Prosperity, 1793–1808: A Reconsideration", *The Journal of Economic History*, Vol. 40, No. 4 (Dec., 1980), pp713–737. Cambridge University Press on behalf of the Economic History Association. http://www.jstor.org/stable/2119997 [Accessed: 19/06/2010] p726.

[27] Donald R. Adams, Jr. "American Neutrality and Prosperity", pp713–737.

The final band of the blockade was of passing Royal Navy vessels that were the escorts to the merchant convoys.[28]

These four layers of Royal Navy vessels engaged in blockading and escorting would harry and chase any French naval vessels that escaped from a harbour. They also attempted to attack and seize any French privateers that wove their way through the lines of the blockade. As the war on commerce escalated, the British made every possible effort to stop all merchant vessels from reaching French ports and to inhibit French vessels in their coastal trade. When one of the blockading ships, usually a frigate, sighted another vessel on the horizon, a "strange sail" as the logbooks report, it would immediately give chase until the vessel's nationality could be identified. A British vessel would be allowed to carry on. French vessels and those of other nationalities, including American, were pursued. By international agreement, civilian fishing boats were supposedly exempt from seizure, though they were often stopped and the fishermen interrogated in order to gain information. In spite of the rule, at times even French fishing boats were seized by blockading vessels and the men taken prisoner. In the words of one French author, the English were the "autocrats of the Channel."[29]

French privateering law is critical to any study of French privateers and their prizes. They have been fully explained by René Worms and Florence Le Guellaff, described and interpreted by Ulane Bonnel, looking at French privateering during the Quasi-War, Patrick Villiers and Patrick Crowhurst, each looking at the financial records of privateers and their prizes, and by Michel Aumont and André Lespagnol in their separate studies of privateers of Granville and Saint Malo.[30] Publications of the laws and procedures, such

---

[28] Wade G. Dudley. *Splintering the Wooden Wall: The British Blockade of the United States, 1812–1815*. Annapolis: Naval Institute Press, 2003, pp26–27.

[29] Georges Lebas. *Histoire d'un Port Normand Sous la Révolution et l'Empire: Dieppe: Vingt Années de Guerres maritimes, les Corsaires de la Manche, la Pêche.* Luneray: Gérard Bertout, 1974, p220.

[30] See René Worms, « La Juridiction des Prises », *Revue des Deux Mondes, 6ème période*, Vol. 30, 1915, pp. 90–115; Florence Le Guellaff, *Armements en course et droit des prises maritimes (1792–1856)* Nancy: PUN-Editions universitaires de Lorraine, 1999. Bonnel, *La France, les États-Unis et la guerre de course*; Patrick Villiers. *Marine royale, corsaires et trafic dans l'Atlantique de Louis XIV à Louis XVI.* Société Dunkerquoise d'Histoire et d'Archéologie, 1991; Patrick Crowhurst, « Profitability in French Privateering, 1793–1815 », *Business History*, Vol. 24 (1982), pp48–60; Chapter 4 in Michel Aumont's *Les corsaires de Granville: Une culture du risque maritime (1688–1815)*. Rennes: Presses universitaires de Rennes, 2013; and André Lespagnol, *Entre l'argent et la gloire: La course malouine au temps de Louis XIV.* Evergreen, 1995. For a very good explanation, in English, of prize law generally, see Donald A. Petrie. *The Prize Game: Lawful Looting on the High Seas in the Days of Fighting Sail.* New York: Berkley, 1999.

as the *Réglement Sur les Armemens en course* (Regulations on Arming for Privateering) and the essays by archivists explaining the series of prize records provide a more precisely detailed understanding of the material.[31]

From as early as 1400, France had legislated privateering procedures that had changed little over the centuries. They had been revised in 1778, to accommodate France's naval aid to the United States in that country's War of Independence, and again in 1803, to suit France's renewed hostilities with Britain.[32] No vessel could arm for war without the approval of the Admiralty and later, the Ministry of Marine, which issued a Letter of Marque to the *armateur* (the shipowner, or owners, or their managing agent),[33] with copies to the captain of the vessel. The Letter of Marque was numbered and was issued only during times of war and authorized aggression against vessels only of enemy nationality. It authorized privateering for a short period, usually three or six months. To obtain the Letter of Marque, the *armateur* had to post a bond which, by 1803 was 37,000 francs for a privateer with a crew fewer than 150, and up to 74,000 francs for larger crews. Privateering without a Letter of Marque or during peacetime was an act of piracy.[34] The Letter of Marque endowed the privateer with military status; if captured, he was considered a legitimate combatant and a prisoner of war, not a pirate to be tried and hung. As a defensive measure, some merchant ships would carry guns to fight off attackers; to show that they were not pirates (being an armed vessel that was not in a navy) they would also carry a Letter of Marque. Only a valuable cargo would justify this added expense.

Privateers as well as the ships they pursued regularly disguised their identities by flying false flags. A French privateer might sail under a false flag in order to avoid frightening off the chase but the true flag was required by law to be flown before the approach and demand to board (however, if the chased vessel were found to be flying a false flag, that was grounds for

---

[31] See especially the essay by François-Xavier Chevignard. « Répertoire numérique: Série FF – Invalides et Prises: Sous–série FF3: Jugements de validité et deliquidation desprises, An V – 1893 » Vincennes, 2012–2013.

[32] Zimmerman, *Impressment of American Seamen*, pp20–21. Both of these revisions would be cited by French ministerial authorities as legal justifications for decisions concerning American prisoners of war.

[33] There is no precisely equal word for *armateur* in English. Patrick Crowhurst's definition is: "The central figure in a privateering venture was the *armateur* or managing owner, who was usually a merchant with considerable experience of buying and fitting out ships and hiring suitable captains. The importance of the *armateur* in privateering cannot be exaggerated, for he took all the major financial decisions and the success or failure of the venture lay to some extent in his hands.", "Profitability in French Privateering", p48.

[34] Aumont, *Les Corsaires de Granville*, pp120–124.

seizure, no matter what flag the privateer had up at the moment).[35] During that chase, the captain of the merchant vessel had very little time to prepare for the boarding. He might have tried to hide or throw overboard anything, whether flags, papers, charts, or logbooks, that could give the pursuer the slightest reason, under one of the many laws, to say that the vessel or its cargo were not neutral but enemy, but he needed to know the nationality of the vessel chasing him in order to know what to keep and what to discard or hide. If the privateer were flying a false flag, he would have to try to guess the nationality by the vessel size and rigging. During the capture, French prize law prohibited any outrageous mistreatment of the captured crew. On pain of death, the captors could not maroon the crew, the ship could not be sunk with people on board, the captured seamen could not be killed or mistreated, but they were prisoners of war.[36] (These things, particularly marooning, did happen, but relatively rarely.)[37] Once captured, most of the crew would be taken off the prize onto the privateer. A prize crew from the privateer would then board and sail the prize, as the merchant vessel had now become, to the nearest friendly port.[38] Speed and good sailing on the part of the prize crew were crucial, for it was possible and often happened that one of the enemy's frigates or privateers could be encountered and, perhaps after another fight, it would take back the prize for its nation.

French captures of merchant vessels were not often made by their navy, except on rare occasions when small squadrons made it out past the blockade. The French relied on privateers to harass, attack and capture merchant vessels of enemy nationalities.[39] The British could not blockade the entire French Atlantic coast. If Brest, Dunkirk, and Le Havre were closely blockaded, Boulogne-sur-Mer, Dieppe and Saint Malo were less so and hundreds of French privateers from those ports attacked British merchant vessels. They were extremely successful at it. In the year of 1808 to 1809, 143 French privateers escaped the blockaded ports and captured vessels and cargo (of which a large number were American, as this was also when the Bayonne

---

[35] *Imprimerie de la République* (Paris), "*Réglement Sur les Armemens en course*", Saint-Cloud, 2 Prairial, an XI, [22 May 1803] p15.

[36] "*Réglement Sur les Armemens en course*", p17.

[37] Reports of being marooned are relatively rare, but that rather begs the question of how many of those marooned survived and then returned and made a report?

[38] Greg H. Williams. *The French Assault on American Shipping, 1793–1813: A History and Comprehensive Record of Merchant Marine Losses.* Jefferson: McFarland, 2009, p4.

[39] Napoléon Gallois. *Les Corsaires français sous la République et L'Empire.* Le Mans: Julien, Lanier et Compagnie, 1847. This monumental work lists all French privateers during the Napoleonic Wars and all of their captures. Only a small percentage are French naval vessels.

Decree was passed, stating that they were no longer neutral) with a value of more than 18,500,000 francs. The value of British captures of French vessels for the same period came to less than twenty per cent of that.[40]

On arrival at a French Empire port, the captain of the privateer took any papers of the captured vessel, or prize (logbooks, ship passports and sea letters, crew lists, bills of lading and all other papers concerning the cargo, etc.) and all of the prisoners (for which he was paid forty francs each)[41] to a justice of the peace, *juge de paix*. He and his crew would be interrogated, as might be the master or crew members of the prize. Those from the prize vessel who were interrogated were almost always officers or passengers, rarely seamen. For those who did not speak French, an interpreter was provided. All present signed the written copies of the interrogations.[42]

The purpose was to record witness statements of exactly how the capture took place, what flags were shown at what point, what the cargo was, what papers the prize vessel was carrying and, most of all, what were the true nationalities of the vessel and its cargo. These interviews were a standard procedure, following a prescribed list of questions that mirror almost identical procedures and questions followed in British prize law.[43] The ship's papers and the interviews went into the prize case file being prepared for the decision of the *Conseil des Prises*, or Prize Council, in truth a court, the decisions of which were enforceable by law. The Prize Council handled only cases of captures by privateers; captures by naval vessels were judged by the Ministry of Marine and Colonies. There were two types of cases, those that were contested and those that were not. All British merchant and naval vessels, being enemy vessels, were, by their nationality, legitimate, or "good" prizes. There could be no contesting of these prizes. Any American vessel that violated any of Napoleon's decrees was deemed to have lost its nationality and so, lost its neutrality, and became legally an enemy vessel and was also judged a good

---

[40] Lebas, *Histoire d'un Port Normand*, p249.

[41] "*Réglement Sur les Armemens en course*", p19.

[42] Margaret Audin. *British Hostages in Napoleonic France, The Evidence: With Particular Reference to Manufacturers and Artisans*, a thesis submitted to the Faculty of Commerce and Social Science of the University of Birmingham, 1987, p41.

[43] Faye Margaret Kert "Prize and Prejudice: Privateering and Naval Prize in Atlantic Canada in the War of 1812". *Research in Maritime History*, No. 11 (1997). International Maritime Economic History Association. Quoting Dr. Christopher Roberts in English Reports, Vol. 165, Appendix 2 gives the complete list of "Standing Interrogatories" used by the Admiralty with British captures during the War of 1812. The equivalent French law, *Réglement Sur le Armemens en course* of 1803, does not stipulate what the interrogation questions should be but of the interrogations of prisoners that survive, it can be seen that they follow a very similar pattern.

prize. Most American captains contested these cases and tried to prove that they, the cargo, the vessel and the crew truly were neutral American.

To contest his case (which enemy captains and owners, for obvious reasons, could not do, but those of neutral nationality could do) the captain had to go to Paris, hire an agent, who was often the United States consul in Paris, and a French lawyer (the Americans usually used a man named Lagrange) who would present his case before the Prize Council. (Prize cases were sometimes sent to the local court at the port, the *Tribunal de Commerce*, for adjudication but more often they went to the Prize Council in Paris.)[44] The Prize Council had been established in 1799 by the Consulate, with the First Consul (Napoleon) selecting the eight members. It was within the Ministry of Marine and Colonies and its primary function was to judge prize cases. By all accounts, it acted at a snail's pace. The entire decision process usually took weeks or even months.[45] The agent/consul wrote numerous letters, attended the court hearings and disputed with the lawyer. In the rare cases where a capture was ruled invalid and the vessel and cargo to be returned, Napoleon had to personally issue his approval. Usually, however, the captures were ruled valid and the ships and cargoes were sold. Meanwhile, the captains enjoyed or languished in Paris, where they tended to lodge near the theatre in rue de la Loi and to gather at the home of the American delegation in rue Vaugirard. While the captains were in hotels in Paris or in the port city of arrival, their crews were in jail.

The Reality for the Crew

To say that a seaman was captured when his ship became the prize of a French privateer partly obscures his experience by speaking of the vessel but not of the man. Being on a vessel that was targeted as a prize could be extremely dangerous.

Though privateersmen were not, because of their Letter of Marque, legally pirates, their behaviour most certainly could be piratical. They were licenced marauders and highwaymen of the seas. Anyone boarding a vessel that was

---

[44] René Guillemin. *Corsaires de la République et de l'Empire*. Paris: Editions France-Empire, 1982, p37. The 1803 revision of the privateering regulations had terminated the procedure of local *Tribunaux de Commerce* judging prizes; all were to be judged by the Prize Council in Paris. This change was not observed in all ports and many times local authorities exploited the confusion to judge a prize as good and sell the cargo and vessel quickly, before a complaint could be made in Paris. See also John Armstrong to James Madison, 29 February 1808, when the law changed again and it was uncertain as to which of the courts would handle American prize cases. United States. Department of State. NARA. *Despatches from United States Ministers to France, 1789–1906*, Vol. 11.

[45] Bonnel, *La France, les États-Unis et la guerre de course*, pp45–47.

to sail the Atlantic during this period feared not only storms and shoals and wrecks, but attacks by pirates and privateers. Privateers were hunters of prey, ideally richly laden merchant vessels that they could outsail and outgun and that were not in a convoy but alone and unprotected. In this period when American merchants were sending out ships laden with goods of value to European customers, ships that were almost never in any convoy (except those sailing to the West Indies) or with protection from one of the United States Navy's few vessels, they were ideal prey.

The privateer, on spotting such a lone vessel, sailed up to the prey at speed, with their guns out. Ideally, the prey would surrender quickly, thus giving the privateersmen an undamaged vessel and pristine cargo to sell at the best prices. However, if the merchant ship refused to surrender immediately, their vessel would be fired upon, canon balls shattering masts, sending large splinters of wood shooting like assassins' knives in every direction, severing limbs, shattering skulls. If the prey still resisted, the privateer, perhaps continuing to fire, would come up close, throw grappling irons to bind the vessels together, then send armed men to board her, attacking and, if necessary to complete the conquest, severely wounding those who resisted. It could be a battle scene, but on the prey vessel the wounded and dead were merchant seamen not armed sailors. Generally, to avoid this very real possibility, the captain of the merchant vessel tried to outsail the privateer but, if that were to fail, then, in order to preserve people, cargo and the vessel, he surrendered without a fight.

There then would be the boarding and the pantomime of looking at papers and determining legality but there are too many stories of ships' papers being thrown overboard to give this full credence. It was at this point that the boarding men stole all of the possessions, including their papers, of the crew and passengers. When the privateers moved the captured crew to their own vessel, as prisoners, the seamen were locked in a hold, possibly with others who had been captured in the same way. They had little hope of anything but jail and prison once they arrived in France. With every chase, if the captain were worried about saving his ship and the cargo, his crew would have been even more anxious for their own papers, for their few possessions and money, for their freedom and possibly for their lives.

Because of the many overlapping maritime laws described here, it was almost certain that the rather common event of an American merchant vessel being stopped at sea could have been disastrous for the seaman. Whether he were impressed onto a Royal Navy ship or taken prisoner by a French privateer, he lost his freedom and entered into a dire situation. A very few seamen were also captured by the French when their ships wrecked on French shores, but the majority were on merchant vessels captured at sea by French privateers.

3

CAPTIVES

Only one American prisoner, John Jea, left an account of his time in a French prison and only one British prisoner, Stephen Clubb, wrote more than a line about the American prisoners he encountered while he was being held. The sources for some of the other details of life in the depots are the accounts written afterward by British prisoners: memoirs, autobiographies or biographies.[1] Most of these British accounts were published after 1815, when the war was over and they returned home. (Some shorter accounts appeared as letters from prison in the British press.) They all contain elements of self-aggrandizement, of demonization of the enemy and of what appear to be marketing ploys. Nearly every title, for example, contains the supposedly alluring word "adventure". Many contain accounts of fantastic and daring escapes that are not always confirmed in French archival sources.[2] Moreover, one depot,

---

[1] Amongst the more than thirty accounts published by those who had been prisoners, see especially Thomas J. Barclay de Mounteney. *The Case of a Détenu.* George Earle, 1838; Edward Boys. *Narrative of a Captivity and Adventures in France and Flanders Between the Years 1808 and 1809.* Richard Long, 1827; Henry Raikes, ed. *Memoir of the Life and Services of Vice-Admiral Sir Jahleel Brenton, Baronet, KCB* London: Hatchard, 1846; James Choyce. *The Log of a Jack Tar; or the Life of James Choyce, Master Mariner, with O'Brien's Captivity in France.* T. Fisher Unwin, 1841, Edward Tagart, *Memoir of the Late Captain Peter Heywood, R.N. with Extracts From His Diaries and Correspondence.* Effingham Wilson, 1832; Seacome Ellison. *Prison Scenes and Narrative of Escape from France, During the Late War.* Whittaker, 1838; William Henry Dillon. *A Narrative of My Professional Adventures*, Michael Lewis, ed. Navy Records Society, 1953 and 1956. For descriptions of time at more prisons, see Richard Langton, *Narrative of a Captivity in France from 1809 to 1814.* Smith, Elder, 1836. All of these, understandably, vilify the French and emphasize the prisoners' sufferings. In nearly all and the many others not listed here, the prison descriptions of Verdun, and secondarily, of Bitche, predominate.

[2] Donat Henchy O'Brien, for example, wrote in *My Adventures During the Late War: a Narrative of Shipwreck, Captivity, Escapes from French Prisons, and Sea Service in 1804–14.* (Edward Arnold, 1902) of more than one remarkable escape. Though the archives at the *Service Historique de la Défense* contain numerous dossiers and much correspondence about escapes and escape attempts, his name never appears amongst them. He appears on lists of prisoners, but not once in the internal memos, reports, surveillance reports or discussions of important or troublesome prisoners.

Verdun, is disproportionately covered in the accounts. They are not the most reliable of sources. Alger, writing in the early twentieth century, commented that "the literature of the Verdun and other captives is disappointing".[3] They are useful for descriptive passages of the depots but otherwise can contribute little to this study of American seamen prisoners who were not at Verdun.

A large part of the details about prisoners in this and later chapters comes from original research in the more than forty cartons of individual prisoner files, many of them on Americans, held in the archives of the *Service Historique de la Défense* (SHD) in Vincennes, and in the correspondence from the prisoners to American consuls and that between American diplomats and French authorities about the American seamen prisoners. (These and other sources are discussed in detail in the Bibliographic Essay below.)

Including Alger, the historiography of the prisoners in Napoleonic France is not a large canon and more than a third of it remains unpublished theses. Michael Lewis, David Rouanet and Didier Houmeau are perhaps the most important and each covers a different aspect. Lewis and Houmeau wrote of the British prisoners, using very different material, Aymes wrote of the Spanish prisoners, numerically the largest nationality of prisoners of war in France, and Rouanet wrote of the prisoners captured in battle and marched to the northeast of France.[4] Arthur Griffiths, writing in 1899, did a still worthy study of the French and British facilities for prisoners of war. Margaret Audin, using the same dossiers in the SHD mentioned above, examined specifically those British prisoners who, because they were artisans with valuable skills, were allowed to live and work in towns under surveillance.[5] More recently, Elodie Duché and Mark J. Gabrielson have studied charitable aid to the prisoners and

---

Though surely he was a prisoner and surely he escaped, most of his claims cannot be confirmed. This is an issue with all of the personal accounts; the claims rarely can be confirmed in other sources.

[3] John Goldworth Alger. *Napoleon's British Visitors and Captives 1801–1815* (Archibald Constable, 1904).

[4] Michael Lewis. *Napoleon and His British Captives*. George Allen & Unwin, 1962; Jean-René Aymes, *La déportation sous le premier Empire: les Espagnols en France (1808–1814)*. Éditions de la Sorbonne, 1983; David Rouanet. *Prisonniers de Napoléon: Les prisonniers de guerre coalisés internés en France de 1803 à 1814*. Unpublished manuscript shared with the author and based on a thesis submitted to Paris IV-Sorbonne, 2009, under the direction of J-O Boudon; Didier Houmeau. *Les prisonniers de guerre britanniques de Napoléon 1er. (1803–1814)*. Draft copy of a doctoral thesis shared with the author, e-mail dated 7 April 2010; Arthur Griffiths. "Old War Prisons in England and France" (*The North American Review*, 168:507 1899); Margaret Audin. *British Hostages in Napoleonic France, The Evidence: With Particular Reference to Manufacturers and Artisans*, a thesis submitted to the Faculty of Commerce and Social Science of the University of Birmingham (1987).

[5] Audin is also to be credited with recognizing the importance of the French bureaucrats in the Ministry of War for the British prisoners. Whatever event made a

a prison school, respectively.[6] Informing all of these rather tightly focused studies is the larger work of Renaud Morieux[7] on prisoners of war in France and Britain during the eighteenth century. The prison depots and policies concerning prisoners of war that he analyzes had changed very little by the early nineteenth century and the Napoleonic Wars.

This chapter delves into the prison experiences of the captured American merchant seamen who, though captured with and held with the British seamen and sailors who were prisoners of war, had different treatment, national identity, and opportunities that are not covered in the historiography outlined above.

Becoming a Captive

The jails, or gaols, found in many Atlantic ports of France tended to be dungeons or vast rooms in large stone towers or arsenals. Some of them had been constructed in medieval times to guard the entrances to the ports. The Tour Solidor, in Saint-Servan, was a grim, three-towered, three-storey keep on a river, built of stone in the fourteenth century, into which the numerous prisoners taken from the privateers returning to Saint Malo were crammed. The Château de Dieppe was a fourteenth-century fort high on a cold, windy cliff above the town, where prisoners were held in one of the stone towers. The Château de Brest, a massive and ancient citadel on the water, had numerous dungeons and prisons within it. There, seamen would have been held with all types of prisoners, both foreign prisoners of war who had escaped and gone to the coast in the hope of finding a boat to smuggle them out of France, and common criminals, condemned to hard labour, the harshest of punishments, bar death. Stephen Clubb, second mate of the *Hyades*, was thrown into the Calais jail, which he described as a place of "filth, damp and stench" and filled with the "clanking of fetters, noise of wooden shoes, and the sight of pale half famished wretches".[8] The prison at Cherbourg, however, was smaller and in the dockyard. There, the prisoners had beds and a daily food allowance

---

person a prisoner, it was these bureaucrats who determined much in their lives during their years in the prison depots. This is discussed much more in Chapter 4.

[6] See Elodie Duché. "Charitable Network Connections: Transnational Financial Networks and Relief for British Prisoners of War in Napoleonic France, 1803–1814". (*Napoleonica. La Revue*. Vol. 3, No. 21, 2014); Mark J. Gabrielson, "Enlightenment in the Darkness: The British Prisoners of War School of Navigation. Givet, France, 1805–1814" (*Northern Mariner/Le marin du nord*, Vol. XXV, 2015).

[7] Renaud Morieux. *The Society of Prisoners: Anglo-French Wars and Incarceration in the Eighteenth Century.* Oxford: Oxford University Press, 2019.

[8] Stephen Clubb. "A Journal: Containing an Account of the Wrongs, Sufferings, and Neglect, Experienced by Americans in France." *The Magazine of History with Notes and Queries*, Extra numbers, Vol. XIII, 1916, p154.

that, in 1806, was "three quarters of a pound of beef, one pound bread, and a pint of cider".[9] The owners of the capturing privateer, or their agents, were required to pay for the food and lodging of the crew, but they did not always do so and even when they did, it often was not for the entire crew.

Those who were sick were sent to the military hospitals, many of which were run by nuns whose religious communities had been disbanded during the Revolution. In a hospital, the conditions could be quite a bit better. The crew of the shipwrecked *Hussar* were rescued and some were taken to the hospital at Brest, where they received what one chronicler called "humane and heavenly treatment".[10] Occasionally, captured seamen were allowed to lodge in town, under police surveillance at the American consul's expense, until the court passed a judgment as to whether or not the capture of their vessel had been legitimate.

The treatment varied greatly from one port to another. For many, it was at this point, when the crew were in a state of uncertainty, that some local authorities conspired to coerce them into signing on to a French privateer. As the war progressed, the British captured more and more French vessels, imprisoning more and more French seamen. This had been a tactic of Britain in wars with France for nearly a century. As Morieux notes, it was "a deliberate strategy, which aimed at incapacitating French manpower at sea".[11] French ships were desperate for men. The French Marine drafted every available seaman, leaving the privateers to find others wherever they could. Leonard Jarvis was the American vice-consul at Cherbourg when he wrote to the Minister Plenipotentiary, John Armstrong, in Paris about this kind of coercion:

> [...our seamen in France]...are...taken [from] English vessels, they are thrown into prison, kept on an insufficient ration of black bread without any food until their spirits are worn down and they have the alternative offered of entering on board a privateer or being marched into the country to a depot of English prisoners.[12]

In an earlier, very similar situation, the vice-consul at Calais, John Appleton, wrote that:

---

[9] Peter Bussell. *The Diary of Peter Bussell (1806–1814)*. London: Peter Davies, 1931, p5.

[10] John Wetherell. *The Adventures of John Wetherell*. New York: Doubleday, 1953, p125.

[11] Morieux, *The Society of Prisoners*, p12.

[12] Jarvis to Armstrong. 18 May 1810. United States. Department of State. *Despatches from United States Ministers to France, 1789–1906*. Vol. 11. Microfilm copy.

> Notwithstanding all my attention to the seamen, and the provision made for their support, nine of them entered on board a French privateer, contrary to my order and every exertion I could make to prevent them...[13]

The harsh treatment of American seamen in port prisons continued throughout the wars. Captain Gorham Coffin's vessel, the *General Lincoln*, of Boston, was captured by the French in February 1812 and taken in to Boulogne-sur-Mer. The captain was allowed to stay in a hotel in order to deal with the legal issues of the ship's capture but the men were put in prison. On their behalf, Coffin complained to the Commissary General of Police:

> ...the Ships company which I have the honor to command, who are now in prison in this place, find their health very fast decaying, owing to the close confinement & small allowance of provisions which they at present have; I beg Sir you will consider that a sailor who requires exercise, is in great danger when he cannot have that exercise & also that you will take into consideration their situation & allow them some relief.[14]

As described above, the judgments of prizes could be long in coming, long enough for a cargo of perishables to rot. The authorities generally sold quickly such cargo and held the money until the final prize judgement should be made. This procedure could be taken too far. At times, the vessel and all cargo were sold immediately and the proceeds kept. It infuriated the owners of the captured vessels but could be beneficial to the seamen. They were often penniless at that point. When a voyage was interrupted in this way and they were captured, they had not yet received their pay and the money to pay them had been seized during the capture, as probably had been any money in their own pockets. Even if they had managed to keep some money at the time of the vessel's capture, it often was spent in jail to buy extra food or fuel for a fire, if that were allowed. The master of their vessel may have gone to Paris to contest his vessel's capture before the Prize Council and may not have chosen or been able to pay the seamen before leaving. The common seaman would not have been able to afford the diligence from a port city to Paris or a hotel when once there, in order to chase his meagre pay from the master. In prison or out, many of the seamen suffered terribly, with some in rags and reduced to begging in the streets. With the authorities' prompt sale of a vessel and perishable cargo, however, courts usually ordered that the crew's

---

[13] Appleton to Armstrong. 16 April 1804. United States. Department of State. *Despatches from United States Consuls in Calais, 1804–1906.* Vol. 1. Microfilm copy.

[14] Coffin to Martin. 27 February 1812, the author's private collection.

maintenance during the wait should be paid for from the proceeds of the sale, ensuring their food and lodging.[15]

When the Prize Council judgment finally came, if the seizure had been ruled illegal, the crew were free to go. With no money at all, they would have needed to take work on the first ships possible, of whatever nationality. If, however, the capture were to have been judged a good prize the crew became prisoners of war.

The March

Condemned as prisoners of war, the captives were then assigned to one of the prisoner of war depots in the interior of the country, away from the coasts. They would go there on foot. France was at war with many countries throughout this period, some of them changing from enemy to ally or from ally to enemy. Tens of thousands of prisoners of war were in France with only a rather small percentage of them being British or American. A very precise and elegantly written report from the Ministry of War to Napoleon in 1807 showed that the prisoners of war came from Prussia, Austria, Britain, Sweden, Russia and elsewhere. This was just after the military campaign of 1805 in Austria, so the greatest number were Austrians (45,675) and Prussians (32,648) compared with 8,224 British prisoners.[16] By the end of the wars, France held over 130,000 prisoners of war, mostly Spanish and Austrian. By then, about 22,000, roughly sixteen per cent, were British or American.[17] Prisoners of war were separated, for the most part, by nationality and were held in regions of France that were as far as possible from any routes back to their own countries. Thus, the British and Americans were held in the north and east of France, far from the Atlantic coast, where they might bribe someone with a boat to take them across the Channel.

To reach these prisons, the prisoners were marched under guard for weeks. Though captured vessels were taken to ports up and down France's Atlantic coast, the port into which most were taken was Brest, followed by

---

[15] Diot to Russell. 26 November 1810. Jonathan Russell Papers. (1795–1832), John Hay Library, Brown University Library.

[16] *"Prisonniers de guerre"* Report submitted by Goulhot. 10 May 1807. *Archives de la Secrétairerie d'État impériale: administration de la Guerre (1800–1814)*. Arch. nat. AF/IV/1158.

[17] Léonce Bernard. *Les Prisonniers de guerre du Premier Empire*. Paris: Editions Christian, 2000, p200. Le Quang puts the total number of prisoners of war taken during the First Empire as somewhere between 140,000 and 270,000. Jeann-Laure Le Quang, « De l'ennemi au nouveau Français: la gestion des étrangers par la police napoléonienne (1799–1814) », *La Révolution française* [En ligne], 22 | 2022, mis en ligne le 20 janvier 2022, consulté le 23 janvier 2022. URL: http://journals.openedition.org/lrf/6034

Dieppe, Cherbourg and Saint Malo. These became the gathering points for prisoners taken in to smaller ports, such as Roscoff. When enough prisoners were accumulated, they were formed into a "convoy" and marched across France. Captains were separated from their crew and sent to different depots. Sailors and common merchant seamen were generally sent to the depots in the fortresses of the towns of Arras, Valenciennes or Cambrai, in the north of France, while merchant captains were sent to the towns of Verdun, Auxonne and later to Longwy. A seaman captured and taken in to the port of Dieppe and then sent to the depot at Arras would have marched about 140 kilometres; to the depot at Cambrai from Dieppe would have been about 175 kilometres. The march from the port of Cherbourg to Arras was over 530 kilometres. From the port of Brest was much longer, being about 635 kilometres to the Arras depot and a bit more to that at Cambrai. Those who had been taken into the ports further south, to Bordeaux or Bayonne, marched the greatest distances, going thence to depots in the northeast. These long marches had been a constant aspect of life in both Britain and France during times of war. Morieux writes: "At any given time, the country roads of France and Britain were criss-crossed by troops of prisoners of war…"[18]

At the same time as captives from ships were being marched to prison depots, thousands of captives from battlefields were being marched across France to different prison depots. David Rouanet describes how much of a hardship these vast columns of prisoners and their guards, needing food, bedding and shelter, were on the communities through which they passed. Local reserves and gendarmes were pulled from their law enforcement duties to escort the columns but often there were not enough available. Hundreds of prisoners might arrive needing many kilos of bread, places to sleep and medical attention, which a town may not have been able to provide.[19] For those towns that were regular stopping places on the routes, this must have been an unbearable burden, being in addition to the loss of men through conscription and to the food shortages brought on by war.

The marches were harsh. The prisoners were marched from dawn to dusk, in all weather, often chained together, and occasionally in company with convicted felons or deserters from the French Army.

> The prisoners were joined, 2 by 2, by a chain in the middle of which there was a ring. The pair of prisoners was joined to the pair in front and to the pair behind by another long chain that passed through the ring. One witness recounted that a procession could have as many as 400 people. The march could last many weeks.… Deaths were frequent (about 10%).[20]

---

[18] Morieux, *The Society of Prisoners*, p165.

[19] David Rouanet. *Prisonniers de Napoléon: Les prisonniers de guerre coalisés internés en France de1803 à 1814*. Unpublished manuscript, p164.

[20] Nicolas Le Boënnec. *Archives anciennes (avant 1790): Inventaire analytique*. Morlaix: Archives Municipales de Morlaix, 2017, p59.

The British ship's surgeon, Daniel Cameron, of the *Biter*, recounted the experience of sharing the march in the winter of 1805 with deserters from the French Army:

> We had about 100 prisoners *Conscrits* with us and severals made their escape such wretched beings could not be imagined to exist, some in carts groaning in the middle of a…fever. Others just worn out… but the two columns of footmen chained by a long chain to each two and a string which ran the middle formed two deep marching in two straight lines.[21]

The marches were done in stages that were rather short in the beginning, until the prisoners became more used to walking all day, and then the stages got longer. Roll call was taken at the beginning and the end of each day. They were allowed a rest at midday. Their guards were advanced money to buy food for the prisoners. Sometimes they did this fairly and the prisoners ate, sometimes they gave them the money and let them find their own food from the hawkers that followed the marchers, and sometimes they kept the money for themselves and the prisoners had no more than bread and water. They slept in local jails, army barracks, dungeons or barns along the way, and were overcharged by their hosts for every bit of food or fuel or extra straw bedding they bought. They were not given clothes or shoes at that point and their own often wore out so that, when they arrived, they were in rags and barefoot. As they marched, the locals sometimes jeered at them but sometimes took pity on them and gave them food.[22] One group of American seamen from the *Ariel* were in such a pitiful state that each was given a pair of shoes (they would have been wooden) before beginning the march.[23]

Peleg Bunker, a Nantucket whaler in his fifties, was marched over 850 kilometres from Bordeaux to Verdun in the winter of 1803 and wrote home that he and the others were treated "like cattle".[24] For some, the march was not so brutal. "Nothing remarkable occurred," wrote one British prisoner, "our conductors, although civil, were unremitting in the watch kept on us … each night they occupied the same room with us, alternately keeping watch."[25] Stephen Clubb, the English mate, was accompanied by his Bostonian wife

---

[21] Cameron dossier. *Archives de la Guerre et Armée de Terre. Prisonniers de guerre français et étrangers* (1792–1874). SHDV. Yj40.

[22] Michael Lewis. *Napoleon and His British Captives*. London: George Allen & Unwin, 1962, pp83–115.

[23] *Guerre et Armée de Terre, Prisonniers de guerre français et étrangers* (1792–1874). SHDV. Yj30. Fulwar Skipwith Papers.

[24] Lydia Bunker Gardner. undated manuscript biography of Peleg Bunker, Edouard Stackpole Collection, Nantucket Historical Association Research Library and Archives, Nantucket.

[25] Richard Langton. *Narrative of Captivity in France from 1809 to 1814*, Vol. 1. London: Smith, Elder, 1838, p156.

and had some money, so he was able to pay for carts and horses on the march from Calais to Arras, and for hotel rooms along the way.[26] The seaman without money would have endured the march at its worst. "The poor sailors," wrote the Methodist Royal Navy man, Cavanagh, on his march to the Cambrai depot, "had but a very scanty allowance of food, and generally very miserable places to sleep in."[27] The surgeon, Cameron, noted that the sailors on the march with him gradually sold the clothes off their backs to get money to buy food.[28]

John Cook was an American seaman who had been impressed by the Royal Navy onto the *Fairie* and then released in England when the American consular agent there was able to prove that he was an American citizen. Afterward, he was stranded in a small harbour town in Devon, where he took a ship to Guernsey, hoping to find there an American vessel to take him home. Captain Robert Crown of the *Jean* was bound for Norfolk, Virginia and agreed to let Cook work his passage. Soon afterward, Cook described his capture by the French and the march, which destroyed his health, in a letter to the American consul in Paris:

> Arras, 29th Jany. 1807
>
> The Humble petition of John Cook, an American & a misfortunate seaman .... Being only two days at sea [we] fell in with two French Man of War brigs who captured the Jean on the 6th March 1806 and landed your Humble Petitioner at Rochefort as a prisoner of war. From thence he was marched to Cambrai ...arriving at Cambrai the 9th May 1806 where he was severely taken ill by a brain fever by which he is rendered unable to walk upon his legs without the assistance of two crutches, & it is the opinion of the surgeons that he ever will continue [thus] and unable to work for his living. He arrived here on the 25th [January 1807] in a most Deplorable situation which will draw Sympathy from any feeling person...[29]

From the naval port of Rochefort to Cambrai, John Cook walked over 600 kilometres. It was during the spring, a time that is usually windy and rainy, so he may have been wet through for much of the march, and probably in chains. A British doctor at one of the depots described the state of most prisoners after such marches:

---

[26] Clubb, "A Journal", p170.

[27] J. Cavanagh. *Some Account of Religious Societies Among the British Prisoners in France, During the Late War. Being an Abstract from the Journal of J. Cavanagh, R.N....* Plymouth: 1826, p12.

[28] Cameron dossier. *Archives de la Guerre et Armée de Terre. Prisonniers de guerre français et étrangers* (1792–1874). SHDV. Yj40.

[29] Fulwar Skipwith Papers. Some of the spelling has been changed to modern usage for ease of comprehension.

I have seen them at different times, to the amount of some hundreds, arrive in a state of comparative nakedness; many under the influence of fever as well as other dangerous complaints; some with very serious accidents....They arrived at all times of the year from the wide extended coasts of the French empire, being en route for weeks, often for months, their usual lodging a jail, perhaps the cachot, sometimes a donjon.[30]

The Depots

There were twelve depots dedicated primarily to British and, with them, American prisoners of war, all of them far from the Atlantic coast and mostly in the northeast quadrant of France. In the northern tip of France were Arras, Cambrai and Valenciennes. Continuing east were Givet, Longwy, Verdun, Sarrelibre (now Saarlouis in Germany) and Bitche, the depot that was furthest east. In the central east were Auxonne and Besançon. Much further south were Briançon and Mont Dauphin. In smaller numbers, British prisoners were also held at Amiens, Bois-le-Duc, Coevorden, Nancy, Sedan and Rennes.

These depots were nearly all in the great, defensive forts built in the seventeenth century by the legendary military architect, Vauban. He served under Louis XIV, whose wars had extended France's boundaries. To secure these boundaries, fortresses and citadels were built around France's perimeters to the north and east, and on the coast. They were all to Vauban's basic design of a walled and bastioned fortress shaped like a pentagon, with surrounding walls that extended the shape to a five-pointed or multi-pointed star. Built on cliffs or hills and with wells for water, they were designed to withstand a siege. They had drawbridges and towers; the walls were five to six meters thick and fifteen to twenty meters high.[31] Flooded ditches or moats surrounded some of them. They were not isolated outposts but attached to large towns. Inside were the barracks and buildings necessary to house, feed, arm and support the soldiers garrisoned there. It was in the towers, dungeons and caverns of these forts that Napoleon decided to place all of his British prisoners of war, including the captured American seamen.

---

[30] Farrell Mulvey. *Sketches of the Character, Conduct, and Treatment of the Prisoners of War at Auxonne, Longwy &c. form the Year 1810 to 1814, with an Account of the Epidemic, As It Appeared in the Latter Place in 1812.* London: Longman, Hurst, Rees, Orme and Brown, 1818, p21.

[31] Marie-Hélène Bloch. *The Citadel of Besançon: Fortifications of Vauban.* Besançon: Editions La Taillanderie, 2008, p10.

One of these depots, Verdun, was designated for British civilian prisoners, shipmasters and officers; it was not a depot for seamen.[32] Only about fifty American prisoners were sent to Verdun, almost all of them masters of their vessels: men such as Richard Cook, of Philadelphia, captain of the *Peace*, and Stephen Waterman, of Nantucket, master of the *Mentor*. This depot also held hundreds of British civilians, and plays a disproportionate part in the historiography about prison life, because most of the people who wrote accounts of their experiences in Napoleon's prisons were held at Verdun. Even though few Americans were held at Verdun, this unusual depot requires some explanation.

The civilians at Verdun had been in prison since the recommencement of war in 1803. As soon as war was declared again, ending the "Peace of Amiens", Napoleon issued a decree to arrest and detain as enemies all British men of military service age who were then in France.[33] He based this on the British law that all men from the ages of eighteen to sixty could be called up to serve in a militia, which he interpreted as their being in the army reserves. During that brief period of peace after the Treaty of Amiens, France, and especially Paris, had filled with British visitors. For them, being rounded up and arrested was sudden and unexpected. It was also very thorough. Businessmen, boys in school, tourists, visiting academics, established immigrants, all British men in France were arrested and held. (Only a very few Americans seem to have been included in these arrests.) The police did not usually arrest women and children but some preferred to remain together as a family and stayed with the men arrested. Those British nationals who were working in France and who could prove that their work was necessary to the French economy were exempt; they were allowed to continue their work and lives as before, albeit under surveillance.[34]

The rounding up of foreign nationals did not originate with Napoleon. In the earlier war with Britain, the Directory had ordered a general arrest of all British nationals in French ports. Napoleon merely extended the geographical application of the law to all of France and not just the port cities. Later, he would apply the same approach to enemy nationals within France's borders when he would round up all the Spanish in France in 1808, when France's war with Spain began.[35]

---

[32] *Guerre et Armée de Terre, Prisonniers de guerre français et étrangers (1792–1874). SHDV. Yj19.*

[33] Audin, *British Hostages*, p15.

[34] Audin, *British Hostages*, p22; *"Exécution de l'arrêté du 2 prairial", Ministère du Grand-juge, Division de Police secrète.*

[35] Bernard, *Les Prisonniers de guerre*, p205.

Estimates as to the number of British détenus, as these civilian prisoners were called,[36] vary according to author and the year. Lewis gives the number as 500,[37] based on 1810 estimates by British commissioners trying to arrange prisoner exchanges. A French list made in 1803 of the names of those arrested in execution of the decree gives the total as a bit less than 1200.[38] The Duke of Rovigo, while Minister of Police, in his regular reports to Napoleon, included a tally of *détenus* at various smaller prisons, with his number consistently at around 5000.[39] The 1807 report to Napoleon mentioned above gave the number at that time as just over 6500.

Initially, the civilian prisoners were assembled in Paris, Fontainebleau, Verdun, Valenciennes and Nîmes.[40] Soon, they were consolidated at Verdun, where they did not have to be in prison cells, but were allowed to live in lodgings in the town.[41] This detaining of civilian foreign nationals cannot be compared to the internment camps of the twentieth century; at Verdun, illogical and frivolous wartime madness reigned and the rich détenus were allowed, even encouraged, to squander all they had. With the arrival of the détenus, the town of Verdun quite quickly became a centre of debauchery. Trapped, bored and some of them very wealthy, the détenus were preyed upon by the Verdun locals. Almost every home rented lodgings, in which the rooms and meals were overpriced. Almost every expensive pastime was encouraged. There were gambling dens, brothels, gentlemen's clubs, horse races, cock-fights, an English library with the latest newspapers from England, English theatre

---

[36] Audin is precise about the terminology (p22). They were not prisoners of war in name at the beginning. Napoleon referred to them as his "hostages" (*ôtages* in French,) but the more common term used for them by the French was "*prisonniers anglais*", "English prisoners". After their status was altered in 1806, they became known as English prisoners of war, "*prisonniers de guerre anglais*", and it is most often under this term that records about them can be found in French archives. Lewis, Audin mistakenly believed, began the use of the French word "*détenus*", or "detained" but long before he wrote his memoir, the 1807 report on prisoners of war to Napoleon uses the word *détenus* for British civilians held as prisoners of war. *Détenus* will be used here.

[37] Lewis, *Napoleon and His British Captives*, p264.

[38] *Guerre et Armée de Terre, Prisonniers de guerre français et étrangers (1792–1874)*. SHDV. Yj33.

[39] Nicole Gotteri. *La Police Secrète du Premier Empire: Bulletins quotidiens adressés par Savary à l'Empereur*, Vols 1–6. Paris, Honoré Champion, 1997.

[40] *Guerre et Armée de Terre, Prisonniers de guerre français et étrangers (1792–1874.* SHDV. Yj33.

[41] Reverend R.B. Wolfe. *English Prisoners in France, Containing Observations on their Manners and Habits, Principally With Reference to Their Religious State, During Nine Years' Residence in the Depots of Fontainbleau, Verdun, Givet, and Valenciennes.* London: J Hatchard and Son, 1830, p59.

productions, and copious amounts of wine and brandy. Everything could be had for a price, always high, and every infraction of rules could lead to a hefty fine, at the very least. One English prisoner wrote:

> Verdun resembles a small fashionable town in England. The lodgings were good and not extravagant...Horses were brought from England and came through Germany at most enormous expense – at last there was a very excellent set of horses, and the course was as fashionable and full of roguery as Newmarket. Drinking and smoking clubs were established in many parts of the town, for all classes...[42]

The people of Verdun enriched themselves to such a degree that other towns, hoping for a similar boon, petitioned to have their fortresses made prisoner depots as well.[43]

The profligate spending of some of the détenus, perhaps coupled with a hatred of the British enemy, would appear to have corrupted the commandant of the depot, General Louis Wirion. Prior to becoming commandant, he had been a respected officer in the Gendarmerie, credited with reorganizing the structure of that branch of the army extremely well. At Verdun, however, he issued harsh punishments to the British prisoners and extorted bribes and illegal payments from many. Eventually, complaints about him were heard and the Ministry of Justice determined that there was enough evidence for a trial. Wirion shot himself in 1810, before the trial could take place. Though justly despised by many of the British prisoners at Verdun, he seems to have treated the American prisoners well. There is no word of complaint about him in the diplomatic or consular correspondence and he signed every release of Americans from Verdun promptly and without, so far as can be known, demanding a bribe or favour.

By contrast, the prison town of Arras was described as being "large and clean" but with "very little commerce".[44] Located in the far north of France, Arras was a regional capital surrounded by farmland where wheat, barley and rye were grown. There were numerous canal boats on the Scarpe River for transport of passengers and goods and in which the townspeople were said to enjoy a Sunday excursion.[45] A small number of British officers lived in the town, as at most depots, but there were few, if any, détenus. A world away, yet adjoining the town, on its southwest side, was the citadel, which was entered by crossing two drawbridges and passing through an imposing

---

[42] Roy and Lesley Adkins. *Jack Tar: The Extraordinary Lives of Ordinary Seamen in Nelson's Navy.* London: Abacus, 2009, p249.

[43] Lewis, *Napoleon and His British Captives*, pp116–136.

[44] Bussell, *The Diary*, p30.

[45] Clubb, "A Journal", p174.

gate that was locked at night. The Arras citadel and barracks were used as a prison depot and received the first prisoners on 13 April 1806.[46]

The initial separation of officers from men and captains from crew, sending them to different depots, that had begun when the prisoners were first taken was maintained throughout their captivity, leading to there being few of low rank at Verdun. Michael Lewis, that very opinionated British naval historian, explains the British prejudices of class, as well as those generally associated with military rank, that affected how the prisoners were distributed:

> Here, as at every other point, a gentleman may expect, and will usually get, one standard of treatment, and a non-gentleman a very different one. A general will be in luxury compared with a private, a naval captain compared with a ship's boy.[47]

Needless to say, the common seaman was barely a notch above a ship's boy and would have received no privileges or preferences at all.

> ...at Verdun, British prisoner of war John Robertson wrote in his journal of the gentlemen's clubs and gambling houses enjoyed by English officers in France. Excluded by his class as a lowly sailor, Robertson criticised the coaches and gold-laced footmen of the "English nobbs" who knew little of captivity.[48]

As Lewis wrote, "Indeed, in the whole history of man there can have been very few prison-places like it. Verdun must be all but unique."[49]

The large majority of American prisoners were common merchant seamen, without wealth, without rank, without the prestige and camaraderie of being in the military. In French eyes they would have been disdained not only because they were of the very lowest order in the hierarchy of a vessel, thought to have been mere muscle without intellect, but also, in a land ruled by an Emperor-General, because they were merchant seamen and not sailors in the Navy or, what might have been considered better yet, soldiers in an army. To the British, class prejudices toward common seamen socially may have been compounded by nationalistic resentment of those from a country that had so recently fought and won a war of independence from their empire. Lines of

---

[46] Jean-Claude Devos. "*Les Prisonniers de Guerre Anglais Sous le Premier Empire*" *Revue de l'Institut Napoléon*, No. 50, January 1954, pp11–21, p14.

[47] Lewis, *Napoleon and His British Captives*, p83.

[48] Anna McKay. "British and French Prisoners of War, 1793–1815". *Museum Blog.* 2 November 2017. Royal Museums Greenwich (NMM ref: JOD/202/1) https://www.rmg.co.uk/explore/blog/british-and-french-prisoners-war-1793–1815. [Accessed 30 March 2020].

[49] Lewis, *Napoleon and His British Captives*, p136.

prejudice were not rigid; guards and prisoners on both sides of the Channel helped one another at times, and some French guards aided some American prisoners. On the whole, however, the American seamen were at the bottom of prison society and would have been separated accordingly.

While merchant captains were sent to Verdun, Auxonne and Longwy, seamen were sent by the hundreds to the overcrowded Arras citadel, where the total number of prisoners soared from 1670 in 1807 to over 3200 two years later.[50] Americans were also sent to the depots at Givet and Valenciennes. The latter was connected by river to Arras and was in a deplorable state, after having been besieged during the Revolutionary Wars. In 1797, the American, William Lee, visited and wrote:

> ...this distressed city, one third of which has been destroyed by the army under the Duke of York...and the misery occasioned by this siege is perhaps as apparent now as ever. The heart of the traveler is melted with pity to see the ragged, wretched conditions of the inhabitants of this once flourishing place. Some houses are without roofs; others without doors and windows; others nothing but a pile of rubbish; and others, being partly destroyed, the remaining half is inhabited. The fortifications are going to ruin, not having had repairs since the siege.[51]

It is unlikely that the fortress had been much repaired or improved for the large number of prisoners placed there. In both Valenciennes and Givet, the number of all nationalities of prisoners was usually about 1500.[52]

To cope with the increasing number of prisoners, the French designated more citadels and fortresses to be used as depots. In 1809, the citadel at Cambrai (which had been housing a Prussian regiment), began to take in prisoners of war. Over 600 seamen, many of them American, were transferred there from Arras at once. Yet that depot, too, quickly became so overcrowded that it was necessary for the prison commandant to request permission to house prisoners in other buildings, even the prison chapel.[53] Troublesome prisoners were moved further inland to other depots, Bitche and Sarrelouis being the most severe. Thus, a seaman could have spent time in three or four prisons before his captivity came to an end.

[50] Arnaud Gabet and Christiane Lepie. "*Cambrai, Camp de Prisonniers de Guerre Anglais (1803–1815)*". Revue Trimestielle de l'Association Cambrésis Terre d'Histoire, No. 5, May 1993, pp4–16, p6. Bussell p28, reports that the numbers when he arrived at Arras was about 1000 men, which Lewis, p152, says rose to 2800.

[51] Lee, *A Yankee Jeffersonian*, p38.

[52] Edward Fraser. *Napoleon the Gaoler: Personal Experiences and Adventures of British Sailors and Soldiers During the Great Captivity*. London: Methuen, 1914, p60.

[53] Gabet and Lepie, "*Cambrai*", p13.

All of the prisons were under the authority of the Ministry of War, which operated them through the Gendarmerie, a policing branch of the Army. Most were governed by officers of the relevant department's Gendarmerie corps, "or even, where necessary, by a reformed or retired officer". Because the British were "of all prisoners of war the most difficult to control, above all those at Verdun and those in the depot at Bitche",[54] the prisons where they were held needed stronger authority and were governed by a Squadron Chief of the Gendarmerie (except for Verdun, run by General Wirion). Thus, because of the fractious nature of the British prisoners with whom they were held, the American seamen prisoners were subject to a generally harsher and stricter discipline than were prisoners of other nationalities in other depots.

The most common punishment for escape attempts, as well as for bad behaviour, was to transfer the culprit to one of the harsher prisons to the east, at Bitche, Sedan or Sarrelibre. "The Place of Tears", Bitche had the reputation among the British prisoner diarists as being the worst of the depots. Although the fortress had been improved by Vauban, it was one of the few that did not follow his design of a pentagon within a star. Surrounded by a ditch, it was of a lumpen, vaguely oval shape on a steep rock that rose 1000 feet into the sky above the surrounding valley and banks of the Rhine. Seen from a distance, it was dark, ominous and grim, looming above the town, on "a lofty rock, with a flat surface, on which a solitary fortress, called Bitche; a place held up as an object of terror…"[55] Inside were all the buildings necessary to house a garrison and to withstand a siege. Below, cut into the rock, were tunnels and caverns originally made for the garrison and for stores. In these half-lit caverns and dark holes were placed the recalcitrant prisoners of war.

The rules of the other prisons seemed not to apply at Bitche. Officers, having become criminals, no longer had any of the rights or freedoms associated with their ranks. In the punishment depots, the men were divided and housed according to their behaviour, not their rank or class. The worst behaved were in the lowest underground, windowless dungeons with seeping walls where "the rocky wall … was in winter time a sheet of ice, the moisture which oozed through having frozen hard".[56] With good behaviour, an officer could work his way up to the slightly better dungeons that had been built to house the garrison. These had high, vaulted ceilings, some windows, and wood plank beds. Common seamen, however, could not, no matter how well behaved,

---

[54] *Prisonniers de guerre* report submitted by Goulhot. 10 May 1807.

[55] James Forbes. *Letters From France, Written in the Years 1803 & 1804: Including a Particular Account of Verdun, and the Situation of the British Captives in That City*, Vol. II. London: J. White, 1806, p258.

[56] Arthur Griffiths. "Old War Prisons in England and France". *The North American Review*, Vol. 168, No. 507 (February 1899), pp. 163–177. University of Northern Iowa. http://www.jstor.org/stable/25119141 [Accessed: 17/04/2020] p176.

hope to rise to better accommodation. In these lowest caverns, the men were nearly abandoned. Among them were any American seamen who could not or would not comply with rules, those men who drank and rioted and fought at any provocation. They, and others like them, devised primitive methods of self-government, which involved boxing matches, sometimes to the death, at the deepest level underground.[57] Guards refused to enter that hole at night and the men there sank to brutality and bestiality.[58]

Sarrelibre (Saarlouis) was at first used to take the overflow of prisoners from other depots but, as time went on, was used for punishment. Roughly sixty-seven kilometres to the northeast of Bitche, Sarrelibre was a fortified city of about 6000 people at the time, situated on the Saar River. Like Givet, the prison was intended to hold 1500 prisoners, most of them of the lowest ranks in the army and seamen.[59] No account by any of the sixty or so American prisoners sent there has survived to tell of the experience. British accounts rate it to have been as bad as or worse than the prison at Bitche, in large part because, yet again, the commandant of the prison was a cruel and corrupt man. Among his abuses was to withhold prisoners' clothing allotment, leaving the men "to stalk about in a blanket," and not to pay them their allowance.[60] For his crimes and cruelty, the commandant of Sarrelibre was eventually condemned to hard labour.[61]

Life in the Prison Depot

Approaching their depot, the men completing the long march would have seen Vauban's looming fortress walls from some distance away and surely would have found the sight daunting. The high walls and towers, the bars on windows, the drawbridges and portcullises all would have communicated a sense of oppression, weight and darkness that could surely have frightened or depressed a seaman whose life had been on the open seas.

On arrival, the prisoners, still in chains, stood in the citadel's courtyard while a roll call was taken. Then, a prisoner number and a room were assigned to each man. All of their details were entered into a ledger or onto a loose-leaf form. The Americans, comparatively few in number, would have encountered a crowd of British prisoners, including many more than the seamen captured from ships or the soldiers taken in battle.

---

[57] Seacome Ellison. *Prison Scenes; and Narrative of Escape from France, During the Late War*. London: Whittaker and Co., 1838, pp84–85.

[58] Lewis, *Napoleon and His British Captives*, p145.

[59] Fraser, *Napoleon the Gaoler*, p145.

[60] Adkins, *Jack Tar*, p253.

[61] Griffiths, "Old War Prisons", p176.

Conditions were more or less the same at the four non-punishment depots where most American seamen were held: Arras, Cambrai, Valenciennes and Givet. Arras and Cambrai may have been more crowded, one commandant or another may have been more corrupt but, on the whole, they followed the same regulations and pattern. At the depots, clothing and bedding, after a fashion, were provided. Each prisoner was given on arrival a woollen vest and trousers, a canvas smock, and a knitted cap. For bedding, a camp blanket and a straw mattress were given to every two men; they were expected to sleep two to a mattress. Where no mattresses were available, each pair received fifteen kilos of straw on which to sleep. The straw was to be changed every four months. For warmth and cooking, fuel "of the most economical type possible" was to be provided.[62] The rooms at both Arras and Givet held eighteen or twenty men and had for furniture "a stove, kettle, table, two long stools, one earthen dish and a pitcher".[63]

As at Verdun, most of the British officers were living outside of the prisons on parole, along with many of the merchant captains, including two or three Americans. The word "parole" comes from the French term for word of honour, *parole d'honneur*, which in the military sense meant that a man gave his word of honour that, if allowed to live in town, he would not try to escape and, if released and repatriated, he would not return to fighting the enemy that had released him. Only officers and merchant captains were allowed parole as, the reasoning went, only they had a sense of honour. Historically, parole was linked with exchange. Prisoner officers of equal rank would be exchanged between belligerents, each man signing a parole document before returning home. Détenus, having no military rank, could not be exchanged. Additionally, Napoleon reduced the number of exchanges greatly, preferring to keep the officers as prisoners (and off the battlefields, for the same reason that the British kept French seamen on prison hulks and away from French vessels by holding them prisoner). Parole during the First Empire came to mean being allowed to live outside of prison but only in the town where the prison was located, not to be exchanged or to leave the country.

In the same way, French prisoners who were officers being held in England were allowed to live outside of prison on parole.[64] In both countries, officers on parole had to be present at every muster or roll call of prisoners or risk having their parole revoked and their being returned to prison. In both countries, they had to pay for their own lodging, meals and other living expenses and neither group found the small allowances adequate. Those who were wealthy

---

[62] Ministère de la Guerre. "*Réglement Sur la Police des Dépots de Prisonniers de guerre du 10 Thermidor, An XI de la République française*". 29 July 1803, Articles LII, LIX and LXII.

[63] Bussell, *The Diary*, p28; Fraser, *Napoleon the Gaoler*, p61.

[64] Bernard, *Les Prisonniers de guerre*, p183.

arranged for their families to send money, quite often using the same Parisian banking house, Perregaux, as was used by the détenus to receive their funds.[65] As parole was only for officers; it was rarely possible for a common soldier or sailor to be exchanged, to sign a parole or to live outside of prison. Very, very few American seaman had the chance to do so.[66] As to exchange, the possibility was available to British officers who were prisoners of war. It was not available to any American, for the simple reason that the United States was not at war with France and had no French prisoners to exchange. Even were the two countries to have been at war, exchange would not have been a hope for a lowly seaman, but only for an officer. The American seamen remained within the prisons, without privileges and without hope of exchange.

Communication with the outside world was limited. No one in all of France was permitted to send any letters outside of the country; to send letters to enemy Britain was punishable by death. This applied to prisoners of war as well. Prisoners had to send any letters for the United States, unsealed, first to the Ministry of War. To be sure, letters could be smuggled out but the cost for this "was prohibitive for all except the best-off among the prisoners".[67] The Americans could and did, however, write to American consuls within France and to the Minister for War directly. From 1806, bilingual prisoners were hired, at seventy-five centimes per day, to work as interpreters.[68] It was their responsibility to open at the post office all letters addressed to prisoners of war and to report on their contents.[69] Their names and comments appear in some of the letters and documents sent by American seamen to the authorities.

The common seamen prisoners' daily lives centred around meals, work and musters. Mustering the prisoners for regular roll calls was an essential part of the prison routine. In the winter, they were mustered twice a day, at eight o'clock in the morning and at four o'clock in the afternoon. In the summer, there were three musters per day, at six in the morning, at midday, and at six in the evening. The punishment for missing a single muster was

[65] Bernard, *Les Prisonniers de guerre*, p183; Elodie Duché. "Charitable Network Connections", p84.

[66] In keeping with Verdun's liberties, American merchant captains there did live in town on parole. Peleg Bunker was on parole when he died in the house of a tanner, Jean Joseph Nicolas, where he was lodging.

[67] Fraser, *Napoleon the Gaoler*, p46.

[68] *Ministère de la Guerre.* "*Réglement pour la Direction, la Police, et le placement des Prisonniers de guerre sur parole, détenus dans les dépôts, où employés comme travailleurs du 8 octobre 1806*". 8 October 1806, Article 15. H. Berriat. *Législation Militaire ou Receuil Méthodique et Raisonné des Lois, Décrêts, Réglemens et Instructions Actuellement en vigueur sur Toutes les Branches de l'état militaire.* Alexandrie: Louis Capriolo, 1812, p372.

[69] Clubb, "A Journal", p176.

close confinement for a minimum of twenty-four hours and up to five days.[70] When there was an escape, musters might be increased to five times per day.[71] Those few allowed to live in town on parole had to appear for musters, often in the central town square or in front of the town hall.

All prisoners who were of the lowest ranks, including the American seamen, were subject to forced labour. Napoleon's policy was that the prisoners should not, on balance, cost the nation.[72] He put thousands of them to work. They worked alongside French labourers on major projects digging canals, on road works, or draining swamps.[73] They also worked in local factories and for local farmers. When a large number of prisoners were expected to arrive, local officials put up notices advising

> ...all...who wish to employ one or more prisoners to work on their farms or in their factories [are] to make their request at the Town Hall, stating 1) how many prisoners are needed 2) what work they will do and 3) how they will be maintained.[74]

At Vincennes, more than 100 prisoners worked for local people.[75] It was a way of compensating the nation's workforce for all of the French men conscripted into the Emperor's army or held on British prison hulks. Some of the work may have been back-breaking but it also afforded the opportunity to get outside of the prison walls and attempt an escape. At Arras, while working under heavy guard late into the night in May 1811, a group of prisoners slipped away in the dark. The guards at all entries to the city were alerted. They did not find the escapees and the sergeant who had been on guard during the escape was demoted.[76]

At least one American prisoner worked in a French factory during part of the time that he was held in France. Hugh Faren, "an honest and quiet man"[77] of New York, was captured in 1804 and sent to the depot at Valenciennes.

---

[70] Ministère de la Guerre. "Réglement Sur la Police des Dépots de Prisonniers de guerre du 10 Thermidor, An XI de la République française". 29 July 1803, Articles II–V. H. Berriat. Législation Militaire ou Receuil Méthodique et Raisonné des Lois, Décrêts, Réglemens et Instructions Actuellement en vigueur sur Toutes les Branches de l'état militaire. Alexandrie: Louis Capriolo, 1812.
[71] Bussell, The Diary, p45.
[72] Bernard, Les Prisonniers de guerre, p197.
[73] Bernard, Les Prisonniers de guerre, p197.
[74] "Prisonniers de Guerre" 4 Brumaire An 14 [26 October 1805] Affaires Militaires – An 9–1810, AD Haute-Vienne, 8R/1.
[75] Bernard, Les Prisonniers de guerre, p207.
[76] Archives de la Guerre et Armée de Terre. Prisonniers de guerre français et étrangers (1792–1874). SHDV. Yj69.
[77] Duquesne to Skipwith, 15 February 1807. Fulwar Skipwith Papers.

Five years later, he was reported to be working in a factory owned by a "Mr. Jolly" in Saint Quentin.[78] This would appear to have been a cotton spinning mill, known as the "Red Mill" because it was built of red brick, run by two Protestant cousins, named Joly.[79] After many years working there, Faren was released in 1813. It could be surmised that the conditions at the factory for Faren and other prisoner of war labourers were only marginally better than those at the Valenciennes depot. After the war, when the Jolys lost these unpaid workers, the locally hired employees had no competition for their employment and could demand better conditions and wages. Only a few months later, the factory workers went on the first of many strikes.[80]

The greatest cause of suffering for most of the prisoners was the shortage of food. "Here is to be seen hunger and distress," wrote Clubb on arriving at Arras, "clothed in tatters, no dainties here, but a scanty allowance is the fare of many an unfortunate captive."[81] The allowance of food per man at Arras, issued every three days, was "one pound of bread, half a pound of beef, about a quarter of a pint of callavances [dried beans] or pease and a little salt, and… about half a pound of coal to cook our meat."[82] Even at rollicking Verdun, the seamen received only "a small square piece of bullock's liver, a slice of black bread, and a glass of new brandy".[83] Prisoners were each given a small allowance based upon their rank, which should have enabled them to purchase a few necessary items and more food. The amount was based on what was paid to men in the French Army or Navy, a prisoner receiving half of what a serving French man of the same rank was paid.[84] Seamen received a pittance of three sous per month, "a sum cruelly inadequate" and one that,

---

[78] "List of American Sailors Detained as Prisoners of War in France". *Spooner's Vermont Journal*, 4 September 1809, Windsor, Vermont, Vol. XXVII, issue 1363, p3. https://www.genealogybank.com/ [Accessed 20 January 2021].

[79] Jean-Marie Wiscart. "*Les Manufactures Protestants en Picardie au XIXe Siècle*", *Revue du Nord*, No. 395, 2012. Association Revue du Nord, pp389–410. https://www.cairn.info/revue-du-nord-2012-2-page-389.htm. [Accessed 20 January 2021] p395.

[80] Wiscart, "*Les Manufactures Protestants*", p407.

[81] Bussell, *The Diary*, p26.

[82] Bussell, *The Diary*, p28.

[83] Thomas James Walker. *The Depot for Prisoners of War at Norman Cross Huntingdonshire. 1796 to 1816*. London: Constable, 1913, p234.

[84] *Ministère de la Guerre.* "*Arrêté relatif au traitement des prisonniers de guerre étrangers de 13 floréal An 7*", 2 May 1799. Article 1. H. Berriat. Législation Militaire ou Receuil Méthodique et Raisonné des Lois, Décrêts, Réglemens et Instructions Actuellement en vigueur sur Toutes les Branches de l'état militaire. Alexandrie: Louis Capriolo, 1812, p363. The sum was based on the payments outlined in the "*Loi du 23 floréal An 5*" [issued by the Directoire], 17 May 1797. See J.B. Duvergier. *Collection complète des lois, Décrets, Ordonnances, Réglemens, Avis du Conseil-d'état*, 2nd edition, Vol. 9. Paris: Guillot at Scribe, 1835, p354.

by all accounts, they immediately spent on getting drunk.[85] Though Army and Navy officers received more (a Post-Captain received the equivalent of four pounds sterling per month) all who had been on the crew of merchant ships, as they were not military, received the same as the seamen.[86] It is likely that three sous per month (a sou, or sol, was equal to five centimes)[87] was the allowance for all of the captive Americans, whether seamen, merchant ship captains or impressed sailors in the Royal Navy.

Contemporary writers agree that even this tiny amount was often given late or not at all. Fraser wrote that "considerable hardship was caused by the payments being often in arrear, while, in addition…dishonest French officials found means of keeping back part of the money, coolly cheating their helpless victims".[88] Clubb, who tried to help the American seamen at Arras, wrote that "half of the provisions and necessaries allowed by the Emperor were withheld from the lower class of prisoners, which was the cause of so much death…".[89] Lest it be thought that the allowance of three sous per month might have enabled a prisoner to supplement his diet by more than a bite, the price of a pound of edible meat, whether beef, mutton or salt pork, at Arras was ten sous, and the price of butter was eighteen sous per pound.[90]

Clubb wrote that his "heart ached for the prisoners that are poor; sickness prevailed, brought in by want and hardship".[91] He estimated that there were fifty to sixty funerals for prisoners each month. While most were British, of course, twenty-eight American deaths were recorded at the Arras depot. At Cambrai, seventeen Americans died. There, the chances of survival were particularly bad for seamen; of the 215 British and American prisoner deaths,

---

[85] Wolfe, *English Prisoners in France*, p64.
[86] Fraser, *Napoleon the Gaoler*, p32.
[87] Thibault Cardon and Frédéric Lemaire. "*Les Sous des Soldats de Napoléon au Camp de Boulogne (1803–1805): Etude des Monnaies Issues des Fouilles des Camps Napoléoniens d'Etaples-sur-Mer et Camiers* (Pas-de-Calais, France)". *The Journal of Archaeological Numismatics,* Vol. 4, 2014. Brussels: CEN – European Centre For Numismatic Studies – Centre Européen D'études Numismatiques, 2015, pp67–176, pp120–122. At this time, both old, *Ancien régime*, money and new French francs were in circulation. The *franc*, divisible into 100 centimes, was created in 1795 with the law of 28 thermidor An III (15 August 1795). The *sou* or *sol* had been in existence for more than 600 years and was still to be found in large numbers, while the centimes had not yet been minted in a large enough quantity. For some years, they were used simultaneously.
[88] Fraser, *Napoleon the Gaoler*, p32. In truth, the French Army were also not receiving their money at this time. See Cardon and Lemaire, "*Les Sous des Soldats de Napoléon*", p121.
[89] Clubb, "A Journal", p180.
[90] Bussell, *The Diary*, p60.
[91] Clubb, "A Journal", p180.

ninety-nine per cent were seamen.⁹² At least ten Americans died in the depot at Givet, where "the prisoners...were sunk in every kind of abomination, half-starved by the French Commissariat, destitute of every comfort, and in a state of mind which aggravated all their external suffering".⁹³ Eight American seamen died in Valenciennes and six in the military hospital at Metz, where they had been sent from the depots at Sarrelibre and Longwy. That journey to the Metz hospital was itself the death of some. One British prisoner wrote of a January 1805 encounter: "On my road to Sarre Louis [Sarrelibre] I met several Englishmen frozen to death, in an open cart, in which they were being conveyed to Metz, a distance of twelve leagues, there being no regular hospital at the former place. However incredible it may appear, this practice was continued for several years."⁹⁴ In all, nearly 100 American seamen died in the French prisons.

They died not only from starvation but from infected wounds and from disease. Toward the end of the war, at the prison town of Longwy (where about sixty Americans were sent), there was an outbreak of plague which, "in less than two months [killed] a tenth of the population".⁹⁵ There was also typhus, known then as "gaol fever", a disease spread by body lice, which nearly every prisoner account says were abundant in every depot. Bussell wrote that, during one epidemic at Arras,

> ...the prisoners at this time [were] very sickly, and numbers continually going to Hospital. The weather is sultry. The rooms is crowded, as a room that measures twenty-three feet by twenty feet has twenty-three to twenty-four prisoners in it, and having scarcely any bedding it is not to be wondered at that sickness prevails amongst us.⁹⁶

Every one of the American men who died in the Metz hospital was recorded as having died of "fever", from the nineteen-year-old African-American Anthony Jacob to the fifty-two-year-old Robert Basset, both seamen from New York.⁹⁷

---

⁹² Gabet and Lepie, *"Cambraï"*, p12.

⁹³ Fraser, *Napoleon the Gaoler*, p65.

⁹⁴ Joshua Done. "Narrative of the Imprisonment and Adventures of Joshua Done, In Various Parts of France". The London Magazine: New Series. Vol. IV, January to April 1826. pp26–37 London: Hunt and Clarke, 1826, p26.

⁹⁵ M.C. *Essai sur l'Histoire de Longwy, par M.C******, suivi de Considérations Relatives à l'Industrie et au Commerce de Cette Ville, et de Notices Biographiques sur les Hommes Illustrés Qui y Ont Pris Naissance*. Metz: Verronnais, 1829, p54. Translation by the author.

⁹⁶ Bussell, *The Diary*, p53. The Spanish prisoners also died of what was probably typhus; Bernard, *Les Prisonniers de guerre*, p210.

⁹⁷ Metz. *Registre de décès, An 13* (Death of Antony Jacob) 22 Nivôse, An 13; Metz *registre de décès*, 1806 (Death of Robert Bassett) 8 February 1806. *Archives municipales de Metz*, https://archives.metz.fr/ [Accessed 6 April 2019].

The Metz death register entries are rare in that they give a cause of death, for French death registers normally do not. Nevertheless, conclusions may be drawn as to the causes of prisoners' deaths in addition to plague and "fever". The proximity of rivers and constant dampness ensured coughs and respiratory infections; the barely heated buildings of thick stone or brick walls ensured a permanent chill; the inhalation of mould spores ensured weakened lungs, the filth ensured infestation; the overcrowding ensured rapid contagion and violence. The common cold, bronchitis, asthma and pneumonia would have been prevalent, especially during the winter months, and, with the chronic malnutrition, would have weakened the immune system further.[98] Truly, what is remarkable is that more did not die.

Punishment was harsh and arbitrary. At Arras, the guards beat prisoners "with great sticks as if we were brute beasts". The more common crimes for which men were punished were stealing, fighting, attacking a guard, smuggling out a letter or even criticizing Napoleon. Attempting to escape, as one would expect, was prohibited. Most escapes by British prisoners were "boring through of walls, iron doors undermined, the descent into deep ditches by cords cunningly prepared from bedding and clothes. In more than one case, a tunnel was driven from the lowest souterrain into the [surrounding] ditch."[99]

Escape attempts were many, but they required money, to bribe guards, to buy decent clothing, to buy food, to pay for transport, to buy false papers, to bribe border guards in the east or a man with a boat on the coast. The seamen did not have money and most of the reports of escapes are by British officers. Nevertheless, at least seventy Americans attempted to escape, of whom twenty-two may have succeeded in leaving France alive.[100] The rest were recaptured, often on the Atlantic coast of France, where every civilian and local officer, from game wardens to local police to fisherman, was on the lookout for enemies. Generally, they were sent to the prison at Brest until there were enough of them to form a convoy and be marched back to a prisoner of war depot. The punishments for the various crimes included being put in irons, being put in the *cachot*, or "Black Hole", but rarely death. There is no record of an American seamen having been executed.

This restraint on the part of the French may have been a fear of retaliation against their own, as posited by Alger.[101] Britain held many more French

---

[98] Elizabeth Heseltine and Jerome Rosen, eds. *WHO guidelines for indoor air quality: Dampness and mould*. World Health Organization, 2009.

[99] Griffiths, "Old War Prisons", p177.

[100] At least, they cease to appear in the French Ministry of War documents after they were recorded as having escaped. Of course, that does not mean that they did not die, nameless, somewhere in France. No record of just how an American escaped has been found.

[101] John Goldworth Alger. *Napoleon's British Visitors and Captives, 1801–1815*. Westminster: Archibald Constable, 1904, pp200–210.

prisoners of war than France did British. By the end of the wars, some 122,000 French were prisoners of war in Britain.[102] Space for them had never been adequate. They were crammed by the hundreds into rotting ships in the harbours of Plymouth, Portsmouth and Chatham, without air, decent food, medical care, or pay. Their only exercise was pacing a space below deck. The vessels, called hulks, were rat-infested and floated in the raw sewage that came from and swilled about them. About 12,000 French prisoners died. The French were appalled. The French authorities determined not to take revenge for this on the British prisoners,[103] but constant stories of the inhumane treatment of the French prisoners increased the intense antipathy felt by the French people and, especially, by the French military.

As explained above, those who attempted to escape, committed a crime or were simply considered dangerous were sent to the punishment prison of Bitche. Some fifty or so American seamen were sent to Bitche. Reuben Hathaway, of Boston, and William Griggs, of New York, died there, as did four others. The man mentioned above, from Boston, who was abandoned at Blaye, John Clarke, was in his early twenties when he was sent to Bitche from Arras. The reason for his having been sent to the punishment depot is not stated in his file, but it may have had to do with his having been entrusted with some money that went missing. While there, one night, in a state of drunkenness, he hid the British Captain Donat Henchy O'Brien, during that man's escape attempt from Bitche.

> I found that I had got into the bed of a servant, an American named Clarke. He was so intolerably intoxicated (they managed that night to get some *snique*, or brandy, smuggled in) that I had a long time before I could rouse him; and when he was awake, I had as much difficulty in making him understand who I was, and why I had got into his bed. I dreaded lest the stupid fellow might utter some ejaculation that might expose everything. Fortunately, however, as soon as he was able to understand what I said, he desired me to cover my face, and assisted me to conceal myself as well as he could. It afterwards appeared that he had gone to bed fully aware of the part he was to play the next morning [to aid in others' escape], and that he had got a little drunk to give him courage for his enterprise; and as drunkenness a little always leads to more, he had got very drunk…[104]

As the wars continued and the men's time in prison stretched into years, there were those who did their best to help one another. Leading this effort were British chaplains and lay preachers who found themselves among the détenus

---

[102] Griffiths, "Old War Prisons", p163.

[103] Bernard, *Les Prisonniers de guerre*, p197.

[104] Donat Henchy O'Brien. *My Adventures During the Late War: a Narrative of Shipwreck, Captivity, Escapes from French Prisons, and Sea Service in 1804–14.* London: Edward Arnold, 1902. p206.

and prisoners of war. There were thirty-four British clerics at Verdun by 1813.[105] Though there must have been prisoners who were of other faiths, only varying forms of Christianity are mentioned in the diaries and memoirs written about the depots. At Cambrai, there was a group of Baptists. At Auxonne and elsewhere, where there was a shortage of Church of England clerics, a prisoner read the service.[106] Many were Methodists; an Englishman named John Taylor formed Methodist Societies at the depots of Arras, Cambrai and Besançon.[107]

The most notable and energetic of the clerics was the Reverend Robert Wolfe. A man with a calling, he dedicated his time and energy to preaching sermons to the prisoner and détenu communities and to trying to give some structure and decency to their lives. He was concerned that civil marriages among prisoners and détenus had not been blessed. He was also distressed by the many children, both the offspring of the civilians and the teens and boys from Royal Navy vessels, who were running wild through the streets, bars and bordellos of Verdun. For a time, as many as forty of the older boys engaged in running stick battles in a sort of gang warfare with the French boys of Verdun. When the gendarmes joined in on the side of the locals, the injuries were serious.[108] The authorities' punishment of these British "turbulent young men" was swift; half were locked up in the citadel and half were sent to Bitche.[109] To put an end to these high jinks, Wolfe established a school. He went on to establish a school at Givet as well, and also one for young midshipmen and lieutenants to study to pass navigation exams.[110] Some British seamen and soldiers attended the lessons in reading and writing for adults. Wolfe wrote that his prison school

> ...became most extensively useful, not only to the poor children, but to persons of all ages...For in some of these schools, persons of all ages enjoyed advantages of general education and professional instruction...[111]

At Auxonne as well, British seamen attended the schools and various lessons.[112]

Wolfe encouraged the many Royal Navy surgeons among the prisoners of war who established hospitals in eight of the depots, with a specific mission

---

[105] Didier Houmeau. *Les prisonniers de guerre britanniques de Napoléon 1er. (1803–1814)*. Draft copy of a doctoral thesis shared with the author, email dated 7 April 2010.

[106] Mulvey, *Sketches*, p24.

[107] Cavanagh, *Some Account of Religious Societies*, p13.

[108] Done, "Narrative", p29.

[109] Bernard, *Les Prisonniers de guerre*, p206. It is not known if the French boys were punished.

[110] Mark J. Gabrielson. "Enlightenment in the Darkness: The British Prisoners of War School of Navigation. Givet, France, 1805–1814." *Northern Mariner/Le marin du nord*, Vol. XXV, No. 1, January 2015, pp1–35.

[111] Wolfe, *English Prisoners*, p6.

[112] Mulvey, *Sketches*, p24.

to "cure prisoners injured during capture or on the march to their depot, and to contain epidemics".[113] Without doubt, the medical care that John Cook received after his disastrous march to Arras was in one of the hospitals set up at Wolfe's direction.

The funding for these charitable endeavours came from Britain and from some of the wealthier détenus themselves. The main source of aid, the Lloyd's Patriotic Fund, was established by the insurers in 1803 to rally the nation to contribute financially to the war effort. Two years later, they added aid to the British prisoners of war in France to their activities. In response to pleas from the prisoners, the Patriotic Fund sent money to support the hospitals.[114] People in Britain donated money, fundraising balls were held, and plays were put on to raise money for the prisoners. The Patriotic Fund sent large sums to be distributed to the prisoners to supplement their small French allowances. The Fund paid the Reverend Wolfe a salary of 200 pounds sterling per year. There were other funds and charities as well, including local charities collecting money specifically for prisoners from their town or area, such as the Fund for the Relief of Guernsey Prisoners in France and the Maritime United Society for prisoners "whose vessels belong to any port in the Bristol Channel".[115]

These contributions surely did help those in need. According to the 1811 *Report of the Committee at Lloyd's*, they were able not only to finance the schools and hospitals, but to send medical supplies. Payments to individuals included daily sums of four to six sous per day to women and children in distress, the same amount to "distressed Masters of Vessels under 80 tons register, who are paid only as Seamen by the French Government", three sous per day went to the aged and elderly prisoners, two sous per day to all prisoners in distress, assistance to those "on their march from the Coast, or from one Depôt to another", and "Occasional aid in Clothes, Bedding, &c to all Prisoners in Distress".[116]

Within the considerable constraints of prison life, a semblance of British normality and their unique social hierarchy was established, in large part because of the substantial charitable aid. British prisoners had church services

---

[113] Duché, "Charitable Network Connections", p109.

[114] Duché, "Charitable Network Connections", pp86–87.

[115] Colin R. Rees and Peter Clark. *Captured At Sea: Merchant Ships Captured in the South West Seas of Britain in the Time of Napoleon, 1803–1815*. Published by the authors, 2011, p141; "The Fund for the Relief of Guernsey Prisoners in France, 1806", Supplement to the *Gazette de Guernesey* of 16 August 1806. https://www.priaulxlibrary.co.uk/articles/article/fund-relief-guernsey-prisoners-france-1806 [Accessed 11 April 2019]; Duché, "Charitable Network Connections", pp99–100.

[116] J. Morley. *A Sermon, Preached in Providence Chapel, Hope-Street, Hull, On Lord's Day, February 24, 1811, To Which Are Added, An Extract of the Circular Letters and the Report of the Committee at Lloyd's, in London*. Hull: published at request, 1811, pp22–23.

and sermons, they received care when they were ill, they received additional funds, clothing, Bibles and *The Book of Common Prayer*[117] from home, and their captive children went to prison schools. Except for some medical care and church attendance, most of the American seamen held prisoner with them, in some cases in prison only because they had worked alongside them, received no share of any of the relief or charity sent to, or participated in schooling arranged for, the British prisoners with whom they were housed.

Farrell Mulvey, the British doctor at Auxonne and Longwy, wrote that, from 1809,

> The mates…had received the same pay as the masters.…With them were included the passengers, or, as they were called, the merchant passenger, as also foreigners in the service of, or belonging to Powers in amity with Great Britain, some families, and a few sailors.…A charitable fund…had been established in England; and it is very creditable to the character of the nation, that it distributed to foreigners of every country in its service, in the same measure as to natives.[118]

If this claim were true, at least a few hundred American seamen should have received payments from the Fund. To be sure, some did, yet the majority of the American seamen, including some of those who had been impressed into the *Hussar*, the *Shannon*, the *Minotaur* and other Royal Navy vessels that wrecked on the French coast, and many American seamen who had signed on with one of the British merchant vessels that were captured, appear to have received nothing. (By contrast, in at least one case, they refused money offered. At Verdun, eighteen American prisoners were released in November 1807. Wirion reported that the British prisoners had taken up a collection for them, which the Americans refused. "Their national spirit was the sole reason for this refusal.")[119]

The 1812 *Report from the Committee for the Relief of the British Prisoners in France* contains a list of the names of all prisoners who received their aid. Of the more than 14,000 names, the *Report* identifies only 132 as American. They include some Nantucket whalers based in Britain, a smattering of the impressed seamen, and some merchant captains and seamen.[120] For the rest, the hundreds of American prisoners locked up as British prisoners of war, there was nothing from the British charities. The French were well aware of this division among the prisoners. The Minister of External Relations wrote

---

[117] Gabrielson, "Enlightenment", p20.

[118] Mulvey, *Sketches*, pp1–2.

[119] d'Hauterive, *La police secrète du premier empire; bulletins quotidiens adressés par Fouché à l'empereur, 3* (Paris: Perrin, 1908), p425.

[120] *Report from the Committee for the Relief of the British Prisoners in France; with A List of the Prisoners.* London: W. Phillips, 1812.

to the Minister of War that between British and American prisoners: "The English Government itself makes a great difference. [The Americans] in the same depots [as the English] have no part in the distribution of charitable funds that they send for prisoners' relief."[121]

At least one American diplomat did try to establish a system of aid for them. For a few short months in 1807, Fulwar Skipwith, the United States commercial agent in Paris, set up a network of agents in the various prison towns to send an allowance to the American prisoners. He had barely begun to establish the network and to outline procedures for proving the American nationality of each seaman requesting aid, when the Minister, John Armstrong, horrified at the soaring number of American prisoners begging for help, cancelled the funding.

> When...I informed you that you might draw upon me for the subsistence of all such persons confined in this country under the denomination of British prisoners as should produce to you sufficient evidence that they were Citizens of the US, I did not mean to authorize either a large or permanent expenditure of Public Monies.[122]

The number of Americans in prison had gone in a few weeks from four to fourteen to sixty-six, and was still climbing. As more and more prisoners wrote to Skipwith and to American consuls in France who, in turn wrote to the Minister asking for guidance as well as for money to send to the men, the problem became more severe, and was two-fold: the funds were inadequate and there was no satisfactory way, from Paris, of determining the nationality of the men requesting assistance from the government of the United States. The difficulty of proving nationality and the diplomats' distrust of the seamen's documents will be discussed in detail below. As for aiding the men in prison, though the ministers and consuls constantly petitioned the French government for the seamen's release, the programme for financial assistance was never resurrected and, as a consequence, the American prisoners suffered even more than they might have done.

Probably the one type of British succour in which American seamen could not only participate but to which they could contribute was religious worship. It seems probable that they were admitted to whatever religious services were available, especially those provided by the Methodists, who were actively proselytizing in the depots.[123] The most impressive account of American

---

[121] Maret to Clark. 30 November 1812. *Correspondance Politique États-unis.* Arch. dip. 39CP/70. Microfilm copy.

[122] Armstrong to Skipwith. 20 February 1807. United States. Department of State. *Despatches from United States Consuls in Paris, 1790–1906.* Vol. 2. Microfilm copy.

[123] Mulvey, *Sketches*, p25.

religious activity tells of John Jea (recorded in all prison documents as John H. Jay). French archives and British prisoner accounts state that he was simply an African-American cook from New York, captured on the *Izette,* sailing from Liverpool, in 1811, and sent to Cambrai, but he was much more than that.

John Jea was, by the time he was taken to France, quite famous in both New England and Britain as an impassioned, eloquent, itinerant preacher. He claimed to have achieved "great success" preaching in Manchester, Lancashire, Yorkshire and Liverpool in England and in Boston, New York and elsewhere in America. Cavanagh's account is one of the few by a listener attesting to Jea's power of oratory:

> 29th [September 1811].... This afternoon I was informed of the arrival of a *Black*, as a prisoner of war; who proved to be an American Methodist, and had a talent for public speaking; so we gave him the right hand of fellowship; and invited him to preach for us.
>
> The circumstances of a black man preaching, attracted an unusual number of hearers...I am thankful to God for this unexpected helper. ...
>
> 30th [September 1811] This afternoon, brother Jay preached again, and the word was attended with much power. Many of the hearers were greatly affected; some convinced of their sin and danger; and others rejoicing in the Lord.
>
> 13th [October 1811] This afternoon brother Jay preached our late brother Avis's funeral sermon...the room was crowded with attentive hearers; many stood at the outside, and many of the wicked were powerfully impressed, and cried aloud for mercy.[124]

In conclusion, captivity for the imprisoned American seamen in France was shared with British sailors and merchant seamen. From the hellish march to a depot, where they were overcrowded and underfed, to a punishment depot if they tried to escape, their years of imprisonment were filled with monotony, deteriorating health and casual brutality. Most were illiterate. None could hope for exchange. Only a handful were permitted parole. Fewer than fifty were at the luxury camp of Verdun. Less than nine per cent of the American prisoners received financial aid from the Committee for Relief. In every aspect of captivity, though they shared the suffering of the British seamen, they did not share in the British relief. They did have, however, something the British prisoners did not, and that was a realistic hope of release.

---

[124] Cavanagh, *Some Account of Religious Societies*, pp19–21.

PART TWO

TRAPPED IN A THORNY MAZE

4

THE FRENCH IN CONTROL

An American seaman usually became a prisoner of war in France because of the judgment on the nationality of the vessel on which he was captured; his possible release would depend upon the judgment on his own nationality and, later, on the reason for his presence on the prize vessel. What was documented about him at every point was referred to repeatedly by the French when making a decision concerning him. Each case was decided individually and depended upon a range of documentation originating with and held by a range of French ministries. This chapter looks at those ministries, at how those decisions were made and at the men who made them.

The Ministry of Marine and Colonies documented a seaman's initial disembarking in France from a prize vessel or his crawling onto a beach from a wrecked vessel. The Ministry of Police General held him in a local jail while a prize was being judged. Once he became a prisoner of war, he was escorted to a depot and detained there by the Ministry of War. Depending upon his fortunes and behaviour, other authorities touched his life. If he broke a civil law (committed murder, theft or affray, for example) it was the Ministry of Police General that pursued him, the Ministry of Justice that prosecuted him, the Ministry of the Interior that jailed him. If he escaped, it was the Gendarmerie that pursued him and the Ministry of War that sent out bulletins with his description to the authorities in the coastal cities (the destinations of most escapees, who hoped to get onto a vessel leaving France). If he were released, the Ministry of External Relations authorized his passport and permission to leave France and from which port, while the Gendarmerie escorted him and the police watched him as he went from the depot to a port and boarded a vessel. American diplomats in France worked for his release, some more vigorously than others, pleading and campaigning on his behalf primarily with the Ministry of External Relations, but also with the Ministry of War and the Ministry of Marine and Colonies.

Some understanding of the French authorities who had the power to make decisions concerning prisoners of war, of the American diplomats in France, and of the cat and mouse game between them is necessary. The Franco-American relationship was heavily tainted by French disappointment, distrust and resentment of the United States. In the endless fight for supremacy over Great Britain, the French had given enormous military aid to America during that country's war for independence from Great Britain. This expense, which the French considered a loan, contributed greatly to the bankruptcy of Louis XVI's realm. The new country, the United States, contained opposing political groups concerning foreign relations, one side thinking it best to establish good relations with Great Britain, the other believing the future lay in a strong alliance with France. Broadly speaking, the former were "Federalists" and the latter "Republicans".[1] The French Revolution and assassination of Louis XVI was used as an excuse by the Americans not to repay the loan (on the grounds that the monarchy and government that had loaned the money no longer existed). The French government, at that point the Directory, badly needing that money, considered this a betrayal. They felt even more betrayed by the 1794 Treaty of Amity, Commerce and Navigation, known as the Jay Treaty, signed between the United States and Great Britain. The French view was that this agreement with the common enemy was a violation of their own, prior agreement with the United States, the Treaty of Amity and Commerce of 1778 (see below). The anger and outrage are palpable in the letter sent to James Monroe, then the Minister Plenipotentiary to France, after his resignation in 1796 and at the time of General Bonaparte's hugely successful campaign in Italy:

> France, rich in her liberty, surrounded by a train of victories, strong in the esteem of her allies, will not abase herself by calculating the consequences of the condescension of the American government to the suggestions of her former tyrants – moreover the French Republic hopes that [the Americans]…always proud of their liberty will never forget that they owe it to France.[2]

In retaliation for what they saw as America's betrayal (as well as to reduce American merchant shipping with Spain and Britain),[3] France's naval vessels and privateers began capturing American ships as early as 1796. The Francophobe, Federalist President John Adams sent envoys to France to try to

---

[1] Looking at today's political parties, these names are confusing even for Americans. The Federalist Party, founded by Alexander Hamilton, John Jay and James Madison, withered and disappeared after the death in a duel of the charismatic Hamilton. The Republican Party, founded by Thomas Jefferson, was the precursor of what is today the Democratic Party. The current Republican Party was founded on anti-slavery principles in 1854. In an unsuccessful effort to avoid confusion, modern writers sometimes refer to Jefferson's party as the Democratic-Republican Party.

[2] United States (1817) *State Papers and Publick Documents of the United States, from the accession of George Washington to the Presidency, exhibiting a complete view of our foreign relations since that time*, Vol. 3. Boston: T.E. Wait and Son, p118.

[3] Patrick Villiers. "Le Commerce maritime des Etats-Unis, ambitions maritimes et commerciales en Atlantique et Méditerranée, 1783–1815", *Storia e attualità della presenza degli Stati Uniti a Livorno e in Toscana, Actes du Colloque (Livorno, 4–6 avril 2002)*. Pisa: Edizione Plus, 2003, p6.

resolve the issue. Four French negotiators were sent by Talleyrand, who had refused to meet them until certain terms were met. The terms were money for impoverished France and a personal bribe for Talleyrand. The American envoys refused and negotiations broke down. War seemed immanent, especially after the American press reported on the bribe request, naming the French negotiators only as W, X, Y and Z and the whole business was known as "The XYZ Affair". The French increased their seizures of hundreds of American ships in the undeclared war known as the "Quasi-War". It all ended sourly with the Convention of 1800, which terminated the 1778 Treaty of Alliance between the Unites States and France.

At the opening of the nineteenth century, there were thousands of Frenchmen who had fought in the American Revolution as a part of the French Expeditionary Force and who might have felt a sense of betrayal. Three amongst them were French ministers whose decisions would concern American seamen held as prisoners of war: Berthier, Decrès and Champagny. A fourth minister, though he never fought in any war, had been embarrassed publicly by the Americans and, for much of the period, held the power to block their diplomats' every step: Talleyrand. There is a permanent note of scorn and disdain, along with a profound distrust, in the correspondence of these four with American diplomats throughout the conflicts.

All of the ministries were based in Paris, most in a cluster around the Invalides on the Left Bank of the Seine, but the Ministry of Marine and Colonies and the Ministry of Justice were further away, on the Right Bank. The Ministry of War was based in rue Saint Dominique, not far from the Ministry of the Interior; unlike the others, this ministry had a second building, which was quite a bit to the north. Many ministries were headed by career army or navy men, some of them of the old nobility, who had been appointed by Napoleon Bonaparte. They were in their forties or fifties and would have been young men during the French Revolution and Terror. Each, at some point in the Revolutionary Wars, had encountered and become a supporter of Napoleon, from the campaigns that he won in Italy, through the coup when he became First Consul, through his establishment of the Empire in 1804. Each was brilliant enough in organization or administration that his talents were recognized by Napoleon and he received his appointment as a minister. For their work in running a ministry under Napoleon's exceedingly watchful eye (they sent him reports almost every day), each minister was ennobled and each was admitted to the Legion of Honour.[4] It cannot be known at exactly what point, or even whether, each lost his enthusiasm for Napoleon but, after his abdication, each of these ministers signed the oath of fealty to the restored Bourbon king. These men were extremely able and highly intelligent; and, with one exception, they were also survivors.

---

[4] Louis Bergeron. *France Under Napoleon*, translated by R.R. Palmer. Princeton: Princeton University Press, 1981, p63.

Ministère de la Marine et des Colonies

The Minister of the Marine and Colonies was Denis Decrès, appointed to the post by Napoleon in 1801. Born in 1761, he entered the French Navy as a midshipman at the age of fourteen and served on vessels around the world, including those that supported the American Revolution, where he showed some heroism in the Battle of the Saintes. He was at sea when the French Revolution began and returned to France to serve in the new legislature, indicating that he supported the ideals of the Revolution. In his fourteen years as Minister, he worked tirelessly, once writing to Napoleon that he worked twelve hours a day. He worked to rebuild the French Navy after the losses at Trafalgar; to root out incompetence, especially among senior officers; to promote men based on merit rather than privilege; and to eliminate nepotism and corruption (he was particularly annoyed by the common practice of doctors writing exaggerated medical certificates of wounds and illnesses endured in service). For all of his honesty and hard work, he was not a pleasant man. He was demanding, harsh and pitilessly critical of his staff. His correspondence is filled with snide, cutting and ironic remarks (such as referring to official American documents as "artefacts"). He endured neither mediocrity nor flattery, yet he could exhibit both in his dealings with Napoleon, who said of him that "his administration was rigorous and…he had a brain…but only for conversation…he created nothing". The Emperor kept him waiting until 1813 for his title of nobility and even then, it was not illustrious, being only his own name, Duke of Decrès. At the end of the Empire, it was he who gave the orders to prepare the frigates at Rochefort that were intended to whisk the defeated Napoleon to America.[5]

Decrès was asked often by the Minister of War to have his staff refer to the lists of captured vessels to confirm that a seaman was American, something he seems to have found tedious. If these requests for further information gave only the name of the seaman or, more often, were a simple list of names, he refused to comply. "To judge the merit of these claims, we need to know from which ships they were taken…because the manifests…are filed by the name of the vessel and not by the names of the prisoners, which are always misspelt."[6] Worse, for the seamen, he was strongly opposed to the release of American prisoners: "For a long time I have fought against requests of this

---

[5] Pierre Lévêque. "*L'Amiral Decrès, un Ministre Courtisan?*". *Revue du Souvenir Napoléonien*. No. 417, mars–avril 1998, pp13–21; Henri Ramé. "*Decrès, Denis, Duc, (1761–1820), Vice-Amiral, Ministre*". *Revue du Souvenir Napoléonien*. No. 353, juin 1987, pp41–43.

[6] Decrès to Maret, the Minister of External Relations. 26 April 1813. *Correspondance Politique États-unis*. Arch. dip. 39CP/70. Microfilm copy. Translation by the author. The misspelling of names and other English words was a serious problem.

nature…". He believed that nothing but confusion as to which seamen were American and which were British would result, as "even the Minister of the United States himself finds it impossible to verify the legitimacy of these claims…".[7]

Ministère de la Police générale

The Ministry of Police General supervised all police activities in all of the Empire, an enormous responsibility. The ministry was run by two successive ministers, the infamous Joseph Fouché, the Duke of Otranto, followed by René Savary, the Duke of Rovigo. Fouché, by all accounts, was a dark, disturbing and sinister character, one of those people who rises to the top in a time of chaos because he can be brutal, and in a time of authoritarianism because he knows how to prey on and increase everyone's fear. He was born in a village at the mouth of the Loire in 1759, the son of a sea captain who was a slave trader. He did not follow his father to sea but studied to become a priest. He left that path and became a professor of science at Arras, where he met and befriended Robespierre.[8] While at Arras, he also became a Freemason.[9] He was an enthusiastic revolutionary, became an atheist, and was instrumental in the vicious crushing of the anti-Revolution insurrection of Lyon.[10] In running the Ministry of Police General, he seems to have continued to use the tools of the Terror: relentless surveillance, suspicion of all, sudden and brutal reprisals. He built a network of spies and informers, the Secret Police, who reported every suspicious event to him, which he condensed into daily reports to Napoleon. He was seen as all-powerful and everyone dreaded his "*Bureau particulier*, where personal details of all those known to the police were kept".[11] He watched everyone, gathered intelligence on all, especially all in power, and intrigued and plotted with all camps. He was denounced as a spy by his rival, Jean Baptiste Dossonville, who was himself secretly backed by the British spy network.[12] Napoleon shut down the Ministry of

---

[7] Decrès to Clarke. 15 January 1813. *Correspondance Politique États-unis.* Arch. dip. 39CP/70. Microfilm copy. Translation by the author.

[8] Emmanuel de Waresquiel. *Fouché. Les Silences de la pieuvre.* Paris: Tallandier, 2014, pp28–38.

[9] Jean Bossu. "*Fichier Bossu*", *Fonds maçonnique, Département des Manuscrits, Bibliothèque nationale de France,* https://gallica.bnf.fr/ark:/12148/btv1b10000111w/f132. image, [Accessed 2 May 2019].

[10] David Andress. *The Terror: Civil War in the French Revolution.* London: Abacus, 2006, pp236–238.

[11] Elizabeth Sparrow. *Secret Service: British Agents in France 1792–1815.* Woodbridge: Boydell Press, 1999, p14.

[12] Sparrow, *Secret Service*, p259.

Police General and Fouché was dismissed in 1802. He was returned to his post in 1804, when the end of the Peace of Amiens and the return of war necessitated the re-establishment of a Ministry of Police General (and of spying), and he remained there until 1810, when his intrigues with all sides at once became too much.

Fouché was succeeded by a man thirteen years younger, Anne Jean Marie René Savary, who had been Napoleon's aide-de-camp after the Battle of Marengo, and been made the Duke of Rovigo in 1809.[13] He had joined the cavalry at the age of seventeen and fought in some of Napoleon's greatest campaigns. He served first in the Army of the Rhine, then in Egypt, at Jena, Ostrolenka, Heilsberg, Friedland and in Spain, reaching the rank of division general.[14] For all that military experience, he had the reputation of being rather useless in the field, but Napoleon seems to have noted that his talents for intelligence gathering were much more impressive and used him to organize unpleasant tasks, including the execution of the Duke of Enghien. Savary, like Fouché, had a reputation for ruthlessness and intrigue. He and his reputedly beautiful wife both engaged in politically strategic love affairs; both were said to have been completely devoted to the Emperor.[15] Savary's first few months in office were spent mostly in hounding his predecessor but in time he did settle in to managing the network of spies.

Neither Fouché nor Savary appear very often in the documentation of the American prisoners of war. A few letters from the Ministry of Police General appear only when internal passports were needed for one or another of the prisoners who was released. Yet everyone, including foreigners, feared the network of the Ministry of Police General.

Fouché had been in charge of the police under the Consulate and at that time had created the Prefecture of the Police of the Seine. Reporting directly to him, this body had powers to police almost every aspect of public life in Paris:

> ...arresting beggars and vagabonds, policing prisons, surveillance of hotels and public houses...preventing or dispersing workers' gatherings and meetings that might disturb the peace, policing bookshops, printing and theatres to protect public morals and safety, surveillance of the sale of gunpowder and arms, pursuit and prosecution of émigrés, surveillance of roads, footpaths, lighting the Stock Market, river traffic...[16]

---

[13] Bergeron, *France Under Napoleon*, p74.

[14] Chandler, *Dictionary of the Napoleonic Wars*, pp402–403.

[15] Bernardine Melchior-Bonnet. "*Savary Remplace Fouché*". *Revue des Deux Mondes* (1829–1971), 1962, pp98–112. www.jstor.org/stable/44590429. [Accessed 3 May 2019] p104.

[16] Louis Madelin. "*La Police générale de l'Empire.*" *Revue des Deux Mondes* (1829–1971), Vol. 60, No. 3, 1940, pp241–267. http://www.jstor.org/stable/44847534, [Accessed 3 May 2019] pp250–251. Translated by the author.

It became so powerful that it was difficult for Fouché to keep it under control. He had also created the *commissaires généraux de police*, or general police commissaries, to be placed with local prefects and sub-prefects across the country. Under them, as direct agents of the Ministry of Police General, all mayors and local officials were required to report on any suspicious activity.[17] The country felt itself to be under siege from the attacking European powers and every foreigner was suspect. The *commissaires spéciaux*, or special commissaries, concentrated specifically on diplomats, foreign agents, royalists, families of émigrés, smugglers, resident foreign merchants and shippers. Fouché referred to these agents as his "guard dogs".

American ministers, consuls and businessmen resident in France were not immune to prosecution and needed to be as wary of the police as did everyone else. When seamen were allowed to live in town, awaiting a prize judgement for example, they were extremely vulnerable to being reported, or "denounced" to the police by the mayor or any local official.

Ministère de la Guerre

Though its responsibilities were vast, covering the support of all of Napoleon's military actions throughout Europe, the Ministry of War was small, with only about 450 staff.[18] When American prisoners began to arrive in France in 1803, the Minister of War was General Louis-Alexandre Berthier, the Prince of Neuchatel, Prince of Wagram, and a Marshal of France, one of the wealthiest and most important men in the Empire. He was born in Versailles in 1753, the son of an engineer who had been ennobled by the king, Louis XVI, in 1763. Either very intelligent or blessed with a powerful mentor, Berthier received his qualifications from the Royal School of Engineering at Mézières at the age of thirteen in 1766. Six years later, he was a lieutenant in the army. He served with Rochambeau in the American Revolution and was a lieutenant-colonel in the army when the French Revolution began.

At that time, he was also in the National Guard at Versailles and may have remained loyal to the king for, in 1791, he was among those who helped two aunts of the king to escape France. The following year, he was dismissed from the service. Remarkably, for one of the nobility, however minor, and one known to have protected the royal family, he survived the Terror and returned to the army as a division general in early 1795. The following year, he met and became a loyal supporter of Napoleon, sixteen years his junior. An experienced soldier, and clever, Berthier also had a reputation for intrigue. He was certainly a man of courage. He fought in the Italian campaign, was wounded

---

[17] Madelin, "*La Police générale*", p251.
[18] Vincent Haegele. "*Le général Clarke au ministère de la Guerre*". Revue historique des armées, Vol. 251. 2008. http://rha.revues.org//index328.html. [Accessed 29 April 2019].

at the Battle of Marengo, and had his horse shot from under him at the Battle of Wagram. As he did with Savary, Napoleon used Berthier on diplomatic and intelligence missions, in Spain and Vienna.[19] Not only was he rewarded for his services with titles but he also acquired great wealth, including an endowment of well over a million francs. He bought a town house worth half a million francs and married a Bavarian duchess, with Napoleon's blessing.[20]

Concurrent with heading the Ministry of War, Berthier was Chief of Staff for the Grand Army. He would seem to have been gifted with an intellectual sympathy and compatibility with the mind of the Emperor and with excellent interpretative and communication skills to be able to transmit quickly and clearly Napoleon's many orders to his staff. He was said to have been not only loyal to Napoleon but his friend. Yet, after the first abdication, he quickly supported the restored monarchy. When Napoleon returned to France from Elba, his old friend and loyal Chief of Staff, perhaps not expecting that resurrection, did not join him. At his chateau in Bavaria, Berthier died by a defenestration that has never been fully explained.[21]

In 1807, when Berthier left the post of Minister of War to concentrate solely on his duties as Chief of Staff, he was replaced by General Henri-Jacques-Guillaume Clarke, later the Duke of Feltre and Count of Hunebourg, who remained as head of the Ministry until 1817, throughout and well beyond the period that American seamen were held prisoner. He was born in 1765 in the far north of France, to a family of Clarkes and O'Shees, descendants of some of the thousands of Irish Catholic refugees who fled to France after the Battle of the Boyne. He entered the army at the age of sixteen and was a lieutenant colonel in the cavalry before the Revolution. He fought with General Custine in the Army of the Vosges during the Revolutionary Wars but was not tainted by the disasters that led to that man being guillotined. He then moved to the Regiment of Bretagne and was promoted to brigadier general.[22] He spoke English and German fluently, which may have been part of the reason he was selected for diplomatic missions in London and elsewhere. He supported Napoleon's coup, in 1799, and became part of the inner circle, serving as Napoleon's personal secretary for four years at the same time that Savary was serving as intelligence specialist and Berthier was Chief of Staff.

---

[19] Gambiez. "*Berthiez, Louis-Alexandre, (1753–1815)*". *Dictionnaire Napoléon*. Paris: Editions Fayard, 1987. http://www.napoleon.org/histoire-des-2-empires/biographies/berthier-louis-alexandre [Accessed 1 May 2019]; Chandler, *Dictionary*, pp54–55.

[20] Bergeron, *France Under Napoleon*, pp74 and 123.

[21] Gambiez, "*Berthiez*".

[22] Henri-Jacques-Guillaume Clarke dossier. Arch. nat. *Base de données Léonore. Légion d'honneur, dossier No.* LH/542/53. http://www2.culture.gouv.fr/documentation/leonore/ [Accessed 3 May 2019].

While Minister of War, Clarke was the man who organized all military activity and administration that was not overseen by Berthier as Chief of Staff. He worked under Napoleon's close direction, seeing him almost daily when the Emperor was in Paris, and exchanging dispatches with him constantly. He managed all of the armies of occupation of lands conquered by Napoleon. He had to deal, as best he could, with the problems that arose from the war in Spain and the failed British invasion of Walcheren Island. Later, he was responsible for the drafting of troops, and for acquiring thousands of horses and cannon for the Russian campaign.

As an administrator, Clarke seems to have excelled. The Ministry had six divisions: Dispatches, Troop Movements, Military Affairs, Inspections, Pensions and Foreign Troops. At times, there was a seventh division concerned with army engineering. Each division head reported to the Minister of War. Each division had numerous bureaux with their own chiefs who reported to the division head. The government was highly centralized under Napoleon. The structure of the divisions and ministries reflected this intense centralization such that each level reported in great detail to the next level up, and the ministers reported frequently to Napoleon, who made almost all decisions personally. The division heads in the Ministry of War have been termed "the eyes and ears of the Grand Army".[23]

The Fifth Division, that for Pensions, was responsible for all military pension funds, calculation and payment of each military pension, veterans' affairs, disabled veterans, and prisoners of war.[24] The division chief was Philippe Jean-Baptiste Nicolas Goulhot. In the files of correspondence concerning individual cases of American prisoners of war, every report from the Fifth Division to Clarke is signed by Goulhot. He was born in Mortain in Normandy, about fifty miles inland from the coast, in 1764, the son of a minor official.[25] At the age of thirteen, he was appointed a *Garde de la porte du Roi*, one of the king's household guards.[26] He left the guards in 1783, before his eighteenth birthday. He did not return to Mortain, but spent the next eight

---

[23] Haegele, "*Le général Clarke*".

[24] Laurent-Etienne Testu, ed. *Almanach impérial pour l'année M.DCCC. XI, présenté à S.M l'Empereur et Roi, par Testu*. Paris: Testu, 1811, p233.

[25] Philippe Jean-Baptiste Nicolas Goulhot dossier. Arch. nat. *Base de données Léonore. Légion d'honneur dossier No.* LH/1177/41. http://www2.culture.gouv.fr/documentation/leonore/ [Accessed 3 May 2019].

[26] This was a man who stood guard at one of the many doors of the king's palace. The guard was not in the military but was a member of the household. No record has been found to explain if the child Goulhot went to Versailles and stood guard, or if he were an apprentice guard, or if the position were merely an honour with a stipend and he stayed at home.

years working in a tax office, the *bureau des aides*, in Marigny, a town over sixty kilometres to the north of his birthplace. That office was closed in 1791.

The year 1791 in France was one of violence, turmoil and chaos as different groups of people strove and disputed over how to create a new government, economy and society: in essence, to redefine an entire country and its people. The royal family were in Paris but would soon attempt and fail to escape. The first constitution would be written. Those who wanted an orderly Revolution struggled against those who wanted to use violence to bring about a swifter and irrevocable change. The violence was most extreme in Paris, where the poor realized their power and mobs rioted whenever they wished to protest what the newly created National Constituent Assembly was doing or not doing. At the same time, royalists tried to protect the king and moderates wanted to maintain order. One of the worst events occurred in July, when the extremists rioted in Paris against the decision by the Assembly to allow Louis XVI to remain king after his escape attempt. The Parisian mob gathered in the Champs de Mars where troops trying to maintain order, led by Lafayette, opened fire on them, killing many. By the end of the year, the king and his family were in prison, many of the nobles were fleeing France, and the extremists, called *sans-culottes*, had acquired a deadly power.

Goulhot was twenty-seven years old when he went to Paris in 1791. He had prepared to find work. In March, two months before the *bureau des aides* was closed, he had taken the precaution of asking his old superior officer from the *Gardes de la porte du Roi* to provide him with a certificate proving his service, and he obtained a similar one from the *bureau des aides*.[27] The National Constituent Assembly gave way to the National Legislative Assembly in the same month that Goulhot was hired by the Ministry of War. Three months before he received his first promotion, in December 1792, pro-Revolution Parisians, distrusting and fearing everyone, broke into prisons and killed hundreds of prisoners in what are known as the September Massacres. The month after Goulhot's promotion, in January 1793, the king was guillotined. That same year, Goulhot was promoted to chief of a bureau. France then declared war on Britain and Holland, while at the same time the country was consumed by civil wars in different locations, but especially in the west, not too far from Goulhot's place of birth.

With France defending her borders from attack and also fighting civil wars, the Ministry of War became of crucial importance and the work within must have been intense. Perhaps it was also very secure. In December, when Fouché

---

[27] *Archives de la Guerre et Armée de Terre. Personnel civil du Ministère de la Guerre* (1806–1853). SHDV. 5YG 1863 (Goulhot). This officer, who had known Goulhot as a boy, was a noble named d'Avrange d'Haugéranville; he was also the brother-in-law of General Berthier, the future Minister of War who would write a letter praising Goulhot's service.

was crushing the rebellion in Lyons, the Terror was raging, and priests were being hunted down, Goulhot married. Eighteen months later, he was promoted to head of the Fifth Division, a post he would hold for many years, through the wars, the glorious gains and finally the defeat of Napoleon and the end of the Empire. In 1798, he was suspended briefly because he did not punish a soldier who had been sent to Rome but who had absconded to Bourges to deal with family affairs, an episode that exhibited the compassion apparent in much of his correspondence concerning American prisoners.[28] At the end of the Napoleonic era, when the Restoration administration was arriving, he destroyed hundreds of files that would have identified men in the Grand Army, who would have been targets for the returning royalists' revenge.[29] He retired in 1817, with many honours and a minor title and having bought a large mansion. He died in 1823, a baron whose son would become a senator.

He was a man who worked steadily, with a tax auditor's precision, and with a cautious compassion. His ministry employment file states that though "this division has a great deal of work…it is, nevertheless, always up to date, because Mr. Goulhot, its head, is of an extreme exactitude and serves as an example to all his subordinates."[30] A letter from Berthier, written in 1801, stated that Goulhot's zeal and talents had contributed to great economies for the country and that his government appreciated his work. Berthier closed the letter with the assurance that he esteemed Goulhot highly.[31] Fine praise indeed, from a man who was, himself, known for his intellectual ability.

The praise of Goulhot's work from many people can seem, at first glance, to imply that his remarkably swift promotions were due to his abilities alone. However, his first promotions were approved, some of them directly, by the Committee for Public Safety, which ruled the country, and coincided with the period when the *sans-culottes* had nearly complete control of the ministry, indicating that, if he did not share their views, he certainly was able to convince them that he did so. He was named by the Committee to the select group of *commissaires des guerres* in 1793, but he was required to choose whether he would stay in that position or in the other to which he had been appointed at the same time, chief of a bureau. His wish was to be a chief of a bureau in the Sixth Division of the ministry, which was concerned with artillery and its

---

[28] Pierre-Dominique Cheynet. *Les Procès-verbaux du Directoire exécutif, an V–an VII: inventaire des registres, tome III, vendémiaire–frimaire, an VI*. Paris. Arch. nat. 2002, p720. This was not the first time he had shown some tolerance.

[29] Jean-Paul Bertaid. "Aperçus sur l'insoumission et la désertion à l'époque révolutionnaire: étude des sources". *Bulletin d'histoire économique et sociale de la Révolution française*. Paris: CTHS, 1969, p29.

[30] Audin, *British Hostages*, pp33–34; *Personnel civil du Ministère de la Guerre* (1806–1853). SHDV. 5YG 1863. (Goulhot).

[31] Goulhot, *Légion d'honneur dossier No.* LH/1177/4.

procurement. However, his division's adjunct, Louis-Alexandre Pille, strongly encouraged him to remain in the Fifth Division. Since a colleague who had argued with Pille had recently been guillotined,[32] Goulhot felt, he wrote years later, that he had no choice but to do as Pille wished. His promotion to chief of the division came when Berthier, who also happened to be the brother-in-law of Goulhot's old superior officer, was Minister of War. After Berthier left the ministry, Goulhot received no promotions under General Clarke. His requests for salary increases and recognition were granted and Clarke even arranged for him to meet the Emperor personally, but he remained chief of the Fifth Division for the rest of his career.[33] If employment can indicate political views, he may have been a true supporter of the Revolution, and perhaps one of the Empire, or perhaps merely an anti-royalist, for he did not stay long at the Ministry after the return of the Bourbons and the monarchy.

Margaret Audin writes that Goulhot was probably the person most involved with the British prisoners (and, consequently, with the American prisoners detained with them). However, it seems likely that two of his subordinates in the Fifth Division were even more directly involved, though neither of their names appears often in the documentation on the American seamen. From as early as 1805, one bureau, headed by Noël Jean Debacq, was responsible for veterans, the disabled or wounded, and prisoners of war. In 1812, that bureau was divided into two, one for veterans and the disabled, still headed by Debacq, and one exclusively concerned with prisoners of war, policing them and exchanging them, headed by Charles Louis Houel. Both men reported directly to Goulhot.

Less is known of these two men than of Goulhot, yet it seems likely that it was they, primarily Debacq, who were the first within the Ministry of War to receive and read the pleading letters from American seamen in prison. Debacq was born in Rouen, one of Normandy's great cities, containing one of France's greatest cathedrals, in 1770 and had arrived in Paris when he was seventeen, before the Revolution.[34] He began as an ordinary clerk at the Ministry of War in 1787 (when Louis XVI was still on the throne and unaware of what was to come, and while young Goulhot was among his house guards). After six years, and soon after Goulhot joined the Bureau, he was promoted to senior clerk.[35]

---

[32] Howard G. Brown. *War, Revolution, and the Bureaucratic State: Politics and Army Administration in France 1791–1799*. Oxford Historical Monographs. Oxford: Clarendon Press, 1995, p309.

[33] *Personnel civil du Ministère de la Guerre*. SHDV. 5YG (Goulhot).

[34] Noël Jean Debacq dossier. Arch. nat. *Base de données Léonore. Légion d'honneur dossier No*. LH/676/57, http://www2.culture.gouv.fr/documentation/leonore/ [Accessed 3 May 2019].

[35] Debacq, *Légion d'honneur dossier No*. LH/676/57.

Like Goulhot, he married in Paris in 1793. At about the same time, he seems to have expunged from his ministry personnel file his early years, those under the monarchy. At his request, a carefully worded note was produced that stated that "1791 is the earliest date for which a payment record for him can be found".[36] (Mention of those early years at the ministry does not appear again until after the Restoration, when he wrote to the minister, asking to be nominated to the Legion of Honour.) He was named chief of the bureau in 1794, replacing Goulhot, who had been promoted to head of the division. He remained at that level until his retirement in 1828; including those early years, he was at the ministry for over forty years. He was the father of five children and cared for his mother in her dotage. Money was always short and his personnel file has many requests, supported by Goulhot, for pay rises. He was able to obtain employment for his son in the ministry and to get a loan to help to pay for that son's marriage.[37]

Debacq and Goulhot were both in the Ministry of War during some of its greatest upheavals. Before the Revolution, from 1787, when Debacq was just beginning his career, numerous reforms of the ministry were made in an effort to control the budget and to make the entire ministry more professional.[38] The staff were reduced by thirty per cent, a purge that Debacq, a lowly clerk at that point, survived. In September 1791, after the entire ministry had been restructured by the War Committee, there were further cost reductions and eliminations of privileges in the effort to change the administration of the ministry from a world of underlings seeking the minister's favour to one of professional bureaucrats, administering according to law and regulation, with their salaries and promotions as their only rewards. Many bureau chiefs who had been in the ministry for thirty years or more were pensioned off, continuing the effort to sweep out the old attitudes. As others moved up to fill the vacant places, new staff were hired, having passed the ministry's new and short-lived proficiency examinations; among the very first of them was Goulhot.

In the next few months, the power struggle between the monarchy and the Legislative Assembly played out in the Ministry of War, with the minister being changed nine times in less than a year. At one point, radical Parisians broke into the ministry and seized two officials who had not acted radically enough and whom they suspected of corruption. Eventually, only those employees who "had passed a security clearance and been issued a special pass" were allowed to enter the ministry.[39] The survival in their positions and their promotions through this chaotic and violent period of restructuring

---

[36] *Personnel civil du Ministère de la Guerre.* (Debacq). SHDV. 5YG 1089.
[37] *Personnel civil du Ministère de la Guerre.* (Debacq). SHDV. 5YG 1089.
[38] Brown, *War, Revolution, and the Bureaucratic State*, p19.
[39] Brown, *War, Revolution, and the Bureaucratic State*, pp21–26, 42–44.

and purges would indicate that Goulhot and Debacq both passed the security clearance and supported the ideals of the Revolution.

In the summer of 1803, Goulhot wrote to the minister explaining that the Pensions Bureau in his division had a great deal of work and that the chief of that bureau, Chauvet, was a sickly man. He asked that Houel, "whom I have known for a long time and who has all of the necessary qualities", be appointed to that bureau as deputy chief (*sous-chef*).[40] Charles Louis Houel was another Norman, born in Saint-Lô in 1769, and had a rather more colourful life than had either Goulhot or Debacq. At the age of fourteen, he had been sent by his mother to study for the priesthood. Apparently an excellent student, he then attended the seminary at Saint-Magloire. In 1789, as the Revolution began, he was still an acolyte. By the turbulent year of 1791, he was a subdeacon and the following year was ordained.[41] In this year, however, all priests were required to swear loyalty to a new, state religion based on reason (rather than on faith); those who did not swear could not perform their functions as priests. Suddenly, in the new France, priests were permitted to marry and priests, monks and nuns were banned from wearing their robes in public.[42] Houel's ordination vows may not even have been valid for, in February 1790, two years before he was ordained, the Assembly had issued a decree forbidding anyone from taking religious vows. This would seem to have suited him very well.

Six months after his ordination, Houel renounced the priesthood and, borrowing 20,000 *assignats* (the currency of Revolutionary France) from his mother, bought a printing house. He began publishing a newspaper called *Le Réhabilitateur ou l'Ami des opprimés*. The views of this publication were certainly in support of the Revolution and its ideals, for he was chosen by the Committee for Public Safety to go, with three others, to Constantinople to spread the word of the Revolution through the French publishing house there, *l'imprimerie française de Constantinople*. This would keep the large French community there informed of how the Revolution was progressing in France and it would, it was hoped, inspire the Turks to have a revolution of their own.[43] After two years, he returned to Paris and picked up printing under his own name again, publishing a long poem by Lavallé, the corrected

---

[40] *Personnel civil du Ministère de la Guerre*. (Houel). SHDV. 5YG 2073. Translation by the author.

[41] Moulin, *Plaidoyer de Me Moulin, Pour M. G. Daguier-Houel, Contre lo M. G. Houel, 2o les Sr et De Lepage. Extrait du journal du Droit du 23 mai 1841. Tribunal Civil de la Seine (3e Chambre) Présidence de M. Pinodel. Audience du 21 mai*. Paris: Bruneau, 1841, p3.

[42] Gérard Desquesses. *Agenda de la Révolution Française, 1790 1990*. Paris: Editions Hibiscus, 1989. [No page numbers. July].

[43] Joëlle Pierre. "La Presse française de Turquie, canal de transmission des idées de la Révolution". *Le Temps des médias*, Vol. 5, No. 2, 2005, pp168–176.

works of Etienne Bonnot de Condillac, and an opera.[44] He then gave up printing and joined the Ministry of War as an ordinary clerk in 1798.[45] In 1812, the Fifth Division expanded and, when the bureau headed by Debacq was divided, Houel was moved from the Pensions Bureau, where he had been for eight years, to become chief of the new bureau devoted exclusively to prisoners of war.[46] After the Restoration, he worked as chief of the Bureau of Military Justice, producing a report proposing the construction of a more humane type of military prison (which was never built).[47] Like Debacq, he retired in 1828. He never married but had a "dear friend" for forty years, a woman who held him in her arms as he died on the last day of 1840.[48] Late in life, he had adopted his nephew and made him his sole heir. When relatives contested his will, a landmark court decision was made, confirming that priests did have the right to adopt.[49]

These three men worked alongside one another in the same division for most of their careers, becoming expert in the application of policy and law to all aspects of their work, including prisoners of war, both French prisoners held by enemy belligerents and the many thousands of prisoners held in France. They were survivors of one of the greatest upheavals any country has known, administrators of military affairs through one of France's most belligerent eras, and responsible for prisoners of war when the concept of what such prisoners were and how they were to be held and treated was being redefined by their Emperor. The American seamen were a tiny proportion of their work but they appear to have given their cases the same scrutiny, attention and effort to be just as they gave to the British, Spanish, Polish, Austrian or Russian prisoners, "never rejecting a request without first examining it".[50]

---

[44] Moulin, *Plaidoyer*, p4.

[45] Charles Louis Houel dossier. Arch. nat. *Base de données Léonore. Légion d'honneur dossier No.* LH/1311/18, http://www2.culture.gouv.fr/documentation/leonore/ [Accessed 3 May 2019]. This unusual move may have been prompted by a possible meeting with Generals Aubert-Dubayet, once a Minister of War, and Carra de Saint-Cyr, who were both in Constantinople when Houel was there.

[46] *Archives de la Guerre et Armée de Terre. Personnel civil du Ministère de la Guerre* (1806–1853). SHDV. 5YG 2073 (Houel).

[47] Report from Houel to the Minister of War. 5 November 1821. *Archives de la Guerre et Armée de Terre. Justice Militaire.* SHDV. C18 44. Can it be that Houel's position in military justice had anything to do with Goulhot's destruction of files that would have sent many to prison?

[48] Moulin, *Plaidoyer*, p2.

[49] *Gazette des Tribunaux: Journal de Jurisprudence et des Débats Judiciaires.* No 1622. 30 January 1842. Paris, p1.

[50] Devos, "Les Prisonniers de Guerre Anglais", p21. Translation by the author.

Ministère des Relations extérieurs

The Ministry of External Relations dealt with all foreign affairs of France during the Napoleonic era. Yet, Napoleon maintained such a tight personal control over all dealings with foreign powers, that historians have long written that there was no French diplomacy and there were no French diplomats other than the Emperor. Nevertheless, for a letter to reach the Emperor, to obtain an audience in order discuss or dispute his decrees, or to make a request concerning a seaman, the American diplomats had to communicate firstly through the Minister of External Relations. From 1804 to 1814, there were four different ministers.

Charles Maurice de Talleyrand-Périgord, later given the title of Prince de Bénévant, was a remarkable man and a wily survivor of France's political turmoil in whom, since the XYZ Affair, Americans had no trust. Born into the nobility in 1754, he was intelligent and extremely perspicacious. Though he walked with a limp and had been scarred by smallpox, he knew what every politician knows: that nothing is more efficacious than confidence. Educated and ordained as a priest, he had no religious calling whatsoever. He was said to have been witty, charming, greedy and licentious; the compliance with his wishes and desires by those with whom he dealt would indicate that he was certainly also persuasive. During the last years of the French Court, he was appointed to the bishopric of Autan but had already insinuated himself into the world of diplomacy. When the Revolution came, he did not emigrate for, though of an aristocratic family, he would appear to have shared some of the revolutionaries' values. He became a member of the Assembly and, though a bishop, it was he who proposed that the State confiscate all of the Church's property. He spent the Terror as an exile in London and America, becoming fluent in English. On his return to France, he was appointed Minister of Foreign Affairs in 1797 and he used the position to enrich himself. When Napoleon became First Consul and then Emperor, he kept Talleyrand as his Minister of Foreign Affairs (in 1804, renamed Minister of External Relations). He remained there for nearly eight years and returned to the post again after the fall of Napoleon (whom he had betrayed).[51]

Jean-Baptiste Nompère de Champagny, the Duke of Cadore (he of the Cadore Letter), was minister from 1807 to 1811, the years during which most American seamen were captured and held as prisoners under the Berlin and Milan Decrees. Born into the nobility in 1756, he had been a Naval officer before the French Revolution and had fought in the American Revolution. He was a representative of the nobility in the Estates General in 1789 and was imprisoned during, but survived, the Terror, no small accomplishment.

---

[51] Duff Cooper. *Talleyrand*. London: Vintage, 2010; Bergeron, *France Under Napoleon*, p76.

After his release and Napoleon's rise to power, he was named ambassador to Austria in 1801. Trusted by Napoleon, he had already served as the Minister of the Interior for three years before moving to External Relations.[52] There, he is said to have carried out Napoleon's will in "executing the replacement of the King of Spain, implementing the Continental Blockade, negotiating the Peace of Vienna, preparing the Emperor's divorce, justifying the annexation of Holland"[53] yet he had time to respond to a number of requests for the release of American seamen. Perhaps he was able to influence the Emperor concerning them, for more were released during Champagny's time at the Ministry than during any other.[54]

Hugues-Bernard Maret, the Duke of Bassano, was born in Dijon in 1763 into the professional class. The son of a doctor, he became a lawyer and married his cousin, the daughter of the mayor of Dijon. When the Revolution came, he went to Paris to join the struggle. Like Houel, but much more successfully, he went into publishing. He was a founder of the *Moniteur Universel*, which gave full reports on the debates and actions of the government and which grew into a publication that would be the chronicle of the First Empire. While still in his twenties, he was appointed to a post in the Ministry of Foreign Affairs in 1792, making him, of all those who ran that ministry during this period, the man who most likely knew it and its staff better than the others. He may have spoken some English as he was sent on a diplomatic mission to London before war was declared in 1793.

While ambassador to Naples, Maret was captured, with many others of the mission, by the Austrians and held as a prisoner of war for two and a half years.[55] He was held in the Ducal Palace of Mantua, probably in some sort of airless dungeon, for he suffered from a convulsive malady for several months while there, and most of those with him fell ill. Fearing that he might die (as the others would do) his captors moved him, in chains that were so tight that he bled, to the hilltop fortress at Kufstein, later an infamous state prison. High on a rock and covered in snow during the winter, the Kufstein fortress is reminiscent of that at Bitche. He had his own cell, "eight feet wide by six

---

[52] Bergeron, *France Under Napoleon*, pp73 and 76.

[53] Lionel Bouchon and Didier Grau. "Jean-Baptiste de Nompère de Champagny (1756–1834)". *Napoléon & Empire*, 2017. https://www.napoleon-empire.net/personnages/champagny.php [Accessed 12 August 2019]. Translation from the French by the author.

[54] Whether this may have been due to a veteran's sympathy with Americans or to a naval officer's sympathy with seamen cannot be known.

[55] Joseph Fr. and Louis Gabriel Michaud. *Biographie universelle, ancienne et moderne, ou Histoire, par ordre alphabétique, de la vie publique et privée de tous les hommes qui se sont fait remarquer par leurs écrits, leurs actions, leurs talents, leurs vertus ou leurs crimes: Supplément,* Vol. 73. Paris: Michaud, 1839, pp104–126.

feet long" with a low, vaulted ceiling. Prisoners were referred to only by their cell numbers, never by their names. Though his situation was in some ways better than that of the American seamen in French prison depots, for there was enough food and a doctor visited weekly, in other ways it was worse, for not once in the twenty-two months that he was at Kufstein was he allowed out of his cell for exercise in a yard.[56] Maret, probably more than any other of all the ministers petitioned by the American minister and consuls on behalf of their seamen, knew very well what it meant to be a prisoner of war.[57]

The Austrians exchanged him, with others, for the daughter of Louis XVI, the last survivor of that family. By December 1796, he was back in France and was soon working in the Ministry of Foreign Affairs alongside Talleyrand. In 1799, he was appointed Secretary General to the Consulate. Among his responsibilities, Maret read and summarized the reports from all ministries into weekly reports to Napoleon. Maret, like Berthier, seems to have had the Emperor's trust and to have understood the way his mind worked. Apparently, Talleyrand despised him,[58] perhaps for this closeness to the Emperor, perhaps for the way that he interpreted Talleyrand's reports in his weekly summaries, or quite possibly for his probity, which may have mystified Talleyrand.

In 1811, Maret was appointed Minister of External Relations, a post he held for two years. He was a man of great stamina, like all those Napoleon selected as ministers; not only did he work long hours, running the ministry and negotiating treaties with allies; he also accompanied Napoleon on most of his campaigns. He remained absolutely loyal to Napoleon to the very end and was exiled during the Restoration. After he was allowed to return, he was made a peer and even, briefly, became the Prime Minister of France. He died in Paris in 1839, survived by four children, including the eldest, whom he had named Napoleon, and a daughter who lived in England.[59] Maret was the Minister of External Relations when the United States declared war against Great Britain in June 1812. It was he who received the requests from the American minister for American privateers against Britain to be permitted to operate from French ports and, in some cases, to be manned by American seamen held prisoner in France.

---

[56] Michaud and Michaud, *Biographie universelle*, Vol. 73, pp109–112.

[57] Maret would also have had a greater awareness than most of the depots where the prisoners of war were held as he had in his youth won second prize in a competition held by the Academy of Dijon for a paper on Vauban; Michaud and Michaud, *Biographie universelle*, Vol. 73, p105.

[58] Bouchon and Grau. "Jean-Baptiste de Nompère de Champagny"; Bergeron, *France Under Napoleon*, p76.

[59] Hugues-Bernard Maret dossier, AN, *Base de données Léonore. Légion d'honneur dossier No. LH/1736/57,* http://www2.culture.gouv.fr/documentation/leonore/ [Accessed 13 August 2019].

The last Minister of External Relations during the period when American seamen were prisoners in France was Armand Augustin Louis de Caulaincourt, in his post only from 1813 to 1814. Born into a noble family in 1773, he entered the Army at the age of fifteen and made his career there. He seems to have had a comportment that revealed his aristocratic origins, for he was distrusted by revolutionaries and, later, would appear to have been selected for some missions on which he was to deal with royalty by Talleyrand and Napoleon, not only for his ability but for his bearing.[60] Yet, perhaps because he was rumoured to have been a party to the arrest and execution of the Duke of Enghien, which he denied to the end of his days, no one seems to have trusted him. He was Minister through the Battle of Paris in March 1814 and was removed the following month, at the fall of the First Empire. The Ministry of External Relations once again became the Ministry of Foreign Affairs. Under the Provisional Government of 1814, a career diplomat, Antoine de Laforêt, held the position of Minister for five weeks, until Talleyrand, that great survivor, resumed the post.

The diplomatic dispatches of American Ministers Plenipotentiary are filled with communiqués to the Ministers of External Relations, Talleyrand, Champagny, Maret and Caulaincourt, as well as d'Hauterive.[61] For the most part, the Americans were disputing the decrees of Napoleon that inhibited the freedom of Americans to trade in Europe. From 1804, as the appeals of American seamen began to reach the American consuls and minister, the requests to the ministry for their release increased. The Minister of External Relations in most cases forwarded these requests to the Ministers of War and Marine, asking them to verify the nationalities of the seamen.

This was complicated by the fact that aspects of the responsibility for the prisoners of war were scattered across different ministries, divisions and bureaux, creating some tension. The "*Almanach impérial*" for 1813 neatly documents this: it has it that the Fifth Division of the Ministry of Marine was in charge of seamen's shares of prize monies, policing prisoners of war and exchanges of naval prisoners of war, while the Ministry of War was also responsible for prisoners of war, for policing them and for any exchanges. At the same time, the Ministry of Police General was responsible for any prisoners who had escaped and the Ministry of the Interior was in charge of

---

[60] Bouchon and Grau. "Armand Augustin Louis de Caulaincourt (1773–1827)". *Napoléon & Empire*, 2017.

[61] From 1798, the name of Alexandre Maurice Blanc de Lanautte, Comte d'Hauterive, a shadowy figure and a powerful man in the political section of the Ministry, appears in the correspondence. Whenever the Minister, whether Talleyrand, Champagny, Maret or Caulaincourt, was away, it was d'Hauterive who stepped in as the temporary Minister.

prisoners of war used in work teams.[62] Adding to the tensions, the Ministers of Police General and of War, Savary and Clarke, disliked one another; the Minister of Marine, Decrès, sneered at everyone; and Clarke was said to be at odds with the Minister of War Administration, Dejean.[63]

In summary, each of the men above had some kind of power over the lives of the American seamen prisoners of war, some of them directly, some peripherally. Each of those who was a minister had the privilege of being able to speak to Napoleon directly and often and was courted by all, including American diplomats because of that ability. They were intelligent men, gifted administrators. However, the confusion, conflicts and rivalries, along with the constant need of all ministers to defer to the absolute authority of the ultimate decision-maker, Napoleon, made it extremely difficult for the American Minister Plenipotentiary and the United States consuls in France to negotiate the release of the seamen, particularly because, as will be seen in the next chapter, the American diplomats were even more fractious amongst themselves.

---

[62] Testu, *Almanach*, pp203–242 and p792.
[63] Haegele, "*Le général Clarke*", p14.

5

THE AMERICAN DIPLOMATS IN FRANCE

The Creation of the Consular Service

The United States established its consular service, as separate from its diplomatic service, at the end of the eighteenth century, in 1792. This was the beginning of an era when the consular services of many nations were large, trusted and influential. During this time, nearly every country of Europe and the Americas had a consular service; the primary functions of them all were the same: to protect their country's commerce and navigation, and their seamen in foreign ports.[1] The fledgling American consular service, before its duties were outlined in an act passed in 1792, was developed, in a very large part, out of the experiences and mistakes of early American diplomats and consuls in France.

In 1776, the Continental Congress appointed three men to be commissioners to France: Silas Deane, a businessman of dubious character who may have been a spy, Benjamin Franklin, a Founding Father of mythological integrity whose Quaker ways reputedly met their match in the Parisian gaiety of pre-Revolutionary France, and Arthur Lee, who had been America's first representative to Great Britain, may also have been a spy and who despised both France and Franklin.[2] Each was given "infinite powers" to negotiate agreements with France that would help America's independence effort.

---

[1] Jörg Ulbert and Lukian Prijac, eds. *Consuls et services consulaires au XIXe siècle*. Hamburg: DOBU Verlag, 2010, pp9–11. Consular history is rarefied historiography; for more on the history of European consular services see Halvard Leira and Iver B. Neumann "Consular Representation in an Emerging State: The Case of Norway", *The Hague Journal of Diplomacy*, Vol. 3 (2008). David Bailie Warden, *On the Origin, Nature, Progress and Influence of Consular Establishments* (1813) which is rather curious, as Warden had been a consul, and not one of the best. He listed and compared the rules and regulations of certain countries' consular services, including requirements for the treatment of seamen. For a more recent effort to describe the history of the British consular service, with almost no mention of the protection of seamen, see John Dickie. *The British Consul: Heir to a Great Tradition.* London: C. Hurst, 2007. The best history of the United States consular service remains that by Emory R. Johnson. "The Early History of the United States Consular Service. 1776–1792". *Political Science Quarterly*, Vol. 13, No. 1, March 1896.

[2] George Dangerfield. *Chancellor Robert R. Livingston of New York, 1746–1813.* New York: Harcourt, Brace, 1960. p254.

The inevitable confusion caused by three distinct representatives with such powers in the same place and at the same time was recognized almost immediately. Within two years, Franklin was urging that the appointments be clarified and regularized under some sort of hierarchy. The needs of American seamen in foreign ports were also instantly apparent; the first of many requests from American representatives in Europe for consuls to be appointed in foreign ports to aid seamen came from the representatives in France.[3]

In spite of their antipathy for one another, Franklin, Deane and Lee managed to negotiate with France the 1778 "Treaty of Amity and Commerce Between the United States and France". It cemented the alliance between the two countries, and granted each the freedom to have consuls in the ports of the other. Crucially for seamen, it also described in detail the documentation, termed "Sea Letters or Passports", that each country's vessels must show when stopped by the warships or privateers of the other, if they wished to prove that they were not the enemy.[4] The French often referred to this treaty, and to violations of it, when discussing American seamen later held as prisoners of war.

In November of the same year, Thomas Jefferson, who had replaced Benjamin Franklin in France, signed the "Convention Defining and Establishing the Functions and Privileges of Consuls and Vice Consuls" at Versailles. In a very large part, it deals with the consuls' responsibilities concerning vessels, merchants, captains, passengers and crews of their nation, and gives them enormous policing, agenting and judicial authority over them.[5]

The Continental Congress appointed a consul general to France in 1778. When he was lost at sea on the voyage to take up his post, the appointment went to Thomas Barclay, an Irishman who had emigrated to Philadelphia and built a fortune as a merchant. Though his responsibilities were clear in the

---

[3] Emory R. Johnson. "The Early History of the United States Consular Service. 1776–1792". *Political Science Quarterly*, Vol. 13, No. 1, March 1896, pp19–40. Academy of Political Science. https://www.jstor.org/stable/2140002 [Accessed 31 July 2019] pp22–23.

[4] For the English version: "Treaty of Alliance Between The United States and France; February 6, 1778". The Avalon Project: Documents in Law, History and Diplomacy, Yale Law School, Lillian Goldman Law Library. https://avalon.law.yale.edu/18th_century/fr1788-1.asp. [Accessed 11 October 2019]. For the French version, which includes the Sea Letters form mentioned in article 25: "Traité d'amitié et de commerce, conclu entre le Roi et les États-Unis de l'Amérique septentrionale, le 6 février 1778". Paris: Imprimerie royale, 1778. Bibliothèque nationale de France, département Droit, économie, politique, F-21249 (37). https://gallica.bnf.fr/ark:/12148/btv1b86259408/f22.image. [Accessed 11 October 2019].

[5] "Convention Defining and Establishing the Functions and Privileges of Consuls and Vice Consuls, November 14, 1788". The Avalon Project: Documents in Law, History and Diplomacy, Yale Law School, Lillian Goldman Law Library. https://avalon.law.yale.edu/18th_century/fr1788.asp #1. [Accessed 11 October 2019].

Convention signed with France, his official position within the budding foreign service of the United States was not. This vagueness was not clarified when, in 1785, Congress passed a resolution creating a consular service but without defining consular duties that would be general to all consuls in all countries. This initial lack of clarity concerning the consular and diplomatic services would create rancorous and spiteful disputes between some of the American consuls and ministers posted to France.

When, in the act of 1792, the responsibilities for all were finally defined, the duties outlined were taken, almost literally, from those in the Convention of 1778 with France. The act also separated the diplomatic service, including the senior diplomats, termed the Ministers Plenipotentiary, from the consular service but, in France, disputes as to responsibilities and authority would continue.

The act of 1792 was entitled "An act concerning consuls and vice-consuls"; it was short, containing just nine sections. The first section addresses ways to ensure compliance with a convention agreed between France and the United States. The following sections deal with consular duties concerning citizens abroad, vessels and the rights of consuls to charge fees. Near the end, sections seven and eight address consular responsibilities toward American seamen in foreign ports.[6]

Firstly, in order "to prevent the mariners and seamen, employed in vessels belonging to citizens of the United States, in cases of shipwreck, sickness, or captivity, from suffering in foreign ports", it was the duty of consuls to provide for them at the expense of the United States, with an allowance of up to twelve cents per day. This was to prove a pitifully inadequate sum for their needs in France.

Secondly, consuls were allowed to request that American masters and captains of vessels belonging to citizens of the United States accept on board stranded seamen to transport back to the United States, free of charge. They could not refuse this request, on pain of a fine of thirty dollars per man refused, but it was limited to two seamen per 100 tons burthen of the vessel and the seamen had to work their passage, if they were not too ill or wounded to do so. Many masters accepted this without complaint. At times, there were so many seamen waiting to be sent home, especially in 1808 and 1809, that vessels were chartered for the purpose. Napoleon allowed at least two such cartels to leave from Livorno and Hamburg in the summer of 1808.[7]

---

[6] Joseph Story. *The Public and General Statutes Passed by the Congress of the United States of America from 1789 to 1827 Inclusive.....* Boston: Wells and Lilly, 1828, pp235–238.

[7] Champagny to Armstrong. 6 August 1808. United States. Department of State. *Despatches from United States Ministers to France, 1789–1906.* Vol. 11. Microfilm copy.

Thirdly, masters of vessels could not abandon their crew in foreign ports but had either to take them back to the state in America from which they had departed or pay for their return passage. If a master refused to do so and the seamen complained to the consul, "the said consul or vice-consul may cause his ship, goods, and person, to be arrested, and held (if the laws of the land permit it) until he shall comply with his duty herein".

The law stated that the people administering this act, e.g., all consuls, vice-consuls and consular agents, were to be American citizens, which was a change from the Convention, which had stated that they could be foreigners. The reality was that, from Barclay's days onward, though consuls and vice-consuls were generally Americans, the consular agent or commercial agent posts were filled by men of either American or French nationality.[8] Jean Diot in Morlaix, François Coffyn in Dunkirk and Etienne Cathalan in Marseilles were three of the most notable and long-standing French nationals who served as consular agents for the United States.

In the opinion of Emory R. Johnson (and of all of the consuls themselves), one of the most grievous flaws in the act was that the consuls were to be unpaid. Their remuneration was indirect in that they were allowed to charge fees for consular services (such as vessel registration) and to use their positions to further their own commercial interests (such as acting as agents for American companies, vessel owners and captains).[9] As will be seen below, this created for many of the consuls situations of glaring conflicts of interest.[10] This lack of remuneration along with a very slow and much disputed system of reimbursing expenses caused a great deal of trouble for the consuls.

The law was revised in 1803, to the disadvantage of seamen. The revision repealed the right of consuls to confiscate the vessels of masters who abandoned seamen, leaving them with no way to enforce compliance. It

---

[8] Not finding enough citizens abroad who could serve as consuls was not unique to the United States. Muller writes of Sweden having the same problem. See Leos Muller, *Consuls, Corsairs, and Commerce. The Swedish Consular Service and Long-distance Shipping, 1720–1815*, Studia Historica Upsaliensia 213. Uppsala: Acta Universitatis Upsaliensis, 2004.

[9] Johnson, "The Early History of the United States Consular Service." p38.

[10] The problem of consuls exploiting their offices of public service for personal gain was not unique to those of the United States in France. Muller writes that Sweden, in an effort to restrain abuse, prohibited consuls from owning vessels or cargo. Pablo Boorsma Mendoza describes the divided loyalties of Dutch consuls in Cadiz who seemingly worked more for local merchants than for their government or citizens. See Leos Muller, *Consuls, Corsairs, and Commerce. The Swedish Consular Service and Long-distance Shipping, 1720–1815*, Studia Historica Upsaliensia 213. Uppsala: Acta Universitatis Upsaliensis, 2004; Pablo Boorsma Mendoza, *Merchant Consuls: Dutch Consuls in Cadiz and their Divided Loyalties (1713–1757)*, Masters thesis in History, University of Leiden, 2015.

also allowed masters to charge for transporting abandoned seamen back to America. Worse for the seamen, the revision repealed the provision of a daily allowance that the consuls could spend to aid stranded seamen. In France, this added to the seamen's sufferings significantly. Aaron Vail, the commercial agent in Lorient, declared that he could not afford to fulfil the part of his consular duties relating to American seamen, having already lost so much money that the government had yet to repay, and he went so far as to refuse to accept the responsibility for seamen sent by agents at other locations to Lorient in order to take a ship home.[11] Jean Diot submitted a number of claims to be compensated for his expenses for clothing, feeding and lodging distressed American seamen.[12] Etienne Cathalan tried to reduce his burden of payments to distressed seamen by giving notice to every American shipmaster who entered the port that he would be holding seamen's wages if they went ashore, to cover any costs incurred:

> ...no Seaman or Seamen will be considered discharged from any American vessel, unless it is done in the United States chancery...[13]

John Appleton, the commercial agent in Calais, responsible for a part of the coast where there were often shipwrecks, wrote to the minister that he was being brought to financial hardship by the costs of helping American seamen who had survived wrecks and that he despaired that, in their impoverishment, they were easily coerced to sign on to French privateers.[14] Five years after Appleton wrote of his efforts to keep Americans from signing on to French privateers, Isaac Cox Barnet, commercial agent at Le Havre, told the stranded seaman John Smith that he should do just that, as he could not help him: "Having no funds from the United States for the aid of seamen in distress, [I advise you] to sign on to a French privateer, being the only way to procure subsistence...".[15] (In his defence, Barnet vigorously denied ever having said such a thing.) A few years earlier, from Antwerp, Barnet had written to Madison, then Secretary of State, that "The allowance of twelve

---

[11] Numerous letters in 1810 and 1811, from Vail to Diot. Jonathan Russell Papers.

[12] Letter from Jean Diot to Jonathan Russell, 31 December 1810. Jonathan Russell Papers.

[13] Notice given by Cathalan to American shipmasters then in the port of Marseilles. 7 December 1807. United States. Department of State. *Despatches from United States Consuls in Marseilles, 1790–1906*. Vol. 2. Microfilm copy.

[14] Appleton to Armstrong. 16 April 1804. United States. Department of State. *Despatches from United States Consuls to Calais, 1804–1906*. Vol. 1. Microfilm copy.

[15] Sworn statement by John Morrison. 20 November 1809. United States. Department of State. *Despatches from United States Ministers to France, 1789–1906*. Vol. 11. Microfilm copy.

cents a day is insufficient for the relief of distressed seamen in this port as in all the ports of France…consuls cannot afford to help them…"[16]

To be sure, there were also times when the consuls had to pay fines for seamen's storied wild behaviour on shore. Christopher Meyer, the chancellor for the United States consulate at Bordeaux, listed with palpable indignation the fines paid to the police for the offences of some men from the crew of the *General Gates*.

> These are to certify that the following Sums have been paid in the Office for Gend'armes fees, prison fees, etc. arising from arrestation, desertion and imprisonment of the hereafter named Seamen belonging to the ship *General Gates* of New York Capt. Richard Marner, vz.
>
> Paid for Thomas Jackson Boatswain arrested for repeated drunkeness. Eleven Dollars Eighty Cents.
>
> Paid for Jacob Barry Seaman arrested for having deserted the Ship. Sixteen Dollars and ten Cents.
>
> Paid for Thomas Wickery arrested by the police having been found ashore at unlawful hours. Two Dollars twenty cents.
>
> Paid for Robert Scott having deserted her and has not been apprehended. Six Dollars.
>
> Paid for John Brown having deserted the ship twice. Eighteen Dollars Eighty Seven Cents.
>
> Paid for James Bonds arrested for having deserted the Ship and for his mutinous conduct. Nineteen Dollars Eighty three cents.
>
> Paid for John S. Pease arrested for mutinous conduct and leaving the Ship. Twelve Dollars Seventy cents.
>
> Paid for Thomas Taylor arrested for having left the Ship and found in places of bad repute by the police. Nine Dollars ten Cents.
>
> Paid for Alexander Kirkwood arrested for deserting the Ship and found in places of bad repute.[17]

---

[16] Barnet to Madison. 12 March 1803. United States. Department of State. *Despatches from United States Consuls in Antwerp, 1802–1906*. Vol. 1. Microfilm copy.

[17] All four men also appear on the captured crew list of the *General Gates*. High Court of Admiralty: Prize Court: Prize Papers. Ships names beginning with this letter: G. *General Gates*. TNA, HCA 32/1771.

By the end of 1810, when many dozens of American vessels had been seized by the French under the Berlin and Milan Decrees, leaving hundreds of American seamen stranded or imprisoned and needing aid, the total cost had risen to 75,000 dollars in claims against the United States Treasury, as listed in the Congressional "Relief of Distressed Seamen in the Ports of Europe". That report shows that William Lee, the consul at Bordeaux, claimed over 13,000 dollars for the aid and repatriation of "one hundred and sixty-four captains, mates and ordinary seamen", and Etienne Cathalan, the consular agent at Marseilles, had had to pay 4000 dollars for the subsistence of American seamen in his area.[18] Some of the consuls never stopped trying to recover their money. Years after the wars ended, in 1822, Fulwar Skipwith, who had tried to help American prisoners with regular payments similar to the charitable funds for the British prisoners, was still petitioning the United States Treasury for the reimbursement of the more than 2000 dollars he had disbursed to American seamen in distress when he was the consul general in Paris during the 1790s.[19]

For American seamen, this irregularity and uncertainty of assistance meant insecurity. They had been led to expect that, in times of need in a foreign port, they could turn to the United States representative in that port for help, but the amount and kind of help varied from country to country, and from port to port. In France, it was a matter of luck as to whether they would receive aid or not, depending upon the nature and personal finances of the man serving as consul, vice-consul or consular agent at the time.

Endless Bickering

There were United States consuls or consular agents at most of the French Empire's main ports throughout the wars. Marseilles, Bordeaux, Lorient, Le Havre, Amsterdam and Antwerp always had a consul or agent. Calais, Brest, Cherbourg, Nantes, La Rochelle and others had sporadic consular services. The consular service in Paris was nothing but confusion. Fulwar Skipwith (who had previously been consul general there) was the commercial agent for the United States in Paris from 1801 to 1808. During that period there was no consul general in Paris, though Skipwith aided American seamen as best he could. From 1809 to 1814, David Bailie Warden was a consul at Paris. For part of this time, Jonathan Russell was the chargé d'affaires at the United States legation in Paris. Somehow, though Warden was consul, Russell, whose responsibility it was not, was more involved with aiding American seamen.

---

[18] "Relief of Distressed Seamen in the Ports of Europe", American State Papers, House of Representatives, 11th Congress, 3rd Session, Commerce and Navigation: Vol. 1, p821–22. https://memory.loc.gov/cgi-bin/ampage?collId=llsp&fileName=014/llsp014.db&recNum=826 [Accessed 29 September 2019].

[19] "Statement of the Claim of FS on Acct of Distressed Seamen", Fulwar Skipwith Papers.

After the abdication of Napoleon, Fulwar Skipwith was back as consul from 1814 to 1815. Though one was desperately needed, there was no United States consul general in Paris at any time during the Napoleonic Wars.

The men who sought the posts as consuls or consular agents, some of them avidly, may not have anticipated just how burdensome would be the responsibility of providing relief to American seamen. They struggled not only with the cost of such relief but with the amount of time and effort required to visit vessels, jails and hospitals, to arrange lodging for and to feed and clothe the seamen in need and to arrange the burials of those who had died. Their intention was not humanitarian work but business and they sought the posts for the access to shipping, the respect they would gain and for the consular fees that they could charge. Their personal businesses generally were in importing, exporting, shipping and serving as local private agents, but when the consuls and consular agents in France added to their activities the consular duties of vessel registration, aiding with prize claims, brokering the sales of ships and cargo, for all of which they charged fees, they may have encountered conflicts of interest, though it is clear that they did not consider it as such at the time. In fact, most of them thought appointments to the posts would make their fortunes.[20]

Generally, they were men with a sound knowledge of French politics and business, having lived in the country for some time. Some, like Nathaniel Cutting, who was briefly the American consul at Le Havre, had been in France since well before the French Revolution, representing British and American mercantile houses. Some already had experience of France, as did Isaac Cox Barnet, who had been spirited away by his father to Nantes as a child during the American Revolution, and who returned to France in 1794 as a supercargo for John R. Livingston and remained, serving as the wordy and ever-injured consul or agent variously at Bordeaux, Brest, Le Havre and Paris.[21] William Lee, commercial agent at Bordeaux, was a businessman from Boston whose

---

[20] Margrit Schulte Beerbühl. *Hard Times: The Economic Activities of American Consuls on the North Sea Coast under the Continental System. German Historical Institute London Bulletin*, Vol. 40, No. 2 (November 2018), pp3–31. Also see Lawrence A. Peskin. "The Blurry Line: Robert Montgomery's Public and Private Interests as U.S. Consul to Alicante", *Cahiers de la Méditerranée*, Vol. 98 (2019) which discusses how one American consul enriched himself in the position, and P.A. Boorsma *Mendoza, Merchant Consuls: Dutch Consuls in Cadiz and Their Divided Loyalties (1713–1757)*, Masters thesis, University of Leiden (2015); and Martin Almbjär, "Swedish consuls in Galicia: the economic function of consuls in turbulent times (1793–1806)", *Scandinavian Economic History Review (2024)* https://doi.org/10.1080/03585522.2024.2347879 showing that it was not a uniquely American issue for consuls to use their positions to further their business interests.

[21] Barnet to Jefferson. 10 September 1801. *The Papers of Thomas Jefferson Digital Edition*, eds Barbara B. Oberg and J. Jefferson Looney. Charlottesville: University of Virginia Press, Rotunda, 2008. Original source: Main Series, Vol. 35 (1 August–30 November 1801).

father-in-law, William Palfrey, had been the unlucky first appointed General Consul to France who had been lost at sea.[22] Aaron Vail, the brother of Moses Vail, a prominent New York merchant, was the consul at Lorient, where he operated a shipping business, often with his brother-in-law, the sea captain Samuel Sherbourne, the two having married French sisters from Saint Servan, a town near the privateering centre of Saint Malo. The sisters' brother was both mayor of and the American consul in Saint Servan.[23] John Appleton, another Bostonian, lived in Paris for a while, dining with Gouverneur Morris and John Paul Jones, before settling in Calais, where he set up business as a ship broker and was the commercial agent there for the United States.[24]

Most were well educated and spoke French. Barnet had acquired fluency during his childhood years in Nantes, as had Skipwith during his years as the American consul in Martinique. Barnet, Skipwith, Vail and Cutting all married French or Belgian women and, presumably, would have spoken some French with them and their families. David Bailie Warden (at first, the private secretary to the minister, John Armstrong) spoke French fluently as did his enemy, William Lee.[25] Those consuls who were French by origin wrote, and probably spoke, perfect English. Jean Diot and Etienne Cathalan wrote English so well, and so often used the English forms of their forenames (John and Stephen, respectively), that some historians thought that they were Americans. However, amongst the Ministers Plenipotentiary to France, there was little success with the language. Robert R. Livingston (brother of John above) could read French but not speak it fluently, and was additionally hampered by deafness. John Armstrong spoke not a word of French and cared not a bit. William H. Crawford also spoke no French and used the American legation's secretary as interpreter.[26] Of the ministers, only Joel Barlow, by the time he took up the post, in 1811, had become fluent.[27]

---

[22] "To Thomas Jefferson from William Lee, [before 9] March 1801," *Founders Online*, NARA [Accessed 29 September 29 2019] https://founders.archives.gov/documents/Jefferson/01-33-02-0180. Note on William Lee.

[23] J. De La Tynna. *Almanach du Commerce de Paris, des Départemens de l'Empire Français et des Principales Villes du Monde.* Paris: De La Tynna, 1811, p652.

[24] Yvon Bizardel. *Les Américains à Paris sous Louis XVI et Pendant la Révolution: notices biographiques.* Printed at Alençon by FD *Imprimerie Alençonnaise*, 1978, pp12–13.

[25] Jolynda Brock Chenicek. *Dereliction Of Diplomacy: The American Consulates In Paris And Bordeaux During The Napoleonic Era, 1804–1815 (A Dissertation Submitted To The Department Of History In Partial Fulfillment Of The Requirements For The Degree Of Doctorate Of Philosophy)*, Florida State University College Of Arts and Sciences, 2008, p68 (Skipwith), p79 (Lee), and p182 (Warden).

[26] John Edgar Dawson Shipp. *Giant Days or the Life and Times of William H. Crawford.* Cambridge: Harvard University Press, 1909, p111.

[27] Conversely, among the French ministers with whom the Americans had contact, many were fluent in English. Talleyrand had lived in Britain and America; Clarke, with his Irish ancestry, spoke English so well that he had been sent to negotiate with

A few were opportunists and speculators, who thought to profit from the collapse of the Old Regime in France and the ensuing chaos of the Revolution and Terror, with Barlow having the most questionable of characters amongst them. He first arrived in France in 1788 as an agent for the infamous Scioto Company, then set up his own company in Paris through which he sold to unsuspecting French investors, desperate to escape the Revolution, deeds to land in Gallipolis, Ohio that he knew the company did not possess.[28]

Barlow joined a community of over 200 Americans who were living in Paris at the time of the Revolution and Terror, many involved in shipping and import-export activities. When the French revolutionaries, following Talleyrand's suggestion, decided to redistribute wealth by the selling off of property confiscated from the Catholic Church and the wealthy émigrés at unbelievably low prices and by lotteries, many of these Americans, including some consuls, made speculative purchases. Barlow bought at least two properties in Paris: one a vast building of shops and apartments that he rented out and the other a grand mansion for himself opposite the Luxembourg Palace.[29] Nathaniel Cutting bought a large house on the Champs Elysées in Paris. Fulwar Skipwith bought numerous mansions and farms in and around Paris, worth millions.[30] He and Daniel Parker both invested with the mysterious Englishwoman, Hannah Wright. Parker, a financier without scruples from Massachusetts, and "constantly on the run from creditors",[31] was in neither the consular nor the diplomatic service but he cultivated friendships with and meddled in the business of all who were. One minister, William H. Crawford, wrote disapprovingly: "He is remarkably attentive to the American ministers, and the Parisians say he has been, in fact, the minister for the last ten years."[32]

---

the English; those who had fought in the American Revolution, Berthier, Decrès and Champagny, may have picked up a few words; while Fouché, the Minister of Police, spoke it so well that he comfortably spied on, and for, the English.

[28] For a full explanation of Barlow's involvement with the Scioto Company, see "Essays" in the *Earlier History of American Corporations*, numbers I–III by Joseph Stancliffe Davis. Cambridge: Harvard University Press, 1917. For a detailed discussion of Barlow's French company and its fraudulent sales, see *Gallipolis: Histoire d'un mirage américain au XVIIIe siècle* by Joselyne Moreau-Zanelli. Paris: l'Harmattan, 2000.

[29] Bizardel, *Les Américains à Paris*, pp24–25.

[30] Bizardel, *Les Américains à Paris*, pp166–170.

[31] Ned Downing. "Revolutionary Idea", *Barron's Mutual Funds Quarterly*, updated 5 April 1999. https://www.barrons.com/articles/SB9231052001071724?tesla=y [Accessed 20 Feb 2020].

[32] Shipp. *Giant Days,* p106. This may have referred only to the entertaining responsibilities of a diplomat, for the American ministers had no budget for grand dinners or receptions, while Parker lived in lavish luxury with Hannah Wright's sister, Frances

At times, some of them combined their business interests and consular duties in improper ways. Aaron Vail handled some of the prizes captured by his brother-in-law, the privateer Benjamin Dubois, and served as the *armateur* at Lorient of some of the privateers Dubois sailed, at the same time that he was the agent helping the captains of the captured vessels with their protests at the Prize Council. At one point, Dubois's captures of three American vessels were contested by the then American consul at Bordeaux, Joseph Fenwick,[33] who may not have approved of Vail's later appointment to the consular service or of Vail's appointment of Benjamin's brother as acting consul of Saint Servan.[34] Fulwar Skipwith was both the United States Commercial Agent in Paris and a private agent when he was accused by a group of American sea captains of charging exorbitant fees, much to the minister's disapproval.[35] Jean Diot, at Morlaix, had been sending out his own privateers since the 1780s and continued to do so. Thus, some consuls were actually financing the privateers that captured and brought in American seamen and, while they may have tried to help the seamen with food and clothing, at the same time, they may have been doing all possible before the Prize Council to have their privateers' prizes declared legitimate, ensuring the seamen would become prisoners of war. The hapless seamen most likely did not suspect that the consul who brought them food and clothing in jail may have been the same man who was lobbying the courts for a decision that would send them to prison.

For reasons that their various biographers have struggled to explain, be it their personalities and quick tempers, their sense of pride or honour, their loyalty to competing home states in America, or their financial woes, many of the consuls, consular agents, and Ministers Plenipotentiary came into conflict with one another and with others in the American community in France. Skipwith began well enough with Livingston, and even invited him to witness his marriage in 1802,[36] but ended in resentful power struggles with him and with his successor, John Armstrong. Barnet took an American to court for

---

(who was concurrently the wife of Henry Preble, brother of Commodore Edward Preble) and entertained often.

[33] Gérard Jolivet. "*1793–1794 Benjamin Dubois, un armateur malouin sous la Terreur*". Published on the website of the *Association Bretonne Généalogie Histoire*, 30 November 2016, http://www.geneabretagne.org/scripts/files/5c2aec9fd11e89.96695907/1-arrestation-de-benjamin-dubois--v4-septo--article-autonome.pdf [Accessed 20 February 2020].

[34] Jarvis to Armstrong. 13 March 1810. United States. Department of State. *Despatches from United States Ministers to France, 1789–1906*. Vol. 11. Microfilm copy.

[35] Armstrong to Madison. 29 February 1808. United States. Department of State. *Despatches from United States Ministers to France, 1789–1906*. Vol. 11. Microfilm copy.

[36] Puteaux, *Registre de mariages, An 10* (Skipwith-Vandenclooster marriage) *13 Prairial*, An 10 (2 June 1802). AD Hauts-de-Seine. http://archives.hauts-de-seine.fr/accueil/ [Accessed 22 March 2022].

assault and accused Armstrong of complicity in the attack.[37] Barnet, no insignificant adversary, also had James Mountflorence jailed for eighteen months, ruining him.[38] Barnet and Fenwick fought over commissions.[39] William Lee, in Bordeaux, and Armstrong's personal secretary, David Bailie Warden, in Paris, had a furious and unseemly dispute not only over who was to be consul general in Paris after Joel Barlow had died but over who should receive the agent's commission fees in a particular prize case.[40] Warden fought with Barnet as well, such that the then minister, Crawford, wrote that they were "at open war with each other".[41] Barnet disparaged Lee when the latter was appointed the consul of Bordeaux in Barnet's place.[42] The incessant bickering caused Armstrong's secretary to write: "Were General Armstrong to interfere officially in all of the personal quarrels which take place between citizens of the United States in France, he would have a new and not very pleasant addition to his public labours."[43] Livingston and Armstrong both reprimanded Skipwith, essentially because his ease with the French seemed to violate their sense of protocol and hierarchy. Livingston "was never reasonable where his pride was concerned"[44] while the militaristic Armstrong never tolerated what he might have considered insubordination.

At times, they took these quarrels to the press in the United States. Because of the political views of the press, some papers being pro-Federalist, and thus anti-French, other papers being pro-Republican, thus anti-British, the subjects of seamen imprisoned in France or impressed by the British became politicised. Republican papers wrote strongly worded and outraged articles against the impressment of American seamen by the British but they also maintained that

[37] Barnet to Armstrong. 14 March 1806. United States. Department of State. *Despatches from United States Consuls in Paris, 1790–1906*. Vol. 2. Microfilm copy.

[38] Mountflorence to Madison. 21 February 1808. United States. Department of State. *Despatches from United States Consuls in Paris, 1790–1906*. Vol. 3. Microfilm copy.

[39] Barnet and Fenwick exchanges. January 1806. United States. Department of State. *Despatches from United States Consuls in Paris, 1790–1906*. Vol. 2. Microfilm copy.

[40] Chenicek, *Dereliction Of Diplomacy*. Chenicek describes the entire battle between Lee and Warden in great detail.

[41] Crawford to Monroe. 20 September 1813. United States. Department of State. *Despatches from United States Ministers to France, 1789–1906*. Vol. 14. Microfilm copy.

[42] Barnet to Jefferson. *The Papers of Thomas Jefferson Digital Edition*, eds Barbara B. Oberg and J. Jefferson Looney. Charlottesville: University of Virginia Press, 2008. http://rotunda.upress.virginia.edu/founders/TSJN-01-35-02-0064-0187/ [Accessed 26 April 2022].

[43] March 1806. United States. Department of State. *Despatches from United States Consuls in Paris, 1790–1906*. Vol. 2. Microfilm copy.

[44] Dangerfield, *Chancellor Robert R. Livingston*, p383.

there were no American seamen held as prisoners of war in France (except those who had lost their privileges of neutral nationality by working on British vessels). Federalist papers reversed the emphasis, claiming that few American seamen were impressed by the British but the French were committing outrages by imprisoning American seamen. For all American seamen, impressed or imprisoned, this befuddlement of the issue of their very real situations was of no help. In just one example, Isaac Cox Barnet, in 1809, sent lists of American seamen held in France to papers in America. A few printed the list without comment. The Republican paper, *The Aurora General Advertiser*, did not publish the list but wrote that it had merely been a fabrication on the part of Barnet in order to show the need for a special agent responsible for prisoners in France, and for himself to be appointed to that office.[45]

In spite of the quarrelling, there were some friendships and even partnerships. Aaron Vail named one of his sons after Livingston.[46] William Lee gave one of his sons the middle name of Barlow and was often a guest at Barlow's home.[47] Lee, Skipwith and Barlow together were involved in an unsuccessful scheme of land speculation in Florida.[48] Crawford was a steadfast supporter of Vail's sons in their careers. All, including the Secretary of State, seem to have completely ignored Cathalan in distant Marseilles, at one point leaving him for two years without consular instructions or replies to any of his letters.[49] On the whole, however, the consuls and ministers competed and disputed with one another constantly, often to the amusement of Talleyrand. Their quarrels did not help and at times hindered the cause of the American seamen held prisoner.

For all of their disputes with one another, for all of their commercial interests, and though they found the seamen that they were charged with aiding to be unclean, unprepossessing, uneducated and uncouth, most of the consuls (except, possibly, Vail) took seriously their responsibility to help the distressed seamen. Most of these men were well aware of the difficulties and risks seamen faced. Their social standing may have been far above that of the seamen but, because ocean voyages were the only form of intercontinental travel at the time, every consul and minister had been on vessels and dependent upon the seamen who sailed them. Merchant vessels were small, with crew and passengers encountering one another constantly during a voyage. It is impossible that they would not have observed, spoken to and formed opinions

---

[45] *Aurora General Advertiser*, Philadelphia, 6 January 1810. https/www.newspapers.com

[46] Lorient. *Registre des naissances*, 1804 (Birth of Robert Livingston Louisiana Vail), 14 February 1804. *AD Morbihan*, https://archives.morbihan.fr/accueil/ [Accessed 26 January 2020]. The child did not live a year.

[47] Lee, *A Yankee Jeffersonian*, p53.

[48] Lee, *A Yankee Jeffersonian*, p106.

[49] Cathalan to Russell. 11 September 1810. Jonathan Russell Papers.

of one another. On vessels, the consuls had seen seamen working, perhaps had been aboard when some were snatched by the Royal Navy, had seen their small and large acts of heroism, may have been rescued by them and possibly had seen one of them die.

In their letters, journals and consular correspondence, there are few words of compassion for the distressed seamen, except from Fulwar Skipwith, who had been aiding them from his earliest consular appointment in Martinique. He had also once shared their plight during an attack. In 1794, he had been a passenger on the *Delaware* when it was captured by a British privateer. The captors stole all of the money and belongings from the passengers and American crew, and then abandoned them on Montserrat to fend for themselves. Skipwith helped some of the stranded seamen to find work or passage home and chartered a ship to take the rest.[50] In Paris, he continued to work on seamen's behalf and wrote to Talleyrand in the Ministry of Foreign Affairs about those American seamen taken prisoner during the Quasi-War:

> ...I must be permitted to say another word in favor of my unfortunate countrymen who are still languishing in different prisons of the Republic....those ill-fated men...without a friend to repeat their sufferings to your ears. Pray let me once more recall them to your memory, citizen minister...lend for a moment, an ear to innocence and distress. ...No crime can be imputed to them, unless, indeed, the speaking of the English language be considered one.[51]

If anything indicates that the consuls, if not compassionate toward the seamen, surely knew that they were truly distressed, it is the fact that, when some in France were hoping for a consular appointment, they did not provide in their applications very much by way of academic or professional qualifications or, more likely to their advantage, their political connections. Instead, they boasted of having freed imprisoned seamen. James Mountflorence, then the chancellor, or secretary, of the Paris consulate under Skipwith and hoping to be appointed consul general, wrote to the Secretary of State:

> I have now the pleasure to inform you, Sir, that all the applications [for seamen to be released, have been] crowned with success. Many of our seamen confined as English prisoners of War having been taken on board English vessels, were immediately released, on my claiming them from the Minister of Marine, and lately seven seamen of that description, confined at Nantes, had found means to effect

---

[50] Henry Bartholomew Cox. *The Parisian American: Fulwar Skipwith of Virginia.* Washington, D.C.: Mount Vernon Publishing, 1964, p42.

[51] Skipwith to Talleyrand. 1 May 1799. United States. Department of State. *Despatches from United States Consuls in Paris, 1790–1906.* Vol. 1. Microfilm copy.

their escape, but were retaken, and thrown then into the common jail with the felons. Mr. Dobrée, our Vice-consul applied there for their release, but without effect. He then addressed himself to the Minister for External Relations; receiving no answer he wrote to me and requested my Interference. My application for these poor fellows had an immediate success, as they are now released.[52]

The Ministers Plenipotentiary

The consuls and consular agents were in their posts throughout the wars. Some moved from one port to another within France, as did Isaac Cox Barnet, but for the most part, they were settled, with families and businesses, very much a part of their local communities. The Ministers Plenipotentiary, however, were temporary, political appointees, who arrived in Paris to represent the American administration. From 1803 to 1815, there were four American Ministers Plenipotentiary in Paris: Robert R. Livingston, John Armstrong, Joel Barlow and William H. Crawford. Livingston, Armstrong and Crawford had been elected to offices previously. Armstrong had served in the army during the American Revolution. Barlow and Armstrong had both known Daniel Parker for many years and continued their friendship with him in Paris. Livingston, Armstrong and Barlow all were members of Masonic lodges in port cities. Their interest in the plight of the imprisoned American seamen varied from one man to another, yet none could claim to have been unaware of seamen, their lives, and their distress in France.

Robert R. Livingston arrived in France in 1801, at the age of fifty-five. He came from a large, prominent, wealthy and politically influential family and was New York's first chief judicial officer, or Chancellor. He was one of the five men, along with Franklin and Jefferson, who drafted the Declaration of Independence and it was he who, as Chancellor, administered the first oath of office to the first President of the United States. He was also known as a man of "deep conservatism" and "somewhat volatile manners",[53] with a haughty bearing, of whom it was said that "politics were…for him, not a matter of power, but a matter of status".[54]

When, eventually, he was offered the post of Minister Plenipotentiary to France, it was not without reason. He had experience in working with the nation's earliest ministers and consuls, including Franklin in France, and he had also been America's first Secretary of Foreign Affairs. He was a Francophile and had been tutored in the French language. He had formed friendships with

---

[52] Mountflorence to Madison. 26 July 1801. United States. Department of State. *Despatches from United States Consuls in Paris, 1790–1906*. Vol. 1. Microfilm copy.
[53] Dangerfield, *Chancellor Robert R. Livingston*, p247.
[54] Dangerfield, *Chancellor Robert R. Livingston*, p320.

French émigrés in New York and his appointment certainly had the support of France's consuls in America.

Most of Livingston's term as minister in France was taken up with negotiating (with Daniel Parker's advice, which some called scheming) the Louisiana Purchase, signed in April 1803. Because of the Peace of Amiens, for the first months of his term, there was no war between France and Great Britain, so almost no American seamen were taken prisoner during his term. With the outbreak of war again in May 1803, however, French naval vessels and privateers began attacking and seizing British merchant vessels, many with American seamen amongst their crew.

Livingston had certainly been aware for years of the troubles of American seamen. Whether impressed by the Royal Navy or, during the American Revolution, made prisoners of war by the British, the woes of American seamen had been brought to his attention. Franklin had kept him informed of his efforts to obtain the release of prisoners of war from Mill and Forton prisons in England. Working with Jean Torris, François Coffyn and Jean Diot, Franklin exploited his proximity to the enemy while in France with an imaginative scheme whereby American privateers operating from French ports, primarily Dunkirk, would capture as many British vessels as possible, taking as many British prisoners as possible, in order to exchange them for American prisoners in Britain. On the whole, because the British never had any intention of honouring the exchange agreements, it did not work, though it did bring great profit to the French owners of the privateers.[55]

Livingston's close friend and a previous minister to France, Gouverneur Morris, surely would have told him that he had gone to London with Thomas Paine in 1790 and had "consulted with Edmund Burke…about how best to help American sailors who had been impressed into the British navy"[56] with the result that Morris was the first to propose that some sort of American citizenship document be created and issued to seamen to protect them from impressment, the idea that led eventually to the creation of the Seaman's Protection Certificates.[57] The chairman of the committee that proposed those certificates and the legislation for the "Relief and Protection of American Seamen" in 1796 was Livingston's brother, Edward. As Livingston had

---

[55] For full discussions of these capers, see William Bell Clark's *Ben Franklin's Privateers: A Naval Epic of the American Revolution*. Baton Rouge: Louisiana State University Press, 1956 and Ruth Y. Johnston's "American Privateers in French Ports, 1776–1778" *The Pennsylvania Magazine of History and Biography*, Vol. 53, No. 4 (1929). Philadelphia: University of Pennsylvania Press. https://www.jstor.org/stable/2008671, pp352–374. [Accessed 71 May 2015].

[56] Richard Brookhiser. *Gentleman Revolutionary: Gouverneur Morris the Rake Who Wrote the Constitution*. New York: Free Press, 2003, p120.

[57] Zimmerman, *Impressment of American Seamen*, pp51–52.

specifically asked this brother, in 1795, to write to him from Congress, so that he could have "the earliest and best intelligence",[58] he would have known in some detail of the preparations for that act. Another brother, John R. Livingston, was a merchant captain and shipowner, some of whose vessels had been captured, and some of their crews imprisoned, by the French. Yet Livingston did very little to help the captive seamen, leaving that to Skipwith, who had less authority.

Livingston left Paris in late 1804 to return to New York and develop steam engines with Robert Fulton, whom he had met in Paris. His replacement as minister was his brother-in-law, John Armstrong, on whom the burden of the increasing number of imprisoned American seamen truly fell. Armstrong had had a frontier childhood in the Cumberland Valley of Pennsylvania. He was well educated at the College of New Jersey, which he left, at the age of seventeen, to join the Continental Army when the American Revolution began, serving under General Horatio Gates.[59] Gates saw himself as the better man than Washington to lead the American army and Armstrong, his loyal young friend and junior officer, agreed. In late 1782, he wrote an anonymous letter to officers of the army, calling them to a meeting to voice their complaints at Congress's failure to pay them. It was the beginning of what became known as the Newburgh Conspiracy, which was quickly and eloquently put down by Washington.

Armstrong then served as the secretary of the Supreme Executive Council of Pennsylvania and joined that state's militia, in which he received the rank of adjutant general. He was selected to represent his state at the Continental Congress in New York in 1787, where he renewed his acquaintances with Daniel Parker and Joel Barlow.[60] There, he settled and married Alida Livingston, the sister of Robert R. Livingston.

He seems to have had a lacklustre political career. His biographer quotes a contemporary as saying that "Armstrong has very superior talents, but they are almost useless, he is so extremely indolent."[61] That sense that he was a man of wasted ability was repeated by many others throughout his life. He also may have been hampered by what seems to have been an unusually prickly character. Aware of his own intelligence, he was arrogant and haughty towards others. He feuded with many, held grudges, was vindictive, "obtuse and mean-spirited".[62] Even Skeen, his largely sympathetic biographer, uses

---

[58] Dangerfield, *Chancellor Robert R. Livingston*. p280.
[59] C. Edward Skeen. *John Armstrong, Jr., 1758–1843: a Biography*. Syracuse: Syracuse University Press, 1981, pp2–4.
[60] Skeen, *John Armstrong, Jr.*, p28.
[61] Skeen, *John Armstrong, Jr.*, p20.
[62] Peter P. Hill. *Napoleon's Troublesome Americans: Franco-American Relations, 1804–1815*. Washington, D.C.: Potomac Books, 2006, p3.

such words about him as "abrasive", "pugnacious", "obstinate", "cynical", "blunt". In Paris, the consul William Lee said of him:

> It is a pity that a man, for whom nature and education has done so much, should be so averse to displaying his powers. This is the effect of early habits, or rather of having never mixed much in society. His conversation is instructive and entertaining; his pen is unequalled; and, with all this, he has a rudeness of character, a stiff republican frankness about him that is not agreeable to strangers, and is the worst commodity a man can bring to Paris.[63]

Some, but certainly not all, of these character flaws might be attributable to pain. From an early age, Armstrong suffered from ill health. His fevers and maladies in early life were not specified but, by the time he was an adult, he was suffering from rheumatism, or joint pain. Pain can warp a personality with depression, a hyper-sensitive snappishness rising quickly to anger, and an incapacity to function (which could appear as indolence), all of which have been attributed to him. When in France, he visited numerous spas, seeking relief, until the French ministers suggested that he really was unfit and requested a healthier man be sent to replace him.[64]

John Armstrong and his family arrived in Paris in October 1804. He brought with him the Irish tutor for his children, David Bailie Warden, a combative man in his own right, to be his personal secretary. He immediately encountered his old acquaintance Daniel Parker and through him rented Joel Barlow's grand house on rue Vaugirard. Very quickly, he realized that, though he was not a poor man, he did not have enough money to entertain or dress in the style then required by Napoleon's court, and as a result he attended few official functions.

It was during Armstrong's six years as the American minister to France that all of the decrees issued by Napoleon that affected American shipping and seamen were passed. The Berlin Decree, the Milan Decree, the Bayonne Decree, the Rambouillet Decree, as well as the Cadore Letter; each resulted in hundreds more American seamen being put in French prisons while Armstrong was minister. In spite of his offensive manner and in spite of the very bad press concerning aid to seamen prisoners that he received at the time in America, Armstrong negotiated the release of many seamen, certainly more than did any of the other ministers who came before or after him.

---

[63] Lee, *A Yankee Jeffersonian*, pp111–112.

[64] It must be added that many of the consuls were also in very bad health, which caused them, when indisposed, to neglect many of their duties. Dobrée, the consul at Nantes, died; John M. Forbes in Hamburg was always very ill; Sylvanus Bourne in Amsterdam wrote of being unwell for long periods as was Jacob Ridgway at Antwerp; William Lee in Bordeaux was ill for seventeen months; Thomas Lowell at La Rochelle simply disappeared.

There is nothing in his background to indicate any particular sympathy with or interest in merchant seamen. Neither he nor anyone in his family was in shipping. The Armstrongs were not a naval family. He had not gone on sea voyages or even once crossed the Atlantic before he went to France. Could it have been that he had, back in the Newburgh days, some real sympathy for the ordinary soldier that, in France, could have been extended to the seaman?

Armstrong left France in September 1810, at the age of fifty-two. The following February, Joel Barlow was appointed to replace him, but he did not present his credentials until November 1811. Barlow was returning to Paris in some small glory. Fluent in French, an honorary French citizen, wealthy, he moved back into his mansion on rue Vaugirard. It was an arrival quite different from that of his first, at Le Havre, more than twenty years previously. In 1788, he was a young, recently married man who had been sent to Europe as a salesman.

Much more has been written about Barlow than about Livingston or Armstrong, too much of it by Barlow himself, making the sifting of facts from self-aggrandizement difficult. He was the son of a Connecticut farmer, and a graduate of Yale. While still in his twenties, he composed and eventually published an epic and largely unreadable poem on the history and supposed moral superiority of America. He was amongst a group of young men who called themselves the Hartford Wits. All of them quite bright, none of them with the literary gifts they imagined themselves to have, they went on to have successful careers in law, education and diplomacy.[65] He continued to write poetry for the rest of his life but only one work, a humorous piece about polenta, entitled "Hasty Pudding", is read today. The rest is heavy, uninspired, without beauty or lyricism; even one of the sponsors of his epic, George Washington, wrote that he could not wade his way to the end of it. Bad poetry did not pay, so Barlow next tried preaching, teaching, publishing and law, in succession, yet none brought him the quick financial success he sought. During his preaching phase, he wrote that too much commercial pursuit was corrupting:

> …it leads the mind to a particular narrowness of thought, which always prevents any eccentric excesses of giving, and superinduces an illiberal turn of mind.[66]

Eight years later, he launched his commercial career as a minor player in a major land speculation scheme.

The problem of paying the soldiers who had fought in the American Revolution, about which John Armstrong had written in the Newburgh Letters,

---

[65] Todd, *Life and Letters of Joel Barlow*, pp1–54.
[66] Todd, *Life and Letters of Joel Barlow*, pp37–38.

had not been resolved. In lieu of the money it did not have, Congress had promised to give each of the men who would stay in the Continental Army through to victory some land in the western territory that it expected to win. At the end of the war, the straightforward land grants became a land speculation enterprise involving the Secretary of the Treasury, a preacher more interested in money than souls, and a few members of Congress, who obligingly passed the Northwest Ordinance in 1787.[67] (In the earliest days of the territory's government, a young John Armstrong had served briefly as a judge in the new territory.)[68] On the formation of the Ohio Company of Associates, as the speculation enterprise was named, Barlow found work in sales and discovered that he was good at convincing people to buy land in Ohio.

It was based on this success that the partners of the Scioto Company, founded by many of the same people who ran the Ohio Company, sent Barlow to Europe to sell plots of American land to Europeans. However, the Scioto plots were not actually owned by the company selling them; it had options to buy the land from Congress, but had not used them before Barlow started selling. Initially, it did not go well for him. No European bank would touch the project and even Daniel Parker, that consummate speculator, who was involved in the Ohio Company from abroad, saw something that indicated failure in either Barlow or the Scioto venture and withdrew. Then the Bastille was stormed and the French Revolution began, giving Barlow and his new partner, a Scot named William Playfair, a swarm of potential clients amongst those desperate to leave the country. Within eighteen months, more than 500 French people arrived in the Ohio wilderness to discover that they had been defrauded by Barlow. No money that they had paid was sent by the Scioto Company in Paris to the Ohio Company in the United States, so the options to buy the land were not taken up. The settlers owned nothing, the town that was to welcome them did not exist and the Native Americans resident on the land did not appreciate their presence.[69]

As would occur with later situations, Barlow had kept his name off most documents and afterward wrote such voluminous denials and justifications that it is his version of events that is presented by most biographers. Historians who have dug deep into the paperwork, however, such as Jocelyne Moreau-Zanelli and Archer B. Hulbert,[70] are convinced of Barlow's guilt. On Barlow's word,

---

[67] Todd, *Life and Letters of Joel Barlow*, p59.

[68] Skeen, *John Armstrong, Jr.*, p27.

[69] Moreau-Zanelli. *Gallipolis.* This work uses French notarial records to document, in great detail, the sales Barlow effected in France.

[70] Archer Butler Hulbert. "The Methods and Operations of the Scioto Group of Speculators". *The Mississippi Valley Historical Review*, Vol. 1, No. 4 (March 1915), pp502–515. Organization of American Historians. http://www.jstor.org/stable/1886952 [Accessed: 19 February 2015].

and that of an auditor sent to Paris to review the Scioto Company files, the blame was put on Playfair.[71] Yet Barlow, who claimed poverty, never tried to take his ex-partner to court. Instead, he moved to London with his wife and lived comfortably without his having to take any employment.

Barlow was amongst a group of foreign enthusiasts of the French Revolution to be given French nationality, early in 1793. This was because he had become such a strong supporter of revolutionary ideals that he ran for office, and the law stated that only French citizens could be elected to public office. He was not elected and he returned to commerce, but kept the nationality. As the Terror and Robespierre's power increased, Barlow profited to an extraordinary degree. Working with Daniel Parker and other Americans in France, he became a shipping broker, moving around Europe but working mostly from the relative safety of Hamburg, handling more French government contracts than anyone except James Swan.[72] He and one of his agents, Gilbert Imlay (who had also been involved in suspect land speculation, in Kentucky),[73] have been identified as the likeliest culprits in the theft of a ship's entire cargo of silver belonging to the French government. Certainly, after the theft, Barlow was a rich man.

In 1795, Barlow encountered in Paris an old friend from his Yale and Hartford Wits days, David Humphreys, who was then the United States Minister Resident to Lisbon and the Special Negotiator to Algiers. Humphreys was leading the efforts of many diplomats and bankers working on resolving the long-standing issues of Algerian privateers capturing American vessels and of their potentate, the Dey of Algiers, enslaving the crews.

The Dey was holding hundreds of foreign seamen as slaves, taken from vessels of many nationalities, all waiting for their countries to make a treaty with Algiers and to pay their ransoms. It was a style of diplomacy pursued in other parts of the Ottoman Empire, in Tripoli, Morocco and Tunis. Access to the Mediterranean trade was so valuable that most nations, including Britain,

---

[71] Recent scholarship has revealed that Playfair may have been no patsy. Bruce Berkowitz writes that he was a canny secret agent in *Playfair: The True Story of the British Secret Agent Who Changed How We See the World*. George Mason: George Mason University, 2018. However, David R. Bellhouse very strongly disputes that in *The Flawed Genius of William Playfair: The Story of the Father of Statistical Graphics*. University of Toronto Press, 2023. Whether or not he was an agent, as to the Scioto scandal, Barlow walked away with the money and Playfair with the blame.

[72] Wil Verhoeven. *Gilbert Imlay: Citizen of the World*. London: Pickering & Chatto, 2008, p173.

[73] Imlay, like Brissot and Barlow, had attempted to encourage settlement of the lands he was trying to sell by publishing a glorious account of the land in question. In his case, it was a long-since forgotten novel, entitled *The Emigrants*, but his name lives on, as something of a cad, only because of the letters of Mary Wollstonecraft.

France, Portugal and Spain, complied, making expensive treaties, ransoming their seamen, paying bribes and presenting lavish gifts to the rulers.[74] With the American Revolution, it became obvious that a new country's vessels were trading in the Mediterranean and the Dey, in order to force the United States to make its own treaty with him, allowed Algerine privateers to prey on American vessels, and they soon captured two, the *Maria* and the *Dolphin*, in 1785.[75]

The American seamen from these two vessels began a period of captivity and enslavement that would last eleven years and that not all of them survived. During that time, though the men believed that they had been abandoned, American diplomats, including Adams, Jefferson and Monroe, struggled to find and finance a solution. In 1793, the Algerine privateers made more captures, resulting in more than 100 American seamen joining those of the *Maria* and the *Dolphin* as enslaved hostages. The efforts to free them increased, as was the Dey's hope, and Congress approved funds for a treaty and for ransoming the seamen. After a month of intense negotiations, a treaty was agreed, in September 1795, stipulating a hefty sum to be paid by the United States to the Dey, in specie, within three months. Then began a frantic race by many Americans throughout Europe to put together more than half a million dollars in coin and bullion and to transport it to Algiers by early December 1795.[76] When Humphreys had gone to Paris in September of that year, not knowing the treaty had just been signed, he had asked Barlow to join the team, appointing him consul general of Algiers. He would be joining the crusty treaty negotiator, Joseph Donaldson.

Six months later, in the same month that the United States Senate ratified the treaty, and three months after the payment was due, Barlow arrived in Algiers, laden with expensive gifts for the Dey, and believing that the money for the ransoms and payment was already arranged. Indeed, he delayed his meeting with the Dey until he should have received confirmation that the money was available,[77] but it was not. He then joined the effort of the other American diplomats in Europe in trying to find money; eventually, they did. Barlow, in his letters recounting the episode, places himself at the centre.[78]

---

[74] Hannah Farber. "Millions for Credit: Peace with Algiers and the Establishment of America's Commercial Reputation Overseas, 1795–96", *Journal of the Early Republic* Vol. 34, No. 2 (Summer 2014), pp187–217. University of Pennsylvania Press on behalf of Society for Historians of the Early American Republic. https://www.jstor.org/stable/24486687 [Accessed 1 March 2020] p201.

[75] Gary E. Wilson. *American Prisoners in the Barbary Nations, 1784–1816*, Dissertation Presented to the Graduate Council of the North Texas State University. May 1979. p38.

[76] Farber, "Millions for Credit", p204.

[77] Wilson, *American Prisoners*, p106.

[78] Todd, *Life and Letters of Joel Barlow*, pp125–141.

He implies that he negotiated the final treaty. He did not. It was negotiated by Donaldson, with the help of a remarkable captive seaman named James Cathcart as translator and go-between (and it was based on an older model of a treaty that had been negotiated by a Scot working for Sweden, whose English son and, particularly, Swedish grandsons in Algiers provided invaluable advice to the Americans).[79] Barlow gave the impression that he was the man who wheedled a banker into paying the ransom of the seamen with the Dey's own specie when, in truth, it was the regular business of the banker (who worked closely with the Dey) to aid consuls in ransoming their country's seamen and he needed no wheedling to do so. That same banker, Bacri, through his connections in Livorno and the credit his cousin there offered to Donaldson, provided the recommendation necessary for Humphreys in Lisbon to borrow a large sum in gold.[80] It was not Barlow's personal triumph, as he claimed, but that of a complicated, international effort involving a dozen or so people.

Barlow returned to Paris, where he and his wife formed an unusually close friendship with Robert Fulton and encouraged his steamship inventions. He continued his business as a shipping broker and was a solid member of the American community in Paris, attending Skipwith's wedding. He returned to America in 1805 and bought a large property near Washington, D.C., naming it Kalorama. He and his wife lived there in elegance until he was nominated to replace John Armstrong as the Minister Plenipotentiary to France in 1811. He would have only fifteen months in the post. Though, from his experience in Algiers, he had the greatest awareness of what imprisoned seamen might endure, Barlow did little for the release of those held in France, leaving the opening of their pleading letters to his wife Ruth.[81]

Barlow died of a sudden chill or illness in Poland in December 1812, having accepted Napoleon's invitation to follow him to Russia in order to discuss a treaty. Thomas Barlow, his nephew and private secretary, was with him and returned to Paris with the news of his death. With no American minister in place, the consuls, the widow and the nephew engaged in one of the most unseemly of battles in American diplomatic history.

Thomas Barlow and the truly distraught Ruth Barlow were taken in by Daniel Parker and Mrs Preble at his estate to the south of Paris. They took with them the diplomatic correspondence and seals. David Bailie Warden made the astonishing move of announcing himself as the consul general to

---

[79] Linda Belabdelouahab-Fernini. "Per Eric Skjöldebrand: The man Towards Whom the United States Is Indebted". Unpublished paper. June 2017. ResearchGate https://www.researchgate.net/publication/333135179_Per_Eric_SkjOldebrand_The_man_Towards_Whom_the_United_States_Is_Indebted [Accessed 25 June 2020] p5.

[80] Farber, "Millions for Credit", p213.

[81] Warden to Graham. 30 January 1813. United States. Department of State. *Despatches from United States Consuls in Paris, 1790–1906.* Vol. 4 Microfilm copy.

Maret, the Duke of Bassano and Minister of External Affairs, who took him at his word and accepted him as such. Warden then asserted that Maret's acceptance constituted legitimation, as if a French minister could appoint an American official. William Lee went to Paris to try to "protect" Ruth Barlow from Warden, while also angling for the post of consul general for himself. Isaac Cox Barnet considered himself a good candidate for the position. Thomas Barlow, having received from the dying minister an appointment, felt that he was to carry on the duties of running the American legation until Barlow's replacement should arrive. Warden demanded the correspondence and seals from the Barlows, who refused to turn them over. He demanded blank passports from Barnet, who refused to surrender them, saying the minister had given them to him specifically for seamen and other Americans. Accusations and insults flew in all directions. It was the middle of the War of 1812, when French ministers saw America as an ally against Britain and began to turn with a kindlier look toward American seamen, but the Barlows and the consuls, especially Barnet and Warden, were so locked in their battles that they went so far as to intentionally block one another's efforts to gain the release of the American prisoners.

William H. Crawford was sent as the next Minister Plenipotentiary to try to clean up the mess. He was tasked with ending the battles between the consuls, finishing Barlow's treaty negotiations, and maintaining good relations with France while America was at war with Britain. Crawford was the first Minister Plenipotentiary to France during the Napoleonic Wars who was a Southerner; he had been born in Virginia, reared in South Carolina and become a resident of and United States senator for Georgia. Born in 1772, he was the youngest of the Ministers during the Napoleonic Wars. One of eleven children, though he was keen to learn, family finances were too short for him to have more than a basic education. He managed to gain a classical education by becoming a teacher at a very good college and learning all that was taught there. He continued teaching until 1799 and then went into law and politics. In 1804, he bought a farm, to which he added acreage over the years, and married a local woman from a French Huguenot family who bore him at least eight children. He was described as being huge, six feet three inches tall and weighing over 200 pounds.[82]

After a number of years as a senator in Washington, D.C., he received his appointment and sailed from New York for France on the United States Navy's sloop of war, the *Argus*, on 18 June 1813, leaving his wife and children in Georgia. It was quite a voyage, his first across the Atlantic, and one which, between his bouts of seasickness, seems to have excited his curiosity

---

[82] Chase C. Mooney. "William H. Crawford: 1772–1834" (1974). United States History. 72. pp2–15. https://uknowledge.uky.edu/upk_united_states_history/72 [Accessed 17 April 2021].

enormously. He was able to observe how Captain Henry Allen, choosing his time carefully, sailed from New York while the British blockading vessels were to the north, off New London, then successfully evaded a British squadron sent to reinforce the blockade of the American coast;[83] he experienced a great storm at sea; he saw the capture of a British crew and the burning of their vessel; he witnessed with frustration as the *Argus* sighted and avoided engagement with armed British vessels blockading France.

He held long conversations with the young captain with whom he shared what surely was a very cramped cabin, made more so by his size, and with many of the young officers. Crawford is not recorded as having had conversations with any of the seamen, of whom there were more than seventy on board the overcrowded vessel.[84] During the storm, which developed into a full gale, Crawford's seasickness kept him below at times, but he rushed onto deck to watch the drama as often as he could. Ira Dye describes it:

> During this dangerous, high-wind sail handling, one of the best topmen, James Hunt, fell from the main yard, forty-five feet above the deck, hit the starboard gunwale, and then went overboard and was lost....At eight that night, 1 July, Henry Allen took in all sail and for five hours scudded under bare poles, rolling, pitching and corkscrewing. While he and the entire crew were using all their energies to keep the ship under control, Minister Crawford...stayed on deck until chased below by the rain and the seas....To him, the storm was a spectacle...[85]

On 12 July, Captain Allen brought the *Argus* and the new minister in to the port of Lorient. A month later, after attacking British shipping and taking or destroying nineteen vessels, the *Argus* would engage in battle with the Royal Navy's *Pelican* and lose dramatically. Captain Allen was killed and many of the seaman were severely wounded. The boatswain, Colin McLeod, was amongst them, surviving but with a mutilated leg. In the following years, he struggled to be released from active duty and to be pensioned off. Dye tells of a letter he wrote to Crawford, reminding him of their acquaintance on the *Argus*, but found no evidence that Crawford, by then Secretary of the Treasury, ever bothered to reply.[86]

On arrival at Lorient, Crawford was ill and remained there for a few days before going on to Paris. During that time, he certainly would have met the United States consul there, Aaron Vail. Very quickly, the two became

---

[83] Dudley, *Splintering the Wooden Wall*, p95.
[84] Ira Dye. *The Fatal Cruise of the Argus: Two Captains in the War of 1812*. Annapolis: Naval Institute Press, 1994, pp133–134.
[85] Dye, *The Fatal Cruise of the Argus*, p141.
[86] Dye, *The Fatal Cruise of the Argus*, p308.

close friends, so much so that Crawford hired Vail's eighteen-year-old son, Eugène, as his personal secretary.[87] Vail seems to have been the only consul he considered worthy. "The acquaintance which I have been compelled to make with several American consuls, has not inspired me with a very high respect for this description of officers", he wrote to the President in late 1814. Barnet, he said, "did many things which were improper"; Warden had "a habitual disregard for the truth"; Lee was a "bankrupt" guilty of "incorrect conduct on money transactions"; Baker, "a man who calls himself consul of the Balearican Islands" was "certainly badly qualified for consul"; and the new consul at Riga "has a very indifferent reputation".[88]

During his brief term as minister, Crawford was in Paris for some of the most momentous events in French history: the battle at the walls of Paris, when the Allies conquered France and the troops sacked much of the city; the return of Napoleon from Elba for the brief Hundred Days; Waterloo; and Wellington's arrival in Paris. As he had done on board the *Argus*, he observed all as a tourist and reported with some acuity to the President and others. This ability to perceive in depth and to summarize clearly would seem to have been his talent of greatest value to those in government. Thomas Jefferson wrote to him:

> I have to thank you for your letter of June 16. it presents those special views of the state of things in Europe, for which we look in vain into newspapers. They tell us only of the downfall of Bonaparte, but nothing of the temper, the views, and secret workings of the high agents in these transactions.[89]

After sorting out the consuls and getting rid of Warden, Crawford's main responsibility was to finish the negotiation of a commercial treaty with the French that would get them to stop seizing American vessels and cargo, to release any being held and to pay for those already sold. He became bogged down in the endless bureaucratic exchanges with the French ministries and achieved very little.

Socially, he formed friendships with Lafayette, Benjamin Constant and, after Napoleon's abdication, with Wellington.[90] While Ruth Barlow was still

---

[87] Eugène Vail. "William H. Crawford", *Southern Literary Messenger*, Vol. 5, No. 6, June 1839, pp361–364.

[88] Crawford to Monroe. 19 December 1814. United States. Department of State. *Despatches from United States Ministers to France, 1789–1906*. Vol. 15. Microfilm copy.

[89] "Thomas Jefferson to William H. Crawford, 14 February 1815", *Founders Online*, NARA [Accessed 24 April 2020]. https://founders.archives.gov/documents/Jefferson/03-08-02-0209; Mooney, "William H. Crawford", p61.

[90] Vail, "William H. Crawford", p362.

staying at Daniel Parker's home, Crawford dined there a few times. Though he and Parker both were keen to have the United States take possession of Florida, they do not seem to have become friends or allies of any sort.[91]

His interest in the American seamen held as prisoners of war in France seems to have been minimal. Like Livingston, but for one or two cases, he made almost no mention of them in the diplomatic dispatches he sent to the Secretary of State. Like Aaron Vail, he bemoaned the cost of aiding seamen but was not entirely insensitive to their difficulties A few weeks after his arrival in Paris, he wrote to Monroe, asking for instruction.

> Several consuls have stated that frequent disputes have arisen between captains and individuals of their crews who have fallen sick in port. The captains deduct the expenses of their illness from their wages and at the same time refuse to allow them their wages during their indisposition.[92]

Crawford left France in April 1815. He returned to his family and to politics, serving as Secretary of War and then Secretary of the Treasury. He continued to try to find employment for Vail's sons. He was a founding member of the American Colonization Society and remained "unflagging in his determination to secure Florida" for the United States.[93] He died in September 1834.

Of the four Ministers Plenipotentiary from 1803 to 1815, two were proud and bad tempered, one was a cheerful thief, and one an observer better at analysing a situation than participating in it. From the early days, personalities rather than policy determined procedure in relation to pleading the cause of the American seaman held prisoner by the French. Initially, it was the consuls, especially the consul in Paris, Skipwith, who spoke directly to Goulhot and even to the Minister of External Affairs, on behalf of the imprisoned American seamen. Soon, however, Livingston and Armstrong both took umbrage with a consul having better access to a French minister than did the Minister Plenipotentiary himself and insisted that a hierarchy be established. Only the Minister Plenipotentiary was to speak to the Minister of External Relations; any subject the consul wished discussed must be presented to the American Minister Plenipotentiary.

The result was that the consuls, who were charged with aiding distressed seamen, could no longer request the seamen prisoners' release, while the Ministers Plenipotentiary, in closing the avenue of access to French officials and making themselves go-betweens, tacitly took from the consuls the task

---

[91] Mooney, "William H. Crawford", pp58–59.

[92] Crawford to Monroe. 20 September 1813. United States. Department of State. *Despatches from United States Ministers to France, 1789–1906*. Vol. 14. Microfilm copy.

[93] Mooney, "William H. Crawford", pp188–195.

of aiding seamen who were prisoners. The consuls were keenly aware that this change was to the detriment of the American seamen:

> …true it is that my fellow Citizens have frequently suffered more inconveniences since His Excellency [Armstrong] has thought proper to exercise exclusively the right of claiming them than when Consuls exercised their legal rights, employed their credit & used their care, in obtaining immediate protection in their favour…[94]

---

[94] Vail to Skipwith. 3 May 1808. United States. Department of State. *Despatches from United States Consuls in Paris, 1790–1906*. Vol. 3. Microfilm copy.

6

A SEAMAN'S CITIZENSHIP

To have any hope of being released from French imprisonment, the American merchant seaman held as a prisoner of war had to be able to prove two things: that he was truly American and not British, and that he had not been working for the British at the time of capture. This is only partially analogous to the plight of the impressed American in the Royal Navy, who had to prove only his nationality, although most of the prisoners in France did not understand that.

There is a substantial amount in the historiography of impressment, of the impressment of Americans by a British institution, and of how that led to the creation of a document designed to prevent it, which in turn influenced the development of a modern understanding of citizenship. The 1924 publication, *Impressment of American Seamen* by James Fulton Zimmerman, remains the foremost study of the British practice as it was used against Americans. Denver Brunsman, in his article "Subjects vs. Citizens" defines its application as a sort of "forced migration", while Jean Choate termed it "involuntary servitude"; but J. Ross Dancy, in opposition to such views, wrote "though impressment was not the tyrannical and evil implement that history has depicted, on some level it did physically deny men their freedom", seeming not to perceive that that denial of freedom was the point of contention or that it required tyrannical and evil behaviour on the part of Royal Navy officers to enforce. Dancy's apology brought disputing responses from other historians, particularly Isaac Land.[1] Because so few of the American seamen who ended up as prisoners of war in France had also been impressed by the Royal Navy, impressment is not the real concern of this chapter.

As a response to British impressment of American citizens, the United States began issuing to merchant seamen a document certifying their American nationality. Whether or not the document was successful in the intended aim, it became central to the new concepts of citizenship occasioned by the American Revolution. With that, a mass of people who had been, in 1775, subjects of the King of England, became by 1783, citizens of the

---

[1] Brunsman, "Subjects vs. Citizens", p561; Choate, ed. *At Sea Under Impressment*; Dancy, *The Myth of the Press Gang*, p152; Isaac Land, "New Scholarship on the Press Gang", *Port Towns and Urban Cultures*, 3 August 2015. https://porttowns.port.ac.uk/press-gang-1/

United States. Current historiography looks intensely at what that change meant, from Denver Brunsman's essay entitled with the contrast, to Nathan Perl-Rosenthal's study of the Seaman's Protection Certificate being a critical early citizenship document, to Sarah Caputo's nuanced discussion of self-identification as opposed to external identification imposed on one by others.[2] This chapter looks at how American merchant seamen of the generation just after the American Revolution were caught up in the differing and changing interpretations of subjecthood and citizenship, not only in the impressment dispute between Britain and the United States concerning kidnapped merchant seamen but in the neutrality and nationality disputes between the United States and France concerning imprisoned merchant seamen.

The difficulties with the verification in France of an American's nationality had changed little since the French Revolutionary Wars, when Skipwith was consul general at Paris and trying to obtain the release of Americans jailed for speaking English. The United States consul at Rouen, F. Carpentier (who had himself been imprisoned the previous year) wrote to Skipwith in 1795:

> …the difficulty of distinguishing an American from an Englishman, the possibility of counterfeit certificates,…these [and other] obstacles must be encounter'd for the release of American citizens.[3]

That same year the Committee for Public Safety

> …recommended expressly that the greatest attention be given to all persons claiming to be Americans…[and that the police] ensure that they truly are, or not, what they claim to be…[4]

Ten years later, after the resumption of war in 1803, this problem was unique to the Americans amongst the prisoners of war of neutral nationalities held in France. The seamen of other neutral countries were not generally suspected of being of a different, enemy nationality. Danes were Danes, Austrians were Austrians and Spaniards were Spaniards. If their government negotiated their release, leaving prison was a straightforward affair, without their consuls having to prove not only their nationality but also, as was the case for Americans, what nationality they were not.

---

[2] Sara Caputo, *Foreign Jack Tars: The British Navy and Transnational Seafarers during the Revolutionary and Napoleonic Wars.* Cambridge: Cambridge University Press, 2023.

[3] Cox, *The Parisian American*, p49, citing a letter from F. Carpentier to Skipwith, 6 March 1795 in the Fulwar Skipwith Papers.

[4] Announcement to the police bureaux of all Paris sections. *12 messidor An 3* [30 June 1795]. Arch. pol. A98.

Seamen's Protection Certificates

In 1796, four years after the consular service was established, Congress authorized the creation and issuance of Seamen's Protection Certificates. The purpose of the document was to serve as proof of the American citizenship of the seaman bearer and so protect him from being impressed by the British Royal Navy. It was not a document intended for international acceptance, as a modern passport is (though Nathan Perl-Rosenthal's *Citizen Sailors* has shown how it was, indeed, the beginnings of that concept); it was intended to communicate with British naval officers and the Admiralty.

The customs collectors of American ports issued the certificates, based on applications by seamen. Affidavits by friends or family confirmed that the seamen was American, whether of native or naturalized citizenship. The certificate issued gave the man's name, age, place of birth and physical description.[5] With this document, the United States consuls and agents in Great Britain and the West Indies had a tool to help them in their claims to the Admiralty for an impressed seaman's release from a Royal Navy vessel, while seamen had something they valued enormously. In our own era of biometric documents, it may be hard to imagine just how precious this piece of paper was to seamen. Its meaning to them is revealed by the fact that they generally referred to the document simply as their "Protection".

What they did not understand is that Congress's creation of the document was not for the purpose of protecting them, as individual persons, but to protect the work force necessary to commerce. It was only as impressment began to inhibit American commerce that the Seaman's Protection Certificate came to be seen as necessary. The United States consul in Jamaica, William Savage, stated it clearly and often:

> The impressing of American seamen is rigidly pursued, to the great distress of the American trade. (30 January 1800)
>
> The American trade, for some months past, has been greatly distressed, in consequence of their seamen being so generally impressed. (February 20 1800)[6]

Some American seamen seemed to believe that their Seaman's Protection Certificate, as proof of their citizenship of the United States, would protect them in situations other than impressment, and that consuls in all countries

---

[5] Ruth Priest Dixon. "Genealogical Fallout from the War of 1812". *Prologue Magazine* 24:1 (Spring 1992). ttps://www.archives.gov/publications/prologue/1992/spring/seamans-protection.html. [Accessed 29 September 2019].

[6] Messages from William Savage. American State Papers: Foreign Relations 2: 293. https://memory.loc.gov/cgi-bin/ampage [Accessed 18 February 2022].

could use the document to obtain their release from foreign vessels or prisons. Certainly, the men captured and held with British prisoners of war in France believed that the consuls, once they had seen their "Protections", would quickly obtain their release. Unfortunately, the Seaman's Protection Certificate served as a very small and frail shelter against the avalanche of 150 years of British and French navigation laws that also defined a seaman's nationality. These laws, along with one business agreement and one treaty that outraged the French, significantly reduced the American seaman's chance of getting out of a French prisoner of war depot, with or without a Seaman's Protection Certificate.

Navigation Laws Pertaining to Citizenship

Beginning in 1651, the British Parliament began to enact a number of laws concerning navigation, initially in an effort to put an end to the Dutch practice of broken voyages and warehousing of goods in their own ports. The 1651 Navigation Act enforced, among other things, that same practice, but via Britain. As a part of the process of putting all imports and exports into Britain under the control of the British crown, the law stipulated that all goods imported into Britain were required to be on British-registered vessels, owned by British subjects, captained by British masters, and manned by crews that were at least seventy-five per cent British, native or naturalized.[7] Nine years later, the 1660 Navigation Act repeated this requirement. In 1793, when war began again, the part of the Navigation Act which concerned the nationality of the crew was suspended.

Subsequent acts and statutes addressed the issue of the nationalities of the seamen. During the reign of Queen Anne, an act in 1707 stated that every foreign mariner or seaman, who shall have "faithfully served on board any of Her Majesty's Ships of War, or any Privateer or Merchant or trading" ships for two years shall be deemed a British subject.[8] This was reiterated in a

---

[7] October 1651: "An Act for increase of Shipping, and Encouragement of the Navigation of this Nation", in *Acts and Ordinances of the Interregnum, 1642–1660*, eds C.H. Firth and R.S. Rait (London, 1911), pp559–562. *British History Online* http://www.british-history.ac.uk/no-series/acts-ordinances-interregnum/, pp559–562 [Accessed 13 October 2019].

[8] "An Act for the Encouragement of the Trade to America". Great Britain, J. Raithby, 1823. *The statutes relating to the Admiralty, Navy, Shipping, and Navigation of the United Kingdom, from 9 Hen. III. to Geo. IV. inclusive.* London: G. Eyre and A. Strahan, p112.

statute of 1740 under George II,[9] and again in a statute of 1794.[10] These laws giving British nationality to foreign seamen applied only in time of war; this part of the statute of 1794 was not repealed any time during the Napoleonic Wars. Thus, an American seaman could have been determined to have become a British subject, simply by having worked on a British naval or merchant vessel in time of war, under impressment or not, for two years. Not only could and did the Royal Navy manipulate the interpretation of these laws when impressing American seamen, but the French also interpreted them as they saw fit when determining an American seaman prisoner's nationality.

In the spring of 1797, in their annoyance at the Jay Treaty, the Directory in France passed a decree that stripped American vessels of their neutrality and made them legitimate prizes if captured by the French. Foreshadowing the Milan Decree, they also ruled that:

> ...every American, who shall hold a commission from the enemies of France, as well as every seaman of that nation, composing the crew of the ships and vessels, shall, by this fact alone be declared piratical, and treated as such, without suffering the party to establish that the act was the consequence of threats or violence...[11]

Thus, well before Napoleon's Milan and Berlin decrees (which in truth, were not as harsh toward seamen as the Directory's decree above, which declared them pirates, not prisoners of war), American seamen were caught in the European wars and could have been seen as British subjects by the French. By serving on a British vessel in time of war for long enough, by being master or mate of a British vessel, by being on the crew of a British vessel or of an American vessel carrying British goods (even if on the crew as a "consequence of threats and violence", e.g., impressed), an American seaman could be held as a de facto British seaman by France. A Seaman's Protection Certificate attesting to his American citizenship did not prove that he had not become British by serving on a British naval vessel or that he was not a British ally by working on a British merchant vessel.

---

[9] "An Act for the better Supply of Mariners and Seamen to serve His Majesty's Ships of War, and on board Merchant Ships, and other Trading Ships, and Privateers, 1740". Great Britain., J. Raithby, T. Edlyne Tomlins (1811). *The statutes at large, of England and of Great Britain: from Magna Carta to the union of the kingdoms of Great Britain and Ireland.* London: G. Eyre and A. Strahan, pp660–662.

[10] "An Act for the further Encouragement of British Mariners; and for other Purposes therein mentioned, 11 June 1794". Great Britain. J. Raithby, 1823. *The statutes relating to the Admiralty, Navy, Shipping, and Navigation of the United Kingdom, from 9 Hen. III. to Geo. IV. inclusive.* London: G. Eyre and A. Strahan, p562.

[11] "*Le décret du 12 ventôse an V* [2 March 1797]". United States. (1817) *State Papers and Publick Documents of the United States*, p121.

To Prove to the French That a Seaman Was American and Not British

The process for a seaman prisoner of war in France to prove that he was American and not British began when a United States consul learned of his having been taken prisoner. The consul may have learned of an American vessel's capture from the moment it arrived in his port, and so immediately visited the imprisoned crew in jail. However, he would not have taken interest in captured British vessels and would not have been aware of the individual American seamen amongst their crews who were marched with the British seamen straight to a prison depot. In that case, the consul only learned of the American seaman prisoner when that seaman wrote to him from the prison depot, a great distance from the port, begging for help. The American consul then had to determine, by post, if the seaman were truly an American. Usually, he demanded that the seaman send his Seaman's Protection Certificate to be verified by someone at the American legation. It had to be the original. Copies, even if notarized, were not accepted. The prisoners were loath to do this, fearing loss of the precious "Protection", but most complied.

The need to see the original was accentuated by the abundance of forged Seaman's Protection Certificates in France. There was, in fact, a booming business in counterfeit certificates that were sold to British prisoners who hoped it would gain them their release. In the spring of 1808, the Minister of Police General, Fouché, wrote to the Minister of War, Clarke, about his investigation into the rumours of these false certificates. "This ruse," Fouché wrote, "whereby English prisoners of war obtain their release as Americans by means of false certificates which they acquire easily" was, indeed, true. His spies had found that British prisoners at Verdun had hired a printer to produce perfect copies of blank Seaman's Protection Certificates, complete with the signature of the customs agent of Boston. He had also found that the printing shop and bookshop run by one Charles Villet, in Paris, was producing them. Fouché ordered his arrest but, warned of the police raid, apparently, Villet made a narrow escape. The police found his shop abandoned and the floor strewn with freshly printed, somewhat torn certificates.[12] Clarke sent Fouché's report about these fakes to Goulhot. Clearly, with so many counterfeits around, the Seaman's Protection Certificate alone would not be enough to prove an American seaman's nationality to the French. The American diplomats were aware of this French distrust. In 1808, Skipwith wrote:

> The French Government are but too well aware that the usual Certificates of Citizenship are often counterfeited, & when genuine, are often transferred by causualty [sic] & by artifice into improper hands...[13]

---

[12] Fouché to Clarke. 5 March 1808. *Archives de la Guerre et Armée de Terre. Prisonniers de guerre français et étrangers* (1792–1874). SHDV. Yj28.

[13] Skipwith to Madison. 7 April 1808. United States. Department of State. *Despatches from United States Consuls in Paris, 1790–1906*. Vol. 3. Microfilm copy.

The French authorities would also not accept the consular Seaman's Protection Certificates issued by American consuls in French ports, even though these were legitimate.[14] Henry Dixon, a seaman from New York, had a consular Seaman's Protection Certificate given him by the American consul in Amsterdam, Sylvanus Bourne, which the French authorities in Calais refused to accept. He was clamped in irons and marched as a British prisoner to Boulogne-sur-Mer, where he was held until he agreed to sign on to a French privateer.[15]

What damaged French trust in the American diplomats even further was the fact that the American consuls and ministers did, at times, give documents of American citizenship to people they knew were not American. These few cases tended to concern persons of some wealth or position, not seamen, but men who owned either land or businesses in the United States.

Joseph Rocher and John Nichols were British prisoners held at Verdun. Both were captured while masters of British vessels and both had their wives with them. Rocher's children were also with him. (The wives and children were not imprisoned but they remained in the town of Verdun by choice, where Mrs Rocher had three more children.) Some years previously, Nichols had been given an American passport[16] by James Madison. Rocher also had "all the correct papers". Minister John Armstrong ordered consul Isaac Cox Barnet to give them American passports. Barnet did so, though he claimed to feel very uncomfortable about it.[17] The men were not released until some years after Armstrong had left and weeks after Barlow had died, in early 1813. They sailed for Charleston, South Carolina on the *Minerva*. Their wives and the children followed them on a different vessel. Once the families were reunited, the Rochers (and possibly also the Nicholses) seem to have sailed immediately for Australia, where their descendants live still.

In another example, George Goodman was a manufacturer from Leeds imprisoned in the round up of British males in France in 1803. He had applied to Armstrong for aid as an American, claiming that he had lived in the United States and owned property there. Armstrong had refused to recognize him as an American because, firstly, his residency in the country had been too short and,

---

[14] In the first years, the format of the certificate was not standard and, as Brunsman explains, could be produced by…"various public officials, courts, and especially notaries…" See "Subjects vs. Citizens: Impressment and Identity in the Anglo-American Atlantic", *Journal of the Early Republic*, Vol. 30 (2010).

[15] Collet to Barnet. 26 May and 18 June 1811. United States. Department of State. *Despatches from United States Consuls in Paris, 1790–1906*. Vol. 3. Microfilm copy.

[16] At this time, the modern passport did not exist. The American legation issued citizens with "passports" to travel to a port in France. It was a paper certificate granting the protection of the American legation to the person for that single journey, after which it was no longer valid.

[17] Barnet to Crawford. 4 September 1813. United States. Department of State. *Despatches from United States Ministers to France, 1789–1906*. Vol. 14. Microfilm copy.

secondly, he did not own real property there, only shares in a business. "This is not adequate to give him the protection of the United States", Armstrong wrote to Clarke.[18]

In 1811, Armstrong was replaced by Joel Barlow. Goodman tried again and this time was more successful. Firstly, Barlow made a request that Goodman be released as a personal favour to him. This was refused by the French. He then claimed Goodman as an American citizen by naturalization and requested his release again. This seeming volte face concerning naturalization law on the part of the American ministers was viewed with suspicion by the French. Clarke referred the question to Napoleon in April 1812. Meanwhile, Goodman's health at Valenciennes was deteriorating and he asked to be allowed to live in Paris or Orléans. An internal memo, of August 1812, in the Ministry of War says that "the Emperor does not permit him to live in either of these cities, but he may go to Arras". In a few months, Napoleon changed his mind. In January 1813, Savary, at the Ministry of Police General, wrote to Clarke at the Ministry of War, that Goodman had been granted release by Napoleon and that he had been issued a passport by the American Legation.

Then, Goodman fell afoul of the battle going on at that time between the American consuls after the death of Barlow. David Bailie Warden, in Paris, denounced the consul Isaac Cox Barnet for having given an American passport falsely to an Englishman, and he reported Goodman to the police as an escaped prisoner. This caused some concern amongst the French. The letters between the Ministries asked if he were an escapee who should be rearrested. It also caused Barnet to write a long (he never wrote anything short) despatch of self-justification to the Secretary of State, James Monroe, which tells how Goodman finally left France:

> Mr. Goodman came to Paris in January 13. He achieved the passport sent him at the office of External Relations whence it was transmitted as usual in such cases to the Police General for the necessary visa. Here it was arrested by Mr. Warden's denunciation. Fortunately for Mr. Goodman he had received one from the Commandant of the Depot at Arras, he was secretly advised to depart with this one and he had left Paris several days before I knew it. Eight days ago I was told he embarked at Nantes. This morning [14 May 1813] a letter was shewed me stating he was taken and carried to England.[19]

---

[18] Armstrong to Clarke. 22 March 1810. *Archives de la Guerre et Armée de Terre. Prisonniers de guerre français et étrangers* (1792–1874). SHDV. Yj52. Clarke to Bonaparte. 1 April 1812. *Archives de la Secrétairerie d'Etat impériale. Rapports du Ministre de la Guerre* (1800–1814). Arch. nat. AF/IV/1158.

[19] Barnet to Monroe. 14 May 1813. United States. Department of State. *Despatches from United States Ministers to France, 1789–1906*. Vol. 14. Microfilm copy.

Goodman is not the only British prisoner Barlow helped. He sent letters filled with blatant lies about John Bamber to the Ministry of War. He claimed that Bamber was an American businessman from Georgetown, South Carolina, who had been living in Buenos Aires for three years, and that he was a passenger on the British merchant ship, *Vedra*, when it was captured by the French privateer, *Brestois*. The dossier on Bamber contains the letters from Barlow, Goulhot's suggestions that Bamber be released, and even a scrubby little note from a "R. Morin" stating that he knew Bamber in Charlestown.[20] While the French considered his case, Bamber was allowed to live on parole at Longwy. Duped by Barlow, they released Bamber, to whom Barlow issued American papers, in June 1812. Bamber immediately returned to his home city of Liverpool, where he was a master mariner whose boastful account of his heroic defence of the *Vedra*, of which he was the captain, would appear soon in British newspapers.[21]

Somewhat different is the case of Joseph Carpenter, who had the grave misfortune to have been captured and imprisoned by the French twice. Originally from Guernsey, he had become a naturalized American in about 1793 and was a resident of Baltimore.[22] He apparently saw himself as a sort of dual national (something not recognized at the time) when it came to his work as a mariner. For many years, he sailed the American merchant vessel, *Rose*, for the owners, Pitcairn and Rogers yet, in December 1804, he was master of the British merchant vessel, *Phoebe*, when it was captured by the French privateer, *Sorcière*.[23] He was sent to Verdun, where he was granted parole and allowed to live in town, a normal privilege for British merchant shipmasters.[24] He was acknowledged as an American citizen by Joseph Pitcairn and John Forbes, consuls at Hamburg and by Skipwith, all of whom wrote on his behalf. He was released with other Americans in 1807 to go to Antwerp to take a ship

---

[20] Dossier on John Bamber. *Archives de la Guerre et Armée de Terre. Prisonniers de guerre français et étrangers (1792–1874).* SHDV. Yj36.

[21] Letter from Brest dated 6 December 1811. *The Hull Packet and Original Weekly Commercial, Literary and Geneal Advertiser*, 17 March 1812, p3. https://www.newspapers.com/ [Accessed 14 May 2024].

[22] Skipwith to the Secretary of State. 7 April 1807. United States. Department of State. NARA. Despatches from United States Consuls in Paris, 1790–1906. Vol. 2. Microfilm copy, 1952, roll T1/2.

[23] Pitcairn to Skipwith. 4 March 1807. Causten-Pickett Papers, Fulwar Skipwith Papers, Correspondence, Library of Congress.

[24] Records of the Admiralty, Naval Forces, Royal Marines, Coastguard, and related bodies, Records of Medical and Prisoner of War Departments, Navy Board and predecessors: Prisoner of War Department and predecessors: Registers of Prisoners of War, France. Nationality: British. Register of prisoners of war. Prisons Verdun, Tours, Tangiers. ADM 103/441, TNA. "Prisoners of War 1715–1945 Napoleonic Wars", *Find My Past* [Accessed 22 March 2023].

for the United States.²⁵ A little over two years later, at the age of forty, as master of the *Stag*, he was captured again by a French privateer, which burned his vessel, and held in the Tour Solidor.²⁶ This time, he was not sent to the relative comfort of Verdun and he was not granted parole. He was marched to Cambrai, which was the normal treatment of American seamen. In July, he was transferred to the prison depot at Auxonne. On 6 September 1810, he escaped. The police bulletin described him as being five feet three inches tall, with brown hair, grey eyes, a black beard, and having a long nose in a long, tanned face. The description was so good that someone recognized him and he was recaptured. As was usual for anyone who had escaped, he was sent to Bitche. He died in the hospital there the following summer.

Of these examples of British nationals having received the protection of the American legation all but Carpenter were merchants of some standing who had been trading with partners in the United States for some years. Only the mariner, Carpenter, was naturalized but all seem to have been considered as naturalized by the American Ministers Plenipotentiary. The question of naturalized American citizens concerns a very small number of the American seamen held in France. Of the four men described above, three, Rocher, Nichols and Goodman, were British civilians who had been captured and held as détenus. They used their American friends and connections to help them to get out of a ghastly situation. Joseph Carpenter was a mariner and was a naturalized American, the only one identified as such in the entire group of over 1500 American merchant seamen.[27]

On seeing that some Americans were released, many British prisoners pretended to be American. A few were quite successful at it. The eminently boastful escapee, Donat Henchy O'Brien, an Irishman in the Royal Navy, wrote that he escaped from the prison fortress at Bitche. In crossing Europe, whenever he and his fellow escapees encountered officials, they pretended to be Americans and were allowed to go on their way.[28]

Less successful was Bedford Russell, who had been captured by the French privateer, the *Loup Marin*, while a passenger on the *Flora*, making a coastal voyage from Littlehampton to Sunderland in late November 1810. On arriving a captive at Dieppe, he already knew to try to pass as an American (possibly

---

[25] Archives de la Guerre et Armée de Terre. Prisonniers de guerre français et étrangers (1792–1874). SHDV. Yj19.

[26] "Listes de prisonniers de guerre anglais détenus à la Tour Solidor de Port-Malo, An VIII–1811". Archives de la Marine. SHDB. 1P10–118.

[27] This is consistent with Brunsman's finding that "fewer than 2 percent" of the American seamen impressed by the Royal Navy between 1796 and 1812 were "British-born sailors who had been naturalized as American citizens". Brunsman, "Subjects vs. Citizens", p573.

[28] O'Brien, *My Adventures*, pp263–275.

advised by the American seaman on the crew of the *Loup Marin*, twenty-year-old Joseph Norris, of Boston, who had been imprisoned at Arras)[29] and told the port officials that he was from Boston. Over the course of his interrogation, he provided names of Bostonians and details of Boston geography. The French might have accepted his story but he ruined his chances of release with two foolhardy escape attempts. In truth, he was from King's Lynn and returned to his family there only after the wars ended.[30]

Most disastrous of the cases of British posing as Americans was that of John Wiltshire who, while a prisoner, somehow had acquired the documents, possibly Seaman's Protection Certificates, of two Americans, Jonathan Bowers and John Riley. During his trial for treason, Wiltshire claimed that Riley had sold him his documents while they were imprisoned together. Posing as Riley, Wiltshire was released with other Americans during the War of 1812 to serve on an American privateer attacking British shipping. He was caught by the Royal Navy while on the prize crew of a recaptured prize vessel, discovered to be English, and tried for piracy and treason. He was convicted and on 18 July 1813, hanged at Newgate.[31] His luck was particularly bad, for more than a dozen others on that privateer were probably also British.[32]

The problem of British prisoners posing as Americans was extremely detrimental to the chances of American seamen being able to gain their own release. Again, this was something much less likely to occur with the other neutral nationalities; the British prisoners did not pretend to be Danish, Norwegian or Portuguese, only American.

The American consuls also had to struggle with some seamen who had no documentation at all. There were a few who had never bothered to acquire a Seaman's Protection Certificate, something Armstrong found to be grounds for suspicion on its own, asking "What citizen of ours now comes to Europe or goes from it without some regular passport which shall ascertain his citizenship?"[33] This is harsh judgment. A seaman may not have been able to afford the certificate fee of twenty-five cents. He may not have had time to

---

[29] High Court of Admiralty: Prize Court: Prize Papers. Ships names beginning with this letter: L. *Loup Marin*. TNA, HCA 32/1245.

[30] Anne Morddel. "Derring-do of seafarer who ran out of lies after capture by French", *Lynn News*, 12 March 2013, p33.

[31] "Trial for Piracy", *The Weekly Register*, Baltimore, 9 October 1813, p90; High Court of Admiralty: Indictments and Other Proceedings (filed), 1812–1814. TNA. HCA 1/90.

[32] Decrès thought there were more than thirty British amongst the prisoners released to crew the *True-Blooded Yankee*; David Bailey Warden thought there were many more.

[33] Armstrong to Barnet. 11 December 1808. United States. Department of State. *Despatches from United States Consuls in Paris, 1790–1906*. Vol. 3. Microfilm copy.

go to the collector's office to get a certificate before sailing. Most, however, said they did have one and that, somehow, it was lost. Their stories of how these documents, so important to them, came to be lost read like a catalogue of abuse of the unfortunate and unwise.

The crews of the *Ann* and of the *Alexander*, for example, when captured by French privateers in August 1809, were hustled from their vessels to the capturing privateers quickly. They were not allowed to go below to fetch their belongings or Seaman's Protection Certificates; they believed that they could do so when the prize vessels and privateers entered port. However, both of the prize vessels, the *Ann* and the *Alexander*, never made it to a French port but were captured by the British, along with their French prize crews and the American seamen's belongings and certificates. The French privateers, with the American seamen on board as prisoners, arrived safely in Dieppe, where the Americans, who now had no documents, were jailed.[34]

John Van, seaman of Boston, had been on the *Two Brothers* when he fell ill, so the master abandoned him at Cork. As soon as he was well, he boarded the *Eliza* for London, hoping to rejoin his original vessel there. The *Eliza* was captured by the French and Van was taken to Morlaix, a prisoner. He asked the master of another vessel, who was going to Paris, to take his Seaman's Protection Certificate to the American consul there. The master did not and Van's certificate was lost.[35]

William Young, of Portsmouth, New Hampshire, was a prisoner in Givet in 1803 when a man claiming to be the American consul asked for his Seaman's Protection Certificate to send to Paris, promising to return it. Young and others handed their certificates to the stranger, who disappeared with the documents, which never turned up in the American legation in Paris.[36] John Rand, held at Valenciennes, was a master from Boston who said his papers went down with his vessel when it sank.[37]

Some French captors were known to have destroyed seamen's papers. William Adam was master of the *Ocean* on a voyage from Virginia to Lisbon when it was captured by the French privateer, *Diligent*. Captain Grassin of the *Diligent* destroyed all of the *Ocean*'s papers and all those of the crew, including their Seaman's Protection Certificates.[38] William Bowes of Whitemarsh, Pennsylvania was forty-five years old when he was captured in 1806 and

---

[34] Le Baron to Barnet. 11–28 August 1809. United States. Department of State. *Despatches from United States Consuls in Paris, 1790–1906*. Vol. 3. Microfilm copy.

[35] Van to Skipwith. 7 and 24 February 1807. Fulwar Skipwith Papers.

[36] *Guerre et Armée de Terre, Prisonniers de guerre français et étrangers* (1792–1874). SHDV. Yj19.

[37] Rand to Skipwith. 23 January 1807. Fulwar Skipwith Papers.

[38] Warden to Maret. 19 January 1813. United States. Department of State. *Despatches from United States Consuls in Paris, 1790–1906*. Vol. 4. Microfilm copy.

sent to Arras; he said he lost all his papers when captured.[39] John Nehill or Neal (of whom more below) was on a brig captured by "two French frigates". When he resisted their pressure to sign on, they "tore up" his papers and sent him to prison.[40] Cathalan commented that "it is known that British officers, when they press American Seamen, keep or destroy their protections."[41]

Some seamen lost their papers through foolishness. Francis Felton, of Marblehead, was a thirty-two-year-old mate on the *Joseph* when he was captured in 1809. After nearly four years as a prisoner of war at Longwy, he was among those released in early 1813. He left the prison, following the required route of stopping at other prisons along the way to have his papers checked. At Verdun, he lost all of his papers, including the release form, which were then used by a British prisoner, Dr William May, to escape prison (he was recaptured at Le Croisic). Helpless, Felton wandered back to the prison at Longwy, where he was interrogated "with force", poor man. He was to have been sent to the punishment depot at Bitche, but the commandant of Longwy, showing some compassion, wrote to the Minister of War asking that he not be transferred there, "for it would surely kill him".[42]

It cannot be denied that some American seamen recycled Seaman's Protection Certificates, though never their own. It may have seemed at the time a desperate ruse that harmed no one, in an individual case, but that certainly did harm the cases of seamen generally for such fraud cost them much in credibility. In July 1807, two American seamen, Joshua Porter and Joshua Linnell, wrote to Fulwar Skipwith from the depot at Givet, begging to receive some aid. Both had been on the Royal Navy frigate, *Hussar*, when it was wrecked and both still had their Seaman's Protection Certificates. The letter appears to have been written by just one person, as all of the signatures are in the same hand, and says that:

> Joshua Linnell an American Seaman Captured at the same time that Joshua Porter was Captured on Board HM Ship Hussar has a protection in his possession obtained from Benjamin Lincoln Collector of the District of Boston and Charlestown and give [sic] sufficient proof that he is a native of the United States and can remit his Protection if thought required.[43]

---

[39] Petition by prisoners at Arras to the President of the United States. 10 September 1808. United States. Department of State. *Despatches from United States Consuls in Amsterdam, 1790–1906*. Vol. 1. Microfilm copy.

[40] Nehill to Skipwith. 10 November 1806. Fulwar Skipwith Papers.

[41] Cathalan to Russell. 25 July 1811. Jonathan Russell Papers.

[42] Dossier on Francis Felton. *Archives de la Guerre et Armée de Terre. Prisonniers de guerre français et étrangers* (1792–1874). SHDV. Yj49.

[43] Pierce, Porter and Linnell to Skipwith. 9 July 1807. Fulwar Skipwith Papers.

Two years later, Linnel's name was on a list of Americans who had proved their nationality with Seaman's Protection Certificates that was dated 26 July 1809 and signed by the Minister Plenipotentiary, John Armstrong. However, he does not appear in any prison register at all. This is because he died months before the ship wrecked on the French coast. The man who claimed assistance from the American consul in France was an imposter using his certificate. Joshua Linnell was, indeed, an American impressed by the Royal Navy. He appears in the *Hussar* muster index as "Josh. Lenale" and in the pay book as "Joseph Lenall" from America, aged twenty-four, transferred from the *Ethalion* on 22 March 1803.[44] His entry shows that he died less than a month after arriving on the *Hussar*, on 12 April 1803, on the Sussex Hospital ship, moored at Sheerness.

Who was the man writing to Fulwar Skipwith asking for aid more than four years after Joshua Linnell died? He could have been any of the prisoners, American or British, yet it is likely that he was a seaman from the *Hussar*. It was the custom in the Royal Navy, when a man died, to sell his few and meagre possessions to his shipmates; if this were done on the *Hussar* after Linnell's death, it could be how another man obtained his Seaman's Protection Certificate. While a dead man's certificate might have been used by another, no American seaman would have given up his own when it was critical to but not always adequate for his release from impressment or imprisonment.

In the cases where the American prisoners in France had no papers or where their documents were doubted, they tried to get letters, documents, and replacement Seaman's Protection Certificates sent from home. This had been the standard procedure for Americans when dealing with the Royal Navy. Proving the nationality of an impressed American seaman only began with his Seaman's Protection Certificate, which the Admiralty professed to distrust claiming that many were fakes. The American agent in London advised the seamen to get further documents proving that they were born, baptized and had family in America.[45] The letters and documents that arrived in reply may have convinced the consuls as to the men's nationality but were rarely successful in convincing the French to release them. In dealing with the Royal Navy, the issue was of citizenship; in dealing with the French there were two issues: citizenship and aiding the enemy.

With lost documents, forgeries and imposters making identification of American merchant seamen so difficult, some additional way to verify nationality was required. Skipwith proposed a sort of American nationality test. After supplying what documents he had to prove he was American, the seaman was to answer the following questions:

---

[44] Records of the Admiralty, Naval Forces, Royal Marines, Coastguard, and related bodies, Records of Service, Admiralty: Royal Navy Ships' Musters (Series I), Ships' Musters: Hussar, 1 May–31 December 1803. TNA. ADM 36/16028.

[45] The files of these letters and proofs form the foundation of research of Nathan Perl-Rosenthal, *Citizen Sailors*. Also see Denver Brunsman, "Subjects vs. Citizens".

What is the name of the notary or notaries in your place of residence? And where do you live in the United States?

What is the name of the Representative to the State Assembly from your town?

Can you name any merchants from your town who will vouch for you?[46]

Skipwith's proposal was that, based on the responses to the questions, he then would judge for himself whether or not the men were American. Armstrong did not feel comfortable with this personal and subjective form of assessment and wrote to Skipwith that "…no evidence other than legal evidence or regular Certificates of Citizenship [meaning Seaman's Protection Certificates] …" would be acceptable as proof of a seaman being American.[47] It appears that Skipwith's test questions were not used.

Ironically, the types of documentation that most satisfied the French that a man was American were produced by Great Britain, not by the United States. Hugh Harrison, of Charleston, South Carolina, was a passenger on the British vessel, *Enterprise*, when it was captured in 1808 by the French privateer *Harmonie*. Though he was not the master of the *Enterprise*, he was a sea captain by trade so he was sent with the crew to the prison depot at Arras. However, he had on him documents proving that, prior to boarding the *Enterprise*, he had been the master of the *Lady Washington*, an American merchant vessel, when it was captured off Gibraltar by the British fifth rate, *Niger*. Since the British had attacked his American vessel, it was fairly certain that he was not aiding the enemy, and since a master had to be of the same nationality as the vessel, it was fairly certain that Harrison was American. The communication and decision-making moved slowly but in August 1809, the Ministers Decrès and Clarke both agreed that he should be released.

The surest documentary proof of an American seaman not being a British subject was the British document, produced by the Admiralty, releasing him from Royal Navy impressment. Even though that release may have been achieved by way of an American consul or agent in London using the impressed American's Seaman's Protection Certificate, to the French, those release papers from the British Admiralty, stating that he was American and could not be made to serve on a Royal Navy vessel, were indisputable. The French knew as well as anyone that the Royal Navy did not release American

---

[46] Skipwith to the Minister of External Relations. 24 July 1806. United States. Department of State. *Despatches from United States Consuls in Paris, 1790–1906*. Vol. 2. Microfilm copy.

[47] Armstrong to Skipwith. 9 December 1806. United States. Department of State. *Despatches from United States Consuls in Paris, 1790–1906*. Vol. 2. Microfilm copy.

impressed sailors easily.[48] Possessing a release from the Royal Navy was proof that the seaman was not aiding the enemy.

John Purcell was first among the very few to be released from a French prison for this reason, in 1804. Never naming any of the vessels involved, he first wrote to the American legation in Paris, in March, from the prison depot at Valenciennes.

> I was cleared from an English Man of War by Mr. G.W. Erving, General Consul in London by being a Native of the United States of America…. Sir, I have my portection [sic] [and my] "Discharge" of Lords Commissioners…[49]

Within six weeks, the Minister Plenipotentiary, Livingston, wrote to Berthier, who had Goulhot check Purcell's papers. Goulhot verified the papers and Purcell's nationality. Berthier then asked the First Consul, Napoleon, for his decision, which was given, on 21 April, to release Purcell.[50] The decision was announced back through all channels (to all except poor Purcell who had heard not a word from anyone and wrote to Livingston that he was "very uneasy") with the Ministry of War informing Livingston on 1 May. Purcell was issued with a passport to travel within France and was released from Valenciennes on the 25th. He was marched for sixteen days to the port of Le Havre. Unfortunately, British vessels had prevented any American ships from entering the port, so Purcell went to one of the smaller havens on the coast, Fécamp, where he found a ship from Boston to take him home.[51]

The remarkable speed with which Purcell was released can be attributed only to his having had Royal Navy discharge papers. At that time, other prisoners had their Seaman's Protection Certificate but were not released and there were others who had been claimed as American citizens by Livingston but were also not released. Only Purcell had British documentation confirming that he was not British. Thus, it was not positive proof of being American that was a seaman's best hope in France, but negative proof, that he was not British and not working for the British; and it was not documents of nationality

---

[48] Brunsman, "Subjects vs. Citizens" estimates that the Royal Navy released only about twenty per cent of the impressed American seamen for whom claims for their release were made.

[49] Purcell to Livingston. 6 March 1804. United States. Department of State. *Despatches from United States Ministers to France, 1789–1906*. Vol. 9. Microfilm copy.

[50] Dossier on John Purcell. *Archives de la Guerre et Armée de Terre. Prisonniers de guerre français et étrangers* (1792–1874). SHDV. Yj67.

[51] Purcell to Livingston. 2 July 1804. United States. Department of State. *Despatches from United States Ministers to France, 1789–1906*. Vol. 9. Microfilm copy.

from a neutral country that were most easily approved, but the documents of a seaman's rejection from France's old enemy that were accepted most readily.

By December 1806, the situation of American seamen prisoners in France was becoming overwhelming for the American diplomats. The British blockade had begun and Napoleon's Berlin Decree forbade all trade with the enemy. As a result, the number of Americans held as prisoners of war in France increased significantly. There was not enough money to continue sending allowances to them all, and there were no instructions from the United States government as to what procedures to follow to identify them clearly and surely and to aid them in prisons. There remained no clarity as to whether the diplomatic or the consular service was ultimately responsible for them, and it was not known just how many of them were imprisoned in France. Finally, in a clear outline of the problem, Skipwith proposed and Armstrong agreed to conducting a census of the American prisoners.

> Sir, I accompany this letter with a Statement up to this date of the Prisoners in France stating themselves to be Citizens and Residents of the US, who have claimed of me, pecuniary succour. These men generally, I am disposed to believe, are in fact what they declare themselves to be, Citizens of the US & have been captured under the particular circumstances detailed in their letters, & which certainly entitle them to the solicitude of our Government; Still, as neither the certificates of Citizenship which they mention, if forwarded to me, & much less, their histories of themselves by letters, can furnish all evidence necessary to satisfy me of their real national characters, and places of abode, I beg leave to suggest the necessity of my being authorized by you to employ a suitable person at the expense of the US to visit and examine them in their respective prisons & to report to you or to me their answers, to a list of interrogations, which I shall propose for the purpose of obtaining a satisfactory & correspondent knowledge upon the points just stated. In this case it will be necessary that you obtain from this Government a Passport or authorization of some kind, to enable the person employed to visit the different prisons. Should you require it, I shall furnish you, as I propose to do our Government with my accounts of the application of the Fund provided by you in my hands for various public uses, at present, I only think it necessary to observe that there is but about four hundred livres remaining; if therefore I continue to supply the Americans, prisoners in France, with succours, you will please let me have an additional sum of three thousand francs, which I calculate will be an adequate supply for the present number of prisoners, for six months, to come in which time & on the report & Statement with respect to these unfortunate sufferers, which I shall forward to the Department of State, our Government will be able to adopt such regulations as may appear expedient & proper.... The person I wish to designate as being

perfectly competent...is Mr. Pacaud, since many years chancellor to this office & I consider intitled to the highest confidence.[52]

The census was completed in early 1807. It seems that Pacaud could not get to Bitche, for that part of the census was completed for the Americans by a British captive in November.[53] The censuses revealed that the number of American prisoners was not the two or three dozen who had received some financial aid from Skipwith, but more than 200 seamen.

Proving a Seaman Was Not Working for the Enemy

Once the American diplomats made their claim for an American seaman's release, having confirmed his nationality, it was the turn of the French to make their own verifications of his nationality and, especially, to confirm that he was not working for the enemy. They did this by checking the captured vessel's crew list and their own lists of those captured, made as soon as the vessel entered a French port.

Maintaining a register of all members of the crew had been a requirement on both French Marine and British Royal Navy vessels from the 1660s. In France, they were part of a naval conscription system inaugurated in 1665, doing away with impressment, which called up a certain number of men each year and put them through training on board different vessels.[54] Consistent crew lists meant that each seaman's career could be followed closely. Both French and British versions, whether *rôles d'équipage* or muster books, gave the man's name, place of birth, when and where he had signed on, his rank and (on Royal Navy ships) if he had been impressed, or "prest", into service. From 1673, French merchant, fishing and coasting vessels were required to maintain crew lists giving the same information, essentially for the purpose of ensuring their contributions to the *Caisse des Invalides*, the fund for wounded or sick seamen and their families.[55] British merchant vessels adopted the practice of contributions much later but for the same reason. The 1747 Disabled Seaman's

---

[52] Skipwith to Armstrong. 4 December 1806. United States. Department of State. *Despatches from United States Consuls in Paris, 1790–1906*. Vol. 2.

[53] William Bienny, who had been an English teacher living in Bayeux at the time of the 1803 arrests of all English men in France.

[54] Ariel Daran. "*Des Ordonnance de Colbert de 1665 et 1668 sur l'enrôlement maritime à l'Ordonnance de juin 2009 – Evolution du droit maritime*", extracted from *Le point sur le Droit du Travail Maritime français*. Published on: Blog Avocats. https://blogavocat.fr/space/ariel.dahan/content/des-ordonnance-de-colbert-de-1665-et-1668-sur-lenrolement-maritime-a-l-ordonnance-de-juin-2009---evolution-du-droit-maritime_1815e07f-fc48-bc62-8fa0-910b60493082 [Accessed 15 October 2019].

[55] Daran, "*Des Ordonnance de Colbert de 1665 et 1668*".

Act, requiring that a portion of every crew member's pay be contributed to a fund for disabled seamen and their families, also required that every master of a merchant vessel "shall keep a Book or Muster Roll" that would include the full name of the seaman, the date and place each signed on, and his previous vessel.[56]

By the beginning of the nineteenth century, when both countries were at war again, crew lists were so much an integral part of a vessel's documentation, or its sea letters, that any vessel that did not have a crew list was immediately suspected of piracy. The nationalities of the crew, as they appeared on a crew list, helped to determine the nationality of the vessel. This was why the French, in the 1778 Treaty between France and the United States, insisted that all vessels maintain a complete crew list, to confirm the nationality of the crew and therefore of the vessel. Unfortunately for American seamen, the United States did not enact the requirement for vessels to carry crew lists until 1803[57] and, even then, it was not always obeyed by American shipmasters.[58]

Even with crew lists, the question of a seaman's nationality was murky. Morieux points out that, from the eighteenth century, "A constant subject was whether the flag under which the prisoners served when they were captured, or their subjecthood, should be the main factor in determining their fate."[59] Britain had determined that the flag overruled subjecthood and so labelled all prisoners as being of the nationality of the flag under which they were captured. The entry books for British prisons during the Napoleonic Wars contain quite a few American seamen labelled as French because they were captured on French privateers. Napoleon was taking the same position with his ruling that all American seamen captured from British vessels be treated as British. The American diplomats in France took the opposite position, that the seaman's citizenship overruled the flag under which he sailed and so, if he were American, he was neutral and should be released, no matter what the nationality of his vessel had been.[60]

---

[56] "An Act for the Relief and Support of maimed and disabled Seamen, and the Widows and Children of such as shall be killed, slain, or drowned in the Merchants Service". Great Britain. J. Raithby, 1823. *The statutes relating to the Admiralty, Navy, Shipping, and Navigation of the United Kingdom, from 9 Hen. III. to Geo. IV. inclusive.* London: G. Eyre and A. Strahan, p225.

[57] Douglas L. Stein. *American Maritime Documents 1776–1860, Illustrated and Described.* Mystic: Mystic Seaport Museum, 1992, p50.

[58] Bonnel, *La France, les États-Unis et la guerre de course*, p71.

[59] Morieux, *The Society of Prisoners*, p16.

[60] Note that, in all cases, the opposite point of view was taken concerning the cargo. Americans maintained that the flag's nationality determined the cargo's, while the French and British maintained that it did not.

The crew lists and an American seaman's name on them became crucial in the French investigation of the American diplomats' claims for prisoners to be released. For each and every claim for a prisoner's release on the grounds that he was American, Goulhot and Debacq or Houel, in the Ministry of War, sent his name and details, along with the name of his vessel, to the Ministry of Marine and Colonies, which would then check the crew and passenger lists of the captured vessel for his name. These would show where he was born and whether or not he had been on the crew or was a passenger. An American on the crew of a British vessel was considered to have been aiding the enemy; an American passenger on the same vessel was not.

The documents about the vessel's capture would also show the vessel's nationality and type. With this information, it would be determined if the prisoner qualified for consideration for release. However, if part of the reason that the vessel had been condemned was false or duplicate ship's papers, the crew list would be considered invalid and the crew as enemy. With all of the many ways that an American seaman could be considered a British subject or as working for the enemy, his chances of release were small. His chances worsened from 1808, when the Bayonne Decree, retaliating for the United States' Embargo Act, authorized the seizure of all American vessels arriving in any port of the French Empire. With that decree, and later, the Rambouillet Decree, American vessels became legitimate prizes and their crew, Americans working on American vessels, were no longer considered neutral but were legitimate prisoners of war. French privateers jumped at the chance to attack American ships, and many more went to sea for that purpose, often from the port of Dieppe, where the British blockade was somewhat thinner than at Brest or Le Havre. They took so many American vessels that the number of American seamen captured in 1809 was over 300, more than double the number taken the year before.

The French position that the crew would be treated as of the same nationality as the vessel was also applied to Americans impressed on Royal Navy vessels. This was because Royal Navy practices toward Americans made it impossible to know if a man were serving willingly or not. Though the simple note of "prest" next to his name would indicate that he had been kidnapped and forced onto the ship, he might have accepted the bounty that the Royal Navy offered to impressed men to join willingly, which changed his status from that of impressed to that of a volunteer. Quite a few Americans had done this, accepting cash with acceptance of their fate.

The determination of an impressed seaman's nationality was made even more difficult by the practice in the Royal Navy of obscuring Americans' identities. At least insofar as concerns impressed American seamen, musters and pay books were not scrupulously kept during the Napoleonic Wars and are not wholly reliable records. Entire columns were left blank. Places of birth were either not given or were falsified, substituting a place in Britain or her colonies for a place in America. On the same vessel, men's identities were altered more than once. Newly impressed men were entered under the names of men who had deserted or died.[61] The constant reassignment of sailors from one vessel to another also aided in beclouding their identities. The Royal Navy's purpose in all of this was to make it extremely difficult for families, friends and consuls to locate an impressed American and to petition the Admiralty for his release.[62] However, it also had the effect of making it difficult, if not impossible, for the impressed seaman to prove his nationality to the French.

On the *Challenger*, Joshua Mariner, who was from New York, appears in the pay books firstly as aged thirty-two from America, then as aged seventeen, from St Kitts.[63] Nine men amongst the survivors of the wreck of the *Shannon* claimed to be Americans who had been impressed in London. Some of their places of birth are given in the *Shannon*'s books as in Britain and not in America. William Knight was from Rhode Island but the muster gave his place of birth as Deptford; the African-American John Williams was from Staten Island, New York but the muster gives no place of birth for him. Henry Green, also African-American, was from Baltimore but the muster said he was from Jamaica.[64] John McChord and John Russell do not appear in the muster under their own names.[65] Only for Samuel Tucker of Philadelphia does the muster agree with his personal identification.[66]

---

[61] For another example of false information entered into musters, see N.A.M. Rodger, *The Wooden World*, p160.

[62] Most of the historiography asserts the likelihood of seamen wilfully using aliases. See Myra C. Glenn. *Jack Tar's Story: The Autobiographies and Memoirs of Sailors in Antebellum America.* Cambridge: Cambridge University Press, 2010, p60: "many mariners who deserted ships and feared recapture…used an alias". Also see Frederick C. Leiner. *Prisoners of the Bashaw: The Nineteen-Month Captivity of American Sailors in Tripoli, 1803–1805*, Yardley: Westholme, 2022, p38. This may have been true of British seamen, but it would not have served the interests of American seamen to take a British alias when they were hoping to be released *because* they were American. There is nothing to be found in the historiography about this consistent practice on the part of ships' clerks and officers of obscuring and falsifying the identities of impressed American seamen, and yet it was very real.

[63] Records of the Admiralty, Naval Forces, Royal Marines, Coastguard, and related bodies, Records of Service, Admiralty: Royal Navy Ships' Musters (Series II), Ships' Musters: Challenger, October 1806–November 1806. TNA. ADM 37/1552 and October 1809–December 1810. TNA. ADM 37/3027.

[64] There are towns called Falmouth in England and in Massachusetts. The muster, by not indicating America, implies the town in England. This occurs often where town names are the same in both countries, as with Plymouth, Portsmouth, Boston, etc.

[65] Records of the Admiralty, Naval Forces, Royal Marines, Coastguard, and related bodies, Records of Service, Admiralty: Royal Navy Ships' Musters (Series I), Ships' Musters: Shannon. September–December 1803. TNA. ADM 36/15531.

[66] Records of the Admiralty, Naval Forces, Royal Marines, Coastguard, and related bodies, Records of Medical and Prisoner of War Departments, Navy Board

In another example, George Adam Cope obtained his first Seaman's Protection certificate at Philadelphia in 1806. It describes him as being twenty years old, with a light complexion and blue eyes. He may have been something of a left-handed pugilist, for he had "scars on all the fingers and thumb of the left hand and One on the Right Thumb, one on the left cheek and one under the left eye".[67] He was not many months at sea before he was nabbed by the Royal Navy and forced onto the *Challenger*. Cope showed his Seaman's Protection Certificate to prove that he was American and the captain burnt it in front of him.[68]

Somehow, he got word to those at home of his predicament and, in February 1808, the United States Department of State included his name in a list of seamen "impressed into the British service" that was published by a number of papers, as was the custom with such lists. The notice said that the men had no documents and asked friends and family to send any such that they had to enable the Secretary of State to help them.[69] George Adam Cope was entered into the *Challenger*'s muster for 1810 as "Nathaniel Lowell", aged twenty-one (by then, his true age was about twenty-four), born in Philadelphia. It stated that he had been "prest" on 25 July 1810 in Curaçao, removing more than two years of his time on board from the already false record.[70] In early 1811, the *Challenger* was captured by the French and the crew sent to prison depots. Cope arrived at Cambrai in May and was registered as "Nathaniel Lowell". He insisted so much and so often that his name was Cope that, at times, both names appear in the prison registers.

In a French prison, Cope had more rights than he had had on a Royal Navy vessel. He was permitted to contact the American consuls in Paris. Through that contact, his relatives and friends, who may have sought him vainly, not

---

and predecessors: Prisoner of War Department and predecessors: Registers of Prisoners of War, TNA. ADM 103/631.

[67] United States. Citizenship Affidavits of US-born Seamen at Select Ports, 1792–1869. Ancestry.com [Accessed 7 November 2021]. Original Publication: Proofs of Citizenship Used to Apply for Seamen's Certificates for the Port of Philadelphia, Pennsylvania, 1792–1861. NARA Microfilm publication M1880, roll 6, frame 372. Records of the U.S. Customs Service, Record Group 36. NARA, Washington, D.C.

[68] United States. Citizenship Affidavits of US-born Seamen at Select Ports, 1792–1869. Ancestry.com [Accessed 7 November 2021]. Original Publication: Proofs of Citizenship Used to Apply for Seamen's Certificates for the Port of Philadelphia, Pennsylvania, 1792–1861. NARA Microfilm publication M1880, roll 17, frame 180. Records of the U.S. Customs Service, Record Group 36. NARA, Washington, D.C.

[69] *Aurora General Advertiser*, Philadelphia. 22 February 1808, p1. https://www.newspapers.com/image/586565789 [Accessed 21 May 2023].

[70] Records of the Admiralty, Naval Forces, Royal Marines, Coastguard, and related bodies, Records of Service, Admiralty: Royal Navy Ships' Musters (Series II), Ships' Musters: Challenger, October 1809–December 1810 TNA. ADM 37/3027.

knowing he was being held under another name, at last could come to his aid. The State Department sent a new Seaman's Protection Certificate. The firm of Smith & Helmuth of Philadelphia offered to pay up to 150 dollars to cover his expenses for returning home.[71] He became the subject of an extensive exchange between the American legation and the Ministry of External Affairs. Alas, he was not freed; to the French, whatever his name, he had been captured on a Royal Navy vessel, serving for the enemy. His anger and resentment at his treatment in the Royal Navy lasted through his years of imprisonment in France. As soon as he returned home, he went to the Customs Service of Philadelphia, where he reported, with an outrage still palpable, how the captain of the *Challenger* had destroyed his Seaman's Protection Certificate.[72]

The French were well aware of the British practice of falsifying the identities of American seamen they had impressed. In February 1809, Goulhot wrote to the Minister of War, Clarke:

> ...the English, who employ them only by force and violence on their ships, are careful to have on their crew lists no indication of anyone being American, in violation of men's rights.[73]

Unfortunately for American prisoners, though the French understood that confusion was intentionally created, they did not consider it their responsibility to sort out the enemy's record-keeping mess. A man captured from a Royal Navy vessel would have had to provide to the French documentary proof, firstly, that he was American and secondly, that he was not serving the British. For the first, he would have had to have been able to retain his Seaman's Protection Certificate, which was possible but rare. For the second, he would have needed a discharge from the Royal Navy, which he would not have had. So he would have been treated as British by the French.

Was he American or British? Was he on the crew or a passenger? Was the vessel American or British? Was he the master of a British vessel? Was the cargo British? Had he been on a good prize? Which of Napoleon's decrees was in effect concerning American shipping when he was captured? All of

---

[71] David Bailey, Warden to the Duke of Bassano, 6 February 1813, *Correspondence Politiques Etats-Unis*. Arch. dip. 69CP/70. Microfilm copy.

[72] United States. Citizenship Affidavits of US-born Seamen at Select Ports, 1792–1869. Ancestry.com [Accessed 7 November 2021]. Original Publication: Proofs of Citizenship Used to Apply for Seamen's Certificates for the Port of Philadelphia, Pennsylvania, 1792–1861. NARA Microfilm publication M1880, roll 17, frame 180. Records of the U.S. Customs Service, Record Group 36. NARA, Washington, D.C.

[73] Report from Goulhot to Clarke, the Minister of War. 14 February 1807. *Archives de la Guerre et Armée de Terre. Prisonniers de guerre français et étrangers* (1792–1874). SHDV. Yj41.

these questions had to be answered, in a certain way, for an American seaman held prisoner to hope for release. It was truly a maze, of French ministerial administration, of strong French and equally strong American personalities, of disputes about vessel neutrality, privateering law, and citizenship definition, with interminable paperwork required in a time of slow communication and war. It was such an entangled situation that no one was likely to have been released and yet, as the following chapters show, a number of Americans were released from French prison depots well before the end of the wars.

PART THREE

ÉLARGISSEMENT – RELEASE

INTRODUCTION

This section looks at the ways that American prisoners of war could hope for release, or *élargissement*. As explained above, though they were held in the same depots as the British prisoners of war, they were not British. Their country was not at war with France and held no French prisoners of war in the United States, so they could not be exchanged. Few of them were taken from Royal Navy vessels and none of those were officers, so they could not be granted parole and return to their own country. There was no set of rules or statutes codifying the release of American prisoners, nor was there any treaty negotiated which outlined conditions for their release. Every prisoner's case was evaluated individually, even if some of them later sailed home as a group. There were five types of release of American prisoners of war.

The first was when a seaman was able to prove that he was not working on the British vessel on which he was captured but merely a passenger. Only a very small number of men were released because they were passengers. The second was release on compassionate grounds, which almost never occurred, yet prisoners seemed to believe that it was a real possibility. The third was when a seaman gave the French valuable information about their enemy, the British. This worked very well, but few men had information that the French could use. The fourth was actually a temporary release but provided excellent opportunities for escape, and that was to volunteer to work on a French privateer attacking British or American merchant vessels. Over 200 men chose this way to get out of the prison depot. Finally, there could be a diplomatically negotiated release. If they had retained their Seaman's Protection Certificates or in some other way could prove that they were American to the American diplomats as well as to the French authorities, the American Minister Plenipotentiary would try to negotiate their release. There were two such releases, of groups of men, in 1807 and 1813. The chapters that follow describe some of these releases.

7

"BAD PRIZES", PASSENGERS AND COMPASSION

"Bad Prizes"

American seamen who were fortunate enough to have been on a captured vessel that the Prize Council declared a "bad prize" (*prise nulle*) would be released from port jails without ever having gone to a prison depot, and were never really prisoners of war, which is not to say that they did not suffer from cold, damp, and bad food. There were not many cases of the capture being judged invalid. Captain Gorham Coffin's vessel, the *General Lincoln*, mentioned above, was one such, and his crew were released from jail after a very long wait.

Another example was the case of the *Saratoga*, Captain Barkir Baker, captured on 26 April 1812, as was the *Massachusetts*, Captain Alan Case, by the *Espadon*, Captain Balidar.[1] Soon afterward, the *Massachusetts* and its prize crew were captured by the Royal Navy's *Helicon* and taken in to an English port as a British prize. The *Saratoga* was sent in to Roscoff, along with the crew and a few of the men who had been taken off the *Massachusetts*. Perhaps because the expected declaration of war by the United States brought some benevolence, the *Massachusetts* crew members were granted permission to leave within weeks and sailed from Morlaix.[2] By the middle of July, the *Saratoga* was judged a bad prize and returned to the owners. The crew were released. (See Appendix A for the released men's names.) Captain Baker sailed the *Saratoga* between France, Britain and America as a cartel, ferrying British seamen captured by American privateers, who brought their prizes in to France, to Britain to be exchanged for American prisoners, who were then taken home to America.

---

[1] High Court of Admiralty: Prize Court: Prize Papers. Ships names beginning with this letter: E. *Espadon*. TNA, HCA 32/1275.

[2] Records of the Admiralty, Naval Forces, Royal Marines, Coastguard, and related bodies, Records of Medical and Prisoner of War Departments, Navy Board and predecessors: Prisoner of War Department and predecessors: Registers of Prisoners of War. Registers by nationality, France. Nationality: British. Register of Prisoners of War. Released Prisoners, 1814–1815. TNA. ADM 103/480.

His original crew may, for the most part, have sailed those journeys with him, for nearly all of them were still in France the following summer, signing on to another cartel, the *Ann Maria*, Captain Campbell, to do the same run with the same types of passengers.[3] (Campbell and his ship had been held at Morlaix for some weeks, for being suspected of aiding in the escape of four prisoners.)[4] Unfortunately, as was reported in the press under the headline "Violation of Cartel", as the *Ann Maria* was leaving Falmouth, where the British prisoners had been deposited, for Dartmouth to collect American seamen released from British prisons, a press gang's boat chased. The gang boarded and hauled off Campbell, whose naturalization as an American, seventeen years earlier, they did not accept.[5]

Cases of Passengers

Americans who had been merely passengers on British vessels had a slight chance of release because they might have been able to prove that they had not been supporting the enemy's cause by working on the crew. Realizing this, some seamen in prison depots changed their stories and claimed that they had not been working the vessel but merely taking passage on it. This was more believable if the captured vessel had been bound for rather than out of the United States, for it was conceivable that an American seaman might have taken passage home but passage, rather than working, on an outward-bound vessel would have made him appear to have been other than American. The lists made by the French port officers of those captured, however, clearly differentiated between crew and passengers so, when they were checked, any lies were usually discovered. The case of Asa Lewis, of Boston, who was captured on the *Santa Maria* in October 1810 and taken in to Morlaix is an example. He and a number of other men from the same vessel swore repeatedly that they were passengers and, as such, the American consul requested their release. It was denied by the French authorities because on the crew list made by the French when the men were landed, Lewis appeared as the captain and the others as members of the crew. As no one else was on board, it is not likely that they were passengers.[6]

---

[3] Crew list written by Jean Diot, 14 July 1813. *Archives de la Marine, Prises – Bâtiments de l'État et corsaires*. SHDV. FF2/10.

[4] Campbell dossier. *Archives de la Guerre et Armée de Terre. Prisonniers de guerre français et étrangers* (1792–1874). SHDV. Yj40.

[5] *Richmond Enquirer*, 12 October 1813. https/www.newspapers.com [Accessed 1 January 2024].

[6] *Archives de la Marine, Affaires maritimes, Quartier de Saint-Malo, 1689–1890*. SHDB. 1P10 85–86.

Legitimate passengers, even if captains and mates, but not working on the voyage, could be released. In March 1810, Alexander Gibson of Connecticut was travelling with Thomas C. Almy of Rhode Island (future hero of the Battle of Lake Erie) and his servant, Thomas Forest, "a man of colour", as passengers on the *Saint Anne*, a Portuguese vessel out of Charleston, when they were captured by the French vessel *Phénix* and taken in to Nantes. It took seven months, but, after the Ministry of Marine and Colonies confirmed that Gibson, Almy and Forest appeared on all lists as passengers, the order was given in October for their release and they were released. Forest, by then aged twenty-seven, travelled to England as Gibson's servant.[7]

Prisoners on the *Minotaur*

Americans who were passengers, or prisoners, on Royal Navy vessels might also be released by the French. As with passengers on merchant vessels, the process of confirming their passenger status could be long but it could work.

The *Minotaur* had been in the battles of Trafalgar and Copenhagen and had been repaired afterward. By 1809, it was in the Baltic Fleet, sent to protect Sweden from invasion by Russia, to contain the Russian and Danish fleets and to protect convoys of merchant vessels in those waters. In July 1809, the crew on board at the time would take part in an attack on Russian gunboats, in which their ship was at the fore and suffered the worst casualties. Two lieutenants, the quartermaster, three seamen and a number of marines were killed and twenty-five men were wounded during that attack.[8] At some time in the following months, the *Minotaur* captured the American ship, *Charles*, of New York, as it was leaving a Lithuanian port. The prize was sent to London,[9] while at least some of the crew, including the captain, Charles Woodward, were held on the *Minotaur* as prisoners of war.[10]

In the early winter of 1810, the *Minotaur* was part of the escort of the last convoy of the year of merchant vessels leaving Gothenburg for British ports. In a storm on the night of 22 December, the *Minotaur*, having lost its way,

[7] Records of the Admiralty, Naval Forces, Royal Marines, Coastguard, and related bodies, Records of Medical and Prisoner of War Departments, Navy Board and predecessors: Prisoner of War Department and predecessors: Registers of Prisoners of War. Registers by nationality, France. Nationality: British. Register of Prisoners of War. Released Prisoners, 1814–1815. TNA. ADM 103/480.

[8] Michael Phillips. *Ships of the Old Navy: a History of the Sailing Ships of the Royal Navy* (Electronic edition, 2007) http://www.ageofnelson.org/MichaelPhillips/

[9] It may have been retaken by remaining American crew members on board, or lost, for there is no prize case file for it in TNA.

[10] *Aurora General Advertiser*, Philadelphia. 12 February 1811, p3. https://www.newspapers.com [Accessed 21 May 2023].

ran aground on sand, some distance from the Dutch shore. As the crashing waves hurled the ship against the sands and the storm raged, some of the men managed to get into boats. By the next morning:

> ...the wind and heavy sea prevented [any boat from the shore] approaching the vessel. She had lost her masts, and was under water from about half-way up the bowsprit to behind the main mast. The waves broke over the remainder of her.[11]

Out of a crew of about 590 men, just 110 made it to shore and survived.[12] There were at least nine Americans amongst the survivors. Three of them were seamen whose names were on the *Minotaur*'s musters and six of them were the prisoners of war, who may have been locked in some sort of cell or brig.

How the French viewed the American seamen who survived the wreck exemplifies their decision-making about Americans found on board British vessels. The three men on the crew were sent to the French prison depot at Valenciennes with other British seamen, even though they almost certainly had been impressed. Of the six other men, four were reported in the press as from the American vessel, *Charles*. The French list of the six men does not give their vessels or their ages or places of birth. It states only that they were American, and were named as: Captain Charles Lodevard [Woodward], Thomas Lunt, William Coffin, John Love, John Milis and Michael Lendrick. All of these prisoners of the British were released.[13] Prisoners of the enemy clearly were not working for the enemy. The men were handed over to the consul at Amsterdam, Sylvanus Bourne, who would have arranged their passage back to the United States.

The three Americans who were on the crew of the *Minotaur* and who were marched to prison depots with the rest of the British crew did not all make it home. John Lexhorn, of "Boston, America", received aid from the Committee for Relief as per the 1812 publication, so he may have survived. He seems never to have written to the American consuls in Paris but to have endured his imprisonment in relative silence to the end of the wars.

James Johnson, was an African-American from Norfolk, Virginia, the son of Richard and Susane [sic] Johnson. Though he was impressed, he may have had little or no sea experience, for he was marked as a landsman on the muster. He had not taken part in the *Minotaur*'s fierce battle with the Russians,

---

[11] Terence Grocott, *Shipwrecks of the Revolutionary & Napoleonic Eras.* London: Chatham, 1997, p302.

[12] Accounts vary from 109, to 110, to 140 to 190 survivors but more give the number of 110.

[13] *Archives de la Guerre et Armée de Terre. Prisonniers de guerre français et étrangers* (1792–1874). SHDV. Yj31.

having been held on the dilapidated *Leyden* in the Scheldt at the time.[14] He and others were transferred from that vessel to the *Minotaur* in September and October 1810, presumably to replace some of the men killed in the battle with the Russian gunboats. He survived the wreck and the winter march to prison, where he was given the prisoner number of 1166 and received some British assistance,[15] only to die at Valenciennes, on 6 January 1812.[16] He was twenty-four years old.

Captured from the *General Gates* by the *Abercrombie*

In early January of 1813, an announcement appeared in British newspapers, that the "beautiful Ship, *General Gates*" was to be auctioned in London. It was described in some detail.

> This ship is about two years old, has a flush deck, and is pierced for 20 guns, and was built in New York of the best materials by an English mechanic. She is coppered and copper fastened, has a bust man-head, and is well found in sails and other stores....
>
> Her large and valuable Cargo, consisting of Cognac, Brandy, Wines, Silks, Crapes, Ribbons, Stationery, Gloves, Silk Stockings &c will shortly be exposed to sale...[17]

The *General Gates* had been captured on 24 May 1812 by the British blockading ships, *Belle Poule*, *Abercrombie* and *Dryad*, as it left Bordeaux for New York. War had not yet been declared by the United States; it was a legitimate prize to the British because it departed from a French port and was carrying French goods. Twenty-eight of the captured crew were placed on the *Abercrombie*, the rest on the other two frigates. Two days later, four of the captives were ordered to go ashore on the island of Hoedic to get water. They wasted no time but grabbed their chance to escape likely impressment, taking one of the boats and rowing toward the Breton shore, more than twenty-five kilometres

---

[14] Records of the Admiralty, Naval Forces, Royal Marines, Coastguard, and related bodies, Records of Service, Admiralty: Royal Navy Ships' Musters (Series III), Ships' Pay books: Minotaur, 1 October 1808–22 December 1810. TNA. ADM 35/2916.

[15] *Report from the Committee for the Relief,* p123.

[16] Valenciennes, *Registre de décès*, 1811–1813 (Death of James Johnson) 6 janvier 1812. *AD Nord*, https://archivesdepartementales.lenord.fr/?id=archives_online [Accessed 30 July 2019].

[17] *The Bristol Mirror*, 2 January 1813, pl, column 4. https://www.newspapers.com [Accessed 21 January 2024].

away. They were pursued by one of the *Abercrombie*'s launches, perhaps half-heartedly, perhaps tardily, for they got away.[18]

Thomas Jackson (the same who had been arrested for repeated drunkenness, costing the consul at Bordeaux more than eleven dollars in fines) aged thirty-seven, from Providence, Rhode Island, had been the boatswain or mate on the *General Gates* and was the leader of the band of escapees. The others were seamen John Harman, aged twenty-four, from Linchester in Maryland, William Jones, aged twenty, from New Jersey, and Robert Brice, aged twenty-two, from New London, Connecticut. They made it to the beaches of Piriac, where they were arrested by the gendarmes and taken to the authorities at Le Croisic. On 2 June, they gave a statement before the mayor, the commandant, the interim naval commissioner, a representative of the seamen's union, an interpreter and the American consul, Frogier. The statement was sent to Clarke, the Minister of War and the men were moved to jail at Nantes to await his decision.

In the usual procedure, the Ministry of War contacted the Ministry of Marine and Colonies for confirmation. Meanwhile, Goulhot contacted the port authorities at Bordeaux. They checked the departing crew list of the *General Gates* and wrote back in August that the four men were, indeed on the crew.[19] Most uncharacteristically, Decrès, the Minister of Marine and Colonies, after writing to Bordeaux himself for the same information, wrote that the men should be released. On 10 September, Clarke wrote of his decision to release the four men.[20] They were placed on the American schooner, *Meteor*, Captain Bartlett, which arrived in Newport, Rhode Island in early October. From there, the men went their separate ways, it would seem, which was fortunate. It meant that they were not amongst the *Meteor*'s crew sent to a British prison when, a few months later, it was captured by the *Briton*.[21]

In a case similar to that of the American seamen who escaped from the *General Gates*, two other men were let go by the French. William Bonny, aged twenty-seven, from Marblehead, and Abraham Dean, aged twenty-four,

---

[18] Jackson's statement. 2 June 1812. Jackson dossier. *Archives de la Guerre et Armée de Terre. Prisonniers de guerre français et étrangers* (1792–1874). SHDV. Yj57.

[19] All four men also appear on the captured crew list of the *General Gates*. High Court of Admiralty: Prize Court: Prize Papers. Ships names beginning with this letter: G. *General Gates*. TNA, HCA 32/1771.

[20] Jackson dossier. *Archives de la Guerre et Armée de Terre. Prisonniers de guerre français et étrangers* (1792–1874). SHDV. Yj57.

[21] General Entry Book of American Prisoners of War at Plymouth, October 1812–May1813. [ADM 103/268] *American Prisoners of War, 1812–1815, Prison Ships and Deports in England, Plymouth, 1812–1814*. British Online Archives. https://microform.digital/boa/collections/58/american-prisoners-of-war-1812–1815. [Accessed 18 December 2020].

from Philadelphia, escaped from the *Regulus* at Guernsey on 24 February 1807. They rowed and drifted some fifty kilometres to the French coast, where they were picked up and taken to Caen. There, interrogations and investigations determined to the authorities' satisfaction that they were Americans and not British and that they had been impressed and held on the *Regulus*. That they had escaped the vessel and preferred landing in France, Britain's enemy but not America's, was also an indicator. They were released in March and sailed home from Cherbourg.[22]

The release of seamen who had taken the risk of escaping Royal Navy vessels, such as those of the *Abercrombie* and the *Regulus*, and of men who were prisoners taken from one or more captured vessels and held on the *Minotaur*, demonstrates how the French differentiated between American seamen willingly on British vessels and those who were not. Even though they understood well that impressed seamen might be working on British vessels against their will, they also, with characteristically French logic, knew that a man's will was not something that could or would be documented on the enemy ship's books and that, once captured, most men would say or do anything to avoid prison, detracting from their credibility somewhat. Thus, those who escaped a Royal Navy vessel or who were imprisoned on board, were considered to be in no way working for the British and were released. Those on the crew, however unwillingly that may have been, were not.

Cases for Compassion

Releases of seamen on compassionate grounds were almost non-existent. It took many requests for Thomas Crippen of Wilmington, North Carolina, blinded and dying after four years as a prisoner of war, two cruises on French privateers and a spell in hospital at Cambrai, to be permitted, by order of Napoleon, to go home. The order was given in August 1812 but six months later, he was still at Cambrai and Barnet was pleading for aid for him:

> Thos. Crippen is blind – he has been discharged some time since but has remained at the Depot on account of the vigour of the season and in order to take the opportunity of some person who might conduct him to a port of embarkation. He is now destitute of every resource in money and it is urgent indeed the calls of humanity require that assistance should be sent him by the mail of this very day.[23]

---

[22] *Archives de la Guerre et Armée de Terre. Prisonniers de guerre français et étrangers* (1792–1874). SHDV. Yj31. d'Hauterive. *La police secrète*, p234 and p243.

[23] Barnet to Warden. 1 February 1813. United States. Department of State. *Despatches from United States Consuls in Paris, 1790–1906*. Vol. 4 Microfilm copy.

James Strawbridge, of Philadelphia, was the mate on a vessel bound for Smyrna (now Izmir), but he left the ship after quarrelling with the captain. He found passage back to America on a British vessel that was then captured by the French. He was very ill, probably with tuberculosis. His family learned of the capture and contacted the French vice-consul in Philadelphia, who personally urged the State Department to do something to get him released. (As Brunsman pointed out, families who contacted the British consul had some success in getting men released from the Royal Navy; Strawbridge's family may have thought the same tactic would work with the French.)[24] The Secretary of State, Monroe, sent instructions to Barlow in March 1812, urging him to do all that he could for Strawbridge's release. Agents of their business in Bordeaux wrote that they were trying to help with Strawbridge's release. The family sent copies of his birth records to Barlow. After the usual exchanges between the various ministries, even Decrès confirmed that he had been a "seaman-passenger". Goulhot proposed that he be released. The poor man died soon after returning home.[25]

It took quite a lot of effort to bring about the release of John Wood Homans, even though he was the cousin of Benjamin Homans, at that time a merchant and shipowner, but who would soon be the Secretary of the Commonwealth of Massachusetts and then the Chief Clerk of the United States Navy. Young Homans had been a passenger, it was claimed, on a British vessel when it was captured. He was sent to the depot at Givet. Friends and family from home provided documents to prove his nationality.[26] His story is not that different from many of those who were not released, nor were his family connections very useful (his cousin had lived in Bordeaux and knew William Lee), but he was lucky. There may also have been an element of compassion when the Emperor approved his release, for the family had begged for his return in the name of his mother, who had already lost two sons to the sea. In June 1806, Napoleon signed his release and Homans returned home soon afterward.[27]

Joseph Allen, a sixteen-year-old boy from Donegal, surely deserved some compassion for his youth. If not Joseph, then his brother, Michael, merited some, for he fought valiantly for his brother to be released. Michael was

---

[24] Brunsman, "Subjects vs. Citizens", p579.

[25] Dossier on James Strawbridge. *Archives de la Guerre et Armée de Terre. Prisonniers de guerre français et étrangers*. SHDV. Yj73.

[26] Dossier on John Wood Homans. *Archives de la Guerre et Armée de Terre. Prisonniers de guerre français et étrangers* (1792–1874). SHDV. Yj56.

[27] This signed release may yet exist. It was amongst items in the Sainsbury autograph collection sold by Sotheby's in 1865. Sainsbury, John, *Catalogue of the… museum formed by John Sainsbury…which will be sold by auction*, 1865, p97. https://books.google.fr/books?id=Zj5bAAAAQAAJ&dq=%22John+Wood+Homans%22&source=gbs_navlinks_s [Accessed 12 May 2024].

established in New York and had become a naturalized American, when he sent for Joseph to join him from Ireland. He boarded the *Prosperity*, along with a group of Irish weavers who were also emigrating, and sailed from Londonderry to start his new life. On 24 December 1807, the ship met a wild storm off Newfoundland that tore it to pieces, leaving it drifting, without rudder or sails, for eleven days. The French frigate, *Patriote*, came along and rescued the crew and passengers and claimed what was left of the *Prosperity* as a prize, making those they rescued prisoners of war.[28]

Joseph, who was not even a seaman, and the crew were taken to Arras. His brother, Michael, somehow found out that Joseph was in France and a prisoner. He began a campaign of letter writing to French ministers that would last five years. Goulhot confirmed and reconfirmed that Joseph had been a passenger on the *Prosperity*, not on the crew. At last, in April 1813, the Emperor agreed to his release. By then, Joseph was a man of twenty-three and probably fluent in French. The explanation for the delay appears in the list of prison depots to which he was sent: Arras, Bitche, Sarrelibre. That he was sent to Bitche indicates that he was either a very fractious prisoner or that he had tried to escape. No one who tried to escape was granted clemency so, in truth, he was a lucky man.

Sailors of the United States Navy

It would seem natural to expect that men who had served in the United States Navy[29] would have been candidates for release. There were two such men, but neither was released.

Henry Green wrote a long, biographical letter to Fulwar Skipwith, given here in full:

> [This is] the Most Humble Petition of Henry Green A Man of Colour Born at Baltimore, in the year 1783 & Served to Sea, under the flag of the United States of America, particular on Board the States frigate La Insurgent Capt. Murry, on the Service of the United States of America, in the West indies, in the year 1798 in the capacity of Wardroom Servent, untill the beginning of 1800, when I received A violent injury by A fall, whose marks is visible, & I was discharged the Service, & in Febry 1803 I sailed from Baltimore, on board the Ship Baltimore, Capt. Smith, bound to Liverpool, & was unfortunately Cast away of Holy Head in Wales, where I went to Liverpool & Shipd myself on Board the Enterprize of Richmond in Virginia, Capt. Stanford, & Saild for

---

[28] Dossier on Joseph Allen. *Archives de la Guerre et Armée de Terre. Prisonniers de guerre français et étrangers*. SHDV. Yj34.

[29] Recall that there was no United States Navy from 1783, when the Continental Navy was disbanded, to 1794, when the Naval Act created a permanent, standing United States Navy, which had six frigates, the first of which was not launched until 1798.

America in March & in July following Sailed from Richmond, on Board the Same Ship Bound to London in August, I was impress at London Octr 15th against the Laws of Nations, & Sent on Board H. Britannick Majestys Ship Shannon, & Capt. Smith informed me he would procure my Liberty on the Ships coming into Port but the Shannon frigate was unfortunately cast away on the Coast of france & made prisoner of War, in the same situation is my fellow petitioner Stephen Sheerwood which I am well acquainted with as A Lawful American; I have frequently Applied for releife [relief, e.g. an allowance] but not being acquainted where to apply to untill lately Some of my countrymen have rec[eive]d releife & informd me where to make application to, as such I hope & trust your honour will Lay my distressed Situation before His Excellency the Plenipotentiary for the United States of America in hopes his Excellency, will take into Consideration my unavoidable Missfortunes, & long Captivity; likewise my long Servitude in the Service of the United States & grant me some releife as my distress is great, & I scorn to go in any Service of my own free will, unless my country calls me in Defence of the Lawful rights of my Country's Cause. I then would cheerfully Venture wherever I might be sent, on board what ever States Ship of War they might think proper to send me, and I hope Hon. Sir, you of your goodness, will favour us with an answer and what his Excellency the Plenipotentiary of the United States may think fit to order us as we wish to abide by his instructions & govern ourselves accordingly & with the Greatest Submission most Humbly beg leave to Subscribe myself your Honour's poor unfortunate petitioner in the citadell of Valenciennes.

Valenciennes

Decr. 1st, 1806

P.S. A List of my Officers on Board the La Insurgent frigate belonging to the United States of America

Capt. Murry

1st Lieut. Mr. King

2nd. D[itt]o Mr. Roberts

Surgeon Mr. Cunningham

Purser Mr. Hughes

I being at the time in the capacity of Wardroom Servent untill Discharged unserviceable[30]

---

[30] Green to Skipwith. 1 December 1806. Fulwar Skipwith Papers.

Like so many seamen, Green was a remarkable survivor. Not only did he survive his fall on board the *Insurgent,* but that "violent injury" and his subsequent dismissal saved his life. The *Insurgent*'s next voyage was a return to patrolling the West Indies seas. Sometime in September 1800, it was hit by a tropical storm and lost, along with the entire crew.[31] Green was very lucky not to have been aboard. He then survived two wrecks, the first, when the *Baltimore* was rammed by the *Northumberland* and sunk in the Holyhead harbour in late 1802 and the second, a year later, when the sparkling new *Shannon*, onto which he had been impressed, smashed on to the rocks off a French island in a storm. He was amongst the crew who were rescued and marched to French prison depots.[32]

He appears to have survived eleven years as a prisoner of war in France, all of them in the depot at Valenciennes. Though Fulwar Skipwith wrote that he took a "deep interest" in Green's case, he was not able to secure his release.[33] Given that he had no papers on him when he was captured to prove that he was American and that he had been serving on an enemy naval vessel, the French authorities had no reason to believe he was not British. It is not clear if the French authorities knew that he was American and offered him the chance to sign on to a French privateer but, as he wrote, he would have "scorned" to serve France in that way.

There is no record that Henry Green received any of the briefly given aid from the American legation but he may possibly have received some from the Committee for Relief. He does not appear under his own name in their 1812 publication, but a "Jeremiah Green", born in London, of the *Shannon*, held at Valenciennes, did receive aid. If the two Greens, Henry and Jeremiah, were one and the same man, which is not at all certain (neither appears in the prison registers), then he would have had some regular allowance to ease his long years in prison. That he did survive is almost certain. Well after the wars ended, in 1819, a "Henry Green, mulatto, born in Baltimore, aged thirty-eight" made a citizenship affidavit in New York so that he could receive a new Seaman's Protection Certificate.[34]

John Nehill wrote at least three times to Skipwith from the prison depot at Arras, saying that he had been the carpenter's mate on the USS *Philadelphia* when it was captured at Tripoli and the crew taken prisoner. He said he then

---

[31] Grocott, *Shipwrecks*, p97.

[32] Grocott, *Shipwrecks*, p162.

[33] Note on the back of Green's letter of 1 December 1806. Fulwar Skipwith Papers.

[34] United States. Citizenship Affidavits of US-born Seamen at Select Ports, 1792–1869. Quarterly Abstracts. New York. Ancestry.com [Accessed 7 November 2021]. Original Publication: *Proofs of Citizenship Used to Apply for Seamen's Certificates for the Port of Philadelphia, Pennsylvania, 1792–1861*. NARA Microfilm publication M2003, roll 1, frame 199. Records of the U.S. Customs Service, Record Group 36. NARA, Washington, D.C.

served on the USS *Constellation*. He was a carpenter on the *Lark* when it was taken by a French privateer off Cuba in February 1806. As recounted above, when he refused to join the privateer (and the pressure would have been intense, as carpenters were highly valued on all vessels), the captain "tore up" his papers, including his Seaman's Protection Certificate and his discharge papers from the United States Navy, signed by Captain William Bainbridge.[35] Because he had no papers and because the *Lark* was a British brig, he was not released.

A Prisoner in Algiers

On 25 July 1785, the schooner, *Maria*, of Boston, with a crew of just six men, was captured by a privateer and taken in to Algiers. They would form a part of the group of enslaved American seamen that Joel Barlow would claim to have rescued almost single-handedly. On the *Maria* was George F. Smith, from Philadelphia. Friends were able to pay his ransom and, after nine years of captivity, he was allowed to leave Algiers. He went back to sea without apparent incident until, in about 1806, the vessel he was on was captured by a French privateer and taken in to Amsterdam. He was marched to Arras, where he received some of the aid Skipwith was sending via the Widow Hurtrel, but that soon ended and his situation became desperate, as Stephen Clubb told:

> An unfortunate man, who told me he had suffered much in the service of the United States, and had been in slavery at Algiers, fell sick and went to the hospital. My wife often went to visit him, and found (I am sorry to say) that nothing ailed the man but the cravings of an empty stomach; he had twice been in the hospital before, was cured and sent to prison again, but for want of nourishing diet as often relapsed, and had not a cent to buy a bit of bread... [36]

Barnet described him as an "old shipmaster"; Clubb thought he looked "prison-worn". He was moved to Valenciennes when the Arras depot was closed. After six years, in 1812, the French finally agreed to his release, but the poor man's troubles were not yet over. He went to Cherbourg to board the *Mary & Eliza* and then endure a voyage of exceptional tribulation. *The Evening Post* reported on 23 January 1813:

> Letter of marque brig Mary & Eliza, 16 guns and 35 men, capt. John White, 61 days from Cherbourg...Was chased one day in the chops of the channel by two [British] frigates. On the 22nd of Nov. was chased by a frigate, and escaped by throwing the guns and anchors overboard, and starting [to throw overboard] part of the water. On

---

[35] Nehill to Skipwith. 10 December 1806, 4 February 1807. Fulwar Skipwith Papers.
[36] Clubb, "A Journal", p189.

> Brown's bank was chased by a brig from 7 A.M. to 5 P.M. when we lost sight of the chace…The Mary & Eliza has experienced extreme heavy gales from the westward, having been obliged to lay too 22 days in the passage.[37]

Smith had already spent a total of fifteen years as a prisoner in Algiers and France; he should have been delighted to have avoided being captured by the British and becoming a prisoner for a third time.

In conclusion, there really was not that much compassion, at least not enough to warrant the release of men who really were suffering more than the others. Green and Nehill were probably not released until the end of the wars in 1814. The others, Crippin, Strawbridge, Homans, Allen and Smith, were released in late 1812, a few months after the United States had declared war. It would appear that compassionate releases were possible only once the United States was also fighting France's enemy. Ordinary passengers on enemy vessels, however, did not need to wait for war. By virtue of their passive presence on the vessel, they were accepted by the French as not supporting the enemy and were allowed to leave.

---

[37] *The Evening Post*, New York, 23 January 1813, p3, column 2.

8

TRADING INFORMATION FOR FREEDOM

A few prisoners discovered that giving information about the British to the French could help prove that they were not British. Desperate to get out of a prison depot, or to avoid being sent to one, they revealed whatever they knew about France's enemy.

The *Geneva Convention on the Treatment of Prisoners of War* was nearly a century and a half in the future. Article Seventeen of that convention states that

> No physical or mental torture, nor any other form of coercion, may be inflicted on prisoners of war to secure from them information of any kind whatever. Prisoners of war who refuse to answer may not be threatened, insulted, or exposed to any unpleasant or disadvantageous treatment of any kind.[1]

The belligerents of the European and American wars of the early nineteenth century would have laughed at such restriction. Brutality toward prisoners of war was exhibited on all sides. Seamen prisoners were starved into signing on to French privateers, heaped together in filth and misery on British hulks, left to starve and freeze, were severely beaten (as was Francis Felton) or shut in the dungeons and prisons of their captors. Though it was standard behaviour, the captors usually had enough sense of what human decency should be to have been ashamed and not to have recorded their own brutality. The documents do not state that the American seamen were beaten or forced to give information but it may have been so. Alternatively, their experiences of forced labour or floggings on board Royal Navy vessels (of which many accounts have been recorded) may have been such that they willingly did what harm they could to the British cause.

---

[1] *International Committee of the Red Cross (ICRC), Geneva Convention Relative to the Treatment of Prisoners of War (Third Geneva Convention)*, 12 August 1949, 75 UNTS 135, available at: https://www.refworld.org/docid/3ae6b36c8.html [Accessed 27 October 2023].

The Courageous George D. Wilson

George D. Wilson was an eighteen-year-old African-American seaman, probably from Virginia, on the three-masted merchant vessel *Minerva*, when it was sailing the Channel in the winter of 1808–9. He was one of four Americans in the crew of nine. The *Minerva* was armed with two twelve-pounder carronades and two swivel guns, the captain clearly intending to defend the vessel and its cargo of shrimp, sugar, rum, cotton, coffee and cocoa should any privateers be encountered.[2] His guns did him no good when, on the cold January seas, two French lugger predators approached: the *Bucaille* and the *Princesse de Bologne*. In the fight that ensued, the captain of the *Minerva* was wounded and forced to surrender his vessel. The prize vessel was sent promptly into Calais, arriving the next day, the 10 January. The cargo and vessel were sold off quickly. The crew had been split up; all were sent to the prison depot of Arras, but arriving there on different dates between late January and late February, having done the march in the coldest months of the year. They may have bemoaned their bad luck but it could have been worse had they been held on the *Bucaille* longer for, a little over two weeks later, on 31 January, that privateer went down.

George D. Wilson arrived at Arras on 25 January 1809.[3] He joined a large contingent of American seamen, including the African-American, Bolen Briggs, another Virginian, who had arrived there a couple of months earlier, and who was about nine years older than Wilson. Within a few weeks, Wilson was transferred to the prison depot at Cambrai. There, with a few other Americans, he signed on to a French privateer, the *Bon Marcel*, sixteen guns, in August 1809. They would have formed part of a crew of sixty, under Captain Denis-Guillaume Lasalle, who had recently escaped from an English prison.[4] The *Bon Marcel* was captured by the British in late 1809, yet Wilson was still in prison in France, so it would appear that he did not join that privateer on its first and only cruise. The experience of signing the recruitment form clearly inspired him, for he repeatedly wrote to Clarke, the Minister of War, asking to be allowed to "serve France" on her privateers.[5]

---

[2] "Nouvelles de Maritime et de Commerce", *Journal du Commerce, de Politique et de Littérature du Département de l'Escaut*, 22 January 1809, No. 1113. *Annonces et avis divers du département de l'Escaut.* Goesin-Verhaeghe. (No page numbers).

[3] Records of the Admiralty, Naval Forces, Royal Marines, Coastguard, and related bodies, Records of Medical and Prisoner of War Departments, Navy Board and predecessors: Prisoner of War Department and predecessors: Registers of Prisoners of War, France. Nationality: British. Register of prisoners of war. Prisons A–G, ADM 103/467. "Prisoners of War 1715–1945 Napoleonic Wars", *Find My Past* [Accessed 22 March 2023].

[4] Henri Malo. *Les Corsaires: Mémoires et Documents Inédits.* Paris: Société du Mercure de France, 1908, p363.

[5] Dossier on George Wilson. *Archives de la Guerre et Armée de Terre. Prisonniers de guerre français et étrangers (1792–1874).* SHDV. Yj79.

He had no Seaman's Protection Certificate but he constantly asserted that he was American. However, he gave his place of birth differently, according to his needs. He told the Committee for Relief that he was from Glasgow, and he received an allowance from them.[6] On the Arras prison entry register, his place of birth is given as Gibraltar.[7] When he signed up for the *Bon Marcel*, he gave his place of birth as Baltimore. When he wrote to the Minister of War, he said that he was a "native of Petersburg" in Virginia.[8]

At some point, he must have attempted to escape, or perhaps he was a fractious and troublesome prisoner at Cambrai, for he was transferred to Bitche. From there, in November 1811, he was sent to Briançon, another of Vauban's fortresses turned prisoner of war depot, in the mountains in the southeast of France, near Italy. Being at an altitude of more than 1300 meters and at the confluence of five rivers, the climate there was cold and damp. Lewis, quoting Stewart, tells of overcrowding and no outdoor exercise. The prison was so snowbound and the roads so icy that the guards apparently did not worry when prisoners escaped in the winter. They let them freeze in the illusion of freedom for a couple of days, then strolled out to collect the weakened and shivering escapees, or their corpses.[9]

By October 1812, Wilson had been at Briançon for at least a year with no prospect of release. Goulhot, in his report to Clarke, best tells how Wilson tried to convince the authorities that he was not British.

> The Commandant of the depot at Briançon gives an account...that one Wilson, American, detained as an English prisoner of war, has unveiled an escape plot which could have been serious. The prisoners locked down in the fort of Trois Têtes [part of the Briançon complex] had managed to saw with the iron spoke of a wheel, the iron grills placed across the fireplaces of two rooms, and had bought 13 yards of new canvas, with which they had already made a ladder. They had planned to throw the Commandant of the fort from the ramparts if he made any resistance. Their preparations were made with such care that the turnkey charged with ascertaining the condition of the fireplace grills could not see that they were sawn because the prisoners had covered them with putty; it was only with the information from Wilson about the grill and the ladder that the plot and the guilty were

---

[6] *Report from the Committee for the Relief*, p89.

[7] Records of the Admiralty, Naval Forces, Royal Marines, Coastguard, and related bodies, Records of Medical and Prisoner of War Departments, Navy Board and predecessors: Prisoner of War Department and predecessors: Registers of Prisoners of War, France. Nationality: British. Register of prisoners of war. Prisons A–G, ADM 103/467. "Prisoners of War 1715–1945 Napoleonic Wars", *Find My Past* [Accessed 22 March 2023].

[8] Dossier on George Wilson. *Archives de la Guerre et Armée de Terre. Prisonniers de guerre français et étrangers (1792–1874)*. SHDV. Yj79.

[9] Lewis, *Napoleon and His British Captives*, pp158–159.

discovered. [As the escape began, Wilson sent a note to the guards he had warned, saying "Come now!" All those who had attempted the escape were thrown into the dungeon, including Wilson, to avoid their suspecting him of being the traitor. However, they soon worked out that it was he and, suddenly, his life was in danger.]

The Commandant of the depot says that he cannot hide Wilson from the fury of the prisoners and has placed him in the civil prison, and he declares that he cannot, without danger to him, return Wilson to the English depot. I beg Your Excellency to let me know if, after verifying the American origins of Wilson, we could hand him over to the Minister Plenipotentiary of the United States to facilitate his return to his country.[10]

This may be the only case in which Goulhot proposed the release of an American who had not yet been claimed by the Minister Plenipotentiary. In betraying the British prisoners, Wilson had found a way to remove all doubts in the minds of his French jailers (except that of Decrès, of course) that he could be British or a British sympathizer. It would seem that this method, of exposing British escape plots, was open to many others in the depots, since quite a few British prisoners did escape, but only Wilson appears to have had the courage, or perhaps the desperation, to risk the vengeance of those whose plot he exposed in order to get out. Goulhot, apparently impressed by Wilson's bravery, suggested kindly treatment for him while he awaited release. "We could, while waiting, place him at Grenoble and give him a junior officer's prison pay of 100 francs." Clarke agreed to this and Wilson was sent to Grenoble while the French authorities decided what to do with him. There, the local commandant said that Wilson would be a good addition to the French Navy. However, Decrès wrote in response to this idea "that a foreigner who was on the crew of a British ship may not be assigned to a ship of His Serene Majesty [Napoleon]". By this point, the United States had been at war with Great Britain for six months and a number of American seamen had been released to march to Brest and crew the American privateer there. It was decided that Wilson should be sent to Brest to join them.

Impressed Americans and the Toulon Conspiracy

Where the Rhone River flows into the Mediterranean Sea, the river's fresh water collects in pools and lagoons that dot the sand spits to the east of the mouth of the river, far from the shore and its towns. The commanders of the British fleet blockading Marseilles and Toulon had discovered this and

---

[10] Dossier on George Wilson. *Archives de la Guerre et Armée de Terre. Prisonniers de guerre français et étrangers (1792–1874)*. SHDV. Yj79.

regularly sent in their boats to take on fresh water from the lagoons. On 8 July 1812, the *Undaunted* (the same frigate that would later transport Napoleon to Elba) sent in seven armed boats of seamen to collect water. One boat was also to collect sand for scrubbing the decks. On it, two midshipmen supervised ten American seamen, not knowing that they had planned their escape.

In the late afternoon, the midshipmen fell asleep on the beach in the summer sun and the Americans took their chance. They extinguished the fuses for the weapons and ran toward a fisherman's boat lying on the beach. The midshipmen awoke, relit the fuse and fired at them, but missed. The escapees rowed upriver in the direction of the town of Port-Saint-Louis, landed and hid behind a sand dune. Such escapes on those spits were not unusual. The previous year, a group of Irish seamen had deserted the Royal Navy at the same place and, regularly, single individuals who had made a dash for freedom were picked up on the dunes. So, when a fisherman named Garcin found them, he knew what to do.

Careful not to touch them, for fear of infectious disease, he took them to the nearby Tour Saint-Louis, where the health officer, Pierre Giot, in charge of quarantining arriving seamen, took charge of them.[11] Plague was still very much a menace in the early nineteenth century, especially at Mediterranean ports. The French had established lazarettos at all of their main ports on the southern coast, and at many of the smaller ones. There, all people arriving by sea, passengers as well as crew, had to stay for two weeks of observation, at their own expense. Only those who appeared to be in good health were allowed to leave the lazaretto to enter France. Originally built in the eighteenth century to house customs offices and to hold captured smugglers, the Tour Saint-Louis was a small, stone tower then being used as the lazaretto for arrivals at the mouth of the Rhone.

Giot placed the American seamen under guard in the tower and immediately wrote to his superior. His report exemplifies the confusion and conflation of the British and the Americans; he referred to them as "ten Englishmen, all American", "English seamen" or "anglo-americans". His superior responded with the usual insistence that the captives prove that they were Americans. Only two of the seamen had their "documents", meaning their Seaman's Protection Certificates. Even though Giot hired an interpreter, their names were

---

[11] Pierre Giot was a captain in the French Marine who had been given an administrative position toward the end of his career. Literate and intelligent, he left a number of papers, log books and letters, covering his career during the Revolution and Napoleonic Wars. These have been published, with superb commentary, and are the main source for the details of the ten American seamen's first days in captivity. Patricia Payn-Echalier and Philippe Rigaud, *Pierre Giot: Capitain marin arlésian "dans la tourmante", journal, livre de bord, correspondance, 1792–1816*. Presses universitaires de Provence, 2017, pp175–190. http//books.openedition.org/pup/44378 [Accessed 7 January 2023].

initially garbled, giving a fine example of the identification problems created by the language barrier, especially at the smaller ports. John Taylor was written as Jean Telle, Andrew Wilson became André Desson, John Wright became Jean Ray, William Richardson was Guillaume Velehisson, Jonathan Johnson was Janeson Sanselme, John Williams was Jean Guillaume, Charles Smith became Charles Esme, Job Ellis Brewster became Alexis Brestel, Edward Bartlett became Edouard Barthene and William Pearson became Guillaume Pelson.[12] It is worth noting that the scribe on the *Undaunted* had followed Royal Navy practice and had intentionally falsified the men's identities. The logbook of the *Undaunted* does not state that any of the escapees were American. Of the names listed as "men's names deserted from the barge", only William Richardson is given under his true name; the other nine names are so completely different that it is impossible to know which man was which.[13]

Giot was an unusually kind-hearted jailer. He begged his superiors to authorize more food for the seamen. When only bread and water were approved for them, he protested, with a prophetic warning. "These deserters are not criminals to be given only bread and water. They arrived here in good health but, if we starve them, they will become ill."[14] Giot obtained proper rations for them from the captain of the gunboat guarding the mouth of the Rhone, the *Tonnante*. In addition to the bread and water, they received wine, cheese and vegetables. Even so, the Americans complained that they were being treated "like animals" and that they never imagined that the French could treat them worse than the British had done. They also had almost no clothing. They explained that they had brought nothing with them from the *Undaunted*, not even shoes, in order to give no hint of their escape plan. Giot requested and was able to obtain clothes and shoes for them. However, in an era when the process of infection was not understood, neither Giot nor his captives knew how dangerous to the latter it could be to sleep in the place where people with plague and other diseases had been quarantined. Plague is spread by fleas living on rats and there surely were rats in that tower. Typhus is spread by lice and, if the straw on which the men slept or the clothing

---

[12] Payn-Echalier and Rigaud, *Pierre Giot*, p180.

[13] Entry for 8 July 1812. Records of the Admiralty, Naval Forces, Royal Marines, Coastguard, and related bodies, Records of HM Ships. Admiralty and Ministry of Defense. Navy Department: Ships' Logs. Undaunted, 13 March 1812–4 February 1813. TNA. ADM 53/1452. The nine false names were: John Cook, Castey Heppen, Jonathan Hanson, Thomas Webster, John Thompson, John Dunn, Ambrose Duffield, Erick Kraft and John Wood. Recall that the men's true names were: John Taylor, Edward Bartlett, Job Ellis Brewster, Jonathan Johnson, William Pearson, Charles Smith, John Williams, Andrew Wilson and John Wright.

[14] Payn-Echalier and Rigaud, *Pierre Giot*, p178.

they were given contained infected lice, they would become ill too. Sadly, something like this is what would happen.

With the help of the interpreter, Giot arranged for the men to write to the United States consular agent at Marseilles, Etienne Cathalan. He wrote back that he would cover all costs of feeding and clothing these Americans, once those who did not have their Seaman's Protection Certificates could prove that they were, truly, American. On 17 July, a French naval official came from Marseilles to interview them. They had already given their names, ages and places of birth. Now poured forth everything they knew about British naval activity in the Mediterranean.

They said that the *Undaunted* (which was at first misunderstood by the French to be the *Ardent*) carried fifty-two twenty-four pounders, had a crew of 270 men and fifty marines. It was captained by Richard Thomas of Plymouth, who was thirty-five years old. They told of other vessels in the British fleet that was blockading Marseilles and Toulon.[15]

Only three months earlier, Thomas, with boats from the *Undaunted* and aided by the ships *Volontaire* and *Blossom*, had directed an attack on twenty-six French vessels at the mouth of the Rhone, destroying a large number of them.[16] (It is likely that some of the Americans giving this information to Giot had taken part in the attack.) The French knew that the attack, along with many other successful raids and attacks by the blockading British could not have been possible without detailed intelligence, but they could not discover the source.[17]

Then the Americans gave their most valuable and consequential piece of information. This was that, occasionally, when the ship signalled with a red flag held in front of a lamp, a small fishing boat sailing from Maire Island, in the south of the Marseilles anchorage, would come up. Two French men dressed as fishermen came aboard and remained for two or three days during each visit. Though they may have been aware that this information was important, the Americans could not have known just how important it was. They gave two crucial details that would allow the police to discover a plot to foment a royalist uprising against Napoleon in the south: the signal on the *Undaunted* that called the spies and which of the many small islands

---

[15] Payn-Echalier and Rigaud, *Pierre Giot*, p175.

[16] William Richard O'Byrne. *A Naval Biographical Dictionary Comprising the Life and Services of Every Living Officer in Her Majesty's Navy, From the Rank of Admiral of The Fleet to That of Lieutenant, Inclusive. Compiled from Authentic and Family Documents.* London: John Murray, 1849. https://en.wikisource.org/wiki/A_Naval_Biographical_Dictionary [Accessed 21 May 2023].

[17] Edouard Guillon. *Les complots militaires sous le Consulat et l'Empire: d'après les documents inédits des archives.* Paris: E. Plon, Nourrit, 1894, p217; "*Affaire Charabot, espionnage*". Arch. nat. F/7/6578.

was their point of departure. A few nights later, the police lay in wait at Maire Island and, when the signal appeared and a fishing boat prepared to sail, they pounced, arresting a young naval officer named Joseph Charabot.

What became known as the "Toulon Conspiracy" was, through the involvement of General Joseph Guidal, linked to the Malet Coup that would take place in Paris in October of that year. Elizabeth Sparrow wrote of the British involvement through their fleet in the Mediterranean:

> Guidal…had moved to Marseilles, where he had made contact with Admiral Sir Charles Cotton in 1811, requesting British naval assistance for the royalist partisans. The admiral approved his plan and… described General Guidal as "worthy of the most entire confidence, to be charged with the Correspondence between the Royalist party in the Midi and the English fleet before Toulon; and to carry various instructions to the King's partisans; that he was employed for the same purpose in the years 1811 and 1812…".[18]

Amongst Guidal's co-conspirators was his wife's cousin, Antoine Charabot, the father of Joseph.

Joseph Charabot was sent to the prison in the Palace of Justice in Marseilles. The police search continued for his father (who was hiding on the *Undaunted*) and for other conspirators. The American seamen had also been sent to Marseilles, where they were held in another coastal tower, the Fort Saint Nicolas, an older, larger, damper and grimmer place than the Tour Saint-Louis. Here, the health officer's predictions began to come true. On 13 August, Charles Smith, from Cape Ann in Massachusetts and twenty-eight years old, succumbed to the bad food, bad lodging and possible bad treatment.[19] Two others, William Richardson and Edward Bartlett, were very ill. (The latter suffered from "extreme dropsy".)

On 11 and 12 September, the seven Americans in good enough health were taken to the Palace of Justice. There, each identified Joseph Charabot as one of the spies who had come aboard the *Undaunted* and each of them gave a statement. The statements were all quite similar, were all made through the same interpreter and all repeated the claims of their original statements to Giot.[20] Johnson added that he had been one of the seamen to escort Charabot from the *Undaunted* to the *Blossom*, to meet with "the English Admiral".[21] The following day, William Richardson died. The rest of the men stayed in the fort as the trial dragged on. On 17 November, Cathalan wrote in his

---

[18] Sparrow, *Secret Service*, p393.
[19] Marseilles, 4, *Actes de décès, août 1812* (death of Charles Smith), 14 August 1812, AD Bouches du Rhône, https://www.archives13.fr/n/consulter-les-archives-numerisees/n:1 [Accessed 31 March 2022].
[20] *Affaire Charabot, espionnage*. Arch. nat. F/7/6578.
[21] Personnel file of Joseph Charabot. SHDV. MV/CC/7 ALPHA 450.

consular dispatches that he was still paying for the eight surviving men, whom the French would not yet release.[22] They must have been released soon afterward because one of them, Job Ellis Brewster, was on the brig, *Mars*, from Baltimore bound for Bordeaux in February 1813, when it was captured by the *Warspite*. After only a few months of freedom from French jails, Brewster was again a prisoner of war. He was sent to Dartmoor Prison, where he remained until the end of the War of 1812.[23] Having gone from being impressed by the British, to being a detained witness held in jails by the French, he was, almost immediately, again a prisoner, now of the British. After his release, he returned to Massachusetts, married and had a family. He died at sea in 1833.[24]

Of all in this group, only William Richardson had already been, briefly, a prisoner in France before his escape from the *Undaunted*. Three years earlier, in October 1809, he was a seaman on the *Polly* when it was captured by the French privateer, *San Joseph*, and brought in to Morlaix. He immediately signed on to the capturing privateer and never went to a prison depot.[25] After eleven months on the privateer, appearing in the *San Joseph* pay list as "William Richard", he was paid over 667 francs of prize money.[26] He was on the prize crew of the captured *Antonia Maria*, sailed it in, and returned to the *San Joseph*. A few days later, the *San Joseph*'s rather brilliant career ended when it was captured by the *Rhin*.[27] Richardson, along with most of the crew, was put on the *Wolverine* and taken in to England a month later. He was entered into the register for Portchester Prison, where he may have been put on a hulk. The register describes a young man of six feet seven inches tall, an extraordinarily unusual height for anyone but especially for a seaman, with a round, fair-skinned face scarred by smallpox, blond hair and blue eyes.[28]

---

[22] Cathalan Accounting Report. 17 November 1812. 234. United States. Department of State. *Despatches from United States Consuls in Marseilles, 1790–1906*. Vol. 2. Microfilm copy.

[23] General Entry Book of American prisoners of war at Dartmoor Prison, April 1813–May 1814, ADM 103/87. "Prison Ship Records from the War of 1812". British Online Archives. https://microform.digital/boa/collections/58/prison-ship-records-from-the-war-of-1812 [Accessed 22 November 2023].

[24] Emma C. Brewster Jones. *The Brewster Genealogy, 1566–1907, a Record of the Descendants of William Brewster*…New York: Grafton, 1908, p375.

[25] *Prisonniers de Guerre à Morlaix, 9 octobre 1809. Archives de la Marine, Prises – Bâtiments de l'État et corsaires*. SHDV. FF2/10.

[26] *Archives de la Marine, Prises (1794–1871), Etats des répartitions, 1811*. SHDB. 2Q 168.

[27] High Court of Admiralty: Prize Court: Prize Papers. Ships names beginning with this letter: S. *San Joseph*. TNA, HCA 32/1193.

[28] Records of the Admiralty, Naval Forces, Royal Marines, Coastguard, and related bodies, Records of Medical and Prisoner of War Departments, Navy Board and predecessors: Prisoner of War Department and predecessors: Registers of Prisoners of War,

He endured four months as a prisoner of war in England, and then, on 27 February 1811, he signed up to the Royal Navy, along with another New Yorker from the *San Joseph* crew named Benjamin Grune. He served Great Britain for seventeen months before he escaped from the *Undaunted* with the others and found himself in France again, imprisoned again. His cause of death is not stated in the documentation but it does state that he was unmarried and twenty-five years old.[29] It is unlikely that his parents, named as John and Bessie Richardson, ever knew what happened to their giant of a son.

In summary, American seamen who freely and fully gave information about enemy activity to the French were able, by that very action, to convince them that they were not British and were not working for the British. They took enormous risks in doing so. The ten American seamen of the *Undaunted* risked French prisons if they were not believed (and two of them died in jails while they were waiting to give evidence) and severe flogging were they to have failed in their escape and been returned to the *Undaunted*. George D. Wilson risked the wrath of his fellow inmates had he not been removed from prison for his own safety by the French. Morieux wrote that "There were many means by which the prisoners could punish the traitors among them." He added that "Ratting on one's companions in captivity was risky, and the ultimate punishment could be death."[30]

To these American seamen, however, the one in prison with British prisoners of war and the ten impressed by the British, there was, it is likely, no sense of having betrayed for they had no sense of companionship or loyalty to the British. Wilson was acting in October 1812, four months after the United States declared war against Great Britain. He almost certainly would have known of the war by then and most likely would have considered the British as the enemy. It is unlikely that the Americans from the *Undaunted* had heard of the declaration of war, on 18 June 1812, when they escaped on 8 July, though it is likely that they had heard some of the many rumours of war that had been circulating for months beforehand. Their primary impetus was the desire to be free of the Royal Navy. In both cases, the French gave no rewards for the information, except freedom.

Portchester Register of Prisoners of War, Certificates. ADM 103/645. "Prisoners of War 1715–1945 Napoleonic Wars", *Find My Past* [Accessed 20 March 2023].

[29] Marseilles, 4, *Actes de décès, septembre 1812* (death of William Richardson). 13 September 1812. AD Bouches du Rhône, https://www.archives13.fr/n/consulter-les-archives-numerisees/n:1 [Accessed 31 March 2022].

[30] Morieux, *The Society of Prisoners*, p319.

9

FIGHTING FOR THE FRENCH

For the prisoners, there was, of course, always the idea of escape, but it was not as simple or easy a thing to achieve as many of the contemporary accounts by British escapees might seem to indicate.[1] Though some British prisoner accounts tell of escapes from the fortresses by climbing out of windows or leaping down walls, most escapees were British officers who were on parole, a privilege not available to most American seamen. These officers were already outside the fortress, having permission to live in town, and were allowed to stroll or ride, even to hunt, outside of the town's perimeters. Many of these British officer escapees simply went out for a stroll one day and did not return. They also used ruses and hired carriages, wore costumes and obtained false papers, had paid tutors to teach them to speak French, all of which cost more money than the American seaman prisoner ever could have hoped to have.

---

[1] For some contemporary accounts of escapes by British prisoners, many of them from the officers' depot of Verdun, see Seacome Ellison. *Prison Scenes; and Narrative of an Escape from France, During the Late War* (Whittaker, 1838); the anonymous account in *Escape from France: A Narrative of the Hardships and Sufferings of Several British Subjects, who effected their escape from Verdun* (1808); Edward Boys. *Narrative of a Captivity, Escape and Adventure in France and Flanders between the years 1803 and 1809* (Richard Long, 1827); George Richard Casse. *Authentic Narrative of the Sufferings of George Richard Casse, as a prisoner in France, during the late war; and of his escape to the Allied Army* (J. Mason, 1828); James Choyce. *The Log of a Jack Tar; or, the Life of James Choyce, Master Mariner* (Unwin, 1891); Joshua Done, who escaped eight times. "Narrative of Done's Imprisonment in France" in *London Magazine* (1826); James Forbes. *Letters from France written in the Years 1803 and 1804, including a particular account of Verdun, and the situation of the British Captives in that City* (J. White, 1806); Peter Gordon. *Narrative of the Imprisonment and Escape of Peter Gordon; Comprising a Journal of the Author's Adventures in his flight through French Territory, from Cambrai to Rotterdam; and thence to the English Coast* (1816); Maurice Hewson. *Escape from the French, Captain Hewson's Narrative, 1803–1809* (Sevenoaks: Hodder and Stoughton, 1981); George Vernon Jackson. *The Perilous Adventures and Vicissitudes of a Naval Officer, 1801–1812; Being part of the Memoirs of Admiral George Vernon Jackson (1787–1876)* (Blackwood, 1927); Edward Proudfoot Montagu. *The Personal Narrative of the Escape of Edward Proudfoot MONTAGU, an English Prisoner of War, from the Citadel of Verdun* (1849).

Most importantly, for the British escapee, home was not all that far away; once he reached the coast, he needed only a fishing boat to take him out to the Royal Navy's blockading vessels and he would be free.

For the American seaman escapee, he would have to get to a port without detection and find an American vessel to take him home by a route that would avoid not only French harbour patrols but also the Royal Navy vessels, which could have impressed him. Nevertheless, between sixty and seventy American prisoners escaped, of whom just twenty-one may have successfully escaped the French Empire. (The names of the escapees are given in Appendix B.) The rest were recaptured, and one of them, Thomas Hudson of Boston, suffered the severe punishment of being condemned to six years in irons for escaping with a false passport.[2] No account of an American escape from a depot or fortress has surfaced, but almost all of those whose escapes were successful made their breaks for freedom while on temporary release to crew a French privateer.

This use of prison labour at sea occurred when the prisoners were recognized by their French captors as being American and neutral (but who would not be released because they had been captured from a British vessel). At times, these men were offered the temporary release of working on a French privateer. Because so many French seamen had been captured and were held in prisons in Britain, the French were finding it increasingly difficult to man their vessels.[3] The Marine did its best to fill its ranks through naval conscription, and tried to keep its sailors with threats of harsh punishment of any deserters, as well as issuing fines to any captains of merchant vessels or privateers that employed naval deserters. On rare occasions, even the Marine used prisoner seamen of neutral nationalities.[4] However, this was discouraged and, were any Americans found to have been forced, impressed, into the French Navy, Napoleon made a great show of ordering their releases immediately. French merchant vessels hired whatever seamen they found in ports; as numerous

---

[2] *Registre du Bagne de Brest*, Register 2 O 23, online image 86, *Bibliothèque numérique du Centre de recherche bretonne et celtique* (CRBC) [Accessed 26 January 2024].

[3] British vessels were suffering the same shortage of manpower and also turned to prisoners. See Patricia K. Crimmin. "Prisoners of War and British Port Communities, 1793–1815" *The Northern Mariner/Le Marin du Nord*, Vol. VI, No. 4 (October 1996); and the account of William Richardson, above, who was recruited by the Royal Navy in prison.

[4] In 1811 Vice-Admiral Missiessy proposed to Decrès to employ on the *Charlemagne* Spanish prisoners of war then working on the fortifications of Antwerp. 25. *Archives de la Marine. dépôt des archives, conseils, cabinet du ministre, commissions.* SHDV. MV BB 8 / 2727-362.

crew lists attest, the resultant crews were multinational and included American merchant seamen.

With naval and merchant vessels hiring most of the available seamen, owners of privateers had to look elsewhere for their crews, especially in 1808 and 1809, when French privateering activity surged. Le Goff writes that French privateers had a long history of signing foreigners onto their crews, at least as early as the mid-eighteenth century.[5] The French rules for privateering allowed for a vessel's crew to be up to two fifths foreigners[6] but with foreign seamen becoming scarce, French agents of privateers were given permission to visit the prison depots where seamen of neutral nationalities were to be found and to coax them to gain a few weeks of temporary freedom sailing on a French privateer and attacking British shipping.[7] An additional reason for Napoleon permitting recruitment at this particular moment was that he had closed the depot of Arras, considering it to be too close to the coast, and had the prisoners marched to the remaining depots, making those prisons quite overcrowded. The recruiters signed up seamen of various neutral nationalities, including Portuguese, Spanish and American. One Saint Malo recruiter signed up over sixty Spanish and Portuguese mariners from the depot at Auxonne.[8] The French privateer, *François*, had a crew of "French, Americans, Danes and Swedes",[9] some of whom were prisoners from the depot of Cambrai. In the same way that Napoleon viewed prisoners of war as manpower for public works projects, so they could be the much-needed manpower on private armed vessels.

The recruiters for French privateers visited the prison depots of Cambrai, Givet and Valenciennes.[10] They offered men the opportunity to work on a privateer during a limited period of time, the length of a cruise under a Letter of Marque usually being from three to six months. Nearly 250 American seamen took up the offer, many of them more than once. It can be imagined that, after months or years in a prison depot, the thoughts of better food, sea air, prize money and, most of all, possible opportunities of escape, were

---

[5] Le Goff, "The Labour Market for Sailors in France", p299.

[6] *Imprimerie de la République (Paris)*. "*Réglement Sur les Armemens en course*", Saint-Cloud, *2 Prairial, an XI* [22 May 1803] p4.

[7] This is comparable to the Transport Board allowing recruitment agents from the Royal Navy and from foreign, allied armies to enter British prisoner of war depots. See the case of William Richardson, above, and Paul Chamberlain, "The Release of Prisoners of War from Britain in 1813 and 1814", *Napoleonica. La Revue,* 3:21 (2014) 118–129, p124.

[8] F. Robidou. *Les Derniers Corsaires Malouins: La Course Sous la République et l'Empire, 1793–1814*. Rennes and Paris: Oberthur, 1919, pp27–28.

[9] High Court of Admiralty: Prize Court: Prize Papers. Ships names beginning with this letter: F. *François*. TNA, HCA 32/1035.

[10] Rouanet, *Prisonniers de Napoléon*, p42.

very tempting. Some men signed on out of desperation. A group of seamen at Arras wrote to Skipwith in 1807, when his payments ceased, "There is no more assistance to come and no clearance [release], so we have entered into the French service."[11] In the same way, in 1811, Peter Carver, a prisoner at Cambrai, wrote to Russell with a list of the names of sixteen American prisoners who were doing the same.[12] Indeed, a prisoner could request to be allowed to work on a privateer. The procedure, as described by Rouanet, was straightforward: he wrote a letter to the Minster of War. Goulhot would check the man's details and advise the Minister. Those most often approved were "model prisoners", of a neutral nationality and among those considered to be in need, e.g., not receiving aid.[13] If the Minister approved, he sent his confirmation to the commandant of the depot where the man was held.[14]

At Verdun, the Reverend Wolfe was surprised but should not have been when he learned of an American seaman who took the opportunity to get out of prison by joining a French privateer. As the seaman told Wolfe, he saw no reason to remain in prison "for a cause which was not that of his country".[15] Wolfe's disapproval would have been stronger in the cases of the somewhat treasonous efforts of the equally desperate British prisoners who, like poor John Wiltshire, by pretending to be American, tried to join French privateers attacking British vessels. The British seaman, Thomas Williams, at Givet was one such, though unsuccessful, and wrote:

> ...the Captain of a French privateer came to the prison to get a crew of foreigners to man his ship, then at Morlaix. Now, as I was registered on the books as an Englishman, I could not go, and not knowing how to act, I at length agreed with an old American, called Thomas Aldridge, of New York, to exchange names in the depot....away we went, about twenty of us of various nations; but before we got far... we were conducted back to the dismal prison...[16]

Some men signed on directly with the privateer that captured their merchant vessel, avoiding going to a prison depot. This was not something new in warfare and had been practiced by other nations: "Many British sailors returning from captivity testified that they had been kept on board the French and Dutch ships

---

[11] Goodman and others. 31 May 1807. Fulwar Skipwith Papers.

[12] Carver to Russell. 15 September 1811. Jonathan Russell Papers.

[13] This would indicate that the French were well aware of which American prisoners were receiving British aid from the Committee for Relief.

[14] Rouanet, *Prisonniers de Napoléon*, p265.

[15] Wolfe, *English Prisoners in France*, p12.

[16] John Tregerthen Short and Thomas Williams. *Prisoners of War in France from 1804 to 1814: Being the Adventures of John Tregerthen Short and Thomas Williams of St Ives, Cornwall*. London: Duckworth, 1914, p79.

of war that had captured them, and forced to work among the captor's crew."[17] Thomas Maky, of Norfolk in Virginia, was a forty-year-old cook on the *Sally* when it was captured by the French privateer, *Adolphe,* in late 1807.[18] They landed at Cherbourg on 13 November. Two weeks later, Maky's name was on the *Adolphe*'s crew list.[19] Of the fifteen American seamen on the crew of the *San Joseph* (which captured the *Exertion*, as mentioned above), in 1809 and 1810, commanded by the experienced privateersman Joseph Wittewronghel, nine of them were not sent from prison depots and probably joined the crew of their captor immediately; six of them had been on the crews of two vessels that the *San Joseph* had just captured and sent in to Morlaix, the *Brutus* and the *Polly*. Four of those six, Louis Fourca and Peter Mark, both of New Orleans, Thomas Stewart of Camden in New Jersey, and William Richard (actually William Richardson, the same man of the *Undaunted* group, above), were duly paid at the end of the cruise and then sent to prison depots, from which some of them signed on to work on privateers again. The other two, Louis Friançon of New Orleans and Thomas Rively of Newport in Rhode Island, chose escape over prize money. They somehow managed to leave the *San Joseph*, abandoning their pay, and never appear in the prisoner lists.[20]

The pay would certainly have been an incentive for a prisoner to sign on to a privateer. Generally, the prisoner seamen received their share of the prize money before they were returned to the depots, where it could make a significant difference to their lives. A seaman on a French privateer received a small, basic wage for the cruise, around 120 to 160 francs, most of it paid, as on merchant vessels in the United States, in advance.[21] If the privateer took a prize, however, his tiny proportion of the prize money could be no small sum.

The division of prize money was based on a system of parts that was agreed amongst the owners and the captain at the outset. In one typical example, the captain received twelve parts plus a sum equal to the value of the contents of the safe in the captured captain's cabin on the prize vessel; first lieutenants received eight parts, second lieutenants and surgeons six parts, and so on down to the seamen, who received less than one part. In one case, the seamen's

---

[17] Morieux, *The Society of Prisoners*, p153.

[18] *Guerre et Armée de Terre, Prisonniers de guerre français et étrangers* (1792–1874). SHDV. Yj30.

[19] High Court of Admiralty: Prize Court: Prize Papers. Ships names beginning with this letter: A. *Adolphe*. TNA, HCA 32/9571.

[20] *Archives de la Marine, Prises (1794–1871), Etats des répartitions, 1811*. SHDB. 2Q 168.

[21] Crowhurst, *The French War on Trade*. p155.

part came to only forty-two francs each.[22] However, for the prizes taken by the *San Joseph*, Peter Mark and Louis Fourca each received just under 445 francs and William Richard [Richardson] and Thomas Stewart each received over 667 francs. Thomas Rively would have received only 187 francs, which may partly explain his having run off.[23] In comparison with the three sous per month that an American seaman prisoner of war received in the depots, these were fortunes.

Working on the French privateers seems to have offered the best opportunity for escape. Joseph Illeman of New York, John Roberts and John Sinclair escaped from the *Loup Marin*. Antony Savage of Baltimore escaped at Dieppe from the *Etoile no. 2*. James Smith escaped from the *Persévérant*.[24] Some managed to jump ship in a port. The best opportunity came if a man were assigned to a prize crew, where he would be one of a small number taking a prize vessel to a French or allied port. Few willingly returned to the privateer but instead they slipped away.

William Cockrane, an African-American from Baltimore, may have been such a one who slipped away. He was prisoner number 5119 at Arras when he and five other American prisoners signed on to the privateer, *Comtesse d'Orsène*, in August 1809.[25] That privateer took at least six prizes, sending two in to Amsterdam to be sold, before it was caught by the British.[26] The Americans may have been on the crew of some of the prizes sent into a port for they seem not to have been on board the *Comtesse d'Orsène*, when it was caught, and their names do not appear in the British prison registers.

Those who may have been successful escapees are those who do not appear in the Ministry of War prisoner records again but there were many Americans who escaped from privateers only to be recaptured and returned to prison. It is clear that signing on to French privateers provided an opportunity of escape but not a guarantee of freedom.

Four American seamen, two of whom would escape, held at Valenciennes and Cambrai, signed a recruitment agreement in 1809 to be on the crew of the *Capricieux*, Captain Daugey. They were marched to Dieppe, where the vessel lay in port. They may have been weakened by the march and by their years in prison depots, or they may have feigned illness, for William Bassett

---

[22] *Ministère de la Marine. "Comptes du corsaire Le Spéculateur"*. Arch. nat. AB/XIX/3193.

[23] *Archives de la Marine, Prises (1794–1871), Etats des répartitions, 1811*. SHDB. 2Q 168.

[24] *Archives de la Marine. "Guerre de l'An II: Prisonniers neutres embarqués sur les corsaires An II"*. SHDV. FF2/104.

[25] *Archives de la Guerre et Armée de Terre. Prisonniers de guerre français et étrangers (1792–1874)*. SHDV. Yj30.

[26] Crowhurst, *The French War on Trade*, p109.

and Samuel Allen were sent immediately to hospital in Dieppe. Bassett, of Norfolk in Virginia, and Edward Gibbs, of Philadelphia, managed to escape in February 1810. How they got out of the country is not recorded. Samuel Allen, of Marblehead, and John Ward were in some way unsuitable to the shipmaster and were sent back to the depot.[27] Thus, they were not on board when the *Capricieux* was captured a few weeks later by the *Echo* and its crew sent to prison in Britain. Back at Cambrai, Allen, in spite of his illness, soon signed on to another privateer, the *Pourvoyeur*.

It was not always necessary to return to a prison depot before signing on to another French privateer. Antoine-Joseph Preira was a privateersman of some renown in France, where he was known by his *nom de guerre*, Balidar. He was captain of the privateer, *Embuscade*, which had a number of American prisoners on its crew. When he moved to the *Indomptable*, he took the American prisoners with him to crew that vessel, along with more American prisoners from the privateers *Pourvoyeur* and *Roi de Naples*, without the men having returned to prison between voyages.

The Cycle of a Seaman's Captures

Working on a French privateer also carried the risk of being captured and imprisoned or impressed by the British. If the British captured a French privateer, it was sold, as was its cargo, and the crew, including any Americans, were sent to hulks or prisons as French prisoners of war. Capture by the British was one of the greatest risks to those who signed on to French privateers.

John Austin, an African-American from Maryland, had been impressed and was on the *Dauntless* when it was captured in May 1807 by the French. He arrived at the Sarrelibre depot in November.[28] Less than two years later, from the depot, he signed on to the French privateer, *Maraudeur*.[29] The privateer was captured by the British on 8 December 1809 and Austin was sent to the prison at Chatham, where he was given the number 10856. He died there in

---

[27] High Court of Admiralty: Prize Court: Prize Papers. Ships names beginning with this letter: C. *Capricieux*. TNA, HCA 32/1112.

[28] Records of the Admiralty, Naval Forces, Royal Marines, Coastguard, and related bodies, Records of Medical and Prisoner of War Departments, Navy Board and predecessors: Prisoner of War Department and predecessors: Registers of Prisoners of War, France. Nationality: British. Register of prisoners of war. Prisons L-VADM 103/468. "Prisoners of War 1715–1945 Napoleonic Wars", *Find My Past* [Accessed 22 March 2023].

[29] *Archives de la Marine.* "Guerre de l'An II: Prisonniers neutres embarqués sur les corsaires An II". SHDV. FF2/104.

November 1810, aged thirty-six, of excessive fluid in his abdomen; apparently, this is most likely brought on by cirrhosis of the liver.[30]

Robert Morris, from either New York or Newport, was the African-American cook on the British merchant vessel the *Tom*, when it was captured by the French privateer *San Joseph* in February 1809.[31] The *San Joseph* had had a most successful cruise, taking at least fourteen prizes. Morris may have been held, with all of the others from the prizes, in the Tour Solidor, near Saint Malo. However, he may not even have gone there; he certainly never went to a French prison depot. Very quickly, he joined the crew of the *San Joseph* as cook on its next cruise, from which he earned prize money, with his name appearing in the pay book.[32] The *San Joseph* was captured by the British in September 1810. Morris was sent to a British prison and died there a year later of a "pain in his side" accompanied by a cough.[33] He was forty-seven years old.

In the same way that a captured seaman might have signed on to the capturing French privateer, as did William Richardson and Thomas Maky, Americans captured by the British, were often offered the opportunity to sign on to the capturing Royal Navy vessel. There were some who chose this. When war was declared between the United States and Great Britain, not all chose to leave the Royal Navy as prisoners of war.

Thomas Martin, an African-American, had been impressed, with four other American seamen, onto the two Royal Navy gun-brigs, the *Teazer* and the *Plumper*. In July 1805, the two vessels had been attempting to patrol the French coast, but the weather was hot and still. The vessels found themselves becalmed and drifting toward the shore near Granville. To avoid being dashed upon the rocks or running aground, they put down their anchors. On shore, the French saw the plight of the anchored vessels, unable to sail away to safety without wind, and realized their opportunity. Seven French gun-boats, with guns of a longer range than those on the British craft, casually rowed out to

---

[30] Records of the Admiralty, Naval Forces, Royal Marines, Coastguard, and related bodies, Records of Medical and Prisoner of War Departments, Navy Board and predecessors: Prisoner of War Department and predecessors: Chatham French of Prisoners of War, ADM 103/646. "Prisoners of War 1715–1945 Napoleonic Wars", *Find My Past* [Accessed 20 March 2023].

[31] *Archives de la Marine, Affaires maritimes, Quartier de Saint-Malo, 1689–1890*. SHDB. 1P10–118.

[32] *Archives de la Marine, Prises (1794–1871)*. SHDB. 2Q 168.

[33] Records of the Admiralty, Naval Forces, Royal Marines, Coastguard, and related bodies, Records of Medical and Prisoner of War Departments, Navy Board and predecessors: Prisoner of War Department and predecessors: Portchester Register of Prisoners of War, Certificates. ADM 103/645. "Prisoners of War 1715–1945 Napoleonic Wars", *Find My Past* [Accessed 20 March 2023].

the *Plumper* and began firing. Its own fire unable to reach the French boats, the *Plumper* impotently endured their attack for an hour and then surrendered.[34] The lieutenant had had his arm blown from its socket and more than a dozen others of the crew were wounded.

The *Teazer* was the next target, but with a rather cruel nonchalance, the French decided to wait for the morrow's daylight and had a good night's sleep while the men on the *Teazer* helplessly awaited the assault they knew was to come. It was still becalmed and could go nowhere. When the assault came at dawn, the *Teazer* lasted less than an hour.[35] The French noted that almost the entire crew of the *Teazer* had been impressed only a month earlier, so it may have been that they were not yet trained to fight or were unwilling to do so.[36] All of them, now prisoners of war, were marched 500 kilometres, in chains, in the summer heat and rainstorms, to the Valenciennes depot.

Only two of the men appear on the prison registers or in the British list of recipients of funds from the Committee for Relief. All five were soon transferred to the depot at Sarrelibre, requiring them to march again, almost certainly in chains, about 300 kilometres to the east. The following spring, one went into the military hospital at Metz and died on 14 May 1806. His death register entry reads: "William Patrick, aged twenty-four, a Negro, tailor on board the royal brig *Teazer*, son of William Patrick and of Anne Ellimback, born and living in New York…died today of fever."[37]

In 1809, four years after his capture, Thomas Martin, with about a dozen other American seamen, signed up to work on the French privateer, *Etoile no. 2*.[38] To go from the depot to the coast, Martin would have been sent on yet another gruelling march, of nearly 700 kilometres due west, from Sarrelibre to La Hougue, where the privateer lay. The prisoners arrived in October and would have been held in the local gaol, or possibly on board, under guard. On 16 November 1809, the *Etoile no. 2* set sail. Just two days later, it was captured off Cherbourg by the *Euryalus*.[39] The crew now became prisoners of war of

---

[34] After capture, the *Plumper* eventually became the French vessel *Argus*, which sailed with the *Medusa* and was the vessel that found the infamous raft, with only 15 survivors of the original 146 abandoned by the *Medusa*.

[35] Edouard Le Héricher. *Avranchin Monumental et Historique*. Avranches: Tostain, 1845, p550.

[36] *Archives de la Guerre et Armée de Terre. Prisonniers de guerre français et étrangers* (1792–1874). SHDV. Yj31.

[37] Metz. *Registre de décès, An 13* (Death of William Patrick) 14 mai 1806; Archives municipales de Metz. https://archives.metz.fr/ [Accessed 6 April 2019].

[38] *Archives de la Marine. "Guerre de l'An II: Prisonniers neutres embarqués sur les corsaires An II"*. SHDV. FF2/104.

[39] *The London Gazette* 16315 (14 November 1809) p1826. https://www.thegazette.co.uk/London/issue/16315/page/1826 [Accessed 2 September 2020].

the British. The French men on the crew were sent to Portsmouth and appear on the prison reception roster.[40] The Americans, including Thomas Martin, remained on the *Euryalus*. Within weeks, all had been induced to join the Royal Navy for they then appear in the muster no longer as supernumeraries but as members of the crew, with Martin on the carpenter's crew. Martin had come full circle. He had been impressed in about June 1805 and put on the *Plumper*, survived the bombardment of its capture, endured forced marches of hundreds of kilometres and four years in French prisoner of war depots, to be captured after but two days at sea and, once again, impressed or coerced to serve the British.

Ambrose Dodd, of Marblehead, Massachusetts, was also on the *Etoile no. 2*, and was captured by the British with Martin. He had been in French prisons since 1803. He had written to Skipwith that his Seaman's Protection Certificate had been lost, left on board the British merchant vessel on which he had been when it was captured by the French. Without any papers and having been captured on an enemy vessel, he had no hope of being released. He attempted an escape but failed and was sent to Bitche as punishment in 1806. By 1809 he was at Sarrelibre, where he signed on to the *Etoile no. 2*, along with Martin, and with Joshua Porter (who had befriended the imposter Joshua Linnell). Soon after the capture of the *Etoile no. 2*, Dodd and Porter also appear as members of the crew on the musters of the *Euryalus*.[41]

Many of these Americans would have been on board when the *Euryalus* joined the Mediterranean fleet off Toulon and certainly would have heard of the ten Americans who had deserted the *Undaunted*. Martin and Dodd remained in the Royal Navy until the end of the War of 1812. From either a failure of national loyalty or an antipathy to yet more years in prisons, they chose not to declare themselves as prisoners of war to be sent to hulks or Dartmoor in Britain.

Was It Treason?

The question of treason worried many American seamen, whether serving on British or French vessels. William Smith was an American seaman who had joined the privateer, *Minute*, at Stralsund. He participated in the *Minute*'s

---

[40] Records of the Admiralty, Naval Forces, Royal Marines, Coastguard, and related bodies, Records of Medical and Prisoner of War Departments, Navy Board and predecessors: Prisoner of War Department and predecessors: Registers of Prisoners of War, Prothée (ship). Nationality: French. Register of prisoners of war, ADM 103/379. "Prisoners of War 1715–1945 Napoleonic Wars", *Find My Past* [Accessed 22 March 2023].

[41] Anne Morddel. *American Merchant Seamen of the Early Nineteenth Century: a Researcher's Guide.* Published by the author. Printer: Lulu, 2020, pp80–86.

capture of two American merchant vessels, the *Hero* and the *Radius* in 1811. When the *Minute* arrived at Copenhagen, the United States consul there, George Erving, wanted the three American seamen on board, including Smith, to be taken off and sent back to America. The captain, one Spings, had already abandoned one of them without pay, an African-American named Daniel Davis. William Smith refused to leave the ship for fear, he said, of being accused of treason because of the "laws in the United States against Americans who served on foreign privateers".[42] Erving, too, was inclined to believe that he should face prosecution. Both he and Smith were mistaken.

The "Neutrality Act of 1794" was in effect at the time and was very clear. It was forbidden for seamen to join foreign privateers from within the United States and to join any privateer of a nationality that was at war with the United States.[43] As Smith had joined the *Minute* at Stralsund and as it was sailing under the flag of France, which was not at war with the United States, he had committed no crime and his fears were unfounded. None of the American seamen who served on French privateers were committing treason, nor were those who had been impressed into the Royal Navy up to the point that Britain and the United States were at war. At that point, they could have turned themselves in as prisoners of war, which all but a few did. An American seaman working on a British privateer during the War of 1812 was also in the position of committing treason.

This was the case of Joseph Fowler, a seaman from New York who was captured at sea by the French in the autumn of 1813. Some months earlier, he had sailed from Philadelphia on a vessel that was captured and burned at sea by the French. He and the rest of the crew were taken into Brest and held in jail, with the usual treatment of starvation into submission. He was released to work for a supposedly Prussian captain. That vessel was captured by a Jersey privateer, the *Success*, and Fowler found himself a captive on Jersey, where he joined the crew of the British privateer, the *Hazard*. When it took a prize, Fowler was on the prize crew, but that prize was taken by the French privateer, *Coureur*. Once again, Fowler was a prisoner in France but one who had committed treason against America by serving on the Jersey privateer when America and Britain were at war. When the American Minister Plenipotentiary, Crawford, learned of Fowler's case, he was outraged and put the blame on the French. Crawford wrote at length to the Duke of Bassano:

---

[42] Desangiers to Erving. 15 and 17 August 1811; Saabye's Report dated 28 August 1811. *Correspondance Consulaire et Commerciale, Copenhague, 1802–1811*. Arch. dip. 92CCC/6.

[43] Act of 5 June 1794. "An act in addition to the act for the punishment of certain crimes against the United States (a)" *United States Statutes at Large*, Vol. 1, 3rd Congress, 1st Session, Chapter 50, 5 June 1794.

> The entrance of this mariner on board an enemy's vessel is an act of treason, for which he is amenable to the government of the United States. To the French government he is accountable only as an English prisoner, and this accountability is the result of the improper & lawless conduct of French Officers…by which an American citizen was thrown into prison, and precluded from all intercourse with those who were disposed to relieve or capable of advising him, until he should engage to enter into foreign service, are the true causes of the reprehensible conduct of this unfortunate man.…Under the circumstances…it is my indisputable duty to request that this mariner may be placed at my disposition, to be sent to the United States, where alone it can be determined whether the circumstances under which this treasonable act has been committed ought to excuse him from the punishment against treason…[44]

Though William Smith and others on French privateers were not committing treason, especially when they were prisoners who had been recruited under the dreadful circumstances of their captivity, doing so could also have been exceedingly hard on those with consciences, for American seamen on French privateers were helping to capture and send to prison not only British seamen but their own compatriots. The privateer, *Furet* of Saint Malo, had at least six American prisoners of war on its crew in the autumn of 1810 during its financially successful cruise.[45] It captured six vessels, at least two of which were American, and sent twenty-six more American seamen to French prisons. The *Capricieux*, with Americans on its crew, captured the *Juno*, and sent two American seamen, one of them a boy of sixteen, to French prisons. The *Rodeur*, with at least seven American prisoners on its crew, captured the *Anthill* and the *Hopewell* and sent five American seamen to the depots.

In the end, though some prisoners may have thought that, by fighting for the French, they would prove that they had no loyalty to the British, and so merited release, there is no evidence that any man who fought on a French privateer was released for this reason. Most men who were not captured by the British or who did not escape or die while on a French privateer were marched back to the prison depots as soon as a privateer's cruise was ended.

To conclude, France's use of seamen prisoners of neutral nationalities to crew privateers is analogous, as concerns motive, to the Royal Navy recruiting men of neutral nationalities from their prisons. In both cases, trained seamen

---

[44] Crawford to Bassano. 15 October 1813. United States. Department of State. *Despatches from United States Ministers to France, 1789–1906*. Vol. 14. Microfilm copy.

[45] *Archives de la Marine. Guerre de l'an II: Prisonniers neutres embarqués sur les corsaires*; [War of Year II: Neutral prisoners embarked on privateers]. SHDV. FF2/104.

were required and being held in such conditions as might induce volunteering. For the seamen, however, the situations were quite different. Life on a Royal Navy vessel would have been one of naval discipline without hope of release until the end of war. Life on a privateer would have been extremely crowded (privateers sailed with dozens of extra men, who would be put on any captured prizes to sail them in to a port) and filled with the anticipation of hunting for richly laden merchant vessels to capture. Both the Royal Navy and a privateer offered the possibility of prize money but a seaman's chance of getting it were much better in the latter, for that was the sole purpose of a privateer.

Most importantly, for an American seaman held prisoner in France, volunteering to work on a privateer offered the opportunity to escape. Even though these were the only successful escapes, little is known of how they were made. It is unlikely that anyone escaped the march from prison to the port where the privateer was anchored, especially if he were in chains. Once they arrived, it seems that some men claimed illness in order to be sent to the port military hospital. Once there, escape was easier. Once aboard the crowded vessel, escape would have been difficult, under so many watchful eyes. The best opportunity would have been to be assigned to a prize crew, to sail a captured vessel in to a port, ideally to a port in the northern reaches of the French Empire, such as Antwerp or the amenable port of Bergen. There, an American seaman might slip away, straight to an American vessel in port.

Many, however, did not escape. Some died in the battles as the privateer attempted to capture a prize or to avoid being captured by a Royal Navy ship. Many failed in this last, and were captured and sent to a British prison, where they were held as French prisoners. Most were returned to a French depot, where they were held as British prisoners.

10

NEGOTIATED RELEASES

With negotiated releases, it is important to differentiate between the arrangements for stranded American seamen to be returned to the United States and those made for prisoners of war to be released and returned. A stranded seaman was one who would have arrived in France legally, having worked a vessel permitted to enter, but who did not find a vessel to work for the return voyage. All Ministers Plenipotentiary were able to arrange for ships to be chartered to send stranded seamen home. Only one Minister was able to send home a ship full of released prisoner seamen and he achieved this only because he circumvented the bickering consuls.

The process of trying to obtain a negotiated release was a painstaking one of letters from seamen to consuls, from consuls to the Minister Plenipotentiary, confirmation of documentation by the Americans, then repeated confirmation by Goulhot and his bureau, letters between the French Ministers of War, of the Marine and Colonies and of External Affairs, and finally a report to Napoleon. Then, communication of his decision went back down the line before any action could be taken. The four American ministers during the period of the Napoleonic Wars had very different rates of success in freeing American seamen prisoners. Livingston did little, but the problem was only beginning while he held the office. Barlow also did little for them, and what he did may have been entirely for self-interest, but he was not in office long before he died. Crawford arrived in Paris just as the wars were ending and the prisons were opened. It was John Armstrong who achieved the most, arranging for the release of at least one large number of prisoners to be sent home.

In the period when Robert R. Livingston was the Minister Plenipotentiary for the United States, the captures of American seamen by the French were just beginning. With his attention taken by the negotiations of the Louisiana Purchase, he left the problem of the seamen to Skipwith, making requests for the release of only a few individuals, including John Purcell, described above.

By the time that he was replaced by his brother-in-law, John Armstrong, the numbers of American prisoners were quickly increasing. At the same time, the disputes amongst the American consuls were intensifying. A close reading of the diplomatic and consular correspondence makes it clear that Armstrong was exasperated with the consuls and distrustful of their handling of the issues concerning American seamen. He disputed all of their fiscal accounts concerning aid to seamen and doubted the integrity of most concerning the verification of American seamen's nationality. He seemed, almost systematically, to wage a war on them all. This chapter examines Armstrong's negotiated release, followed by the release occasioned by the outbreak of the War of 1812 and examines why the latter was, in truth, a betrayal of the imprisoned American seamen.

The 1807 Release

Initially, Armstrong worked with Skipwith to try to help the seamen, though the animosity between the two had become so extreme that Skipwith often wrote to the Secretary of State complaining about Armstrong, while Armstrong was about to publish a pamphlet in America attacking Skipwith. In August 1807, after Pacaud had completed his census of American prisoners, Armstrong submitted a request to the Minister of Marine and Colonies, Decrès, for the release of "50 or 60" American prisoners.

> Your Excellency cannot but know that among the people known as English prisoners of war in France can be found about 50 or 60 American seamen who, during the course of the current war, were found aboard vessels of Great Britain and are today in the depots; some of these are men with little intelligence and without attachment to their country, and have signed on to the vessels, perhaps willingly, but Your Excellency can be sure that they were very few in number. Their treatment, their food, their pay all are better on American vessels than on those of England, thus it must be presumed that these seamen are what they declare themselves to be, either impressed or only passengers on their return to the United States. In either case, my instructions enjoin me to request, and I dare to hope, that in the present circumstances His Majesty the Emperor would please release them according to the rules established concerning these men and give me the liberty to send them directly to the United States. There is at the moment the opportunity to fulfil this goal promptly and securely; an American schooner will arrive in one of the Channel ports in 10 or 15 days.
>
> It is useless to represent to Your Excellency how precious will be the restoring of these men to the United States of America and what obligations my government will have to His Majesty. The truth is, (and it is in confidence that I say this to Your Excellency) that the United States have no hope of resolving their differences with Great

Britain, and that they use all means possible to pursue war with energy and success; and one of these means is the recovery of her seamen.[1]

Five years before the War of 1812, the representative of the United States was holding out the hope of his country entering the war against Britain and promising that the released prisoners would join the fray to France's benefit.

Two days later, Decrès reported Armstrong's request to Napoleon, whose decision was

> If this is requested as a right, it is not possible. If it is requested as a grace in the name of the President of the United States of America, then His Majesty agrees.[2]

Decrès wrote of the Emperor's decision to Armstrong, who sent a list of the names of not "50 or 60" but of more than 100 Americans held in the depots. He added that the vessel that was to take the men could take only about thirty. The rest would have to leave "from Antwerp and ports of Holland". Trusting that this would be acceptable, he had already given orders to the American consul there to prepare to receive the men.[3] Perhaps having learned the flowery style of the Empire, the proud General added:

> Permit me to take this opportunity to thank Your Excellency personally for the obliging manner in which you have accepted my request in favor of these unhappy souls and more particularly for what you will no doubt wish to undertake in presenting to His Majesty the tribute of thanks that my Government owes him for the kindness with which he deigned to pronounce their freedom.

The Minister of Marine and Colonies, Decrès, wrote to the Minister of War, Clarke, asking for the prisoners to be released and included Armstrong's list. However, the Minister of War replied that, while the request was for fifty or sixty men to be released, the list contained 102 names. This discrepancy, along with the fact that no documents proving the men's nationality were attached, "seems to me sufficient reason to again ask His Majesty for his orders".[4] It was Goulhot who wrote to the Emperor, who again agreed to the men's release "not

---

[1] Armstrong to Decrès. 31 August 1807. *Archives de la Guerre et Armée de Terre. Prisonniers de guerre français et étrangers* (1792–1874). SHDV. Yj19.

[2] Decrès to Bonaparte. 2 September 1807. *Archives de la Guerre et Armée de Terre. Prisonniers de guerre français et étrangers* (1792–1874). SHDV. Yj19.

[3] Armstrong to Decrès. 8 September 1807. *Archives de la Guerre et Armée de Terre. Prisonniers de guerre français et étrangers* (1792–1874). SHDV. Yj41.

[4] Clarke to Decrès. Undated, September 1807. *Archives de la Guerre et Armée de Terre. Prisonniers de guerre français et étrangers* (1792–1874). SHDV. Yj19.

as a right but by my favor".⁵ Goulhot then wrote to Armstrong asking him to rewrite the list to include the names of the vessels from which the men were captured. Armstrong complied and sent the new list to the Ministry of War on 28 September. The list now held only sixty-nine names, being those men who had documentary proof of American nationality, their Seaman's Protection Certificates, and for whom the name of their vessel could be determined. Left off the list were the many men whom Pacaud noted in his census as "surely American" but who had no documents to prove it.

Because it now contained yet again a different number of prisoners claimed as American, the new list caused more doubt and suspicion for the French. Two weeks later, Clarke wrote to Decrès that he thought it was Decrès's responsibility to follow the Emperor's orders concerning the release of the American prisoners, that he had received a new list and it now required clarification. He asked that Decrès send him the first list, a copy of the report he sent to the Emperor and a copy of the Emperor's decision, "so that I may comply with it exactly".⁶ Decrès did so, sending the copies and pointing out that the Emperor had not seen the list of names and had made his decision based on the number of men only. Thus, sixty was the maximum number of seamen that could be released.

Armstrong wrote to the Minister of External Relations, asking if the number of men released could be raised to sixty-nine. On 21 October, the Minister of External Relations replied that the Emperor had agreed.⁷ Finally, on 22 October, the sixty-nine proven Americans began to be released from the various depots. They made their way, on foot and under guard, in the autumn rains, north to Antwerp, which had been selected by Armstrong as their port of departure (the American schooner initially designated to take some of them had long since sailed). To the end of October, the French ministers were still communicating about the release and writing a report about the change in numbers. Goulhot reported that he was sending word to the authorities at Antwerp to allow the men to sail. In November, the commandants of the depots sent to Clarke confirmation of the departures of the Americans: eighteen left from Verdun, twenty-one from Arras, ten from Valenciennes, eighteen from Mezières, four from Sarrelouis, two remained in hospital (they had recovered by January 1808 and begged to be allowed to leave), two had been sent to Bitche (from which no one in this group was released), five were unknown

---

⁵ Goulhot to Clarke. 14 September 1807. *Archives de la Guerre et Armée de Terre. Prisonniers de guerre français et étrangers* (1792–1874). SHDV. Yj19.

⁶ Clarke to Decrès. 10 October 1807. *Archives de la Guerre et Armée de Terre. Prisonniers de guerre français et étrangers* (1792–1874). SHDV. Yj19.

⁷ Unsigned letter to Armstrong. 21 October 1807. *Correspondance Politique États-unis*. Arch. dip. 39CP/60. Microfilm copy.

to the prison commandants, one pushed his luck and asked to go to Quebec instead. As ever, the numbers do not quite add up.

The seamen were sent from Antwerp to Amsterdam, where they were joined by "a great number of destitute American seamen…from every quarter of Europe", abandoned as a consequence of the Embargo Act and costing the American consul in Amsterdam, Bourne, "about 40 dollars per day for their support".[8] They wrote to him in desperation, as in this letter from four American seamen writing (with wondrous spelling) in February 1808:

> In Regard to the ships not being allowed to Depart for the Unighted States of America we are under the Necessaty to Ask your assistance as we are Destitute of the Wharewith to Support our selves any longer.

In the same winter month, Thomas Perkins wrote:

> …I am in want of a suit [of] Clothes and i hope that you will let me have them as whe are going on a winters Coast and as i have not in my health… [9]

Bourne also included some American prisoners held at the Breda prison, whose release he had negotiated.[10]

He chartered the ship *Eliza* of Baltimore, Captain Huffington, to take them all to America, at no small cost.

> Capt. Huffington contracted with me to take these passengers free on condition of my laying in provisions for them & furnishing them with hammocks & for their accommodation which I thought to be the best arrangement that could be made for the publick interest…[11]

After two months at sea, the *Eliza* arrived in Baltimore on 2 May 1808,[12] with an undetermined number of Armstrong's released prisoners finally arriving home. (See Appendix A).

---

[8] Bourne to Madison. 22 February 1808. United States. Department of State. *Despatches from United States Consuls in Amsterdam, 1790–1906*. Vol. 1. Microfilm copy.

[9] William Glover and others to Bourne, 9 February 1808 and Thomas Perkins and John Shiply to Bourne, 24 February 1808. Sylvanus Bourne Papers (1775–1859). Library of Congress. MSS13367. Carton 25.

[10] Bourne to Madison. 14 April 1808. United States. Department of State. *Despatches from United States Consuls in Amsterdam, 1790–1906*. Vol. 1. Microfilm copy.

[11] Bourne to Madison. 5 March 1808. United States. Department of State. *Despatches from United States Consuls in Amsterdam, 1790–1906*. Vol. 1. Microfilm copy.

[12] *L'Oracle and Daily Advertiser* 109 (7 May 1808) Shipping announcement, p2.

It is clear from the belaboured and tedious trail of correspondence with the French authorities that, even though his health plagued him, the irascible and arrogant John Armstrong worked hard for the release of American seamen. However, amongst the American prisoners who were not released, there was an understandable frustration, despair and fury and, somewhat unfairly, it was directed at Armstrong. In September 1808, a number of American prisoners at Arras wrote a petition addressed to the President of the United States, accusing Armstrong of neglecting them.

> Letter to the President of the United States, a Petition from prisoners of war at Arras....having repeatedly petitioned General Armstrong... for our liberation but finding all our applications abortive after having sent the Protection of those who had them, our last recourse is the present application to Your Excellency....Our situations are now very deplorable.....[We who have] seen numbers of our fellow citizens and natives liberated since our unfortunate confinement, deem it very hard we have not benefitted by the perseverance of Genl Armstrong that he has given to others ...[13]

They attached a table with their names, Seaman's Protection Certificate numbers and ports of issue, their places of birth, and even names of references in the United States. (John Nehill, who had been a prisoner in Tripoli, cited the eminent Bainbridge as his reference.) They added that "We receive no benefits or subscriptions which have been sent to the English Prisoners of War." (That is, none of the aid from the Committee for Relief.) Armstrong's many political enemies in the United States ensured that the petition appeared in the press. Of this same episode and complaint, Stephen Clubb claimed that American seamen prisoners at Arras told him of Armstrong arranging for the release of a number of British prisoners under the guise of their being American:

> Went into the citadel to inquire after the Americans. Some of them came to me, and I asked why they were not liberated with their countrymen, who were sent away about a month before. They said that those men were liberated as Americans at the instance of Gen. Armstrong; but that the greatest part of them were English captains, some of whom had since wrote letters to France, and that these things being known to the Minister at war, he had spoke to Gen. Armstrong, advising him to take more care to discriminate, and find out who had legal protection of the American flag, and to liberate none other...[14]

---

[13] Bourne to Madison. 10 September 1808. United States. Department of State. *Despatches from United States Consuls in Amsterdam, 1790–1906.* Vol. 1. Microfilm copy.

[14] Clubb, "A Journal", p175.

Was this claim true? Some eighteen of the men named in the surviving lists of those Americans released in 1807 were shipmasters. That is much less than half the number of those released but still a significant number of shipmasters. Of those, three were British. One of these, Daniel Hayes, promptly returned to Britain and signed on as the captain of another vessel, ending up in South Africa. He was master of the infamous *William & Emma*, the vessel that was to have carried the abused Saartje Baartman, an African who was to be sent to England and put on display, but she did not board. The vessel was captured by the French, and Hayes, for a second time, was sent to Verdun. With some restraint, Hayes's return is reported in the Police Bulletin for 25 April 1809.

> At Verdun: 5 English prisoners have arrived, including Hayes, identified by Wirion as the captain, already taken, released in 1807 as an American, returned to the English merchant marine, taken on the William & Emma.[15]

Also amongst the shipmasters released in 1807 was the even more reprehensible William Shaw and his young "servant" (probably slave), the unnamed "son of the king of Congo". Shaw was an American slave trader working for a British consortium, master on the vessel *Sir William Douglas*, which was registered in Britain, who bought locally kidnapped people in West Africa and sold them as slaves in the United States. Returning to London from Charleston in South Carolina, the ship was captured in 1804 by the French privateer *Vaillant* and sent in to Puerto Pasajes (which the French called "Le Passage") in Spain. Shaw and the young prince were marched north to Verdun, where Shaw was allowed to live on parole with some financial aid from Skipwith, presumably keeping his servant with him.

The British prisoner at Verdun, Lieutenant William Henry Dillon, wrote in his long and tedious journal of captivity an account of this young prince of Congo being used, atrociously, as a decorative carriage servant:

> General [Wirion, the commandant of Verdun] wishing to cut a figure at Bonaparte's coronation, Borrowed [a] Gentleman's carriage for that purpose, in which He went off to Paris accompanied by [his wife]. There happened to be a young negro at Verdun, the son of an African King. That Prince wishing to have his son educated in England, had placed him under the care of the Master of one of our trading Vessels, which being captured on her way Home the unfortunate black, who had a pecuniary allowance, was sent to our depot, the General dressed this prince in a Splendid livery, and made him attend behind the carriage on that occasion. [As an African] he could

---

[15] d'Hauterive, *La Police Secrète*, Vol. 5, p29.

not be considered as a prisoner of war, nevertheless, He was detained and treated as such.[16]

Shaw, as an American, and the son of the king of Congo were released from Verdun in November 1807 and they, too, were marched to Antwerp, to take the cartel to America. It is unclear if the young African endured a life of slavery in America or if he were taken to Britain to be educated.

In addition to these, there were, amongst those released, the names of four whaling men linked to a group of Quaker whalers from Nantucket who had lived in Dunkirk, training French whalers, in the 1780s, as a part of an agreement made by William Rotch and the King of France. However, during the French Revolution and Terror, they had abandoned France and gone to Britain. When Peleg, Christopher and Henry Bunker, and Christopher Folger were captured by the French, they were all on British owned and registered whaling vessels, returning from the South Seas whaling grounds with holds filled with whale oil to be sold in Britain. As all four of these men were living in Britain, masters or mates of British owned vessels, carrying British cargo to be sold in Britain, they should not have been released for they were the very definition of Americans aiding France's enemy. The American consular agent in Dunkirk, François Coffyn, who may have known them well, was instrumental in gaining their release. He arranged for many upstanding citizens of Dunkirk to sign a notarized affidavit affirming the good characters of the men and the good work they once had done for France.[17] Peleg and Henry Bunker died before the departure for Antwerp but Christopher Bunker and Christopher Folger were released.

After the 1807 release of some American prisoners, Armstrong's relationships with the consuls worsened, and his distrust of them concerning finances increased. He continued to dispute Skipwith's financial claims and those of other American consuls and agents. In September 1808, he appointed David Bailie Warden, the Irish tutor who had become his secretary, and whom he apparently trusted, as temporary consul at Paris.[18] In June 1809, he suspended

---

[16] Unpublished Journal of Lt. William Henry Dillon, RN, Vol. 3, entry for July 1806. Papers of Professor Michael Arthur Lewis. Caird Library, National Maritime Museum. Manuscript LES/6/7/(8).

[17] Undated and unsigned list of American prisoners. *Archives de la Guerre et Armée de Terre. Prisonniers de guerre français et étrangers (1792–1874)*. SHDV. Yj41. There also exists one further explanation, by Peleg Bunker's granddaughter, which claims that Napoleon was convinced by Quaker negotiators to release them, but no official record could be found to confirm this. See Lydia Bunker Gardner. undated manuscript biography of Peleg Bunker, Edouard Stackpole Collection, Nantucket Historical Association Research Library and Archives, Nantucket, Massachusetts.

[18] Warden to Madison. 2 September 1808. United States. Department of State. *Despatches from United States Consuls in Paris, 1790–1906*. Vol. 3. Microfilm copy.

Isaac Cox Barnet from consular duties and later denounced him to the Secretary of State for issuing a United States passport to a British citizen.[19] He persecuted the others so much that, in August 1809, Coffyn, who was a second generation United States consular agent at Dunkirk, was said to be so disillusioned that he was considering selling up and moving to Spain.[20] In early 1810, Armstrong sent Leonard Jarvis to report on conditions at Cherbourg and at Morlaix, suspecting Jean Diot, who had been serving the United States there since Benjamin Franklin had been in Paris. (Jarvis ultimately praised Diot and recommended that he continue in his post. See more about his character below.)[21] That same year, the French refused the credentials of the consul proposed at Nantes, William Patterson, who believed that they had been influenced to do so by Armstrong.[22]

Some part of Armstrong's increase in distrust and animosity of the consuls would seem to be due to that reprimand from Clarke, the Minister of War, for his having included some British prisoners amongst the list of Americans to be released. Certainly, after this, Armstrong became excessively cautious about any prisoner who could possibly be construed as British. As seen above, he refused Goodman an American passport and, though he could not refuse to recognize the passport Madison had given Nichols and he gave a certificate of nationality to Rocher, he did not request their release. They had to wait for Barlow's arrival. Particularly thorny for Armstrong was the issue of naturalized Americans. As with Goodman, he applied the rules of the law concerning residency very strictly. In one case of his doing so, that of James McClure, he occasioned much debate in the American press. McClure's father was Scottish and had taken American citizenship in South Carolina. His son, James was born in the United States, and so had citizenship by birth. However, both men had returned to Britain more than fifteen years before ending up in France in 1807 and 1808. Armstrong thought that this lack of residency meant that both had forfeited their citizenship. He denied James McClure the papers necessary to leave France as an American. The French authorities allowed him to live in Paris as they observed the American debate on the issue. As with the others, it was Barlow, on Monroe's instructions, who gave James McClure an American passport, enabling him to leave France after four years in limbo.

---

[19] Armstrong to Barnet. 3 June 1809. United States. Department of State. *Despatches from United States Consuls in Paris, 1790–1906*. Vol. 3. Microfilm copy.

[20] J. Collet to Barnet. 4 August 1809. United States. Department of State. *Despatches from United States Consuls in Paris, 1790–1906*. Vol. 3. Microfilm copy.

[21] Jarvis to Armstrong. 13 March 1810. United States. Department of State. *Despatches from United States Ministers to France, 1789–1906*. Vol. 11. Microfilm copy.

[22] Patterson to Armstrong. 14 February 1810. United States. Department of State. *Despatches from United States Consuls in Nantes, 1790–1906*. Vol. 1. Microfilm copy.

The issue of naturalization was also the reason for Armstrong refusing to recognize Stephen Clubb as an American citizen or to request his release. Clubb was English and had married Mary Carpenter, the daughter of the Salem captain and merchant, Benjamin Carpenter. They were living in Britain, where her father had spent a number of years, and then decided to move to Boston. The vessel on which they planned to sail ran into trouble, so Clubb took a job as mate on an American vessel, the *Hyades*. This paid for his wife's passage and for the transport of their belongings with them. The *Hyades* was captured by the French privateer, *Sauvage*, in December 1807, and Clubb was taken prisoner. His claim was that his marriage to an American woman, as well as his intention to emigrate, in effect, naturalized him. By no interpretation of the law, which required a residency of five years, was this so. He also offered the interesting argument that, since the nationality of the vessel applied to the crew, he should be considered an American because he was working on an American vessel.

As Armstrong did not support him, Clubb tried the consul, Isaac Cox Barnet, who was more amenable. Barnet wrote directly to the Minister of War in April 1809, claiming Clubb as an American, in defiance of Armstrong. In May, Goulhot advised the Minister of War that, of course, Madame Carpenter (Clubb) was free to go, but that Clubb, being English, should remain in prison. In spite of this, Clubb was released by direct order of the Emperor, in June.[23] Who was able to speak on Clubb's behalf to the Emperor and obtain this remarkable release? In the preface to his published account of his time as a prisoner of war in France (which was vitriolically critical of Armstrong), republished by the Freemasons, Clubb states that he is a member and that it is his duty to publish his account "in gratitude to French Free Masons". He also states that Isaac Cox Barnet "took an active part in his liberation".[24] The Masonic Lodge in Arras at the time that Clubb was a prisoner there, *Sophie Madeleine, Reine de Suède*, had an illustrious member, Joseph Fouché, the Duke of Otranto and the Minister of the Police General.[25] No record has been found to prove that he intervened for Clubb but the path of communication from Clubb to Fouché existed with the Freemasons and Fouché certainly spoke to Napoleon regularly. As for Isaac Cox Barnet, this was not the only British prisoner he helped.

The Clubb and McClure cases reveal more than a young country's uncertainty about naturalization. They also show how cautious Armstrong had

---

[23] Dossier on Stephen Clubb. *Archives de la Guerre et Armée de Terre. Prisonniers de guerre français et étrangers (1792–1874).* SHDV. Yj42.

[24] Clubb, "A Journal", p148.

[25] It does not appear that Isaac Cox Barnet was a Freemason. However, John Armstrong was a member of a lodge in New York; if only because of his inability to speak French, it is unlikely that he would have joined a lodge in Paris.

become, determined to ensure that he did not claim any British nationals as American, lest the French grow angry and cease to release any Americans at all which, in the end, is exactly what was to happen.

The 1809 Failure

Armstrong continued to request from the French authorities releases of individual prisoners, working on his own and without the consuls wherever possible. "It seems that your minister wants entirely to do your business", the consular agent in Dieppe wrote to Barnet.[26] By 1809, Armstrong had developed another list of names of prisoners whose release he requested. He hoped to send them back not on a vessel chartered by a consul, but on one he arranged directly with Nathan Haley.

Nathan Haley was an American, from Stonington, Connecticut, who had been based in Dieppe for a dozen years. He seems first to have seen France in about 1794, when he was master of an American merchant vessel captured by a French privateer and taken in to Brest. Haley soon returned to New York to carry on as master of vessels voyaging between New York and London. In 1797, while master of the *Hare*, a vessel laden with a fairly rich cargo sailing from London, he outraged the maritime community with the not uncommon trick of "capturing" his own vessel with a phantom privateer; in essence, he simply sailed it into a French port as his "prize". At that time, even British merchant captains used a similar ruse, and would "by a previous agreement… allow themselves to be captured [by the French] off Dieppe, Le Havre, or Saint-Valéry."[27] Haley used his prize money to settle in France. In becoming an American privateer based in France, Haley was joining a small but active group that included William Cowell, captain of the privateer, *Hardi*, who was preying upon American merchant vessels and taking them in to Lorient; Benjamin Lewis, of Marblehead;[28] and, in Dunkirk, both Vickary Sparrow of Massachusetts and William Ripner of Hartford, Connecticut[29] (who had sailed the *Black Prince* and other vessels in the 1780s for Franklin's privateer

---

[26] LeBaron to Barnet. 28 August 1809. United States. Department of State. *Despatches from United States Consuls in Paris, 1790–1906*. Vol. 3. Microfilm copy.

[27] Howard C. Rice. "James Swan: Agent of the French Republic 1794–1796." *The New England Quarterly*, Vol. 10, No. 3, New England Quarterly, Inc., 1937, pp464–486, https://doi.org/10.2307/360316 [Accessed 3 December 2021].

[28] Mountflorence to Pinckney, 14 and 21 February 1797. *American State Papers: Foreign Relations*. 2:11. https://memory.loc.gov/cgi-bin/ampage?collId=llsp&fileName=002/llsp002.db&recNum=16 [Accessed 12 December 2021].

[29] J. Lemoine and Henri Bourde de la Rogerie. *Inventaire Sommaire des Archives Départementales Antérieures à 1790: Finistère, Archives Civiles, Série B*, Tome III. Quimper: Imprimerie Brevetée-A. Jaouen, 1902, pLXV; Dunkerque. *Registre des*

outfitter, the man who was also Diot's first employer, Jean François Torris).[30] The people Haley robbed in his first privateering act would pursue him in courts for the rest of his life and made it impossible for him, had he wanted to do so, to return permanently to the United States. He married a Belgian woman and remained in France.

He acquired some wealth, as both a captain of merchant ships and, reputedly, as a privateer. There has been speculation that he was an associate of Gilbert Imlay and that some of his wealth may have come from involvement in the silver theft, though no document shows that.[31] Certainly, he would have encountered Barlow, if not through Imlay, then through their mutual friend, Fulton. He had attempted to join the French Navy and had nearly succeeded but Decrès, the Minister of Marine and Colonies, stopped that by ordering an investigation into how an American could have been considered for an appointment in the French Navy when foreigners were forbidden to join at all (with the notable exceptions of Joshua Barney and William Ripner, both of whom were well entrenched in the French Navy before Decrès became Minister). Though uneducated, he must have had some charm, for he formed friendships with Thomas Paine, Robert Fulton and Jonathan Russell, shared investments with Talleyrand, and was trusted by LaTouche-Tréville. At the same time, he was denounced to Livingston by James Swan, and repeatedly attacked in the press by Isaac Doolittle (a close friend of Barnet's), by the people he had robbed, and others. His primary motivations in life seem to have been the acquisition of money and a searing hatred of the British. Haley could be both cruel and kind to seamen, as evidenced by his fraudulent denouncement of the mate, Benjamin F. Seaver as a British spy, and by his taking into his home and caring for an impoverished, elderly seaman.

Haley and Armstrong had probably met through mutual American acquaintances in Paris but Armstrong did not employ Haley in any official capacity until after the latter had been given diplomatic dispatches by President Jefferson. This came about because, in April 1808, Joel Barlow wrote to Jefferson recommending as a messenger "Captain Nathan Haley…well known to me these many years."[32] It was not unusual for captains wishing the protective cover

---

mariages, 1780. (Ripner-Popgay marriage). 17 August 1784. *AD Nord*. https://archives-departementales.lenord.fr/ [Accessed 12 December 2021].

[30] Alain Demerliac. *La Marine du Consulat et du Premier Empire: Nomenclature des Navires Français de 1800 à 1815*. Nice: Editions A.N.C.R.E., 2003.

[31] Lola Lóbula. "Ciudadana Frankenstein [II]: La última corsaria", *CES Alcant Obrera*, 14 July 2021. https://alacantobrera.com/2021/07/14/ciudadana-frankenstein-ii-la-ultima-corsaria/ [Accessed 10 November 2021], p7.

[32] Barlow to Jefferson. 15 April 1808. United States. Department of State. *Despatches from United States Consuls in Nantes, 1790–1906*. Vol. 1. Microfilm copy.

given a diplomatic messenger to make such a request, as this request by a Captain John Doric to Thomas Jefferson explains bluntly:

> Circumstances as We are the travellers must take as much security as they can have. Therefore I take the liberty of solliciting Your patronage to make me to have some dispatches from the Secretary of State Either for the charge d'affaire of the U.S. at Paris or for the French minister any Kind of dispatches will be a good passport against the British cruizers...[33]

Haley was given dispatches to carry to Armstrong in July 1808. Armstrong then employed him to take Skipwith on the unhappy voyage ending with his arrest. Except for his services as a sea captain, Haley's abilities were held in low opinion by Armstrong for two reasons: he could not keep a secret and he was but semi-literate and had to have others write letters for him:

> ...Haly [sic] was found to be leaky and incapable of keeping his own secrets...Haly's letter was written by an Irish priest by the name of Ferris...[34]

In spite of these failings, Haley was no fool and was just as capable of using the diplomats as of being used by them. If carrying dispatches would provide protection for a vessel, carrying dispatches and returned prisoners for the United States would provide even more. Realizing that Armstrong was working for the release of more seamen, Haley speculatively bought, with Henry Preble, a vessel in Dieppe and fitted it out for the purpose, giving it the common cartel name of *Happy Return*. Armstrong agreed to pay 5000 francs for it to carry dispatches and as many American seamen as possible.[35] Nathan Haley also loaded the hold with sixty-three boxes of merchandise, which cartels and ships under flags of truce were forbidden to carry.[36] At that time, voyages diplomatic and voyages commercial were to be separated.

---

[33] John Doric to Thomas Jefferson. 16 May 1811. *Founders Online*, NARA, https://founders.archives.gov/documents/Jefferson/03-03-02-0500. [Original source: *The Papers of Thomas Jefferson*, Retirement Series, Vol. 3, *12 August 1810 to 17 June 1811*, ed. J. Jefferson Looney. Princeton: Princeton University Press, 2006, pp619–620.]

[34] Armstrong to Madison. 24 November 1808. United States. Department of State. *Despatches from United States Ministers to France, 1789–1906*. Vol. 11. Microfilm copy.

[35] Preble to Madison. 15 October 1809. United States. Department of State. *Despatches from United States Ministers to France, 1789–1906*. Vol. 11. Microfilm copy.

[36] Armstrong to Delarue. 10 October 1809. United States. Department of State. *Despatches from United States Ministers to France, 1789–1906*. Vol. 11. Microfilm copy.

For months, as he had done in 1807, Armstrong had been writing letters to the various French ministers requesting the release of American prisoners. By this time, he had formed a good working relationship with Clarke (surely aided by Clarke's fluency in English), whom he admired.

> ...this minister, who by the way is now Duke of Feltry [Feltre], is not only a man of the best talents in the Empire, but of the best temper also—that is, his temper is always regulated by his understanding & he accordingly does many agreeable things, not to promote the wishes of the individual, but to promote the interests of the State. He is truly an able Man.[37]

By July 1809, Armstrong had sent to Clarke another list of the names of more than 100 American prisoners whose documentation had been verified (their original Seaman's Protection Certificates seen). He asked that the same principle of the Emperor's favour as had been the basis for the release in 1807 be once again applied for a second batch of prisoners to be released. In November, Clarke presented a list of only fifty American prisoners and wrote to Napoleon to ask his orders.[38] Permission was refused. According to Barnet, the refusal was because the request was not made through the correct channels. Armstrong had written directly to the Minister of War and not to the Minister of External Affairs, who was at that point Champagny, the Duke of Cadore.[39]

The *Happy Return* sailed from Dieppe, arriving in New York, not with Armstrong's second group of freed prisoners, but with a few seamen who had been stranded in port. Armstrong left France the following September, without gaining further large releases, though he did manage occasional releases of fewer than ten men at a time.

In 1811, during the interim between Ministers Plenipotentiary, Jonathan Russell, the chargé d'affaires in Paris, gained permission from Napoleon for at least two vessels, the *Union*, from Dunkirk, and the *Vigilant*, to take stranded American seamen back to the United States, but it seems that no prisoners were included.

Joel Barlow's credentials as Minister were presented in November 1811. The following June, the United States declared war against Great Britain. In

---

[37] Armstrong to Jefferson. 19 September 1809. *The Papers of Thomas Jefferson Digital Edition*, ed. James P. McClure and J. Jefferson Looney. Charlottesville: University of Virginia Press, Rotunda, 2008–2021. CanonicURL: https://rotunda.upress.virginia.edu/founders/TSJN-03-01-02-0426 [Accessed 03 Dec 2021]. Original source: Retirement Series, Vol. 1 (4 March–15 November 1809).

[38] Clarke to Bonaparte. 22 November 1809. *Archives de la Secrétairerie d'Etat impériale. Rapports du Ministre de la Guerre (1800–1814)*. Arch. nat. AF/IV/1157.

[39] Barnet to Russell. 15 August 1811. Jonathan Russell Papers (1795–1832), John Hay Library, Brown University Library.

October 1812, Barlow left Paris on a journey to meet with Napoleon, who was on the Russian campaign. He never caught up with him and, by December, he was dead. He had spent most of his brief tenure working on a treaty with the French, against the orders of the Secretary of State and without success. While the dispatches and correspondence of Armstrong were filled with requests for the release of American seamen, and those of Livingston contained a few, but for one grand episode to be discussed below, those of Barlow contained hardly any, and some of these were rather dubious.

The 1813 Release

But for the writings of Lawrence S. Kaplan, the historiography of the War of 1812 insofar as that small war between the United States and Great Britain concerned France or was influenced by France is nearly non-existent. French historians who have written of Napoleon's interest in America, such as Schalck de la Faverie and Murat, stop with the Louisiana Purchase of 1803.[40] The bicentennial of the war, in 2012, brought a large number of publications in English, not one of which gives more than a few lines to the role of France in the conflict. Kaplan's comment about an earlier generation of historians of the war still applies: "Although every account of the war gives France attention as a causal factor, France seemingly disappears once the war has begun."[41]

This is because France's and Napoleon's attention were elsewhere. Though for years, Napoleon had been trying to manipulate the United States into a war with Great Britain, when it finally came, it was too late; he and his Grand Army had already marched two thirds of the way to Moscow and the disaster that would befall him there. "When war was declared," Kaplan notes, "French newspaper attention centred on Russia not Washington." The war was fought largely in North America, far from France, and at the same time that there was a coup attempt against Napoleon, he came racing back from Russia, the First Empire crumbled, Paris was invaded, and Napoleon was sent into exile on Elba. Yet, during these quite cataclysmic events happening around them, to a small group of Americans living in France and to all of the American seamen held prisoner in France, America's war was of enormous importance.

---

[40] Lawrence S. Kaplan. "France and the War of 1812", *The Journal of American History*, Vol. 57, No. 1 (Jun., 1970), pp. 36–47 and "France and Madison's Decision for War, 1812", *The Mississippi Valley Historical Review*, Vol. 50, No.4 (Mar., 1964); Alfred Schalck de la Faverie, *Napoléon et l'Amérique: Histoire des relations franco-américaines spécialement envisagé au point de vue de l'influence napoléonienne (1688–1815)* (Paris: Librairie Payot, 1917); Inès Murat, *Napoléon et le Rêve américain* (Paris: Fayard, 1976).

[41] Kaplan, "France and the War of 1812", p36.

For the American community in France, the commercial agents, shipping agents and consuls, war with Britain brought the thrilling opportunity to get rich quick through privateering raids on British merchant vessels. Many of them, including consuls, began investigating the purchase of suitable vessels even before they had received official notification that war was declared. (Indeed, Jonathan Russell, the American chargé d'affaires in Paris, was offered the *Yarico* as a privateer by Diot, nine months before war was declared.)[42]

No one, it seems, was more enthusiastic about American privateers based in France than the Minister Plenipotentiary, Joel Barlow. Henry Preble wrote that Barlow

> ...mentioned several times that he was surprised that the Americans in France had not sufficient spirit to fit out a privateer, that such an enterprize would please this Government ...[43]

Before his death, Barlow requested from the French the necessary permissions for any American privateers that would be based in France. Writing to Maret, the Minister of External Relations, he requested that American privateers be permitted to operate from and bring their prizes into all ports of the French Empire, and that the American consuls in those ports have the authority to rule on the legitimacy of those prizes.[44] Permission was granted, to the outrage of the British. John Bennet, junior, Secretary of Lloyd's, reported to the Admiralty from Le Havre that the American consuls have "the very extraordinary power of condemning vessels sent in by American Privateers, without the interference of the French Courts".[45] This permission gave the American privateers an encouragement they hardly needed, for it increased their chances of sending in prizes that were captured in the seas around Britain with a greater chance of their not being recaptured than if they had to be sent across the Atlantic to an American port.

Though the United States Navy had grown, and by 1812 had developed an impressive new type of frigate design that would do serious damage to Royal Navy vessels in sea battles during the war,[46] there was also an expec-

---

[42] Diot to Russell. 23 September 1811. Jonathan Russell Papers. Diot had bought the *Yarico* at auction; it had been chartered by the consul at Bordeaux, William Lee, who lost his investment when the *Yarico* was taken as a prize by the French and sold.

[43] Preble to Barnet. 23 November 1812. United States. Department of State. *Despatches from United States Consuls in Paris, 1790–1906*. Vol. 4 Microfilm copy.

[44] Barlow to Maret. 8 August 1812. *Despatches from United States Ministers to France, 1789–1906*. Vol. 13. Microfilm copy.

[45] Bennett to Croker. 11 May 1814. Admiralty and Ministry of Defence. Navy Department. Correspondence and Papers. Letters from Lloyds. TNA. ADM 1/3994.

[46] For explanations of this design see Tyrone G. Martin and John C. Roach, "Humphreys's Real Innovation". *Naval History*, Vol. 8, No.2 (Apr 1994); Ian W. Toll,

tation that private, armed vessels, privateers, would engage in attacking trade and taking prizes. Both sides took hundreds of prizes, though Britain was far more successful at this than was America.[47] Barlow received at least eight American Letters of Marque, signed by President Madison, to issue to American registered vessels then in European ports that would sail as privateers. He reported that he had issued them all and wrote that "I...could place as many more if I had them".[48] At least two had been issued to Henry Preble, one for a vessel purchased at Brest with Nathan Haley, and named the *True-Blooded Yankee*, the other owned by Preble alone, the *Bunker Hill*.[49]

They were then confronted with the significant problem of finding enough American seamen in French ports to crew the privateers that would sail under the American flag, and to man any prizes they might take. For this, they needed between 100 and 150 men for each privateer. The *Bunker Hill* was able to find enough seamen in port, but the *True-Blooded Yankee* could not. Initially, Haley and Preble colluded with local gendarmes, who rounded up in the port of Brest nearly two dozen American seamen and arrested them for being without papers, then delivered them to the *True-Blooded Yankee*,[50] yet many more men were needed. Looking to hire American seamen found in other ports of France, Henry Preble asserted that Barlow had intended to use the consular service to act almost as crimps in pushing American seamen to work on his privateer.

> Mr. Barlow told me as agent for the concerned that he had given orders to all the consuls to send the seamen who might be found in their respective districts to Brest. Such orders I know have been given to many. And I supposed to you also, but a proof that you have been left in ignorance of such a step is your sending to Cherbourg a man whom Mr. Barlow had ordered to Paris for this privateer, and that you have prevented another who is now in Paris from engaging to go in her.[51]

Six Frigates: The Epic History of the Founding of the U.S. Navy (New York: W.W. Norton, 2008) Nicholas James Kaizer, *Revenge in the Name of Honour: The Royal Navy's Quest for Vengeance in the Single Ship Actions of the War of 1812* (Warwick: Helion, 2020).

[47] Kaizer, *Revenge in the Name of Honour*, p175.

[48] Barlow to Monroe. 20 August 1812. *Despatches from United States Ministers to France, 1789–1906*. Vol. 13. Microfilm copy.

[49] The first vessel's name apparently had some significance to the Haley family. Nathan Haley's younger brother, Simeon Haley, named a boat the *True-Blooded Yankee*. He acquired a Letter of Marque for it and with it captured some British marines in Long Island Sound. Amos Wheeler Papers, 1810–1818, New York State Library, SC20914. Folders 3 and 9.

[50] High Court of Admiralty: Oyer and Terminer Records. Minutes of Proceedings, 1759–1824. Trial of John Wiltshire. Testimony of George Brown. TNA. HCA 1/61.

[51] Preble to Barnet. 23 November 1812. United States. Department of State. *Despatches from United States Consuls in Paris, 1790–1906*. Vol. 4. Microfilm copy.

This is a strange volte face on Preble's part. Only a year previously, in applying for the position of United States consul at Nantes (which he did not get), he wrote to the Secretary of State, disapproving that

> There are many of the persons now acting as Vice Consul in the small Ports of the Channel that are highly improper; in lieu of protecting our seamen they contrive to get them on board of Privateers in which they have shares.[52]

This is precisely what Preble was doing in late 1812. Barnet strongly disagreed and refused to be bullied by Preble, replying:

> With respect to Mr. Barlow's sentiments and opinions on such armements I can say nothing. Nor did I know before that he had given orders to all the consuls of the U.S. in France to send on all the American seamen who might be found in their respective districts to Brest to assist in manning such a privateer! To me he gave no such <u>orders</u> – leaving me to follow the Instructions of the Law of our Government in relation to distrest seamen.[53]

Frustrated and getting ever more desperate for men, Preble turned to the prison depots.

As early as August 1812, Barlow was writing to the Ministry of War requesting the release of the prisoners, promising that, if the American prisoners were to be set free, he would send them home on an American vessel so that they would be available for the first call of men to serve in the war against Britain.[54] Thus, indirectly, they would be aiding France. A couple of weeks later, Barlow tried a new argument, as revealed in a report, signed by Houel and Goulhot, that was sent to Napoleon, which said that Barlow, as Minister Plenipotentiary, claimed that *all* American prisoners taken from English or Spanish ships had been either impressed or were voyaging as passengers when taken, meaning that they had not been serving Britain willingly. He was countering the argument that all seamen taken from British vessels had been serving Britain. However, as everyone knew, merchant vessels did not impress seamen; only Royal Navy vessels did so, making Barlow's claim patently untrue. "He assures," the report went on, "that he will take all precautions necessary [in order for the prisoners] not to be mistaken as to their

---

[52] Preble to Madison. 25 November 1811. United States. Department of State. *Letters of Application and Recommendation During the Administration of James Madison, 1809–1817.* Microfilm copy.

[53] Barnet to Preble. 25 November 1812. United States. Department of State. *Despatches from United States Consuls in Paris, 1790–1906.* Vol. 4. Microfilm copy.

[54] La Bessardière to Clarke. 4 August 1812. *Archives de la Guerre et Armée de Terre. Prisonniers de guerre français et étrangers (1792–1874).* SHDV. Yj19.

nationality."[55] What were the Emperor's wishes, the report asked. The Emperor granted Barlow's request.

On 18 October 1812, Napoleon ordered the release of all American seamen held as prisoners of war.[56] They would have to prove their nationality beyond any doubt, but they were all to be released. The Minister of War, Clarke, was to release them in groups to be marched, under guard as always, to the ports of Brest, Nantes, Bordeaux and Genès.[57] The word spread quickly round the prison depots and American seamen rejoiced. Unjustly and sadly, it was not to be.

In November 1812, Barlow had submitted to the Minister of External Affairs, Maret, his lists of prisoners' names with a request that they be released, not to take a ship home, as he had promised in August, but directly to Haley, in Brest. Maret took up the cause and wrote to Clarke at the Ministry of War, quoting Barlow verbatim:

> ...The situation of the USA in relation to the UK has changed since these men became prisoners. The two governments are today at war and one of the causes of this war is the treatment by one government of the American seamen...these...men will be used against England. Capt. Haley tells me he proposes to cruise only in European waters and to bring any prizes only to French ports...I beg of you to help Capt. Haley in any way possible.[58]

Napoleon's order had been to release all American seamen prisoners but now, Napoleon was on his way to Moscow. Preble and Haley wanted the prisoners to be released directly to the *True-Blooded Yankee*, in effect, to be impressed, and Barlow made the official request for them. Following Maret's parroted request, Clarke released the first group of more than 100 American seamen prisoners. They could have gone home. There were more than enough vessels that could have taken them, including numerous American vessels at Nantes that could not sail because of a lack of seamen to crew them. Yet, because of the pressure of Preble, Haley and Preble's nephew, Thomas Oxnard (initially the lieutenant and later master of the *True-Blooded Yankee*), it was determined

---

[55] Houel and Goulhot to Napoleon. Minute of a report. 27 August 1812. *Archives de la Guerre et Armée de Terre. Prisonniers de guerre français et étrangers (1792–1874)*. SHDV. Yj19.

[56] *Rapport à Sa Majesté l'Empereur et Roi de la Ministère de la Guerre du 23 Janvier 1813. Correspondance Politique États-unis*. Arch. dip. 39CP/70. Microfilm copy.

[57] Minister of External Relations to Barlow. 11 January 1813. *Correspondance Politique États-unis*. Arch. dip. 39CP/70. Microfilm copy.

[58] Maret to Clarke. 30 November 1812. *Correspondance Politique États-unis*. Arch. dip. 39CP/70. Microfilm copy.

that the released prisoners be marched straight to the privateer. They had left the depots by January 1813.

Once there, they had little choice. Haley was encouraging them to sign on with the usual promises of prize wealth. Jean Diot and Aaron Vail were involved as well, with such intensity that some financial investment in the privateer on their part might be suspected. John Jea, the gifted African-American preacher, who was also something of a pacifist, was amongst those released and his may be the only surviving words of those seamen:

> We arrived safe at Brest, thanks be to God, but we had great trials and difficulties on our march thither, being obliged to walk without shoes, and having no more provisions than what we could buy by our scanty allowance, which was a half-penny per mile; and when our feet were so sore that we could not march, we were not allowed any thing. Some of us had no clothes to cover our nakedness; and our lodgings at nights were in barns and cow-houses, and we were obliged to lay down the same as beasts, and indeed not so comfortable, for we were not allowed straw nor any thing else to lay on.
>
> As soon as we arrived at Brest we were sent on board of a French corvette[sic], under American colours [the *True-Blooded Yankee*], to go and fight against the English, but twenty, out of near two hundred that were sent on board, would not enlist under the banner of the tyrants of this world; for far be it from me ever to fight against Old England, unless it be with the sword of the gospel, under the captain of our salvation, Jesus Christ. Those of us who would not fight against the English, were sent on board of a French man of war, that they should punish us, but they would not, but sent us to Morlaix, about thirty miles from Brest, where they put us in prison, and kept us upon bread and water for a fortnight, then all the rest consented to go back on board of the corvette [the *True-Blooded Yankee*], rather than be sent again to the depot, for we were to be sent back loaded with chains, and under joint arms. I was the only one that stood out; and I told them I was determined not to fight against any one and that I would rather suffer any thing than do it. They said they would send me back to Cambria [the prison depot of Cambrai], and they would keep me upon bread and water, until the wars were over. I said I was willing to suffer any thing, rather than fight. They then took me before the council [consul], and the head minister of the Americans, to examine me. They asked me which I liked to do, to go back to the ship, or to be marched to Cambria. I told them they might send me on board of the vessel, if they liked; but if they did I was determined not to do any work, for I would rather suffer any thing than fight or kill any one. They then consulted together what they should do with me; and made up their minds to turn me out of prison....So they turned me out of their office; and said that I had liberty to go any where in the

town, but not out of the town; that they would not give me any work, provisions, or lodgings, but that I should provide it myself. ...

I was two days without food, walking about without any home, and I went into the hospitals, gaols, and open streets,...on the second day of my distress, after I was turned out of Morlaix prison into the streets, by order of the American counsellor Mr. Dyeott [Diot], and Mr. Veal [Vail] ... [59]

Jea was released from jail onto the streets of Morlaix, without money, forbidden to leave the town, forbidden to work, forbidden to beg. The intention clearly was to continue to starve him into submission, copying the French behaviour about which so many American consuls had complained. This despicable performance reveals the dark side of the American consular agent in Morlaix, Jean Diot, of whom Jea gives numerous examples of viciousness, and of the American consul of Lorient, Aaron Vail, who exhorted Jea to join the privateer, both of whom owned interests in privateers.[60] It also makes very plain the cynical indifference to the conflict of interest occasioned by a consul or agent for the United States, one of whose primary functions was to aid distressed American seamen, also being in the privateering business, which often led to them being the causes of that very distress.

From internal correspondence, it seems that the Minister of Marine and Colonies, Decrès, was kept unaware of all of this. In early January, he received a letter from the Minister of War, Clarke, informing him that Napoleon had authorized the release and that the majority of the first group were going to Brest where an American privateer was readying. Decrès wrote in a note to his secretary "Remind me why am I having to fight this same battle?" [That of releasing Americans] Then: "What is this about an American privateer at Brest?"[61] He was furious that the Americans had been released. As soon as Napoleon had approved the release of Americans, Decrès began trying to get

---

[59] Jea, *The Life*, p88–91.

[60] Jea eventually obtained permission from the mayor (at that point someone other than Diot, who previously had held that office) to preach in the streets, which inspired some of his listeners to help him. He survived fourteen months on their charity. At last, after the abdication of Napoleon in April 1814, when Morlaix filled with conquering British vessels and captains, one of them took Jea back to England, where he reunited with his wife and wrote his autobiography. His wife died not long afterward; he married a fourth time and became the father of a daughter. He died while on a preaching mission in St Helier, Jersey in late 1817 and is buried there. "John and Mary Jea". *The Mixed Museum*. Published 15 June 2022. https://mixedmuseum.org.uk/amri-exhibition/john-and-mary-jea/ [Accessed 20 October 2023].

[61] Clarke to Decrès. 7 January 1813. *Archives de la Marine, Prises – Bâtiments de l'État et corsaires.* SHDV. FF2/10.

him to rescind the order, saying that some British prisoners would inevitably be released with the Americans. Clarke disputed this: "I do not share the disquiet of the Minister of Marine in this regard as I took every precaution to ascertain the origins of these prisoners."[62] To the great disappointment of the Americans, Decrès managed to have further releases suspended until there could be an investigation.[63] In April 1813, he sent a detailed report to Napoleon on the release that had already occurred. 125 men had been released, he wrote. Of those, thirty-two were "known to be British"; ninety-two were Americans who had been taken from enemy vessels; just one, he asserted, was an American taken from an American vessel. He urged Napoleon to release no more prisoners.[64] Convinced by Decrès, Napoleon rescinded the order, and forbade any further releases of Americans, reverting to his original position that all Americans taken from British vessels were voluntarily serving the enemy and were to be considered and held as British prisoners of war.[65]

How could the American diplomats have done this? When Napoleon gave the order for the release, in October, Barlow was still in Paris and submitted lists of names of men to be released. By the time that Goulhot, at the Ministry of War, had gone over the list and Clarke had ordered the release, Barlow had died and Warden, Barnet, Lee and the rest of the consuls were engaged in their unseemly power struggle to temporarily replace him.

The lists of the men released to Haley survive in the archives, and show at least twenty-six men clearly born in Ireland, England or Scotland. This inclusion of British men should have had to have been justified by the Americans to Goulhot. Naturalizations should have had to have been proved, yet no documentation or correspondence of such proofs has survived. Amongst the many dozens of individuals discussed and disputed in the exchanges between the American diplomats and the French officials, not a word about these British men can be found. Without any attempt to hide their British origins, it seems, they were simply let go with the Americans. Someone, amongst the Americans, put the British names on the lists submitted to the French and someone, amongst the French in the Ministry of War, did not take their names off the lists, but approved them for release.

On the part of the American diplomats and those involved with the *True-Blooded Yankee*, it was a grievous betrayal of the American seamen

---

[62] Clarke to Bonaparte. 23 January 1813. *Archives de la Secrétairerie d'Etat impériale. Rapports du Ministre de la Guerre (1800–1814)*. Arch. nat. AF/IV/1194.

[63] Barnet to Monroe. 23 February 1813. United States. Department of State. *Despatches from United States Consuls in Paris, 1790–1906*. Vol. 4. Microfilm copy.

[64] Decrès to Bonaparte. 10 April 1813. *Archives de la Secrétairerie d'Etat impériale. Rapports du Ministre de la Guerre (1800–1814)*. Arch. nat. AF/IV/1194.

[65] La Bessardière to Warden. 25 June 1813. United States. Department of State. *Despatches from United States Consuls in Paris, 1790–1906*. Vol. 4. Microfilm copy.

prisoners. Had it been made clear that all the men in that first group were to be put on a cartel taking them to the United States, no British prisoner would have wanted to join them, since the two countries were at war and they would have been imprisoned on arrival. Instead, everyone in the prisons had heard the rumours that those released were to go to Brest to join a privateer that would sail around Britain. Had the American Minister Plenipotentiary and the consuls not so eagerly supported (and probably invested in) the privateer, and instead concentrated on ensuring that only Americans were on their lists of prisoners whose freedom they requested, Decrès would have had no grounds for complaint and Napoleon would not have rescinded his order. Most likely, had the American diplomats been more conscientious, the rest of the American seamen would have been released in 1813. Instead, those diplomats added British names to the list of those whose release to serve on the privateer was requested. Preble, Oxnard, Haley, Barlow, Diot, as well as Isaac Cox Barnet,[66] bear a large part of the responsibility for the fact that no further Americans were allowed to leave prison until the general release of all prisoners of war held in France after Napoleon's abdication in the spring of 1814, more than a year later, with more suffering and more deaths.

In summing up the negotiated releases, it is clear that Napoleon was never going to allow the release of any seaman taken from a British vessel, whether merchant or naval. Only Americans taken from American vessels that had been carrying American or other neutral cargo and that had not been to a British port or been visited by a Royal Navy ship and that had perfect ships' papers in perfect order might be released. The number of such men was small. Even these were prevented from being released as much as possible by Decrès. Of the American diplomats, it is the irascible, unfriendly and unpopular Armstrong who emerges as something of a saviour. In 1807, he managed to restrain his surly ways to be able to go through the arduous and frustrating ordeal of complying with the French requirements for ever more documented proof. The cynical abuse of the truly helpless prisoners by the American diplomats and community involved in the 1813 release is shameful. The men who were released were not allowed to go home but had to work a privateer. To be sure, it is likely that some welcomed the chance to fight or at least to gain some prize money, but others, like John Jea, did not. They had no choice; in truth it was no release but more of a transfer of prisoners. The consequence of including some British prisoners in the group released was for Napoleon to rescind his order for the release of Americans and for the hundreds still in prison to have to stay there, betrayed by their own consuls and Minister.

---

[66] Warden places the blame for the inclusion of British prisoners amongst the Americans entirely on Barnet. Warden to Crawford. 1 September 1813. United States. Department of State. *Despatches from United States Consuls in Paris, 1790–1906*. Vol. 5. Microfilm copy. However, Clubb said he was "that friend of the real American", "A Journal", p189.

CONCLUSION

The experience of the American merchant seamen in the prison depots intended for British prisoners of war sheds new light on life in those depots. Compared with the British seamen together with whom they were held, the experience of the American seamen was more difficult: most received no aid, they could attend no school, they had no hope of exchange, almost none could hope for parole and they were so far from home that, though many tried, escape was almost pointless. They were, however, able to attend British church services and British hospitals that were established in the depots. Diplomatically, the British and French authorities had the formalities and structure for discussing and arranging the exchange of prisoners on both sides and there was regular communication between the Ministry of Marine and Colonies and the Royal Navy's Transport Board, comfortable as old adversaries. The American ministers and consuls had no such precedent, no treaties or formalities concerning prisoners held by a country with which theirs was not at war, and they struggled to argue every case individually.

The individuality of the cases of these American merchant seamen is what this study has revealed most of all. As prisoners of war in France, they were temporarily a distinct group. Before and after that, like all merchant seamen, they individually moved across other temporarily distinct groups. Evidence in the various sources used here has shown how a seaman could have moved from one merchant vessel to another, from one flag, or vessel nationality, to another, from a merchant vessel to a privateer, from being impressed onto a Royal Navy vessel to joining the Navy and serving on a United States Navy vessel, and back to any one of them again. They moved in rank, or shipboard job, as well, from ordinary seaman to able-bodied seaman to mate to prize captain; some were carpenters or sailmakers; a few were shipmasters. During the Napoleonic Wars and the War of 1812, they could end up in French or British prisons or both. They were more than tattoos or names on crew lists or prison registers; each was a complex individual with a unique past and a unique career at sea.

They were not an anonymous mass; but researching them, as this study has shown, requires delving into a variety of record types in different collections in different countries, for each seaman left traces in different places as he voyaged, and in different categories of documentation as he moved from one type of employment to another. In truth, there is enough information on

Early Republic merchant seamen, though scattered around the Atlantic world, to be able to construct biographies about many of them.

Their imprisonment in France revealed the critical flaw in the consular service of the Early Republic, that of expecting consuls to consider the fees they charged as their salary. The inevitable corruption that ensued when *armateurs* and shipping agents were given the position of consul or consular agent was compounded by the conflict of interest in their working in the interests of both the capturers of and the captured ships, most seriously because that led them, in many cases, to work against the interests of the seamen they were pledged to help. If most of the American consular service in France have been shown to have been stained, it is hoped that the reputation of one Minister Plenipotentiary, John Armstrong, usually depicted as impossibly bad tempered and unable to get things done, may be somewhat rehabilitated by this study.

The efforts of Armstrong and, less so, of the others, to gain the release from French prisons of the American merchant seamen highlight but do not significantly contribute to the developing sense of citizenship and nationality as discussed in Brunsman, Alonso and Perl-Rosenthal. Brunsman points out that impressment ironically created a stronger sense of citizenship amongst American seamen, while Perl-Rosenthal makes the case that the Seaman's Protection Certificate was the precursor of the passport as a citizenship document instead of the single journey travel document passports had been. However, for the American seamen trapped in French prisons, the issue was not only their nationality but their individual, personal (as opposed to their country's) neutrality, which could have been lost if they had been on British vessels. In most cases, no one doubted their American nationality; it simply made no difference. Though they could not be freed without proving that they were American, that proof did not guarantee their freedom. They were trapped by wars, and their suffering ended only when the wars did, regardless of their citizenship.

Future Work

This study covers almost exclusively the American seamen held prisoner in France who had been captured in the English Channel or the Atlantic. There were an estimated 200 French privateers in the Mediterranean Sea during the First Empire. It appears that they may have deposited their prisoners in military prisons; prisoners taken in the Mediterranean are almost entirely absent from the British prisoner of war depots.[1] A study of what they did with the prisoners they took is warranted. The same is true of prisoners captured

---

[1] I am indebted to Dr Patrick Villiers for this information.

by French West Indies privateers. Their prisoners seem not to have been sent to France; what happened to them?

Moving from those captured by French privateers to those on the crews of French privateers, no study has been done of the American seamen or those of other nationalities who were held in British prisons as French prisoners of war because they had been working on French privateers or merchant vessels. The multinational origins of prisoners could take on a different character when more might be understood about the flags of the vessels from which they were taken.

Finally, a very interesting study would be to compare the details about the American seamen who left Royal Navy vessels, once the War of 1812 began, as they were noted in the General Entry books of Dartmoor, Chatham and other British prisons with the details about the same men in the muster books of the vessels from which they came. How much agreement would there be between the two record types as to name, place of birth, dates, age, and whether or not impressed?

EPILOGUE

Opening the Prison Gates

The remaining hundreds of American seamen held in French prisons had to await the order for the release of all prisoners of war in France, which was not published by the provisional government until 13 April 1814.[1] Britain and the coalition had conquered France, and Napoleon was on Elba, but the United States and Britain were still at war. From the declaration of the War of 1812 in June of that year to Napoleon's first abdication in April 1814, France and the United States were both at war with Great Britain and aided one another. Most importantly for American seamen, American vessels were allowed into French ports and American privateers could sail from and send their prizes in to French ports. From April 1814, those permissions were rescinded by the provisional and later the Bourbon government and France suddenly was declared neutral in the War of 1812. Orders went out to seize any American privateers that entered French ports.[2] Thus, when the prison gates were opened and the prisoners walked out of the depots and headed for the Atlantic coast, though there were many ships to take British prisoners across the Channel, there were no American vessels in French ports to take the American seamen home.

By that time, William H. Crawford had arrived as Minister Plenipotentiary and had begun to get some control over the warring consuls. He dismissed David Bailie Warden and promoted Barnet from consul of Le Havre to consul general at Paris. He also vastly preferred the occupying, English force to his French hosts and, as noted, enjoyed spending time with Wellington. The fact that his country was at war with Britain seemed in no way to diminish this preference but it may help to explain the sudden silence, which lasted for most of his term in office, in the diplomatic dispatches from France. Not only was their new minister ruling with a firm hand, but he had to work with his new hosts, the Bourbon government and the British, while at the same time

---

[1] France. *Bulletin des lois de la République française.* Paris: *Imprimerie nationale des lois*, 1814, p39.
[2] Crawford to Talleyrand. 26 May 1814. United States. Department of State. *Despatches from United States Ministers to France, 1789–1906.* Vol. 15. Microfilm copy.

many of the consular agents, such as Diot, had been ardent revolutionaries and *armateurs* of privateers; many of the consuls, such as Aaron Vail, had been actively involved in financing privateers that had attacked and would still attack British shipping.

To his credit, Crawford did try to arrange for cartels to take the American prisoners home, but not until months after they were released. He pointed out to the French that, as the United States was not at war with France, American vessels should be free to enter French ports. The provisional government, directed by his friend, Wellington, speaking through Talleyrand (once again the Minister of Foreign Affairs), remained adamant in its refusal.[3] Keeping over 1000 released American seamen trapped in France and unable to man American vessels in their war with the United States was to Britain's benefit.

Distressed Seamen Once More

As the months passed, the indigent seamen gathering at the ports, unable to find a vessel and without sustenance, became a concern to all. Two more groups of American seamen added to the problem. Firstly, the American prisoners who had signed on to French privateers that were then captured by the Royal Navy and who had been imprisoned as French were released from British prisons (Crawford was mistaken when he wrote that they had escaped, below) in April and May 1814. They were sent to French ports, such as Calais and Morlaix, with the rest of the released French prisoners of war. Secondly, many Royal Navy vessels that had captured American seamen at sea could not be bothered to send them in to overcrowded British prisons but dumped them in French ports, where they joined the massing, destitute American seamen unable to find a passage home.[4] In July, shipmasters in New York were requesting permission from Monroe to sail cartels to France to bring the seamen home[5] but, three months later, Crawford was writing that

> The number of distressed seamen now in France occasions expenditure of the public money much greater I fear than you had anticipated. The discharge of them from their French depots threw a number upon the hands of the Consuls, naked and penniless. This number has been considerably increased by those who have escaped from the prison ships of England. The *Wasp* took off about fifteen and I intend to

[3] Crawford to Talleyrand. 30 September 1814. United States. Department of State. *Despatches from United States Ministers to France, 1789–1906*. Vol. 15. Microfilm copy.
[4] Crawford to Monroe. 8 June 1814. United States. Department of State. *Despatches from United States Ministers to France, 1789–1906*. Vol. 15. Microfilm copy.
[5] Daniel Preston, ed, *A Comprehensive Catalogue of the Correspondence and Papers of James Monroe*, Vol. 3 (Greenwood: Greenwood Press, 2001), p406. Knox to Monroe. 18 July 1814; Rogers to Monroe. 20 July 1814.

send home as many as can be stowed into the Transit unless I am prevented by the French govt. I think it would be judicious to order the first frigate which makes a cruize to touch in one of the ports of France for the purpose of taking off these destitute seamen.[6]

The released British prisoners went to the Atlantic ports of Morlaix, Saint Malo, Boulogne, Calais, Dieppe, Lorient and Le Havre, where cartels were ready to take them across the Channel. Most American seamen were frantic to avoid being included with them, as it would take them to the enemy country where they would immediately be sent to a British prison. Some, inevitably, did end up in Britain where, accepting their fate apparently, a few simply walked to the prisons and turned themselves in. The American seamen who had been prisoners of war in France and who ended up prisoners of war in Britain were held on prison hulks and in prisons at Chatham, at Portsmouth and at Dartmoor.[7] There they would have encountered Americans who had been captured from privateers and merchant vessels, just as they had done in France, but also the hundreds of American seamen who had been impressed by the Royal Navy and who, once war was declared, refused to serve against their own country.

For those who had been forced onto the *True-Blooded Yankee*, the fates of many are not known but some ended up in Dartmoor. The *True-Blooded Yankee* sailed on four cruises out of Brest during the War of 1812, and captured approximately thirty-six prizes.[8] Of those, three were given up to the crews (loaded with unwanted prisoners taken from the prizes and let go), eight or more were burnt, sunk, or driven on shore to wreck, and perhaps sixteen were sold in France or Norway. At least nine, however, plus the privateer's tender, were recaptured by Royal Navy ships, sending their prize crews, about thirty American seamen, to prison in Britain. Of the British who had been released with the American prisoners in 1813 in France and were on one of the *True-Blooded Yankee*'s retaken prizes, only one, John Wiltshire, described above, was discovered to be British and hung for treason.

---

[6] Crawford to Monroe. 21 October 1814. United States. Department of State. *Despatches from United States Ministers to France, 1789–1906*. Vol. 15. Microfilm copy.

[7] The story of the American prisoners held by the British at Dartmoor, and of the "Dartmoor Massacre" has been told often and thoroughly elsewhere and does not fall under the purview of this study of American prisoners of Napoleon. See Neil Davie's *French and American Prisoners of War at Dartmoor Prison, 1805–1816: The Strangest Experiment*. (London: Palgrave Macmillan, 2021); and Charles Andrews's *The Prisoners' Memoirs, or Dartmoor Prison…1815*, New York.

[8] Because the accounts of the *True-Blooded Yankee*'s prizes do not all agree and do not name all of the vessels, the total number of its prizes can only be approximate.

Most of the released American prisoners in France probably did not find a passage home until the end of 1814 or later, when the war between the United States and Britain was nearly over. There really was no one amongst the diplomats who had understood their situation previously who was available at this time to help them. All were occupied elsewhere. In late 1814, John Armstrong, who had arranged the release of many, was in no position to assist in their return, having just been removed from office as Secretary for War and blamed for the British Army's burning of Washington, D.C. and the White House in what was surely America's most enduringly humiliating memory of the War of 1812. Fulwar Skipwith, who possibly was the man who showed them the most compassion, was busy in the politics of Louisiana. Jonathan Russell, who had done what he could for them during his short stay in Paris, was in Ghent, one of the Americans negotiating the treaty that would end the war. After Crawford had dismissed him, David Bailie Warden remained in France and returned to his true calling of science and scholarship. None showed any residual interest in the American seamen prisoners.

In France, Napoleon had abdicated, Paris had been ransacked by Cossacks, and the British were guiding the restored Bourbon monarchy, many of whose aristocratic supporters fervently sought revenge on both the revolutionaries and all who supported the First Empire, in what became known as the "White Terror", white being the colour of the Bourbon flag. The United States consuls and consular agents most surely had to be very circumspect. Previously, their war efforts for the United States against Great Britain had been compatible with France's war against the same enemy; now, defeated France was run by a provisional government directed by Great Britain, which declared France neutral in the ongoing war between the United States and Great Britain. The consuls in France were paralyzed, threatened with arrest if they violated the neutrality, and American privateers in French ports were ordered to be seized. For those who had financed privateers attacking British vessels, such as Diot (Aaron Vail had died in 1813), they were doubly suspect. None seems to have stepped forward to provide a vessel to take the seamen home.

The American prisoners of Napoleon received no heroes' welcome when they managed to straggle home. Those who returned home from British prisons in 1815 received slightly more attention than any who made it home from France; their country's press, better at outrage than accolades, wrote much about the "Dartmoor massacre" in Britain and precious little about the returning seamen who had manned one of the privateers of which it was so proud, or about the men who had bravely exchanged impressment for imprisonment, or about those seamen who had been in French prisons for ten years longer than those held in Dartmoor. But for rare mentions of a few in family histories, such as those of Job Ellis Brewster and Francis Felton, both of whom would die at sea, the fates of nearly all of the American prisoners in France are unknown. They disappear back into the population of labourers at sea.

APPENDIX A:
AMERICAN PRISONERS WHO WERE RELEASED

Lists for the men released in 1807 as a result of John Armstrong's diplomatic efforts and of those released in early 1813 and sent to Brest survive in the archives of the *Service Historique de la Défense* at Vincennes, scattered amongst different cartons in the Yj series. It is not clear if these lists are complete. No departing passenger lists for the vessels on which they left France survive. The twenty-six British or Irish men released with the 1813 group are not included here. The names of a small number of men who were released individually are given at the end.

Seamen Prisoners of War released in 1807

These men were released in November 1807 and marched to Dieppe or Antwerp; most of them took ships to America. Because of the complaints of seamen in Arras that most were masters, those who were have their status as such indicated in bold type.

Ash, Robert, of Baltimore, **shipmaster**, held at Verdun and Valenciennes
Barnes, William, of Boston, seaman, held at Arras
Bunker, Christopher, of Nantucket, **shipmaster**, held at Verdun and Valenciennes
Carpenter, Joseph, of Baltimore, **shipmaster**, held at Verdun
Carteret, Samuel, of Boston, seaman, held at Valenciennes and Verdun
Chute, David, of Salem, held at Arras
Clemens, William, of Salem, seaman, held at Arras
Conner, John, of New York, seaman, held at Arras
Cook, Richard, of Philadelphia, **shipmaster**, held at Verdun
Dodds, Thomas, of Falmouth, Massachusetts, held at Arras
Dunlop, Robert, **shipmaster**, held at Valenciennes and Verdun
Eatton, John, **shipmaster**, held at Verdun
Folger, Christopher, of Nantucket, mate, held at Verdun and Sarrelibre
Folger, Obadiah, **shipmaster**, held at Verdun
Gilmore, John, **shipmaster**, held at Verdun
Gutteridge, William, of Washington, D.C., held at Arras
Haig, John, possibly of Quebec, **passenger**, held at Verdun and Sarrelibre

Hayes, Daniel, **shipmaster, British**, held at Sarrelibre and Verdun
Hickman, David or Daniel, of Philadelphia, seaman, held at Arras
Holly, John, **shipmaster**, held at Verdun
Jacob, Jean or John, of Baltimore, seaman, held at Arras
Kerr, Berkley, seaman
Kerridge, Thomas, of New York, seaman, held at Arras
LePrevost, Job, mate, **British**, held at Sarrelibre, Verdun, Valenciennes
LeFevre, Edward, possibly a marine, held at Verdun
McAdore, James, of New York, seaman, held at Arras
Merry, Benjamin, of Boston, mate, held at Valenciennes, Verdun, Sarrelibre
Milton, John, of Boston, seaman, held at Arras
Neil, George, **shipmaster**, held at Verdun
Page, Christopher, of Rhode Island, seaman, held at Arras
Russel (Rosal?), Peter, of New York, **officer**, held at Arras
Saulman, William, of Marblehead, seaman, held at Arras
Scott, John, of Boston, **officer or passenger**, held at Arras
Amery, a **child**, escorted by Scott, above, of New York
Shaw, William, **shipmaster, British**, held at Verdun
a Prince of the Congo, **slave**?, with Shaw, above
Shipley, John, of Boston, seaman, held at Arras
Snow, John, of Charleston, seaman, South Carolina, held at Arras
Stewart, William, of Norfolk, Virginia, seaman, held at Arras
Thomas, John, of Bridge Town, Maryland, seaman, held at Arras
Thompson, Edward, **shipmaster**, held at Verdun
Wells, Dickson, of George's Street, New York City, **officer**, held at Arras
Wilson, John, **shipmaster**, held at Verdun
Wise, George, of New York, held at Arras

Seamen Prisoners of War Released in 1813

The various prison depots confirmed that these men were released in January 1813. They were marched to Brest but they did not all join the American privateer there. Some took work on different vessels.

Adams, John or James, of New York, held at Arras and Cambrai
Amber, Joseph, of New Orleans
Anderson, John, of Jamaica, New York, held at Arras
Andrews, Jeremiah, of New York, held at Arras
Atchinson, Thomas, of Norfolk, Virginia, held at Arras
Ayres, Robert, of Philadelphia, held at Arras

Bacchus, Peter, of New York, held at Arras and Cambrai
Barden, Mitchell or Michael, of New York, held at Arras
Beaston, Robert, of Alexandria, Virginia, held at Cambrai

Benton, Elias, of New York, held at Arras
Bradley, John, of Norfolk, Virginia, held at Cambrai and Valenciennes
Briggs, Bolen, of Virginia, held at Arras and Cambrai
Briggs, John, of Windham, Connecticut, held at Givet
Brook, Philip L., of New York, held at Arras and Cambrai
Brown, John, of Marblehead
Brown, Seth, of Bristol [unclear which state], held at Arras
Bryan, George, of Derry [New Hampshire?]
Bryan, Thomas, of New York, held at Briançon
Buck, Jonathan, of Boston, held at Auxonne and Longwy

Cadich, Henry, of Baltimore, held at Cambrai
Carnes or Cernes, Thomas, of Virginia, held at Arras, Valenciennes, Calais
Carver, Peter, of Maryland, held at Cambrai
Christie, John, of Wilmington [unclear which state], held at Arras
Churchill, Stephen, of Richmond, Virginia, held at Arras and Valenciennes
Clark, Abraham Daniel, of Fishkill, New York, held at Auxonne and Longwy
Cole, Nathan, of Barrington, Rhode Island
Cole, William, of Alexandria, Virginia, held at Cambrai
Cooper, Isaac, of Long Island, New York, held at Arras
Cooper, James, of Long Island, New York, held at Arras
Coxson, John, of Baltimore, held at Arras and Cambrai

Daniels, James or Samuel, of Norfolk, Virginia, held at Cambrai and Arras
Davy, George, held at Arras
Dennis, Thomas, of New York or Marblehead, held at Sedan
Devereux, Benjamin, of Boston or Salem, held at Arras and Cambrai
Dyer, Jonathan, of Boston or Cape Cod, held at Cambrai and Valenciennes

Farren, Hugh, of Irish Town Parish, New York, held at Valenciennes
Farret, George, of Georgetown or Charleston, held at Arras
Follingsbee, William, of Newburyport, held at Valenciennes and Cambrai
Forrester, William, of Salem, held at Longwy and Bitche
Fox, James, of Alexandria, Virginia, held at Valenciennes
Franklin, George, of Alexandria, Virginia, held at Arras
Freeman, Edmond, of Virginia, held at Arras
Fromager, Samuel, held at Verdun
Fuller, John, of Salem, held at Givet

Gerald, John, of Washington or North Carolina, held at Arras and Cambrai
Gibson, George, of Savannah, held at Valenciennes
Godfrey, Cesar of Newport, Rhode Island, held at Arras and Cambrai
Griffin, Thomas, of Norfolk or Petersburg, Virginia, held at Arras, Cambrai, Verdun

Hall, John, of Baltimore, held at Arras and Cambrai
Hastings, Thomas, of Sedgwick, Massachusetts [now in Maine], held at Arras
Hatch, John, of New York, held at Arras
Hearl, Hiram, of Berwig, Massachusetts [now in Maine], held at Longwy
Holland, James, held at Givet
Hornewater, Henry, of Wappin's Creek, New York, held at Givet
Hubble, James, of Connecticut or New York, held at Cambrai
Hudson, Thomas, of Boston, held at Valenciennes, Bagne de Brest, Bitche

Ingersoll, Abraham, of Boston, held at Cambrai

Jackson, John, of Norfolk, Virginia, held at Arras
Jea or Jay, John H., of Africa or New York, held at Cambrai
Johnson, Nicholas, of Albany, New York, held at Bitche
Johnson, Robert, of Norfolk, Virginia, held at Arras, Valenciennes, Sarrelibre
Jones, Thomas, of Philadelphia, held at Cambrai and Valenciennes

Lawson, Lawrence, of New York, held at Cambrai and Valenciennes
LeBaron, Peter, of Cape Ann, Massachusetts, held at Valenciennes
Ley or Lay, William, of Boston, held at Arras
Little, John, of Philadelphia, held at Valenciennes and Cambrai
Livermore, Arthur, of Pembroke, Massachusetts, held at Valenciennes
Love, John, Of New Haven, Connecticut, held at Givet
Lovett, William, of Eastport and Passamaquoddy, held at Longwy

Macguire, Daniel, of Baltimore, held at Mont Dauphin
Marr, John, of Waterford
Matthews, Lewis of Dover, Pennsylvania, held at Arras
Mayo, Nathaniel, of Cape Cod, held at Longwy
Mead, John, of Philadelphia, held at Valenciennes
Meaton, John, held at Verdun
Metford, Philip, of Perth Amboy, New Jersey, held at Cambrai
Millroy, Richard (or Bennett, Thomas), held at Bitche
Moore, George, of New York, held at Arras
Moore, John, of Norwich, Connecticut, held at Mont Dauphin and Briançon
Morris, Elias, of New York, held at Cambrai

Nicholson, Samuel, of Philadelphia, held at Valenciennes

Pickham, Nelson or Lazard, held at Arras
Pollard, John, of New Hampshire, held at Givet
Porter, Humphrey, of New York, held at Givet
Potts, William, of Wilmington, Delaware, held at Arras and Cambrai
Powers, Morgan, held at Cambrai

Richards, John William, of Boston, held at Arras
Rider, Henry, of Boston, held at Auxonne, Sarrelibre, Bitche
Riley, John (alias used by John Wiltshire) of New York, held at Arras and Cambrai
Robson, Robert, held at Longwy
Rogers, Francis, of Philadelphia, held at Arras
Ross, James, of New York, held at Cambrai and Arras
Ross, Jeremiah, of Massachusetts, held at Givet

Shepherd, James, of New York, held at Arras
Skinner, Ebenezer, of Nantucket, held at Valenciennes and Cambrai
Smith, James, of Germantown [unclear which state], held at Arras and Cambrai
Smith, John, of Boston, held at Cambrai and Arras
Snelling, James, of New York or Philadelphia, held at Cambrai
Stevens, William, of Connecticut, held at Cambrai
Story, William, of Philadelphia, held at Arras, Longwy, Verdun
Suttman, Martin, of New Bedford, held at Givet

Taylor, Thomas, of Philadelphia, held at Valenciennes

Walker, Thomas, of Boston, held at Cambrai
Warner, Joseph, held at Arras, Valenciennes, Givet
Warner, Philip, held at Verdun
Waterman, Stephen, of Nantucket, held at Verdun
Watson, Henry, of Newport or New York, held at Givet
Weeks, James, held at Briançon
Welch, William, of Virginia, held at Cambrai
White, James, of Stillwater, New York, held at Cambrai
Wilkinson, Benjamin, of Virginia, held at Cambrai
Willey, Ebenezer, of Doron, New Hampshire, held at Briançon
Williams, Charles, held at Cambrai
Williams, John, of Staten Island, New York
Williamson, John, held at Cambrai
Wilson, George D., of Petersburg, Virginia, held at Arras, Cambrai, Bitche, Briançon
Woodbury, Samuel, of Baltimore, held at Mont Dauphin

Seamen of the *Massachusetts* and *Saratoga*, released from the jail at Roscoff, July 1812

Massachusetts

Baron, Lasard or Lazard
Case, Allen (shipmaster)
Herrinton or Herrington, John

Milles, William
Skilding, Samuel
Stewart, Isaac

Saratoga

Allan or Allen, Abishai
Alwood or Atwood, David
Baker, Barkir or Barker (shipmaster)
Capy, John
Cole, Nathan
Gaitworth, James
Jacobs, Peter
Knowles, Caleb
Knowles, Smith
Smith, Samuel H.
Taylor, George
Williston, Samuel

Individually Released

Almy, Thomas C., of New York
Bradley, John, held at Briançon and Cambrai, released in 1812
Clark, John of Charles County, Maryland, released in 1812
Clubb, Stephen, British, released in 1809
Forrest, Thomas, of Long Island, New York
Gibson, Alexander
Gunton, Thomas, of New York, released in 1812
Harrison, Hugh, of Charleston, South Carolina, released in 1809
Hazzard, William, Irish resident of Baltimore, released in 1810
Henderson, Robert, his wife and five children, of Philadelphia, released in 1809
Tent, William, held at Valenciennes
Turner, John, held at Cambrai
Watson, Thomas, released in 1808

APPENDIX B:
AMERICAN PRISONERS WHO ESCAPED

Those marked with an asterisk * were recaptured.
No account of an escape by an American seaman has been found. Note by the asterisks below that most were recaptured.

*Adams, John, from Edenton, North Carolina, escaped from Auxonne
*Archer, Edward, from Baltimore, escaped from Cambrai
*Ash, Richard, from Baltimore, escaped from Auxonne

*Barnes, William, from Boston, escaped from Arras
*Barnet, Charles, of New York, escaped from a French privateer at Amsterdam
*Bassett, William, from Norfolk, Virginia, escaped from Valenciennes
*Brosse, Henry, of Baltimore, escaped from Givet
*Brown, John, of Boston, escaped from a French privateer at Dieppe

*Caggin, Solomon, of Georgetown, escaped from a French privateer at Boulogne-sur-Mer
*Campbell, Samuel, of Portsmouth, escaped from Longwy
*Carpenter, Joseph, of Baltimore, escaped from Auxonne
*Care or Carr, James, from New York, escaped from Arras
Cook, Richard, of Philadelphia, escaped from Arras
*Correl, Samuel, of Boston, escaped from Arras
Cowing, Charles, of Boston, escaped from a French privateer at Boulogne-sur-Mer

*Deal, Louis, of Annapolis, escaped from Cambrai

Ellicot, Charles, of Dumfries, Virginia, escaped from a French privateer

Gambles, William, escaped from a French privateer
*Griggs, William, of New York, escaped from Arras

*Hall, John, of Baltimore, escaped from a French privateer
*Harrison, Thomas, escaped from the hospital at Briançon

*Hartnell, Francis, of New York, escaped from Cambrai
*Hatch, John, of New York, escaped from Cambrai
*Hattridge, Robert Charles M., of New York, escaped from Auxonne
*Hathaway, Reuben, of Boston, escaped from Valenciennes
*Hayes, Daniel, escaped from Sarrelibre
*Henderson, James, escaped from Arras
Hill, Thomas, of New York, escaped at Amiens while being marched to a prison depot
*Hudson, Thomas, escaped from Valenciennes, sent to the Bagne de Brest, the to Bitche
*Hughes, John, of Whitehaven, Maryland, escaped from a French privateer at Dieppe

Illeman, Joseph, of New York, escaped from a French privateer

Low or Law, Daniel, of Newbury, escaped from a French privateer at Calais

*MacPherson, David, of Philadelphia, escaped from Arras
*Marsh, Samuel, of Marblehead, escaped from Arras
Marshall, John, of Philadelphia, escaped from a French privateer at Dieppe
Martin, John, escaped from a French privateer at Amsterdam
*Martin, Thomas, of New Jersey, escaped from a French privateer at Dieppe
McPherson, John, from New York, escaped from Auxonne

*Ormerod, Richard, of Norfolk, Virginia, escaped from Cambrai
Owise, Joseph, escaped from the hospital at Briançon

Patisen [Patterson?], George, escaped from Briançon
Pearat, Elias, of Charleston, South Carolina, escaped from a French privateer
Penning, Charles, of Baltimore, escaped from Cambrai
Perry, Edward, of New York, escaped from a French privateer at Amsterdam
*Potts, William, of Wilmington, Delaware, escaped from Cambrai

*Rider, Henry, of Boston, escaped from Longwy
Roberts, John, escaped from a French privateer
*Russell, Thomas, of Charleston, South Carolina, escaped from Valenciennes

Savage, Antony, of Baltimore, escaped from a French privateer at Dieppe
*Sharp, John, of Baltimore, escaped from a French privateer at Lorient
Sinclair, John, of Philadelphia, escaped from a French privateer
Smith, James, of City Point, Virginia, escaped from a French privateer
Smith, William, of New York, escaped from the Tour Solidor

*Spurrings, Thomas, of Plymouth, Massachusetts, escaped from a French privateer
Swift, John, of New York, escaped from a French privateer

*Tait, William, escaped from a French privateer at Dunkirk

Welch, William, of Virginia, escaped from a French privateer
*Williams, John, of Philadelphia, escaped from Vincennes
*Williams, John, of Boston, escaped from Arras

APPENDIX C:
AMERICAN PRISONERS WHO DIED IN FRANCE

Nearly all of the deaths listed below can be found online on the websites of the Departmental Archives, which have made available the civil registers of births, marriages and deaths from 1792 through to at least 1902. Many of the registers of Givet have been lost. Some, but not all, of the deaths also appear in the ADM series.

Abbot, Ephraim, of Plainfields, New Jersey, died at Cambrai in 1811
Allen, Joseph, of Boston, died at La Rochelle in 1810
Anderson, George, of Alexandria, Virginia, died at Sedan in 1811
Annable, Samuel, of Charlestown, Massachusetts, died at Bayonne in 1808
Archer, Edward, of Baltimore, died at Besançon in 1813
Baggs, Daniel, of Charleston, South Carolina, died at Bordeaux in 1802
Bailie, Elias, died at Arras in 1808
Bassett, Robert, of New York, died at Metz in 1805
Bayley, John, of New York, died at Givet in 1807
Beach, Joseph, of Boston, died at Cambrai in 1813
Boston, Prince, of Nantucket, died at Cambrai in 1813
Bowen, Seth, of West Jersey, died at Arras in 1807
Bradfield, Thomas, of New York, died at Metz in 1810
Brogen, Thomas, of New York, died at Givet in 1814
Brosse, Henry, of Baltimore, died at Givet in 1808
Brown, William, of Boston, died at Mont Dauphin in 1811
Bruce, Robert, of Rhode Island, died at Arras in 1811
Buck, Jonathan, of Boston, died at Metz in 1813
Bunker, Henry, died at Metz in 1807
Bunker, Peleg, of Nantucket, died at Verdun in 1806
Carpenter, Joseph, of Baltimore, died at Bitche in 1811
Charleton, William, died at Mont Dauphin in 1812
Clark, Henry, of Boston, died at Arras in 1812
Clark, Thomas, of Portsmouth, New Hampshire, died at Arras in 1809
Clark, William, of Philadelphia, died at Givet in 1810
Cloberts, Joseph, of Philadelphia, died at Mont Dauphin in 1810
Clowburn, John, died at Arras in 1809

Colbertson, John of New York or Newark, died at Cambrai in 1811
Cooper, Isaac, of Philadelphia, died at Arras in 1813
Cornell or Connell, James, of Flushing, New York, died at Arras in 1807
Cowen, John, of Boston, died at Arras in 1808
Dickson, or Dixon, Richard, of Charlestown, had been released to join the privateer, *Indomptable*, died at Roscoff of wounds received during the privateer's battle with a British cutter in 1810
Direndal, John Prents, of Philadelphia, died at Metz in 1813
Dougherty, Paul, of Boston, died at Arras in 1809
Drickle, Richard, of Boston, died at Arras in 1807
Francis, David, of New York, died at Bitche in 1805
Freeman, Elijah, of New York, died at Arras in 1807
Frisby, Archibald, died at Arras in 1807
Gibson, Thomas, of New York, died at Cambrai in 1813
Glough, Isaac, died at Bordeaux in 1806
Gregory, Thomas, of Baltimore or Fredericksburg, died at Auxonne in 1810
Griggs, William, of New York, died at Bitche in 1809
Grubb, George, of Philadelphia, died at Arras in 1812
Hamilton, John, of Baltimore, died at Arras in 1807
Harper, Richard, of Boston, died at Bayonne in 1805
Hartley, Jeremiah, of New York, died at Arras in 1808
Hathaway, Reuben, of Boston, died at Bitche in 1809
Hawkesmore, Robert, of New York, died at Cambrai in 1813
Haylene, Joseph, of Newburyport, died at Arras in 1814
Hayman, John, of Boston, died at Arras in 1808
Jacob, Antony, of New York, died at Metz in 1804
Johnson, James, of Norfolk, Virginia, died at Valenciennes in 1812
Johnson, John, of Charleston, South Carolina, died at Bitche in 1805
Johnson, William, of New York, died at Cambrai in 1811
Joseph, John, of "New England", died at Arras in 1806
Kenny, Stephen, of Philadelphia, died at Arras in 1807
King, Joseph, of Rhode Island, died at Cambrai in 1812
Lawson, Henry, of Virginia, died at Givet in 1811
Lewis, William, of Philadelphia, died at Cambrai in 1813
Macdonald, Daniel, of Richmond County, North Carolina, died at Sedan in 1813
Macy, Aston, of Charlestown, Massachusetts, died at Bitche in 1807
Manchester, Daniel, of Rhode Island, died at Cambrai in 1811
Maurel, Antoine, of Philadelphia, died at Marseilles in 1814
Mayhill, John, of Rhode Island, died at Valenciennes in 1805
McKinnon, John, of New York, died at Dieppe in 1809
Melvin, Hezekiah, of Norfolk, Virginia, died at Cambrai in 1813
Miller, Kelless, of Philadelphia, died at Toulouse in 1804
Miller, Robert, of New York, died at Cambrai in 1811

Mitchell, John, of Boston, died at Cambrai in 1812
Morris, Joseph, of Nantucket, died at Arras in 1807
Mumford or Manford, James, of New York, died at Givet in 1807
Nelson, John, died at Metz in 1808
Netterville, William, of Portsmouth, New Hampshire, died at Cambrai in 1811
Patrick, William, of New York, died at Metz in 1806
Preston, Edward, died at Arras in 1808
Richardson, Robert, of New York, died at Arras in 1808
Richardson, William, of New York (Heldeberg?), died at Marseilles in 1812
Robinson, John, of Norfolk, Virginia, died at Givet in 1813
Robinson or Robertson, David, of Exeter, New Hampshire, died at Arras in 1809
Robinson, Thomas, of Baltimore, died at Grenoble in 1812
Rosar, John, of Bangor (Maine or New York?), died at Besançon in 1812
Rowe, Zebulon, of Massachusetts, died at Givet in 1812
Rudman, Daniel, of Rhode Island, died at Arras in 1808
Sauls, Benjamin, died at Arras in 1808
Seymour, John, of New York, died at Cambrai in 1811
Sharp, John, of Baltimore, died at Arras in 1812
Shaw, John, of Baltimore, died at Cambrai in 1810
Smith, Charles, of Massachusetts, died at Marseilles in 1812
Smith, John, of Boston, died at Valenciennes in 1806
Smith, Peter, of Cambridge, Massachusetts, died at Arras in 1807
Smith, Samuel, of Boston, died at Givet in 1813
Speed, Samuel, of Philadelphia, died at Valenciennes in 1810
Stewart, John, of Philadelphia, died at Valenciennes in 1813
Taylor, Joseph, of Germantown, died at Arras in 1808
Thomas, John, of Salem, died at Arras in 1809
Thomas, William, of Providence, Rhode Island, died at Valenciennes in 1804
Thompson, John, died at Arras in 1813
Thompson, Nathaniel, of Baltimore, died at Brest in 1810
Torril, John, of Boston, died at Arras in 1808
White, James of Charleston or Charlestown, died at Givet in 1813
Williams, Andrew, of New Orleans, died at Bitche in 1809
Williams, James, of New York, died at Givet in 1804 or 1805
Williamson, Charles, of New York, died at Cambrai in 1812
Winegrove, John, of Chester, Pennsylvania, died at Montreuil-sur-Mer in 1810
Woitter, John Samuel, of Philadelphia, died at Metz in 1805
Wood, William, of New York, died at Valenciennes in 1805
Woodger, William, of Baltimore, died at Mont Dauphin in 1812
Yankey, Benjamin, of Kensington, Pennsylvania, died at Arras in 1810
Young, Richard, of Providence, Rhode Island, died at Valenciennes in 1810

BIBLIOGRAPHIC ESSAY

Though much published material has been used for this research, it was more helpful in researching vessels, politics and historiography, not individual American seamen. Newspapers, histories and prisoners' memoirs, as explained below, provide limited information on American prisoners. It is the original, archival material that reveals who they were, their plight, and the diplomatic efforts to help them.

Contemporary newspapers of all nations, viewed on various online databases of historic newspapers, are invaluable in tracing and identifying a vessel. Their daily reports of shipping arrivals in and departures from ports helped to track voyages. Their regular reports of vessels captured by privateers also helped to confirm information found in other sources and the captives' own accounts. *La Gazette nationale ou le Moniteur Universel*, the French government's mouthpiece, published reports of captures by French privateers. In many cases, these reports give more information than those about the same captures in the British *Lloyd's List* or the various American papers. However, they only rarely mention a ship's master and never the seamen by name.

Nineteenth and early twentieth century works about privateers of the War of 1812, such as Maclay's *A History of American Privateers* and Coggeshall's *History of the American Privateers and Letters of Marque During the War with England in the Years 1812, '13 and '14*, are filled with mistakes about the privateers sailing from France. These have been copied into Wikipedia and numerous other works and websites, perpetuating the spread of misinformation. (For example, in the case of just one privateer, Henry Preble was not from Rhode Island; the *True-Blooded Yankee* was not a French brig nor was it built in France; American seamen were not released by "the connivance of French authorities" but after exhaustive diplomatic negotiations; the *True-Blooded Yankee* was not captured and the crew were not sent to a prison in Gibraltar.[1] Neither Joshua nor Simeon Haley was the master of the France-based *True-Blooded Yankee*, yet even the United States Navy was caught by

---

[1] Edgar Stanton Maclay. *A History of American Privateers*. D. Appleton, 1899, pp276–277.

this confusion.)² Everything in these books and similar accounts has to be checked and verified with more reliable, usually original, archival sources.

The numerous memoirs of captivity in France written after the war are almost all by British clergymen, British officers or British civilian détenus held at Verdun, where there were few American seamen. Their descriptions of their relatively comfortable lives on parole in town bear no resemblance to the captivity endured by lowly seamen, whether American or British, within fortress prisons or dungeons. Only John Jea's memoir gives a picture of what American seamen endured, while Stephen Clubb (who was a British first mate, married to an American) described their suffering with great sympathy. No other published account by an American prisoner has been discovered.

Modern historians writing about the British prisoners in France, such as Michael Lewis, Margaret Audin, David Rouanet, Didier Houmeau and Elodie Duché, are interested solely in the British experience. None mentions Americans or seems aware that a number of prisoners were American.

The single published work that attempted to list all British prisoners that is worthwhile – although not infallible – is the *Report from the Committee for the Relief of the British Prisoners in France; with A List of the Prisoners*, published in 1812. Many researchers consider this to be one of the best sources on British prisoners in France, reasoning that, because it was written by English speakers within the prison depots, the spelling of names and vessels and other information will be better than anything created by the French (for many of whom, indeed, English, Scottish and Irish names were very difficult to spell). Yet, as was common for many nineteenth-century publications, there are numerous spelling and typographical errors.

For each prisoner, the Committee for Relief's list gives the first and last name, rank, home town, ship or regiment and the depot where he was held. However, only a little over 500 of the American prisoners appear in the publication, while there were hundreds more held in the same depots as the British captives. They were omitted because they were not recipients of the Committee's aid. For many of those Americans who are included in the list, an incorrect, British, place of birth is given. It is impossible to know with certainty why this was done. Perhaps, as this was a list of those receiving British aid, the men lied in order to receive it. That may have been the only way open to them to access the payments; it is very clear that many American men held in the same prisons were not receiving Lloyd's relief and were in desperate need. Perhaps, though they had been born in the United States, they considered themselves to be British; certainly, some men born in America who are included in the Committee's list as receiving relief never made any

---

² "Hailey (DD-556)". *Naval History and Heritage Command.* United States Navy. https://www.history.navy.mil/research/histories/ship-histories/danfs/h/hailey.html [Accessed 26 October 2023].

claim for aid or recognition from the American diplomats. (Recall that, after 1807, there was no American aid to request.) Lastly, the *Report* is based on a count of prisoners in depots receiving aid that was done in about 1811, and so would not have included any Americans released in 1807 or any who were temporarily released to a French privateer. Thus, the *Report from the Committee for the Relief of the British Prisoners in France*, though helpful, is not at all the best of sources on American prisoners.

It is unpublished records and archives that form the main sources used for this study. They come primarily from French archival material, secondarily from archives and libraries in the United States and, lastly, from the archives in Great Britain. Even in the original material, however, there were disappointments. The digitized archival collections relating to the Seaman's Protection Certificates were rarely useful concerning the Americans held in France. Though most of the American seamen who were prisoners would have had their Seaman's Protection Certificate at some point, almost none of the originals have survived and no original was found in any of the prisoner dossiers. In the archives of applications for the certificates, many of which can be accessed on Ancestry.com or as extracts on the website of the Mystic Seaport Museum, fewer than a dozen could be connected with any certainty to an American prisoner in France. Either the names are too common (John Brown, John Smith, etc.) or there are not enough details in the prison records to make identification possible. Another disappointment was Britain's National Maritime Museum, which has a superb collection. Unfortunately, but for one list of prisoners held at one depot, almost none of it has any bearing on American prisoners of war in France.

Below are described the most important, but certainly not all, of the dozens of different series used.

French Sources

The French sources are, naturally, the richest on the subject of prisoners of war in France but they are quite scattered amongst different archive facilities. They were created in different locations, under the authority of different ministries, for different purposes, as the individual seamen were moved about and were considered variously as crew members, foreigners under surveillance, prisoners of war, escapees or even criminals.

The documentation varies greatly in the spelling of English names. In some cases, the lists of prisoners or seamen are an abysmal mystery of names mangled by efforts at phonetic spelling; in others, especially at the major ports, where many professional translators could be found, every name is perfectly spelt.

Service Historique de la Défense (SHD)

This is the combined archives of all arms of the French military: the Army, Marine (Navy), Gendarmerie, Air Force, Coast Guard, etc. The main archive facility is at the Château de Vincennes, just east of Paris. Branch naval archives are in the naval port cities of Cherbourg, Brest, Lorient, Rochefort and Toulon. All but Toulon were visited for this study.

At the Vincennes facility, the archives of the Army contain cartons of lists of prisoners of war of all nationalities in the record series Yj. These cartons are filled with loose slips of paper, correspondence and small notebooks; (the actual prison depot registers of British prisoners were taken to England and now form the bulk of the Admiralty archives on prisoners of war in France). Many appear to be the initial lists made by prison personnel when a convoy of prisoners would arrive, but there are nowhere near enough to account for all of the prisoners of war of the First Empire. There are fewer than ten cartons of such lists. The names of American prisoners are intermingled with those of British prisoners, with the city of birth often being the only piece of information that indicates a man was American. Carton Yj19 contains a copy of the census of American prisoners in the depots made by Pacaud in 1807.

Series Yj also includes some forty-eight cartons of dossiers on specific British or American prisoners. There are by no means individual dossiers on each and every prisoner, only on those who, for some reason, were brought to the attention of the Minister of War. Notices from depot commandants about troublesome prisoners or escapees, letters from prisoners or their families and correspondence between officials about prisoners are the types of documents found within these dossiers. The dossiers on Americans are intermingled, alphabetically, with those on British prisoners. In some cases, it was noted on the file cover that the prisoner was from the United States; in most cases, however, each dossier had to be opened and read to determine the nationality of the prisoner. The contents of the files on Americans are usually correspondence from the American Minister Plenipotentiary requesting a man's release and memoranda of communications between French officials to determine the prisoner's nationality and capture details in order to decide whether or not he could be released.

Also in Vincennes can be found some of the files of the Marine on prisoners of war taken from the prize vessels captured by privateers, in the sub-series FF2 and FF3.[3] This sub-series also contains numerous forms listing vessels captured by privateers. Files on shipwrecks during the First Empire can be found in the Marine series CC3. Many seamen became prisoners on being rescued from a wreck and, while their names are not in these lists, the date

---

[3] As of late 2023, at least part of the FF2 series has been relocated to the Marine archives in Rochefort. (SHDR).

and place of each wreck can be confirmed. The documents about vessels in the FF2 and CC3 series help to pinpoint when a man was brought into France and, if there is also a crew list, the precise details about him as the French recorded them on his entry.

A particularly valuable resource is a register of seamen of many neutral nationalities (American, Swedish, Portuguese, etc.) who signed on to French privateers, something that enemy British prisoners were not allowed to do.[4] The information that it gives is minimal: the man's name, the prison where he was located, and the privateer he volunteered to join. It is not, however, wholly reliable on its own. Many of those privateers were captured by Royal Navy vessels and sent in to English ports as prizes. The prize case files survive and often contain the French crew lists. Comparing these with the register, it can be seen that, in some cases, none of the prisoners who volunteered were on the crew list, while in other cases many more American seamen prisoners turned up on the crew lists than are in this register. For this study, the real value of the register is that it helps to confirm the neutral nationality of those permitted to volunteer, whether or not they actually joined the vessel.

Included in the FF2 series but also scattered in other archives, from the Brest branch of the SHD to the National Archives, to various Departmental Archives (see below) are prize liquidation files. These show the payments of the prize monies, from what the *armateurs* received, to what went to the creditors, to the tiny sums paid to the seamen. Where the crew payment lists (*états des répartitions*) survive, each recipient's name is given along with his station or rank on board and often his place of birth. Quite a few Americans appear on the crew payment lists of French privateers. This, combined with the register of seamen of neutral nationalities who signed on to French privateers already mentioned, and the crew lists of French privateers captured in the prize cases at TNA, below, made it possible to follow a seaman's movements.

While the prisoner lists in the Yj series give only names and a few details about a man, and while the crew lists in the Marine archives give little more, the individual dossiers in the Yj series can tell much more about him, in some cases. There are few letters from the seamen themselves, but the American minister often wrote what he had learned from their relatives or their documents in pleading for the man's release. In this way, the growing collection of detail begins to reveal the man's identity and part of his story.

At the branch SHD facility at Brest, in series 1P10, can be found a register of privateers' captures and the crew lists from the captured vessels of those brought in to Saint Malo as well as correspondence about them. The series also contains an early register of captured seamen sent to the local jail, Tour Solidor, while they awaited the judgement on the capture of their vessel.

---

[4] This is the source for Bonnel's list of « Prisonniers américains embarqués sur les corsaires » in *La France, les États-Unis, et la Guerre de Course*, pp442–451.

Series 2Q contains the payment record for the privateer *San Joseph*, showing the names of some American seamen who had been recruited from a prison depot. All of the SHD branch facilities (except Lorient, which lost most of its archives when it was bombed during World War Two) contain files of local port officers' communications with the Ministry, which can contain queries about individual seamen in the port, some of them American.

Archives nationales (Arch. nat.)

The *Archives nationales* branch in Pierrefitte-sur-Seine contains all the French National Archives collections of the nineteenth century, except notarial records. Of particular interest are the Archives of Executive Power, series AF/IV, which include ministerial reports to Napoleon. Here can be found Decrès's outraged report on British prisoners who were included in the group of American prisoners released in 1813 (AF/IV/1194). A few American seamen's names are scattered amongst those of the British in these reports.

The archives of the Police General, series F/7, which are within the archives of the Ministry of the Interior, contain the documentation of the many types of spying and surveillance conducted by the Police General under Fouché and Savary during the First Empire. There are a dozen or more registers of passport requests, permissions to reside in Paris, people under surveillance, etc., many of them concerning the British, with whom the Americans were inevitably grouped. This series also contains the condensed reports of any activity of interest, anywhere in the Empire, sent to Napoleon. An edited version of these reports has been published as *La Police Secrète du Premier Empire*. They give a fascinating picture of life in the First Empire through the eyes of the police and their surveillance officers. They covered all types of events, including escaped prisoners, captured foreigners, suicides, reports from the Army and from the ports, and events large and small, from battles to local thefts. Mentions of Americans are very few but, occasionally, there are some mentions of captured American vessels with the names of the crew taken prisoner.

Archives diplomatiques (Arch. dip.)

The series *Correspondance politique – Etats-unis* contains the French side of the exchanges between the American Ministers Plenipotentiary and the French Minister of External Affairs concerning Americans held as British prisoners of war. Duplicates of some of the lists of prisoners released that have not survived (or, at least, have not been microfilmed) in American records can be found here.

Archives Departmentales (AD)

When the First Empire fell, there were approximately 140,000 prisoners of war in France, of many different nationalities. They had been marched across France from ports and battlefields to depots in different parts of the country. A few had escaped and could have been found anywhere, as they tried to reach a coast or border. Because prisoners of one nationality or another were in every one of the departments of the country, documents about them can turn up in any of the Departmental Archives of continental France. The archival classification system is standard for all Departmental Archives; those series most likely to contain information on prisoners of war are as follows.

Series 9R contains records concerning enemy prisoners of war. Here will be found correspondence from local officials concerning the use of Spanish prisoners for farm labour, the use of skilled British or American prisoners in textile factories, bulletins with descriptions of escaped prisoners, etc.

Series 6U contains the Commercial Court (*Tribunal de Commerce*) records. Here are found files of the sales of a privateer's prizes which rarely name the crew but at least name the captain and first mate of the prize. In the archives of those departments on the coasts, this series will also contain many complete prize cases. It was the practice, especially if the validity of the prize were thought to have been questionable, to try to have the case judged in the local Commercial Court rather than in the central Prize Court in Paris (*Conseil des Prises*). As many of the judges were also part or whole owners of privateering vessels, or were the agents for selling the prizes, or were relatives of the captains and crews of the privateers, the chances of a ruling in the captor's favour were much higher in these local courts.[5]

Certainly, the series in the Departmental Archives that are the easiest to access are the civil registers of births, marriages and deaths, in Series E. All of them can be accessed online. For every prisoner who died in France, there will be a civil death register entry, giving as much information as possible to identify the deceased: his full name, his parents' names, his date and place of birth, sometimes even the name of his vessel and his prisoner number. The information is not always complete, spelling can be wildly phonetic and British towns can be confused with American towns of the same name (e.g., Cambridge, England with Cambridge, Massachusetts). Still, these entries can be very helpful in identifying a prisoner. Though many British prisoners living on parole in Verdun and at other depots married and had children, making

---

[5] As in the case of Jean Diot of Morlaix, who, while he was mayor and head of the Commercial Court, also owned a number of privateers and was the prize agent for others. As he was also the consular agent for the United States in the port of Morlaix, when an American prize was being judged, he, at times, would excuse himself from those cases.

the entries in the birth and marriage registers useful in researching them, no American prisoners did so. It is the sad declarations in the death registers that help to tell some of their tales.

United States Sources

Libraries

The correspondence, especially that retained in the personal papers of American consuls, is filled with personal details in the letters from the seamen. The private correspondence used for this research survives in the Fulwar Skipwith Papers within the Causten-Pickett Papers in the Library of Congress (LOC), in the papers of David Bailie Warden held by the Nimitz Library, United States Naval Academy and, in the Jonathan Russell Papers, John Hay Library, Brown University. The seamen wrote to the three men while they were consuls in Paris, describing their plights and begging for help. The Skipwith collection also contains correspondence with the local agents he hired to manage the allowances given to American seamen.

National Archives and Records Administration (NARA)

The Diplomatic and Consular Dispatches of the United States Ministers Plenipotentiary and of the United States Consuls and Consular Agents in France are held by NARA and reveal the discussions of American prisoners, as well as with the acrimonious exchanges between diplomats and consuls that exhibit the disputes, personal attacks and power struggles amongst them. I was able to access these in microfilm form at the *Archives nationales* in Pierrefitte. For the dispatches from consuls based in cities outside of modern France, such as Amsterdam or Antwerp, I was able to access them online from NARA. In many cases, by matching letters found in the Diplomatic Dispatches with their replies in the *Archives diplomatiques*, it was possible to understand the entire, written discussion of a seaman's case.

Prize Cases

To a limited degree, War of 1812 prize case judgements, in the different district courts of states, especially New York, have provided a small amount of information on the few seamen who had been prisoners of war in France and who ended up on an American vessel that both sailed from France and captured a prize to be judged. The documentation in these cases is much less than that included in British prize cases (see below) and rarely includes all of the captured ships' papers.

British Sources

The two main British sources for prisoner names are the prison registers and the 1812 publication by the Committee for Relief (discussed above), yet they are imperfect. The hundreds of incorrect details that they contain reflect the disorder, deception, disarray and chaos of the situation in the depots at the time. Concerning American prisoners, only a little over a third of them, some 535, are mentioned in one or both of the two sources, and many of them are incorrectly or incompletely identified.

The National Archives (TNA)

The Admiralty records in TNA are an enormous collection, of which four series contributed to this work: the registers of the British prisoners of war in France, the prize cases judged by the High Court of Admiralty, the muster books for Royal Navy vessels and the registers of American prisoners of the War of 1812. Three of these series of pertinent British records are concerned with listing prisoners. Of those, only one is concerned exclusively with Americans.

The registers of prison entries, of releases and of prisoner deaths for the prisoner of war depots in France are French. It is unclear how these registers travelled from the various French prison depots to the Admiralty but all of them did so; no such register can be found in the *Service Historique de la Défense*. They are all in the ADM 103 series and can be viewed and searched on the commercial genealogy website, FindMyPast.co.uk. They give a prisoner's name, place of origin, rank and vessel or regiment. Insofar as they concern Americans, they are not entirely reliable. As detailed in many cases above, though some of the Americans in the registers may be correctly identified, with the home town correctly given, in many cases, especially but not only with men who were impressed into the Royal Navy, a false, British, home town will be given and the man's name may be partially or wholly incorrect.

Hundreds of French prize cases judged by the High Court of Admiralty are in the HCA series of TNA. Often, they include the papers of the captured ship which sometimes include the French crew list, as was the case with the captured *San Joseph*, the *Etoile no. 2*, the *Maraudeur* and others mentioned in this study. These crew lists made it possible to confirm that some of the American seamen who, while in a prison depot, signed on to a French privateer that was then captured, were indeed on that vessel (and were then sent to a British prison or impressed into the crew of the capturing Royal Navy vessel).

The musters and pay books of Royal Navy vessels (within the Admiralty, or ADM, series) list the crew members, their place of birth, when they joined a vessel and whether or not they were impressed ("prest") as well as other details. As described above, they are most unreliable concerning American seamen. In many cases, only the man's name is given, with no other details. Americans were often given false names. Places of birth, if given, were falsified, as were dates showing when the man joined the vessel. In spite of all of this effort to obscure the Americans, if other sources provide enough detail about a man, he can be found in these books, and thus be confirmed as having been on a Royal Navy vessel.

When the War of 1812 broke out, the Royal Navy and British privateers began attacking any and all American merchant vessels (not just those leaving France or carrying French cargo) as well as the few ships of the United States Navy. They sent the captured crews to England or Canada as prisoners of war. Additionally, hundreds of American seamen who had been impressed onto Royal Navy vessels, on learning of the war, turned themselves in, saying that they were now prisoners of war and could not be forced to fight against their own country; they demanded to be sent to prison (which is quite a testament to how dreadful their treatment on board must have been). Those who were sent to England went to prisons at Plymouth, Portsmouth, Chatham, on hulks and, eventually, Dartmoor. They were entered into the prison registers as Americans, including their name, age, place of birth, vessel and any distinguishing marks. These registers, too, are in the ADM 103 series (Prisoner of War Department of the Navy Board). They may be viewed online on the website British Online Archives. Many of the American prisoners of war released by the French were on vessels that were captured by the Royal Navy and became prisoners of war of the British. The details about a man in the British prisoner of war registers can help to confirm those about him in the French records.

Sources on African-American Seamen Prisoners

The documentation of African-American seamen is unique in that the men were often singled out for identification by their skin colour. The reasons why merit some explanation.

Some fifty-three of the captured American seamen were African-American. This is about three per cent of the total number of American seamen prisoners held in France, a proportion consistent with Foy's calculations of Black seamen amongst the crews of British merchant vessels of the eighteenth century, which he found to be at three per cent.[6] Putney's numbers were much higher, averaging sixteen per cent for the years of the Napoleonic Wars, but the crew lists that she examined were of vessels that sailed the eastern coast of America and to the West Indies.[7] Few of the vessels she studied crossed the Atlantic. W. Jeffrey Bolster's estimates, based on an examination of 50,000 names in

---

[6] Charles R. Foy. "Eighteenth Century French Black Seamen", *Lumières*, No. 35, 2020, pp17–34.

[7] Martha S. Putney. *Black Sailors: Afro-American Merchant Seamen and Whalemen Prior to the Civil War*. New York: Greenwood Press, 1987, p120.

crew lists, are much higher, with the numbers of African-Americans amongst crews averaging twenty per cent.[8] It is unclear how much of what he examined covered vessels sailing coastal and Caribbean waters and how much covered vessels crossing the Atlantic. Thus, comparisons with the statistical findings of other researchers can only be partially conclusive.

The documents found for this study that identify the men's race are not of a single type, as were those used by the authors cited above. They come from a wide variety of document types. Many are lists; much is correspondence. The French documents include ministerial correspondence and lists of captives made by port officers. The American documents include diplomatic and consular correspondence, letters from the seamen, Pacaud's census of Americans in prison depots and handwritten copies made by the seamen (or for them, possibly by letter-writers) of their Seaman's Protection Certificates. The British documentation includes primarily the prison entry and death registers (many of which were written by French prison officials) of British captives in France and the published 1812 list of prisoners receiving money from the Committee for Relief. All differ widely in whether or how they mention a seaman's race.

British records concerning prisoners in France do not mention race, but in some of their falsehoods about American seamen impressed into the Royal Navy they indicate that a man was an African-American seaman. In falsifying the names and obscuring the origins of impressed American seamen in the vessel musters and pay books, Royal Navy officers often used, as the place of birth of African-American seamen, Jamaica or Bermuda, making the seamen appear to have been born in British territories, and so not to be American citizens. This, on its own, is not enough to identify a man's race but, combined with information from other sources, can be an indicative addition to the information about his race. Recall that Henry Green appears on the muster of the *Shannon* with no indication as to his race and as born in Jamaica.[9] He wrote to the American consul describing himself as "a man of colour", born in Baltimore.

Americans were more inclined than either the French or the British to mention race in their correspondence and lists of prisoners. The Seaman's Protection Certificates always either state the seaman's race, such as "free black", "mulatto", etc., or give descriptions uniquely associated with race. The Seaman's Protection Certificate of Peter Anderson, for example, describes

---

[8] W. Jeffrey Bolster. *Black Jacks: African American Seamen in the Age of Sail.* Cambridge: Harvard University Press, 1997, p238.

[9] Records of the Admiralty, Naval Forces, Royal Marines, Coastguard, and related bodies, Records of Service, Admiralty: Royal Navy Ships' Musters (Series I), Ships' Musters: Shannon September–December 1803. TNA. ADM 36/15531.

him as "…a free black American seaman…with black, woolly hair and a dark complexion…".[10]

The French were required to mention race in census returns, lists and prison registers though, in practice, they did not always do so. The French noting of race has its origins in Napoleon's attitude toward slavery and "people of colour" ("*gens de couleur*"). During the Revolution, the law of *16 pluviôse An II* (4 February 1794) had abolished slavery throughout the French colonies. However, in 1802, when Napoleon was First Consul, he reinstated slavery through a series of decrees concerning "*gens de couleur*" that were increasingly restrictive.

One law in particular affected foreign seamen. The decree of *13 messidor An X* (2 July 1802), stated that no foreign "black, mulatto, or other people of colour" ("*noir, mulâtre, ou autre gens de couleur*") could enter France under any circumstances; additionally, except for those in the service of France, no "people of colour" from the colonies could enter continental France without specific permission from the authorities. Finally, it gave that any "people of colour" who entered France in violation of this decree would be detained and deported. There were specific instructions for how this law applied to foreign seamen:

> …the Blacks or Mulattos belonging to the crews of foreign Ships are to be confined on Board and will be sent to a [prison] depot if they are found on Shore.[11]

Thus, any foreign seaman who was Black had to stay on his vessel for as long as it was in port; any African-American found strolling the streets of a port town, for example, or escaped from a prison, could have been questioned by the gendarmes simply for being Black.

This decree also began a new phase of documenting "people of colour" in France.[12] It became the practice, whenever lists were made by officials, whether population lists, crew lists or lists of prisoners, to indicate next to the name

---

[10] United States. Citizenship Affidavits of US-born Seamen at Select Ports, 1792–1869. Ancestry.com [Accessed 30 November 2021]. Original Publication: *Proofs of Citizenship Used to Apply for Seamen's Certificates for the Port of Philadelphia, Pennsylvania, 1792–1861*. NARA Microfilm publication M1880, roll 9, frame 390. Records of the U.S. Customs Service, Record Group 36. NARA, Washington, D.C.

[11] "*Arreté du Gouvernement du 13 Messidor An 10 qui interdit à tous les gens de couleur des deux sexes l'entrée du Territoire Continental de l'Empire.*" AD Charente-Maritime, 5M7, art. 1.

[12] "*Actes du Gouvernement. Arrêt du 13 messidor An 10*". *La Gazette nationale ou le Moniteur universel*, 1 October 1802, p2. RetroNews, le site de presse de la BnF. https://www.retronews.fr/?gad=1&gclid=EAIaIQobChMI76XcwIjS_wIVKp9oCR-3j9wkKEAAYASAAEgJ_qvD_BwE [Accessed 25 March 2023].

if someone were a non-white person. Thus, on many, but certainly not all, of the lists that include American seamen, can be found such indications as "*noir*", "*mulâtre*", "*homme de couleur*" or, more rarely, "*nègre*" next to some of the names.[13] The notation was not applied universally or even most of the time, where prisoners were concerned. For two of the men (Prince Boston, who is known to have been African-American and Native American, the other presumed to have been African as he gave his place of birth as the Coast of Guinea) no document noting their race at all could be found. They may not have been the only African-American seamen for whom this was the case, so it must be considered that there may have been more African-American seamen imprisoned in France who were not identified as such. However, it can be said that there were at least fifty-three men who were identified as non-white.

For those fifty-three African-American seamen, 260 documents mentioning one or more of them were found, but only sixty-four of those, less than a quarter, noted a man's race. Though the average number of documents on each man is five, with just one mentioning his race, there can be as many as nineteen documents on a man, of which only one mentions his race. On no man are there more than three documentary mentions of his race.

More than half of the African-American seamen were sent to French prisons from merchant vessels, usually either British or American, with a few that were Portuguese ships. Twelve African-American seamen were taken from captured or wrecked Royal Navy vessels onto which they had been impressed. None was taken from a whaling vessel. (Though Prince Boston came from a family of African-American whalers of some renown, he was captured on a British merchant vessel.) As to rank, most were regular seamen on board; six were cooks, one each a mate, a merchant, a tailor and a carpenter. One was the unnamed servant of William S. Shaw said to have been the son of the king of Congo. One African-American seaman was not a prisoner of war but a criminal who died in irons.

Putney writes of how, from 1822, fewer African-American seamen had Seamen's Protection Certificates and that they were entered into crew lists with

---

[13] Literally, "Black, mulatto, man of colour, Negro". The terminology, in relation to Black American seamen was complicated by the customary use of the word "Amérique" to mean France's colonies in the Caribbean, especially Saint Domingue (now Haiti). While "américain" as an adjective, definitively meant someone or something from the United States, to say that a person "looked as if he came from Amérique" meant that he was dark skinned, like the enslaved people in Saint Domingue. In the exchanges between the authorities at Grenoble and Goulhot about how to be sure that George D. Wilson was American and not British, when the officer in Grenoble wrote that Wilson looked like "he came from Amérique" ("qu'il vient de l'Amérique"), he meant that he was Black, not that he was from the United States, "un américain".

the note "no proofs" to indicate this.[14] The decade when African-American American seamen were prisoners in France was well before the passage of acts in America that were intended to restrict their movements first began in southern states in 1822. Yet, even at this earlier period, only fifteen of the men had their Seamen's Protection Certificates at the time they were sent to a prison depot.[15] Their documents were confirmed as seen by one of the consuls or their representatives and noted on the lists and in the correspondence next to the man's name as "has proofs".

Many of these African-American seamen received allowances from the British Committee for Relief, according to the list of recipients published in 1812 by the Committee, but there seems to be no correlation between a man's having proved his American citizenship and his receiving, or not, the aid for British seamen. Of the African-American seamen who had proved their American citizenship, three also received money from the Committee for Relief, but eleven did not. Of those who could not prove their American nationality, ten also received money from the Committee for Relief, while twenty-six did not.

Nor does there seem to be any connection between receiving British aid and the nationality of the vessel on which the man was taken, though this is difficult to ascertain as not many of the documents showing the merchant vessels' nationalities have survived. Looking at the twelve African-American men taken from Royal Navy ships (vessels of which the nationality cannot be in question), only five received money from the Committee for Relief. Thus, seven, who had been forced to serve Britain, would seem to have received no British aid.

To receive aid from the American legation in France, proof of nationality was crucial. However, these funds were distributed for such a short period of time in 1806 and 1807 that few American seamen received any money from the legation. Nor did proving American nationality guarantee release from French prisons. Repeatedly, the French authorities insisted that prisoners claiming American nationality have documentary proof of it if they were to be considered for release, yet this requirement seems not to have been applied to actual releases. Of the African-American seamen, only three who had their Seaman's Protection Certificate were released. Twelve others had that certificate and were not released. A further twelve who did not have their certificates were released.

Added to the group of those released must be those who had the temporary release to work on a French privateer. Six African-American seamen signed

---

[14] Putney. *Black Sailors*, p11.

[15] Unfortunately, none of the documents seems to have survived but three seamen copied out or had copied their Seaman's Protection Certificates when they wrote for help to the American consuls.

on to French privateers, three from a prison depot and three from the port gaols, the latter group signing almost as soon as they were captured. Not one of the six was returned to French prison depots. At least four of the French privateers were captured by the British; if the men were still on the crews at the time of capture, they either would have been pressed into the crew of the Royal Navy captor or sent to British prisons as French prisoners of war. Of the two remaining men who signed on, no further record was found and their fates are unknown.

Both Putney and Bolster have discussed how some African-American seamen on American merchant vessels were slaves. None of the African-American seamen held prisoner in France was clearly identified as a slave. However, two men, Thomas Forrest and Charles Cornwie, were described as the "servants" of, respectively, Thomas C. Almy and a Captain Laad (possibly Ladd), and they may have been slaves. If having a single name can be seen as an indication that a seaman was a slave, then three more of the African-American seamen may have been slaves: Jupiter, Fletcher and Francis. However, there is not enough information about these men to be certain of their status. Jupiter and Francis were the two men mentioned above who signed on to French privateers and disappeared from French prison records. Fletcher and Cornwie each appear only once. Only Forrest appears again, when he was released to travel to England as the "domestic" of Alexander Gibson.

Ten of the African-American men died in prison. Two died of "fever" in the military hospital at Metz; the thief died in irons, at Brest. Prince Boston died very soon after the long march to his depot. French death register entries never usually give a cause of death.[16] Thus, there is no way of knowing if a man died of illness or exhaustion, or of wounds received during the battle at sea that resulted in his capture, or in a fight in prison.

None of the sources is infallible and all have lacunae. This is so concerning the African-American prisoners as much as it is for others. Any who died or were released before 1812 will not appear in the publication of the Committee for Relief compiled the previous year. The prison registers of British prisoners miss out hundreds of Americans; though there were African-Americans in nearly all of the prisons, primarily Arras, Givet and Cambrai, the prison registers of British prisoners of war held by the Navy Board miss many of them, even where they were taken from British vessels. Of the fifty-three men, twenty-three, or nearly half, do not appear in the prison registers. Conversely, some African-Americans appear only in the prison registers and not in the American records at all.

Though the African-Americans often had their race noted on French or American documentation, except for the young prince of the Congo, they were

---

[16] The Metz death register entries are most unusual in that they give a cause of death, albeit the same cause for every man: fever.

in no other way treated differently from the other American seamen prisoners in France, at least insofar as can be determined from the documentation.[17] They were held in the same port jails as other American seamen, marched together to the same prison depots, joined the same French privateers. If lucky, they were released and sent home on the same vessels; if unlucky, they died in the same hospitals.

Lastly, it must be repeated that the records and archival material used in this work contain outdated, racist and discriminatory language. The documents cited show the historical racism of Britain, the United States and Napoleonic France, with the terms in them that describe African-American seamen being offensive and inappropriate. These words have been included only where necessary for illustrative purposes and are denoted with inverted commas.

---

[17] Of the fact that racism existed amongst seamen, there can be no doubt, and this could have resulted in racist behaviour. See the very ugly racism of the author in the autobiography of Nathaniel Ames, *A Mariner's Sketches*.

PRIMARY SOURCES

1. Manuscript and Archival Collections

Repository abbreviations

Arch. pol.	*Archives de la préfecture de Police de Paris*
AD	*Archives départementales*
Arch. dip.	*Archives diplomatiques*
Arch. nat.	*Archives nationales*
BNF	*Bibliothèque nationale de France*
SHDB	*Service Historique de la Défense à Brest* *Archives de la Marine*
SHDR	*Service Historique de la Défense à Rochefort* *Archives de la Marine*

SHDV	*Service Historique de la Défense à Vincennes,*
	    Archives de la Guerre et Armée de Terre
	    Archives de la Marine

TNA	The National Archives of the United Kingdom of Great Britain and Northern Ireland at Kew
NARA	National Archives and Records Administration of the United States

A. France

    Archives de la préfecture de Police de Paris

A98

    Archives diplomatiques, La Courneuve

92CCC/6
39CP volumes 60–70

    Archives départementales

AD Ardennes
Série E – *Actes d'état civil*

AD Bouches–du-Rhône
Série E – *Actes d'état civil*
AD Charente-Maritime
5M7
AD Finistère
Série E – *Actes d'état civil*
AD Haute-Vienne
8R/1
AD Hauts-de-Seine
Série E – *Actes d'état civil*
AD Morbihan
Série E – *Actes d'état civil*
AD Nord
Série E – *Actes d'état civil*
AD Pas-de-Calais
Série E – *Actes d'état civil*
AD Seine-Maritime
6U 1/246

Archives municipales

Metz – *Actes d'état civil*

Archives nationales

AB/XIX/3193
AF/IV/1157
AF/IV/1158
AF/IV/1194
F/7 6578
LH/542/53 (Clarke)
LH/676/57 (Debacq)
LH/1177/41 (Goulhot)
LH/1311/18 (Houel)
LH/1736/57 (Maret)

Bibliothèque nationale de France

Jean Bossu. *"Fichier Bossu", Fonds maçonnique, Département des Manuscrits, Bibliothèque nationale de France*, https://gallica.bnf.fr/ark:/12148/btv1b10000111w/f132.image

Service Historique de la Défense, Vincennes (SHDV)

BB8
C18 44
MV/CC/7 (Charabot)
5YG 1089 (Debacq)
5YG 1863 (Goulhot)

5YG 2073 (Houel)
Yj19–81
> *Service Historique de la Défense, Brest* (SHDB)

1P10 85–86
1P10 118
2Q 168
> *Service Historique de la Défense, Rochefort* (SHDR)

FF2/8
FF2/10
FF2/11
FF2/12
FF2/104
FF3/1 to FF3/8

B. United States

> *National Archives and Records Administration* (NARA)

All Department of State Ministerial and Consular Dispatches were viewed on microfilm, either in the *Archives nationales*, where they have their own codes, or as digital copies ordered from NARA. The following are the NARA roll numbers assigned:

M34/11 to /18
T1/1 to T1/5
T164/2
T181/1
T220/2
T223/1
T373
T446/1

Additionally:
M38
M1180/7

> *John Hay Library, Brown University Library*

Jonathan Russell Papers (1795–1832)

> *Library of Congress*

MSS13367 – Sylvanus Bourne Papers
MSS15420 – Causten-Pickett Papers, Fulwar Skipwith Papers

> *Nantucket Historical Association Research Library and Archives*

Edouard Stackpole Collection

PRIMARY SOURCES

New York State Library

Amos Wheeler Papers, SC20914

C. Britain

National Archives (TNA)

ADM 1/1550
ADM 1/3994
ADM 36/15531
ADM 36/16028
ADM 37/3027
ADM 53/1452
ADM 103/87
ADM 103/379
ADM 103/432
ADM 103/441
ADM 103/467
ADM 103/468
ADM 103/631
ADM 103/645
ADM 103/646
HCA 1/61
HCA 1/90
HCA 32/992
HCA 32/993
HCA 32/1019
HCA 32/1035
HCA 32/1083
HCA 32/1104
HCA 32/1112
HCA 32/1164
HCA 32/1193
HCA 32/1245
HCA 32/1246
HCA 32/1275
HCA 32/1307
HCA 32/1552
HCA 32/1771
HCA 32/9571

Caird Library, National Maritime Museum

Manuscript LES/6/7/(8)

2. Printed Primary Sources

A. Books and Articles

Adams, Donald R., Jr., "American Neutrality and Prosperity, 1793–1808: A Reconsideration", *The Journal of Economic History*, 40:4 (Dec., 1980).

Adams, Henry, *History of the United States of America During the Administrations of James Madison* (New York: Literary Classics of the United States, 1986).

Adkins, Roy and Lesley, *Jack Tar: The Extraordinary Lives of Ordinary Seamen in Nelson's Navy* (London: Abacus, 2009).

Albion, Robert Greenhalgh, *Square-riggers on schedule; the New York sailing packets to England, France, and the cotton ports* (Princeton: Princeton University Press, 1938).

Alger, John Goldworth, *Napoleon's British Visitors and Captives, 1801–1815* (Westminster: Archibald Constable, 1904).

Almbjär, Martin, "Swedish consuls in Galicia: the economic function of consuls in turbulent times (1793–1806)", *Scandinavian Economic History Review (2024)* https://doi.org/10.1080/03585522.2024.2347879

Andress, David, *The Terror: Civil War in the French Revolution* (London: Abacus, 2006).

Andrews, Charles, *The Prisoners' Memoirs; Or, Dartmoor Prison; Containing a Complete and Impartial History of the Entire Captivity of the Americans in England…* (New York: printed for the author, 1815).

Anonymous, *Escape from France: A Narrative of the Hardships and Sufferings of Several British Subjects, who effected their escape from Verdun* (1808).

Aumont, Michel, *Les corsaires de Granville: Une culture du risque maritime (1688–1815)* (Rennes: Presses universitaires de Rennes, 2013).

Bartolomei, Arnaud, et al., *De l'utilité commerciale des consuls. L'institution consulaire et les marchands dans le monde méditerranéen (XVIIe–XXe siècle)* (Rome: École française de Rome, 2017).

Beerbühl, Margrit Schulte, "Hard Times: The Economic Activities of American Consuls on the North Sea Coast under the Continental System", *German Historical Institute London Bulletin*, 40:2 (November 2018).

Bellhouse, David R., *The Flawed Genius of William Playfair: The Story of the Father of Statistical Graphics* (Toronto: University of Toronto Press, 2023).

Bergeron, Louis, *France Under Napoleon*, Translated by R.R. Palmer (Princeton: Princeton UP, 1981).

Berkowitz, Bruce, *Playfair: The True Story of the British Secret Agent Who Changed How We See the World* (George Mason: George Mason University, 2018).

Bernard, Léonce, *Les Prisonniers de guerre du Premier Empire* (Paris: Editions Christian, 2000).

Berriat, H, *Législation Militaire ou Recueil Méthodique et Raisonné des Lois, Décrêts, Réglemens et Instructions Actuellement en vigueur sur Toutes les Branches de l'état militaire* (Alexandrie: Louis Capriolo, 1812).

Bertaid, Jean-Paul, "Aperçus sur l'insoumission et la désertion à l'époque révolutionnaire: étude des sources", *Bulletin d'histoire économique et sociale de la Révolution française*. Paris: CTHS, 1969,

Bizardel, Yvon, *Les Américains à Paris sous Louis XVI et Pendant la Révolution: notices biographiques* (Alençon: FD Imprimerie Alençonnaise, 1978).

Bloch, Marie-Hélène, *The Citadel of Besançon: Fortifications of Vauban* (Besançon: Editions La Taillanderie, 2008).

Bolster, W. Jeffrey, *Black Jacks: African American Seamen in the Age of Sail* (Cambridge: Harvard UP, 1997).

Bonnel, Ulane, *La France, les États-Unis et la guerre de course (1797–1813)* (Paris: Nouvelles Éditions Latines, 1961).

Bouchon, Lionel and Didier Grau, "Armand Augustin Louis de Caulaincourt (1773–1827)", *Napoléon & Empire* (2017). https://www.napoleon-empire.net/personnages/caulaincourt.php

Bouchon, Lionel and Didier Grau, "Hugues Bernard Maret", *Napoléon & Empire* (2017). https://www.napoleon-empire.net/personnages/maret.php

Bouchon, Lionel and Didier Grau, "Jean-Baptiste de Nompère de Champagny", *Napoléon & Empire* (2017). https://www.napoleon-empire.net/personnages/champagny.php

Bower, Beth, "'Captivity with ye Barbarous Turks': Seventeenth-Century New Englanders Held Hostage", *American Ancestors: New England, New York, and Beyond,* 13:2 (New England Historic Genealogical Society, 2012).

Boys, Edward, *Narrative of a Captivity and Adventures in France and Flanders during the Years 1808 and 1809* (London: Richard Long, 1827).

Brookhiser, Richard, *Gentleman Revolutionary: Gouverneur Morris the Rake Who Wrote the Constitution* (New York: Free Press, 2003).

Brown, Howard G., *War, Revolution, and the Bureaucratic State: Politics and Army Administration in France 1791–1799*, Oxford Historical Monographs (Oxford: Clarendon Press, 1995).

Brunsman, Denver, The *Evil Necessity: British Naval Impressment in the Eighteenth-century Atlantic World* (Charlottesville: University of Virginia Press, 2013).

Brunsman, Denver. "Subjects vs. Citizens: Impressment and Identity in the Anglo-American Atlantic", *Journal of the Early Republic* 30, No. 4 (2010): 557–586. http://www.jstor.org/stable/40926065.

Burrows, Edwin G., *Forgotten Patriots: the Untold Story of American Prisoners During the Revolutionary War* (New York: Basic Books, 2008).

Burt, Roger, "'Wherever Dispersed': The Travelling Mason in the Nineteenth Century", Prestonian Lecture 2015 (Exeter: privately printed, 2015).

Bussell, Peter, *The Diary of Peter Bussell (1806–1814)* (London: Peter Davies, 1931).

Buti, Gilbert and Philippe Hrodej eds, *Dictionnaire des Corsaires et Pirates* (Paris: CNRS Editions, 2013).

C., M., *Essai sur l'Histoire de Longwy, par M.C******, suivi de Considérations Relatives à l'Industrie et au Commerce de Cette Ville, et de Notices Biographiques sur les Hommes Illustrés Qui y Ont Pris Naissance* (Metz: Verronnais, 1829).

Cacchione, Victoria, "Gene Winter Chapter Presents: Victoria Cacchione", *MassArchaeology*, https://www.youtube.com/watch?v=QB9X92lwy3g

Caputo, Sara, *Foreign Jack Tars: The British Navy and Transnational Seafarers during the Revolutionary and Napoleonic Wars* (Cambridge: Cambridge UP, 2023).

Cardon, Thibault and Frédéric Lemaire, "Les Sous des Soldats de Napoléon au Camp de Boulogne (1803–1805): Etude des Monnaies Issues des Fouilles des Camps Napoléoniens d'Etaples-sur-Mer et Camiers (Pas-de-Calais, France)", *The Journal of Archaeological Numismatics*, 4, 2014 (Brussels: CEN – European Centre For Numismatic Studies Centre Européen D'études Numismatiques, 2015).

Casse, George Richard, *Authentic Narrative of the Sufferings of George Richard Casse, as a prisoner in France, during the late war; and of his escape to the Allied Army* (J. Mason, 1828)

Cathcart, James Leander. *The captives, by James Leander Cathcart, eleven years a prisoner in Algiers, Compiled by his daughter, J.B. Newkir* (La Porte: Herald Print. 1899).

Cavanagh, J., *Some Account of Religious Societies Among the British Prisoners in France, During the Late War. Being an Abstract from the Journal of J. Cavanagh, R.N....* (Plymouth, 1826).

Chamberlain, Paul, "The Release of Prisoners of War From Britain in 1813 and 1814", *Napoleonica. La Revue*, 3:21 (2014) 118–129.

Chandler, David G., *Dictionary of the Napoleonic Wars* (London: Arms and Armour Press, 1979).

Choate, Jean ed., *At Sea Under Impressment: Accounts of Involuntary Service Aboard Navy and Pirate Vessels, 1700–1820* (Jefferson: McFarland, 2010).

Choyce, James, *The Log of a Jack Tar; or, the Life of James Choyce, Master Mariner* (London: T Fisher Unwin, 1841).

Clark, William Bell, *Ben Franklin's Privateers: A Naval Epic of the American Revolution* (Baton Rouge: Louisiana State UP, 1956).

Clayton, Jane, "Nantucket Whalers of Milford Haven, Wales". *Historic Nantucket*. 56:7 (Winter 2007).

Clubb, Stephen, "A Journal: Containing an Account of the Wrongs, Sufferings, and Neglect, Experienced by Americans in France", *The Magazine of History with Notes and Queries*, Extra numbers, XIII (1916).

Coggeshall, George, *History of the American Privateers and Letters of Marque During the War with England in the Years 1812, '13 and '14* (New York: published by the author, 1856).

Cooper, Duff, *Talleyrand* (London: Vintage, 2010).

Cormack, William S., *Revolution and Political Conflict in the French Navy, 1780–1794* (Cambridge UP, 1995).

Cox, Henry Bartholomew, *The Parisian American: Fulwar Skipwith of Virginia* (Washington, D.C.: Mount Vernon Publishing, 1964).

Creighton, Margaret, "Fraternity in the American Forecastle, 1830–1870", *The New England Quarterly*, 63:4 (December 1990).

Crimmin, Patricia K., "Prisoners of War and British Port Communities, 1793–1815", *The Northern Mariner/Le Marin du Nord*, VI, No. 4 (October 1996), pp17–27.

Crowhurst, Patrick, *The French War on Trade: Privateering 1793–1815* (Aldershot: Scolar Press, 1989).

Crowhurst, Patrick, "Profitability in French Privateering, 1793–1815", *Business History*, Vol. 24 (1982), pp48–60.

Dana, Richard Henry, Jr., *A Seaman's Friend: Containing a Treatise on Practical Seamanship, with Plates; a Dictionary of Sea Terms; Customs and Usages of the Merchant Service; Laws Relating to the Practical Duties of Master and Mariners* (Boston: Thomas Groom & Co., 1851).

Dana, Richard Henry, Jr., *Two Years Before the Mast and Twenty-four Years After* (New York: P.F. Collier, 1937).
Dancy, J. Ross, *The Myth of the Press Gang: Volunteers, Impressment and the Naval Manpower Problem in the Late Eighteenth Century* (Woodbridge: Boydell Press, 2015).
Dangerfield, George, *Chancellor Robert R. Livingston of New York, 1746–1813* (New York: Harcourt, Brace, 1960).
Davey, James. *In Nelson's Wake: the Navy and the Napoleonic Wars* (New Haven: Yale University Press, 2015).
Davey, James. *Tempest: The Royal Navy and the Age of Revolutions* (New Haven: Yale University Press, 2023).
Davie, Niel, *French and American Prisoners of War at Dartmoor Prison, 1805–1816: The Strangest Experiment*. (London: Palgrave Macmillan, 2021).
Davis, Joseph Stancliffe, *Earlier History of American Corporations*, numbers I–III (Cambridge: Harvard University Press, 1917).
De La Tynna, J., *Almanach du Commerce de Paris, des Départemens de l'Empire Français et des Principales Villes du Monde* (Paris: De La Tynna, 1811).
Demerliac, Alain, *La Marine du Consulat et du Premier Empire: Nomenclature des Navires Français de 1800 à 1815* (Nice: Editions A.N.C.R.E., 2003).
de Monteney, Barclay, *The Case of a Détenu* (London: George Earle, 1838).
Department of State. "A Diplomatic Tradition", *A Short History of The Department of State* (Office of the Historian, Bureau of Public Affairs, United States Department of State). https://history.state.gov/departmenthistory/short-history/style.
Desquesses, Gérard, *Agenda de la Révolution Française, 1790 1990* (Paris: Editions Hibiscus, 1989).
Devos, Jean-Claude, "Les Prisonniers de Guerre Anglais Sous le Premier Empire", *Revue de l'Institut Napoléon*, 50 (January 1954).
de Waresquiel, Emmanuel, *Fouché: Les Silences de la pieuvre* (Paris: Tallandier, 2014).
d' Hauterive, Ernest. *La police secrète du premier empire; bulletins quotidiens adressés par Fouché à l'empereur*, 3 (Paris: Perrin, 1908).
Dickie, John. *The British Consul: Heir to a Great Tradition* (London: Hurst, 2007).
Dixon, Ruth Priest, "Genealogical Fallout from the War of 1812", *Prologue Magazine,* 24:1 (Spring 1992).
Done, Joshua, "Narrative of the Imprisonment and Adventures of Joshua Done, In Various Parts of France", *The London Magazine*, New Series, IV (January to April, 1826) 26–37.
Doré, Alain, "Histoire des Loges Maritimes, Première Partie". *Triple-Point* (18 April 2008), http://triple-point.xooit.com/t2322-Les-loges-maritimes-18e-19e-s.htm
Downing, Ned, "Revolutionary Idea", *Barron's Mutual Funds Quarterly* (April 1999). https://www.barrons.com/articles/SB9231052001071724?tesla=y
Duché, Elodie, "Charitable Network Connections: Transnational Financial Networks and Relief for British Prisoners of War in Napoleonic France, 1803–1814", *Napoleonica, La Revue*, 3:21 (2014).
Dudley, Wade G., *Splintering the Wooden Wall: The British Blockade of the United States, 1812–1815* (Annapolis: Naval Institute Press, 2003).

Durand, James, *The Life and Adventures of James R. Durand: During a Period of Fifteen Years, from 1801 to 1816: in which times he was impressed on board the British fleet and held in detestable bondage for more than seven years* (Sandwich: Chapman Billies, 199).

Duvergier, J.B., *Collection complète des lois, Décrets, Ordonnances, Réglemens, Avis du Conseil-d'état.* 2nd edition, 9 (Paris: Guillot at Scribe, 1835).

Dye, Ira, "Early American Merchant Seafarers", *Proceedings of the American Philosophical Society*, 120:5 (15 October 1976) 331–360.

Dye, Ira, *The Fatal Cruise of the Argus: Two Captains in the War of 1812* (Annapolis: Naval Institute Press, 1994).

Ellison, Seacome, *Prison Scenes; and Narrative of Escape from France, During the Late War* (London: Whittaker, 1838).

Falconer, William and William Burney, *A New and Universal Dictionary of the Marine...* (London: T. Cadell and W. Davies, 1830).

Farber, Hannah, "Millions for Credit: Peace with Algiers and the Establishment of America's Commercial Reputation Overseas, 1795–96", *Journal of the Early Republic* 34:2 (Summer 2014).

Forbes, James, *Letters From France, Written in the Years 1803 & 1804: Including a Particular Account of Verdun, and the Situation of the British Captives in That City*, II (London: J. White, 1806).

Foy, Charles R., "Eighteenth-Century French Black Seamen", *Lumières* (2020). https://www.cairn.info/revue-lumieres-2020-1-page-17.htm

France, *Bulletin des lois de la République française (*Paris: Imprimerie nationale des lois, 1814).

Fraser, Edward, *Napoleon the Gaoler: Personal Experiences and Adventures of British Sailors and Soldiers During the Great Captivity* (London: Methuen, 1914).

Friedenberg, Zachary B., *Medicine Under Sail* (Annapolis: Naval Institute Press, 2002).

Fury, Cheryl ed., *Social History of English Seamen* (Woodbridge: Boydell Press, 2012).

Gabet, Arnaud and Christiane Lepie, "Cambrai, Camp de Prisonniers de Guerre Anglais (1803–1815)". *Revue Trimestielle de l'Association Cambrésis Terre d'Histoire*, 5 (May 1993).

Gabrielson, Mark J., "Enlightenment in the Darkness: The British Prisoners of War School of Navigation. Givet, France, 1805–1814", *Northern Mariner/Le marin du nord*, Vol. XXV (January 2015).

Gallois, Napoléon, *Les Corsaires français sous la République et L'Empire* (Le Mans: Julien, Lanier et Compagnie, 1847).

Gambiez, "Berthiez, Louis-Alexandre (1753–1815)", *Dictionnaire Napoléon* (Paris: Editions Fayard, 1987).

Gilje, Paul A. and William Pencak eds, *Pirates, Jack Tar, and Memory: new directions in American maritime history* (Mystic: Mystic Seaport, 2007).

Gilje, Paul A., "On the Waterfront: Maritime Workers in New York City in the Early Republic, 1800 –1850", *New York History*, 77:4 (October 1996) 395–126.

Glenn, Myra C., *Jack Tar's Story: The Autobiographies and Memoirs of Sailors in Antebellum America* (Cambridge UP, 2010).

Gordon, Peter, *Narrative of the Imprisonment and Escape of Peter Gordon; Comprising a Journal of the Author's Adventures in his flight through French Territory, from Cambrai to Rotterdam; and thence to the English Coast* (1816).

Gotteri, Nicole, *La Police Secrète du Premier Empire: Bulletins quotidiens adressés par Savary à l'Empereur*, Vols 1–6 (Paris, Honoré Champion, 1997).

Greenfield, Robert A., "A Brief History of Marine Lodge" (Marine Lodge AF&AM) https://www.marinelodge.org/about-the-lodge/a-brief-history-of-marine-lodge/

Griffiths, Arthur, "Old War Prisons in England and France", *The North American Review*, 168:507 (Feb., 1899) 163–177.

Grob, Gerald N., *The Deadly Truth: a History of Disease in America* (Cambridge: Harvard UP, 2002).

Grocott, Terence, *Shipwrecks of the Revolutionary & Napoleonic Eras* (London: Chatham, 1997).

Guillemin, René, *Corsaires de la République et de l'Empire* (Paris: Editions France-Empire, 1982).

Guillon, Edouard, *Les complots militaires sous le Consulat et l'Empire: d'après les documents inédits des archives* (Paris: E. Plon, Nourrit, 1894).

Haegele, Vincent, "Le général Clarke au ministère de la Guerre", *Revue historique des armées*, 251 (2008).

Henwood, Philippe and Edmond Monange, *Brest un Port en Révolution, 1789–1799* (Rennes: Editions Ouest-France, 1989).

Heseltine, Elizabeth and Jerome Rosen eds, *WHO guidelines for indoor air quality: Dampness and mould* (World Health Organization, 2009).

Hesselman, L.W., "Some Selective Service Aspects Of Interest To The Navy", *Proceedings*, Vol. 68, No. 12 (U.S. Naval Institute, December 1942).

Hewson, Maurice, *Escape from the French, Captain Hewson's Narrative, 1803–1809* (Sevenoaks: Hodder and Stoughton, 1981).

Hickey, Donald R., *The War of 1812: a Forgotten Conflict, Bicentennial Edition.* (Urbana: University of Illinois Press, 2012).

Hill, Peter P., *Napoleon's Troublesome Americans: Franco-American Relations, 1804–1815* (Washington, D.C.: Potomac Books, 2006).

Hirrien, Jean-Pierre, *Corsaires!: Guerre et Course en Léon, 1689–1815* (Morlaix: Skol Vreizh, 2004).

Howell, Colin and Richard Twomey, *Jack Tar in History: Essays in the History of Maritime Life and Labour* (Fredericton: Acadiensis Press, 1991).

Hulbert, Archer Butler, "The Methods and Operations of the Scioto Group of Speculators", *Mississippi Valley Historical Review*, 1:4 (March 1915). http://www.jstor.org/stable/188695

International Committee of the Red Cross (ICRC), Geneva Convention Relative to the Treatment of Prisoners of War (Third Geneva Convention), 12 August 1949, 75 UNTS 135, available at: https://www.refworld.org/docid/3ae6b36c8.html [Accessed 27 October 2023].

Jackson, George Vernon, *The Perilous Adventures and Vicissitudes of a Naval Officer, 1801–1812; Being part of the Memoirs of Admiral George Vernon Jackson (1787–1876)* (Blackwood, 1927).

Jansen, Jan C. "In Search of Atlantic Sociability: Freemasons, Empires, and Atlantic History", *Bulletin of the GHI* [German Historical Institute], 57 (Fall, 2015).

Jea, John, "The Life, History, and Unparalleled Sufferings of John Jea, the African Preacher", *Pioneers of the Black Atlantic: Five Slave Narratives from the Enlightenment, 1772–1815*, eds Henry Louis Gates, Jr., and William L. Andrews (Washington, D.C.: Civitas Press, 1998) 367–463.

Jea, John. "The Life, History, and Unparalleled Sufferings of John Jea, the African Preacher. Compiled and Written by Himself. Printed for the Author", *Documenting the American South*, https://docsouth.unc.edu/neh/jeajohn/jeajohn.html

"John and Mary Jea", *The Mixed Museum* (15 June 2022) https://mixedmuseum.org.uk/amri-exhibition/john-and-mary-jea/

Johnson, Emory R., "The Early History of the United States Consular Service. 1776–1792", *Political Science Quarterly*, 13:1 (March 1896) 19–40.

Johnson, Robert, "Black–White Relations on Nantucket", *Historical Nantucket*, 51:2 (Spring 2002) 5–9 https://nha.org/research/nantucket-history/historic-nantucket-magazine/other-islanders/

Johnston, Ruth Y., "American Privateers in French Ports, 1776–1778", *The Pennsylvania Magazine of History and Biography,* 53:4 (1929) 352–374. https://www.jstor.org/stable/2008671

Jolivet, Gérard, "1793–1794 Benjamin Dubois, un armateur malouin sous la Terreur". *Association Bretonne Généalogie Histoire* (30 November 2016) http://www.geneabretagne.org/scripts/files/5c2aec9fd11e89.96695907/l-arrestation-de-benjamin-dubois--v4-septo--article-autonome.pdf

Jones, Emma C. Brewster, *The Brewster Genealogy, 1566–1907, a Record of the Descendants of William Brewster…* (New York: Grafton, 1908).

Kaizer, Nicholas James, *Revenge in the Name of Honour: The Royal Navy's Quest for Vengeance in the Single Ship Actions of the War of 1812* (Warwick: Helion, 2020).

Kaplan, Lawrence S., "France and Madison's Decision for War, 1812", *The Mississippi Valley Historical Review,* Vol. 50, No. 4 (Mar 1964).

Kaplan, Lawrence S., "France and the War of 1812", *The Journal of American History*, Vol. 57, No. 1 (Jun., 1970).

Kert, Faye Margaret, "Prize and Prejudice: Privateering and Naval Prize in Atlantic Canada in the War of 1812", *Research in Maritime History*, 11 (1997).

Knight, Roger. *Convoys: the British Struggle Against Napoleonic Europe and America* (New Haven: Yale University Press, 2022).

Langley, Harold D., *Social Reform in the United States Navy, 1798–1862* (Urbana: University of Illinois Press, 1967).

Langton, Richard, *Narrative of Captivity in France from 1809 to 1814* (London: Smith, Elder, 1838).

Lebas, Georges *Histoire d'un Port Normand Sous la Révolution et l'Empire: Dieppe: Vingt Années de Guerres maritimes, les Corsaires de la Manche, la Pêche* (Luneray: Gérard Bertout, 1974).

Le Bihan, Alain and Alain Doré, "Histoire des Loges Maritimes, Quatrième Partie", *Triple-Point* (18 April 2008) http://triple-point.xooit.com/t2322-Les-loges-maritimes-18e-19e-s.htm

Le Boënnec, Nicolas, *Archives anciennes (avant 1790): Inventaire analytique* (Morlaix: Archives Municipales de Morlaix, 2017) 59.

Lee, William, Mary Lee Mann, ed., *A Yankee Jeffersonian: Selections from the Diary and Letters of William Lee of Massachusetts, Written from 1796 to 1840* (Cambridge: Belknap Press, 1958).
Le Goff, T.J.A., "The Labour Market for Sailors in France", *Merchant Organization and Maritime Trade in the North Atlantic, 1660–1815*, Research in Maritime History, No. 15, Olaf Uwe Janzen, ed. (St. John's, Newfoundland: International Maritime Economic History Association, 1998).
Le Héricher, Edouard, *Avranchin Monumental et Historique.* (Avranches: Tostain, 1845).
Leiner, Frederick C., *Prisoners of the Bashaw: The Nineteen-Month Captivity of American Sailors in Tripoli, 1803–1805* (Yardley: Westholme, 2022).
Leira, Halvard and Iver B. Neumann, "Consular Representation in an Emerging State: The Case of Norway", *The Hague Journal of Diplomacy*, Vol. 3 (2008).
Lemisch, Jesse, "Jack Tar in the Streets: Merchant Seamen in the Politics of Revolutionary America", *The William and Mary Quarterly,* 25:3 (July 1968) 371–407. https://www.jstor.org/stable/1921773
Lemoine, J. and Bourde de la Rogerie, *Inventaire Sommaire des Archives Départementales Antérieures à 1790: Finistère, Archives Civiles, Série B,* III (Quimper: Imprimerie Brevetée-A. Jaouen, 1902).
Lespagnol, André, *Entre l'argent et la gloire: La course malouine au temps de Louis XIV* (Evergreen, 1995).
Lévêque, Pierre, "L'Amiral Decrès, un Ministre Courtisan?", *Revue du Souvenir Napoléonien,* 417 (mars–avril 1998) 13–21.
Lewis, Michael, *Napoleon and His British Captives* (London: George Allen & Unwin, 1962).
"List of American Sailors Detained as Prisoners of War in France", *Spooner's Vermont Journal,* XXVII:1363 (4 September 1809) Windsor, Vermont, 3. https://www.genealogybank.com/
Lóbula, Lola, "Ciudadana Frankenstein [II]: La última corsaria", *CES Alcant Obrera* (14 July 2021). https://alacantobrera.com/2021/07/14/ciudadana-frankenstein-ii-la-ultima-corsaria/
Louis, Jeanne H., "The Nantucket Quakers' Message as an Alternative to Benjamin Franklin's Message to the French Revolution", *Quaker Studies,* 5:1 (2000) 15–16. http://digitalcommons.georgefox.edu/quakerstudies/vol5/iss1/2
MacArthur, Walter, *The Seaman's Contract, 1790–1918, a complete reprint of the laws relating to American seamen, enacted, amended, and repealed by the Congress of the United States, as originally published in the U. S. statutes at large…* (San Francisco: Walter MacArthur, 1919).
Maclay, Edgar Stanton, *A History of American Privateers* (New York: D. Appleton, 1899).
Madelin, Louis, "La Police générale de l'Empire". *Revue des Deux Mondes*, 60: 3 (1940). http://www.jstor.org/stable/44847534
Maistre, *Les Corsaires de la Manche sous la République et l'Empire*, Travail pour la Promotion à l'Ecole de Guerre Navale (1923).
Malo, Henri, *Les Corsaires: Mémoires et Documents Inédits* (Paris: Société du Mercure de France, 1908).

Martin, Tyrone G. and John C. Roach, "Humphreys's Real Innovation", *Naval History,* Vol. 8, No.2 (Apr 1994).

Marzagalli, Silvia, "The Continental System", *The Journal of Economic History*, 40:4 (Dec, 1980). http://www.jstor.org/stable/2119997

Marzagalli, Silvia, "The Continental System: A view from the sea", Johan Joor and Katherine Aaslestad eds, *Revisiting Napoleon's Continental System: Local, Regional, and European Experiences* (Basingstoke: Palgrave, 2014).

Maxwell, John Irving, *The Spirit of Marine Law, or, Compendium of the Statutes relating to the Admiralty [etc.]* (London: Joyce Gold, 1808).

McClure, James P. and J. Jefferson Looney, eds, *The Papers of Thomas Jefferson Digital Edition*, Charlottesville: University of Virginia Press, Rotunda, 2008–2021. https://jeffersonpapers.princeton.edu/editions/digital-editions/

McKay, Anna, "British and French Prisoners of War, 1793–1815", *Museum Blog*. (2 November 2017). https://www.rmg.co.uk/explore/blog/british-and-french-prisoners-war-1793–1815

Melchior-Bonnet, Bernardine, "Savary Remplace Fouché", *Revue des Deux Mondes* (1962). www.jstor.org/stable/44590429

"More Than a List of Crew", *Memorial University of Newfoundland*. https://www.mun.ca/mha/mlc/articles/shipmasters/

Merchants' Lodge of Liverpool, "Our History", http://www.merchantslodge.co.uk/our-history.html

Michaud, Joseph Fr. and Louis Gabriel Michaud, *Biographie universelle, ancienne et moderne, ou Histoire, par ordre alphabétique, de la vie publique et privée de tous les hommes qui se sont fait remarquer par leurs écrits, leurs actions, leurs talents, leurs vertus ou leurs crimes: Supplément* (Paris: Michaud, 1839).

Montagu, Edward Proudfoot, *The Personal Narrative of the Escape of Edward Proudfoot MONTAGU, an English Prisoner of War, from the Citadel of Verdun* (1849).

Mooney, Chase C., "William H. Crawford: 1772–1834" (1974). *United States History,* 72. https://uknowledge.uky.edu/upk_united_states_history/72

Morddel, Anne, *American Merchant Seamen of the Early Nineteenth Century: a Researcher's Guide* (Lulu, 2020).

Morddel, Anne, "Nathaniel Mayo: Documenting an American Merchant Seaman of the Early Nineteenth Century", *Coriolis: the Interdisciplinary Journal of Maritime Studies*. 10:2 (2021) https://ijms.nmdl.org/article/view/21629.

Moreau-Zanelli, Jocelyne, *Gallipolis: Histoire d'un mirage américain au XVIIIe siècle* (Paris: L'Harmattan, 2000).

Morel, Anne, *Catalogue de Liquidations des Courses des Corsaires Armés à Saint-Malo (1799–1835)* (Paris: Imprimerie de la Marine, 1966).

Morieux, Renaud, *The Society of Prisoners: Anglo-French Wars and Incarceration in the Eighteenth Century"* (Oxford: Oxford UP, 2019).

Morison, Samuel Eliot, *John Paul Jones: A Sailor's Biography* (Boston: Little, Brown, 1959).

Morley, J., *A Sermon, Preached in Providence Chapel, Hope-Street, Hull, On Lord's Day, February 24, 1811, To Which Are Added, An Extract of the Circular Letters and the Report of the Committee at Lloyd's, in London* (Hull: published at request, 1811).

Moulin, *Plaidoyer de Me Moulin, Pour M. G. Daguier-Houel, Contre 1o M. G. Houel, 2o les Sr et De Lepage. Extrait du journal du Droit du 23 mai 1841. Tribunal Civil de la Seine (3e Chambre) Présidence de M. Pinodel. Audience du 21 mai* (Paris: Bruneau, 1841).

Muller, Leos, *Consuls, Corsairs, and Commerce. The Swedish Consular Service and Long-distance Shipping, 1720–1815*, Studia Historica Upsaliensia 213 (Uppsala, 2004).

Mulvey, Farrell. *Sketches of the Character, Conduct, and Treatment of the Prisoners of War at Auxonne, Longwy &c. from the Year 1810 to 1814, with an Account of the Epidemic, As It Appeared in the Latter Place in 1812* (London: Longman, Hurst, Rees, Orme, and Brown, 1818).

Murat, Inès, *Napoléon et le Rêve américain* (Paris: Fayard, 1976).

Newman, Simon, "Reading the Bodies of Early American Seafarers", *William and Mary Quarterly*, 55:1 (January 1998).

Norman, C.B., *The Corsairs of France* (London: Sampson Low, Marston, Searle & Rivington, 1887).

Oberg, Barbara B. and J. Jefferson Looney, eds, *The Papers of Thomas Jefferson Digital Edition* (Charlottesville: University of Virginia Press, Rotunda, 2008). https://jeffersonpapers.princeton.edu/editions/digital-editions/

O'Brien, Donat Henchy, *My Adventures During the Late War: a Narrative of Shipwreck, Captivity, Escapes from French Prisons, and Sea Service in 1804–14* (London: Edward Arnold, 1902).

O'Byrne, William Richard, *A Naval Biographical Dictionary Comprising the Life and Services of Every Living Officer in Her Majesty's Navy, From the Rank of Admiral of The Fleet to That of Lieutenant, Inclusive. Compiled from Authentic and Family Documents* (London: John Murray, 1849).

Parker, Richard B., *Uncle Sam in Barbary: a Diplomatic History* (Gainesville: University Press of Florida, 2004).

Payn-Echalier, Patricia and Philippe Rigaud, *Pierre Giot: Capitain marin arlésian "dans la tourmante", journal, livre de bord, correspondance, 1792–1816* (Presses universitaires de Provence, 2017). http//books.openedition.org/pup/44378

Perl-Rosenthal, Nathan, *Citizen Sailors: Becoming American in the Age of Revolution* (Cambridge: Belknap Press, 2015).

Peskin, Lawrence A., "The Blurry Line: Robert Montgomery's Public and Private Interests as U.S. Consul to Alicante", *Cahiers de la Méditerranée*, Vol. 98 (2019).

Petrie, Donald A., *The Prize Game: Lawful Looting on the High Seas in the Days of Fighting Sail* (New York: Berkley Books, 1999).

Phillips, Michael, *Ships of the Old Navy: a History of the Sailing Ships of the Royal Navy* (Electronic edition, 2007) http://www.ageofnelson.org/MichaelPhillips/

Pierre, Joëlle, "La Presse française de Turquie, canal de transmission des idées de la Révolution", *Le Temps des médias*, 5:2 (2005).

Preston, Daniel, ed., *A Comprehensive Catalogue of the Correspondence and Papers of James Monroe*, Vol. 3 (Greenwood: Greenwood Press, 2001).

Putney, Martha S., *Black Sailors: Afro-American Merchant Seamen and Whalemen Prior to the Civil War* (Greenwood: Greenwood Press, 1987).

Raikes, Henry, ed., *Memoire of the Life and Services of Vice-Admiral Sir Jahleel Brenton, Baronet, KCB* (London: Hatchard and Son, 1846).

Raithby, J. and T. Edlyne Tomlins. (1811). *The statutes at large, of England and of Great Britain: from Magna Carta to the union of the kingdoms of Great Britain and Ireland.* (London: G. Eyre and A. Strahan).

Raithby, J. (1823). *The statutes relating to the Admiralty, Navy, Shipping, and Navigation of the United Kingdon, from 9 Hen.III. to Geo. IV. inclusive.* (London: G. Eyre and A. Strahan).

Ramé, Henri, "Decrès, Denis, Duc, (1761–1820), Vice-Amiral, Ministre", *Revue du Souvenir Napoléonien,* 353 (juin 1987).

Reddie, James, *An Historical View of the Law of Maritime Commerce* (London: Blackwood, 1841).

Rediker, Marcus, *Between the Devil and the Deep Blue Sea* (Cambridge: Cambridge University Press, 1987).

Rees, Colin R. and Peter Clark, *Captured At Sea: Merchant Ships Captured in the South West Seas of Britain in the Time of Napoleon, 1803–1815*. (Published by the authors, 2011).

Reeves, *A History of the Law of Shipping and Navigation* (London: E. and R. Brooke, 1792).

Reisenberg, Felix, "Merchant Seamen", *Proceedings*, Vol. 58, No. 5 (U.S. Naval Institute, May 1932).

Report from the Committee for the Relief of the British Prisoners in France; with A List of the Prisoners (London: W. Phillips, 1812).

Rice, Howard C., "James Swan: Agent of the French Republic 1794–1796" *The New England Quarterly*, 10:3 (1937) 464–86. https://doi.org/10.2307/360316

Robidou, F., *Les Derniers Corsaires Malouins: La Course Sous la République et l'Empire, 1793–1814* (Rennes and Paris: Oberthur, 1919).

Rodger, N.A.M., *The Wooden World: an Anatomy of the Georgian Navy* (London: Fontana, 1988).

Russell, Edward Frederick Langley, *The French Corsairs* (London: Robert Hale, 1970).

Schalck de la Faverie, Alfred, *Napoléon et l'Amérique: Histoire des rélations franco-américaines spécialement envisagé au point de vue de l'influence napoléonienne* (1688–1815) (Paris: Librairie Payot, 1917).

Shipp, John Edgar Dawson, *Giant Days or the Life and Times of William H. Crawford* (Cambridge: Harvard UP, 1909).

Short, John Tregerthen and Thomas Williams, *Prisoners of War in France from 1804 to 1814: Being the Adventures of John Tregerthen Short and Thomas Williams of St. Ives, Cornwall* (London: Duckworth, 1914).

Skeen, C. Edward, *John Armstrong, Jr., 1758–1843: a Biography* (Syracuse: Syracuse UP, 1981).

Sparrow, Elizabeth, *Secret Service: British Agents in France 1792–1815* (Woodbridge: Boydell Press, 1999).

Stein, Douglas L., *American Maritime Documents 1776–1860, Illustrated and Described* (Mystic: Mystic Seaport Museum, 1992).

Story, Joseph, *The Public and General Statutes Passed by the Congress of the United States of America from 1789 to 1827 Inclusive....* Boston: Wells and Lilly, 1828, pp235–238.

Tagart, Edward, *Memoir of the late Captain Peter Heywood, R.N., with extracts from his diaries and correspondence* (London: Effingham Wilson, 1832).
Taylor, Alan. *The Civil War of 1812: American Citizens, British Subjects, Irish Rebels, & Indian Allies* (New York: Vantage Books, 2011).
Testu, Laurent-Etienne, ed., *Almanach impérial pour l'année M.DCCC. XI, présente à S.M l'Empereur et Roi, par Testu* (Paris: Testu, 1811).
Testu, Laurent-Etienne, ed., *Almanach impérial pour l'année M.DCCC. XIII, présente à S.M l'Empereur et Roi, par Testu,* (Paris: Testu, 1813).
Thayer, Jonathan, "Mapping New York City's Sailortown", *Seamen's Church Institute* (1 August 2016). https://seamenschurch.org/article/mapping-new-york-citys-sailortown
Todd, Charles Burr, *Life and Letters of Joel Barlow, LL.D. Poet, Statesman, Philosopher* (New York: Putnam's Sons, 1886).
Toll, Ian W., *Six Frigates: The Epic History of the Founding of the U.S. Navy* (New York: W.W. Norton, 2008).
Tyler, Royall, *The Algerine Captive: the Life and Adventures of Doctor Updike Underhill: Six Years a Prisoner among the Algerines* (New York: Cosimo Classics, 2009).
Tyng, Charles, *Before the Wind: The Memoire of an American Sea Captain, 1808–1833* (New York: Penguin Books, 1999).
Ulbert, Jörg and Lukian Prijac, eds, *Consuls et services consulaires au XIXe siècle* (Hamburg: DOBU Verlag, 2010).
Vail, Eugène, "William H. Crawford", *Southern Literary Messenger*, 5:6 (June 1839).
Van Hille, Jean-Marc, "*Les baleiniers quakers du Nantucket à Dunkerque en 1786, un pionnier: William Rotch*" (Synthèse d'une conférence faite à Bruxelles le 24 mai 2014) *Acta Macionica*, 24 (2014). http://www.swiss-quakers.ch/ge/library/edocuments/ 8378-BaleiniersQuakersDunkerque.pdf
Verhoeven, Wil, *Gilbert Imlay: Citizen of the World* (London: Pickering & Chatto, 2008).
Vickers, Daniel, *Farmers & Fishermen: Two Centuries of Work in Essex County, Massachusetts, 1630–1850* (Omohundro Institute and University of North Carolina Press, 1994).
Villiers, Patrick, *Marine royale, corsaires et trafic dans l'Atlantique de Louis XIV à Louis XVI* Société Dunkerquoise d'Histoire et d'Archéologie, 1991.
Villiers, Patrick. "Le Commerce maritime des Etats-Unis, ambitions maritimes et commerciales en Atlantique et Méditerranée, 1783–1815", *Storia e attualità della presenza degli Stati Uniti a Livorno e in Toscana, Actes du Colloque (Livorno, 4–6 avril 2002).* Pisa: Edizione Plus, 2003.
Villiers, Patrick, *Les Corsaires: des origines au traité de Paris du 16 avril 1856* (Quintin: Editions Jean-Paul Gisserot, 2007).
Volo, Dorothy Denneen and James M. Volo, *Daily Life in the Age of Sail* (Westport: Greenwood, 2002).
Wait, Thomas Baker and George Washington, *State Papers and Publick Documents of the United States, from the accession of George Washington to the Presidency, exhibiting a complete view of our foreign relations since that time,* Vol. 3 (Boston: T.E. Wait and Son, 1817).

Walker, Thomas James, *The Depot for Prisoners of War at Norman Cross Huntingdonshire. 1796 to 1816* (London: Constable, 1913).
Warden, David Bailie, *On the Origin, Nature, Progress and Influence of Consular Establishments* (Paris, 1813).
Watt, Helen, with Anne Hawkins, *Letters of Seamen in the Wars with France, 1793–1815* (Woodbridge: Boydell Press, 2016).
Wetherell, John, *The Adventures of John Wetherell* (Garden City: Doubleday, 1953).
Williams, Greg H., *The French Assault on American Shipping, 1793–1813: A History and Comprehensive Record of Merchant Marine Losses* (Jefferson: McFarland, 2009).
Winfield, Rif, *British Warships in the Age of Sail 1793–1817: Design, Construction, Careers and Fates* (Barnsley: Seaforth Publishing, 2008).
Wiscart, Jean-Marie, "Les Manufactures Protestants en Picardie au XIXe Siècle", *Revue du Nord*, 395 (2012) 389–410. https://www.cairn.info/revue-du-nord-2012-2-page-389.htm
Wolfe, R.B., Rev., *English Prisoners in France, Containing Observations on their Manners and Habits, Principally With Reference to Their Religious State, During Nine Years' Residence in the Depots of Fontainebleau, Verdun, Givet, and Valenciennes* (London: J. Hatchard and Son, 1830).
Worms, René, « La Juridiction des Prises », *Revue des Deux Mondes, 6ème période*, Vol. 30 (1915) pp. 90–115.
Zimmerman, James Fulton, *Impressment of American Seamen* (Port Washington: Kennikat Press, 1966).

B. Official Documents and Publications

France

"*2ème décret de Milan, 17 décembre 1807*". *Histoire des Deux Empires. Le Site d'Histoire de la Fondation Napoléon*. Napoleon.org. https://www.napoleon.org/histoire-des-2-empires/articles/2eme-decret-de-milan-17-decembre-1807/

"*Actes du Gouvernement. Arrêt du 13 messidor An 10*". *La Gazette nationale ou le Moniteur universel* (1 October 1802, p. 2). RetroNews, le site de presse de la BnF. https://www.retronews.fr/

"*Arrêté relatif au traitement des prisonniers de guerre étrangers de 13 floréal An 7*". (H. Berriat, *Législation Militaire ou Receuil Méthodique et Raisonné des Lois, Décrêts, Réglemens et Instructions Actuellement en vigueur sur Toutes les Branches de l'état militaire*. (Alexandrie: Louis Capriolo, 1812.)

"*Le décret du 12 ventôse an V [2 March 1797]*", United States. (1817) *State Papers and Publick Documents of the United States.*

"*Décret du Blocus Continental du 21 novembre 1806*", *Histoire des Deux Empires, Le Site d'Histoire de la Fondation Napoléon*, Napoleon.org. https://www.napoleon.org/histoire-des-2-empires/articles/decret-du-blocus-continental-du-21-novembre-1806/ Quoting *Le Moniteur*, 4 December 1806.

"*Réglement Sur la Police des Dépots de Prisonniers de guerre du 10 Thermidor, An XI de la République française*". H. Berriat, *Législation Militaire ou Receuil Méthodique et Raisonné des Lois, Décrêts, Réglemens et Instructions Actuellement en vigueur sur Toutes les Branches de l'état militaire*. (Alexandrie: Louis Capriolo, 1812.)

"*Réglement Sur les Armemens en course*" (Saint-Cloud, 2 Prairial, an XI. Paris: Imprimerie de la République, 1803).

"*Traité d'amitié et de commerce, conclu entre le Roi et les États-Unis de l'Amérique septentrionale, le 6 février 1778.*" Paris: Imprimerie royale, 1778. BNF, *département Droit, économie, politique*, F-21249 (37). https://gallica.bnf.fr/ark:/12148/btv1b86259408/f22.image

United States

"Convention Defining and Establishing the Functions and Privileges of Consuls and Vice Consuls, November 14, 1788". The Avalon Project: Documents in Law, History and Diplomacy, Yale Law School, Lillian Goldman Law Library. https://avalon.law.yale.edu/18th_century/fr1788.asp #1.

Joint Army and Navy Selective Service Committee, *American Selective Service: a Brief Account of Its Historical Background and Its Probable Future Form* (October 1939).

"Treaty of Alliance Between the United States and France; February 6, 1778". The Avalon Project: Documents in Law, History and Diplomacy, Yale Law School, Lillian Goldman Law Library. https://avalon.law.yale.edu/18th_century/fr1788-1.asp

United States Congress. *American State Papers: Foreign Relations* (Buffalo: W.S. Hein, 1998).

https://www.loc.gov/item/97080286/

United States Congressional Serial Set. "Relief of Distressed Seamen in the Ports of Europe", H.R. Doc. No. 152–153, 11th Cong., 3rd Sess. (1810) Commerce and Navigation: 1:821–22.

United States Statutes at Large

Act of 31 July 1789. "An Act to regulate the Collection of the Duties imposed by law on the tonnage of ships or vessels, and on goods, wares and merchandises imported into the United States." ch.5, Stat.1. https://memory.loc.gov/cgi–bin/ampage?collId=llsl&fileName=001/llsl001.db&recNum=152

Act of 5 June 1794. "An act in addition to the act for the punishment of certain crimes against the United States (a)" *United States Statutes at Large*, Vol. 1, 3rd Congress, 1st Session, Chapter 50, 5 June 1794.

Act of 18 April 1806. "An Act to prohibit the importation of certain goods, wares and merchandise." ch.29, Stat.1. https://memory.loc.gov/cgi–bin/ampage?collId=llsl&fileName=002/llsl002.db&recNum=416

Act of 22 December 1807. "An Embargo laid on Ships and Vessels in the Ports and Harbors of the United States." ch.5, Stat.1. https://memory.loc.gov/cgi-bin/ampage?collId=llsl&fileName=002/llsl002.db&recNum=488

Act of 1 March 1809. "An Act to interdict the commercial intercourse between the United States and Great Britain and France, and their dependencies; and for other purposes." ch.24, Stat.2. https://memory.loc.gov/cgi-bin/ampage?collId=llsl&fileName=002/llsl002.db&recNum=565

Act of 1 May 1810. "An Act concerning the commercial intercourse between the United States and Great Britain and France, and their dependencies, and for other purposes." ch.39, Stat.2. https://memory.loc.gov/cgi-bin/ampage?collId=llsl&fileName=002/llsl002.db&recNum=642

Great Britain

"An Act for the better Supply of Mariners and Seamen to serve His Majesty's Ships of War, and on board Merchant Ships, and other Trading Ships, and Privateers, 1740", J. Raithby, T. Edlyne Tomlins (1811). *The statutes at large, of England and of Great Britain: from Magna Carta to the union of the kingdoms of Great Britain and Ireland.*

"An Act for the Encouragement of the Trade to America". Great Britain., J. Raithby (1823). *The statutes relating to the Admiralty, Navy, Shipping, and Navigation of the United Kingdom, from 9 Hen. III. to Geo. IV. inclusive.* (London: G. Eyre and A. Strahan).

"An Act for the further Encouragement of British Mariners; and for other Purposes therein mentioned, 11 June 1794", J. Raithby (1823). *The statutes relating to the Admiralty, Navy, Shipping, and Navigation of the United Kingdom, from 9 Hen. III. to Geo. IV. inclusive.* (London: G. Eyre and A. Strahan).

"October 1651: An Act for increase of Shipping, and Encouragement of the Navigation of this Nation", *Acts and Ordinances of the Interregnum, 1642–1660*, eds C.H. Firth and R.S. Rait (London, 1911) 559–562. *British History Online* http://www.british-history.ac.uk/no-series/acts-ordinances-interregnum/pp559–562

"The Orders of Council, and Instructions for Imposing the Restrictions of Blockade; and for Regulating The Navigation of the Sea...." (London: N. Shury, 1808).

C. Newspapers and Periodicals

Aurora General Advertiser (22 Feb, 1808), (12 Feb, 1811)
Barron's Mutual Funds Quarterly updated (5 Apr, 1999)
The Bristol Mirror (2 Jan, 1813)
Bulletin d'histoire économique et sociale de la Révolution française (1969)
Bulletin of the GHI [German Historical Institute] No. 57 (Fall, 2015)
Coriolis: the Interdisciplinary Journal of Maritime Studies. Vol. 10, No. 2 (2021)
Commonplace: the journal of early American life issue 12.4 (Jul, 2012)
The Evening Post (23 Jan, 1813)
Gazette de Guernesey (16 Aug, 1806)
Gazette des Tribunaux: Journal de Jurisprudence et des Débats Judiciaires 1622 (30 Jan, 1842)
La Gazette nationale ou le Moniteur universel (1 Oct, 1802), (22 Dec, 1803)
German Historical Institute London Bulletin Vol. 4, No. 2 (Nov, 2018)
Historic Nantucket Vol. 69, No. 4 (Fall, 2019)
The Hull Packet and Original Weekly Commercial, Literary and General Advertiser (17 Mar, 1812)
The Journal of Economic History Vol. 40, No. 4 (Dec, 1980)
Journal of the Early Republic Vol. 34, No. 2 (Summer 2014)
The London Gazette No. 16315 (14 Nov, 1809), 16903 (31 May, 1814)
The Mississippi Valley Historical Review Vo.l.1, No. 4 (Mar, 1915)
Napoleonica. La Revue. Vol. 3, No. 21 (2014)
The New England Quarterly Vol. 10, No. 3 (1937), Vol. 63, No. 4 (Dec, 1990)
New York History Vol. 77, No. 4 (Oct, 1996)

The North American Review Vol. 168, No. 507 (Feb, 1899)
The Northern Mariner/Le Marin du nord VI, No. 4 (Oct, 1996)
L'Oracle and Daily Advertiser 109 (7 May, 1808)
The Pennsylvania Magazine of History and Biography Vol. 53, No. 4 (1929)
Political Science Quarterly Vol. 13, No. 1 (Mar, 1896)
Proceedings Vol. 58, No. 5 (1932); Vol. 68, No. 12 (1942)
Proceedings of the American Philosophical Society Vol. 120, No. 5 (Oct, 15, 1976)
Revue des Deux Mondes (1915, 1940, 1962)
Revue du Nord No. 395 (2012)
Revue historique des armées Vol. 251 (2008)
Richmond Enquirer
Spooner's Vermont Journal Vol. XXVII, No. 1363 (4 Sept, 1809)
The Weekly Register (9 Oct, 1813)
The William and Mary Quarterly Vol. 25, No. 3 (Jul, 1968)

3. Unpublished Theses, Papers and Archivists' Essays

Audin, Margaret. *British Hostages in Napoleonic France, The Evidence: With Particular Reference to Manufacturers and Artisans, a thesis submitted to the Faculty of Commerce and Social Science of the University of Birmingham* (1987).
Belabdelouahab-Fernini, Linda. (2017). "Per Eric Skjöldebrand: The man Towards Whom the United States Is Indebted." Unpublished paper (June 2017).
Boorsma Mendoza, Pablo, *Merchant Consuls: Dutch Consuls in Cadiz and their Divided Loyalties (1713–1757)*, Masters thesis in History, University of Leiden, 2015.
Chenicek, Jolynda Brock. *Dereliction Of Diplomacy: The American Consulates in Paris and Bordeaux During the Napoleonic Era, 1804–1815 (A Dissertation Submitted to the Department of History in Partial Fulfillment of the Requirements for the Degree of Doctorate of Philosophy)*, Florida State University College of Arts and Science (2008).
Chevignard, François-Xavier, « Répertoire numérique: Série FF – Invalides et Prises: Sous-série FF3: Jugements de validité et de liquidation des prises, An V – 1893 » (Vincennes, 2012–2013).
Cheynet, Pierre-Dominique. *Les Procès-verbaux du Directoire exécutif, an V–an VII: inventaire des registres, tome III, vendémiaire–frimaire, an VI*. Paris: Arch. nat. 2002.
Corn, Tony. "Global Napoléon" (work in progress, Academia.edu, 2021) https://www.academia.edu/45556643/Global_Napol%C3%A9on
Daran, Ariel. *"Des Ordonnances de Colbert de 1665 et 1668 sur l'enrôlement maritime à l'Ordonnance de juin 2009 – Evolution du droit maritime"*, extracted from *Le point sur le Droit du Travail Maritime français*. Published on: *Blog Avocats*. https://blogavocat.fr/space/ariel.dahan/content/des-ordonnance-de-colbert-de-1665-et-1668-sur-lenrolement-maritime-a-l-ordonnance-de-juin-2009---evolution-du-droit-maritime_1815e07f-fc48-bc62-8fa0-910b60493082

Delobette, Edouard. *Ces "Messieurs du Havre". Négociants, Commissionaires et Armateurs de 1680 à 1830. Thèse de doctorat de IIIe cycle préparée sous la direction de Monsieur le Professeur André ZYSBERG, soutenue à l'Université de Caen le samedi 26 novembre* (2005).

Dillon, William Henry. Unpublished journal. Vol. 3, entry for July 1806. Papers of Professor Michael Arthur Lewis. Caird Library, National Maritime Museum. Manuscript LES/6/7/(8).

Gordinier, Glenn Stine. *Versatility in Crisis: The Merchants of New London Customs District Respond to the Embargo of 1807–1809*. Doctoral thesis, University of Connecticut (2001).

Houmeau, Didier. *Les prisonniers de guerre britanniques de Napoléon 1er. (1803–1814)*. Draft copy of a doctoral thesis shared with the author, email dated 7 April 2010.

Johnson, Kenneth. "1804–1814: 'Harassing the British with expenses & fatigue'— Napoleon's Naval Strategy" (Academia.edu, 2023) https://www.academia.edu/102597966/1804_1814_Harassing_the_British_with_expenses_and_fatigue_Napoleon_s_Naval_Strategy

Rouanet, David. *Prisonniers de Napoléon: Les prisonniers de guerre coalisés internés en France de1803 à 1814*. Unpublished manuscript shared with the author and based on a thesis submitted to Paris IV-Sorbonne, 2009, under the direction of J-O Boudon.

Wilson, Gary E., *American Prisoners in the Barbary Nations, 1784-1816*. Dissertation Presented to the Graduate Council of the North Texas State University (May 1979).

BIBLIOGRAPHY

Abbot, Abiel, *Sermons to Mariners* (Boston: Samuel T. Armstrong, 1812).
Abell, Francis, *Prisoners of War in Britain, 1756 to 1815* (Oxford UP, 1914).
Adams, Jr., Donald R., "American Neutrality and Prosperity, 1793–1808: A Reconsideration", *The Journal of Economic History*, 40:4 (Dec, 1980) 713–737.
Alonso, William, "Citizenship, Nationality and Other Identities", *Journal of International Affairs*, Vol. 48, No. 2 (Winter 1995) pp585–599.
Ames, Nathaniel, *A Mariner's Sketches* (Providence: Cory, Marshall, and Hammond, 1830).
Andrews, Edward L., "Napoleon and America". *The Magazine of History with Notes and Queries*, 6 (July–Dec, 1907).
Armstrong, John, *Notices of the War of 1812* (New York: Wiley & Putman, 1840).
Astorquia, Madeline, et al., *Guide des Sources de l'Histoire des Etats-Unis dans les archives françaises* (Paris: France Expansion, 1976).
Aymes, Jean-René, *La déportation sous le premier Empire: les Espagnols en France (1808–1814)* (Paris: Éditions de la Sorbonne, 1983).
Barnes, James, *Yankee Ships and Yankee Sailors: Tales of 1812* (New York: Macmillan, 1897).
Baron, Bruno, "Aspets Principaux de la Vie politique à Morlaix de 1759 à 1815", Mémoire de maitrise effectué (undated).
Bauer, Jean Ann, *Republicans of Letters: The Early American Foreign Service as Information Network, 1775–1825*, A Dissertation presented to the Graduate Faculty of the University of Virginia in Candidacy for the Degree of Doctor of Philosophy, Corcoran Department of History, University of Virginia (August 2015).
Bégaud, Stéphane, Marc Belissa, and Joseph Visser, *Aux Origines d'une Alliance Improbable: Le réseau consulaire français aux Etats-Unis (1776–1815)* (Brussels: P.I.E. Peter Lang, 2005).
Bizardel, Yvon, *Les Américains à Paris Pendant la Révolution* (Paris: Calmann-Lévy, 1972).
Blayney, Andrew Thomas, *Napoleon's Prisoner of War: Experiences of a British officer during the Napoleonic Wars in Spain and France* (Driffield: Leonaur, 2009).
Bolster, W. Jeffrey, "To Feel Like a Man: Black Seamen in the Northern States, 1800–1860", *The Journal of American History*, 76:4 (Mar, 1990) 1173–1199.
Bonnel, Ulane, "La Marine Marchande des Etats-Unis et le Blocus Continental", *Revue de l'Institut Napoléon*, 76 (July 1960) 225–229.
Bouchon, Lionel and Didier Grau, "Freemasonry Under the French First Empire", *Napoléon & Empire* (2017). https://www.napoleon-empire.net/en/freemason.php

Bourgogne, Adrien, *Memoirs of Sergeant Bourgogne, 1812–1813* (London: Constable, 1996).

Boutet de Monvel, Roger, *Les Anglais à Paris 1800–1850* (Paris: Librairie Plon, 1911).

Brenckle, Matthew, *British and American Naval Prisoners of War During the War of 1812* (Boston: USS Constitution Museum, 2005).

Bruns, Craig, *Skin & Bones: Tattoos in the Life of the American Sailor* (Philadelphia: Independence Seaport Museum, 2009).

Burrill, Gary, *Away: Maritimer in Massachusetts, Ontario, and Alberta* (Montreal: McGill-Queen's UP, 1992).

Burt, Roger, "'Wherever Dispersed': The Travelling Mason in the Nineteenth Century", Prestonian Lecture 2015 (Exeter, privately printed, 2015).

Cabantous, Alain, *La mer et les hommes: pêcheurs et matelots dunkerquois de Louis XIV à la Révolution* (Dunkirk: Westhoek-Editions, 1980).

Cantor, Milton. "Joel Barlow's Mission to Algiers." *The Historian* 25, No. 2 (1963): 172–94. http://www.jstor.org/stable/24442368.

Caputo, Sara, "Alien Seamen in the British Navy, British Law, and the British State, c.1793 – c.1815", *The Historical Journal*, 62:3 (September 2019) 685–707. doi:10.1017/S0018246X18000298

Cavignac, Jean, Jean-Pierre Bériac and Mauricette Laprie, *Bordeaux, la Guyenne et les États-Unis, 1750–1820: exposition organisée aux archives départementales de la Gironde…Bordeaux, du 26 octobre au 19 décembre 1987* (Bordeaux: AD Gironde, 1987).

Charles-Roux, François, *Les Travaux d'Herculais ou une Extraordinaire Mission en Barbarie* (Paris: Leroux, 1929?).

Colley, Linda, *Captives: Britain, Empire, and the World, 1600–1850* (New York: Anchor Books, 2004).

Colombos, C.J., "Some Notes on the Decisions of the French Prize Courts", *Journal of the Society of Comparative Legislation, New Series*, 16: 2 (1916), 300–321. http://www.jstor.org/stable/752429

Coquelle, P., *Napoleon & England, 1803–1813: a Study from Unprinted Documents* (London: George Bell and Sons, 1904).

Cox, Henry Bartholomew, "A Nineteenth-Century Archival Search: The History of the French Spoliation Claims Papers", *The American Archivist*, 33:4 (October 1970) 389–401. http://www.jstor.org/stable/40291271

Creighton, Margaret, *Dogwatch & Liberty Days: Seafaring Life in the Nineteenth Century* (Salem: Peabody Museum of Salem, 1982).

Cuffe, Paul, Narrative of the Life and Adventures of Paul Cuffe, a Pequot Indian: During Thirty Years Spent at Sea, and in Travelling in Foreign Lands. (Vernon: 1839).

Cutler, Carl C., *Greyhounds of the Sea: The Story of the American Clipper Ship* (Annapolis: United States Naval Institute, 1930).

Dague, Everett, "Henri Clarke, Minister of War, and the Malet Conspiracy", Originally published in *Selected papers of the Consortium on Revolutionary Europe* (1996) *The Napoleon Series*. https://www.napoleon-series.org/ins/scholarship98/c_clarke.html

Davis, Joshua, *A Narrative of Joshua Davis, an American Citizen, Who Was Pressed and Served on Board Six Ships of the British Navy* (Boston: B. True, 1811).
de Feyster, Frederic, *A Biographical Sketch of Robert R. Livingston, read before the N.Y. Historical Society, October 3, 1876* (New York, 1876).
de Gasquet, André, "Etienne Cathalan: vice-consul des Etats-Unis à Marseille de 1789 à 1819", *Cahiers du Comité du Vieux Marseille*, 78 (1989).
de la Gravière, E. Jurien, *Guerres Maritimes sous la République et l'Empire*, 2 (Paris: Charpentier, 1860).
Doyle, William, *The Oxford History of the French Revolution* (Oxford: Oxford UP, 1990).
Driault Édouard, "L'histoire de la politique extérieure de Napoléon Ier. État des travaux et questions à traiter", *Revue d'histoire moderne et contemporaine*, 3:4 (1901) 377–394. https://www.persee.fr/doc/rhmc_0996-2743_1901_num_3_4_4407
Duché, Elodie Marie, *A passage to imprisonment: the British prisoners of war in Verdun under the First French Empire*, A thesis submitted in fulfilment of the requirements for the degree of Doctor of Philosophy in History, University of Warwick, Department of History (September 2014).
du Pasquier, Thierry, *Les Baleiniers français de Louis XVI à Napoléon* (Paris: Henri Veyrier, 1990).
Durden, Robert F., "Joel Barlow in the French Revolution", *The William and Mary Quarterly, Third Series,* 8:3 (1951) 327–354.
Dutton, Thomas, *The Captive Muse, a Collection of Poems* (London: Sherwood, Neely and Jones, 1814).
Fabel, Robin F.A., "Self-Help in Dartmoor: Black and White Prisoners in the War of 1812", *Journal of the Early Republic*, 9:2 (Summer 1989). 165–190. https://www.jstor.org/stable/3123202
Farr, James Barker, *Black Odyssey: The Seafaring Traditions of Afro-Americans* (New York: Peter Lang, 1989).
Fink, Leon, *Sweatshops at Sea: Merchant Seamen in the World's First Globalized Industry, from 1812 to the Present* (Chapel Hill: University of North Carolina, 2012).
Fischer, Lewis R., ed., *Research in Maritime History No. 7: The Market for Seamen in the Age of Sail* (St. John's, Newfoundland: International Maritime Economic History Association, 1994).
Fischer, Lewis R. and Walter Minchinton, eds, *Research in Maritime History No. 3: People of the Northern Seas* (St. John's, Newfoundland: International Maritime Economic History Association, 1992).
Foss, John, *A journal, of the captivity and sufferings of John Foss; several years a prisoner at Algiers: together with some account of the treatment of Christian slaves when sick:-- and observations of the manners and customs of the Algerines* (Newburyport, Angier: March, 1798). https://quod.lib.umich.edu/e/evans/N25429.0001.001/1:1?rgn=div1;view=fulltext
Foy, Charles R., "The Royal Navy's employment of black mariners and maritime workers, 1754–1783", *The International Journal of Maritime History* 28:1 (2016) 6–35.

Frykman, Niklas, "Seamen on Late Eighteenth-Century European Warships", *International Review of Social History*, 54:1 (2009) 67–93.

Garrioch, David, *The Making of Revolutionary Paris* (Berkeley: University of California Press, 2002).

Gibbs, Christopher John. *Friends and Enemies: the Underground War Between Great Britain and France, 1793–1802*, thesis submitted as part of the Final Honours Examination, History Program, La Trobe University (2010).

Gilje, Paul A. "'Free Trade and Sailors' Rights': The Rhetoric of the War of 1812" *Journal of the Early Republic*, 30, No. 1 (2010) pp1–23. http://www.jstor.org/stable/40662251

Gilje, Paul A., *To Swear Like a Sailor: Maritime Culture in America, 1750–1850* (New York: Cambridge UP, 2016).

Girard, Philippe R., "The Ugly Duckling: The French Navy and the Saint-Domingue Expedition, 1801–1803", *International Journal of Naval History* 9:1–3 (April–December 2010).

Glover, Richard, "The French Fleet, 1807–1814; Britain's Problem; and Madison's Opportunity", *The Journal of Modern History*, 39:3 (September 1967) 233–252. http://www.jstor.org/stable/1876579

Glover, Richard, *Britain at Bay: Defence against Bonaparte, 1803–14* (London: George Allen & Unwin, 1973).

Grasilier, Léonce, *Evasions de Prisonniers de Guerre favorisées par le Francs-Maçons sous Napoléon 1er* (Paris: H. Daragon, 1913).

Gregory, Charles Noble, "Right of the Master and Crew of a Captured Ship to Effect Her Rescue", *The American Journal of International Law*, 11:2 (April 1917) 315–326. https://www.jstor.org/stable/2188052

Griffith, Paddy, *The Vauban Fortifications of France* (Oxford, Osprey, 2006).

Griffiths, Arthur, "Old War Prisons in England and France", *The North American Review*, 168:507 (Feb, 1899) 163–177. http://www.jstor.org/stable/2511914

Hamilton, Archibald, and Nial Osborough. "A Treatise on Impressing." *Irish Jurist (1966–)* 8, No. 1 (1973): 117–42. http://www.jstor.org/stable/44026613

Hantraye, Jacques, *Les Cosaques aux Champs-Élysées: l'Occupation de la France après la chute de Napoléon* (Paris: Belin, 2005).

Heuvel, Sean M. and John A. Rodgaard, eds, *From Across the Sea: North Americans in Nelson's Navy* (Warwick: Helion, 2020).

Hewson, Maurice and Antony Brett-James, *Escape from the French: Captain Hewson's Narrative (1803–1809)* (Sevenoaks: Hodder and Stoughton, 1981).

Hibbert, Christopher, *The Days of the French Revolution* (New York: Morrow Quill, 1981).

Hicks, Dan, *True Born Columbians: The Promises and Perils of National Identity for American Seafarers of The Early Republican Period*, Submitted in Partial Fulfillment of the Requirements for the Degree of Doctor of Philosophy, College of Liberal Arts, The Graduate School, Pennsylvania State University (May 2007).

Hill, Peter P., "The Savannah Riots: a Burning Issue in Franco-American Hostility, 1811–1812", *The Georgia Historical Quarterly*, 88:4 (Winter 2004) 499–510.

Hill, Peter P., *Joel Barlow: American Diplomat and Nation Builder* (Washington, D.C.: Potomac Books, 2012).

Hillman, Henning and Christina Gathmann, "Overseas Trade and the Decline of Privateering", *The Journal of Economic History*, 71:3 (September 2011) 730–761. https://www.jstor.org/stable/23018337

Hohman, Elmo Paul, *History of American Merchant Seamen* (Hamden: Shoe String Press, 1956).

James, Trevor, *American Prisoners of War at Dartmoor War Depot (1813–1815)* (Crediton: Hedgerow Print, 2007).

Johnson, Niall, "Taking French Leave: Masonic English Napoleonic Prisoners 1803–1814", *Ars Quatuor Coronatorum,* 135 (2022) 1–18.

Lambert, Andrew and John Keegan, eds, *War at Sea in the Age of Sail* (London: Cassell, 2000).

Lane, Horace, *The Wandering Boy, Careless Sailor, and Result of Inconsideration, a True Narrative* (Skaneateles: Luther A. Pratt, 1839).

Lane, John, *Masonic Records, 1717–1894* (London: Freemason Hall, 1895).

Lansing, Charles (attributed). *The Narraganset Chief, or the Adventures of a Wanderer, Written by Himself.* (New York: J.K. Porter, 1832).

Laugel, Auguste. "Les Corsaires confédérés et le droit des gens." *Revue Des Deux Mondes (1829–1971)* 52, No. 1 (1864): 224–48. http://www.jstor.org/stable/44726306.

Lawrence, James Henry, *A Picture of Verdun, or the English detained in France* (London: T. Hookham Jun. and E.T. Hookham, 1810).

Le Carvèse, Patrick, "Les Prisonniers Français en Grande-Bretagne de 1803 à 1814: Étude statistique à partir des archives centrales de la Marine", *Napoleonica. La Revue,* 8 (2010) 3–29.

Leech, Samuel, *Thirty Years From Home, or a Voice From the Main Deck...* (Boston: Tappan, Whittemore & Mason, 1843).

Le Guellaff, Florence, *Armements en course et droit des prises maritimes (1792–1856)* (Nancy: PUN-Editions universitaires de Lorraine, 1999).

Lemisch, Jesse. "Listening to the 'Inarticulate': William Widger's Dream and the Loyalties of American Revolutionary Seamen in British Prisons" *Journal of Social History* 3, No. 1 (1969): 1–29. http://www.jstor.org/stable/3786643.

Le Quang, Jeanne-Laure, De l'ennemi au nouveau Français: la gestion des étrangers par la police napoléonienne (1799–1814), *La Révolution française: Cahiers de l'Institut d'histoire de la Révolution française,* 22 (2022).

Logan, Rayford W. "The Negro in the Quasi War 1798–1800." *Negro History Bulletin* 14, No. 6 (1951): 128–43. http://www.jstor.org/stable/44212448.

Malloy, Mary, *African Americans in the Maritime Trades: A Guide to Resources in New England* (Sharon: Kendall Whaling Museum, 1990).

Mancini, Jason R. and LaRose, Silvermoon Mars. "'The Narraganset Chief, or the Adventures of a Wanderer': Recovering an Indigenous Autobiography", *Mainsheet*, No.1 (2024), 124–149.

Marquis, Hugues, "La Convention et les Prisonniers de Guerre des Armées Etrangères", *Histoire, économie & société,* 3 (2008)) 65–81. https://www.cairn.info/revue-histoire-economie-et-societe-2008-3-page-65.htm

Marzagalli, Silvia, "Port Cities in the French Wars: The Responses of Merchants in Bordeaux, Hamburg and Livorno to Napoleon's Continental Blockade, 1806–1813", *The Northern Mariner/Le Marin du Nord,* VI:4 (October 1996) 68–73.

Marzagalli, Silvia, "Establishing Transatlantic Trade Networks in Time of War: Bordeaux and the United States, 1793–1815", *Business History Review*, 79:4 (Winter 2005) 811–844.

Marzagalli, Silvia, "The Failure of a Transatlantic Alliance? Franco-American Trade, 1783–1815" (Pre-print version) *History of European Ideas*, 34:4 (Dec, 2008) 456–464.

Marzagalli, Silvia, "La Circulation de l'Information et les Réseaux marchands à l'Epoque moderne", Sébastien Laurent, ed., *Entre l'État et le marché. L'information et l'intelligence économique en France* (Paris: Nouveau Monde éditions, 2010) 13–43.

Marzagalli, Silvia, "American shipping and trade in warfare, or the benefits of European conflicts for neutral merchants: The experience of the Revolutionary and Napoleonic wars, 1793–1815", *Kyoto Sangyo University Economic Review* 1 (Mar, 2014).

Marzagalli, Silvia, *Bordeaux et les Etats-Unis, 1776–1815: Politique et stratégies négotiantes dans la genèse d'un réseau commercial* (Geneva: Librairie Droz, 2015).

Marzagalli, Silvia and James R. Sofka, John McCusker, eds, *Research in Maritime History No. 44: Rough Waters: American Involvement with the Mediterranean in the Eighteenth and Nineteenth Centuries* (St. John's, Newfoundland: International Maritime Economic History Association, 2010).

Massachusetts, House of Representatives, *Report of the Committee of the House of Representatives of Massachusetts on the Subject of Impressed Seamen…* (Boston: Russell and Cutler, 1813).

Maude, John Barnabas, "Journal 1802–1814" (unpublished), Queen's College Library, Oxford, GB/NNAF/P144289

Melvin, Frank Edgar, *Napoleon's Navigation System: The Study of Trade Control During the Continental Blockade* (New York: D. Appleton, 1919).

Miège, Jean-Louis, ed., *Navigations et Migrations en Méditerranée: de la Préhistoire à nos Jours* (Paris: CNRS Editions, 1990).

Moore, John Bassett, "A Hundred Years of American Diplomacy", *Harvard Law Review*, 14:3 (November 1900) 165–183. http://www.jstor.org/stable/1323898

Morison, Samuel Eliot, *The Maritime History of Massachusetts, 1783–1860* (Boston: Houghton Mifflin, 1921).

Morley, J., *A Sermon, preached in Providence Chapel, Hope-Street, Hull…* (Hull: J. Ferraby, 1811).

Morriss, Roger, *The Channel Fleet and the Blockade of Brest 1793–1801* (Abingdon: Taylor and Francis, 2020).

The Naval Chronicle (London: Joyce Gold, 1813 and 1815).

Nixon, J.A., "British Prisoners Released by Napoleon at Jenner's Request", *Proceedings of the Royal Society of Medicine*, XXXII: 8 (June 1939) 877–883.

Office of the Historian, Bureau of Public Affairs, United States Department of State, "A New Framework for Foreign Affairs", *A Short History of the Department of State: Foundations of Foreign Affairs, 1775–1823*. https://history.state.gov/departmenthistory/short-history/framework

Paine, Ralph D., *The Old Merchant Marine – a Chronicle of American Ships and Sailors* (New Haven: Yale UP, 1919).

Parry-Wingfield, John, *Napoleon's Prisoner: a Country Parson's Ten-Year Detention in France* (Torrs Park: Arthur H. Stockwell, 2012).
Pierson, Harry H. "Excerpts from the Consular Register in the American Consulate General, Paris, France", *The New England Historical and Genealogical Register*, 111 (April 1956) 128–134.
Pigeard A., "Le service des vivres dans les armées du première empire (1804–1815)", *Annales historiques de la Révolution française*, 303 (1996) 144–147. https://www.persee.fr/doc/ahrf_0003-4436_1996_num_303_1_3426
Porter, Kenneth Wiggins, *The Jacksons and the Lees: Two Generations of Massachusetts Merchants, 17765–1844* (New York: Russell & Russell, 1937).
Poussou, Jean-Pierre, ed., *Les Constructions navales dans l'Histoire* (Paris: Sorbonne UP, 2007).
Putney, Martha, "Black Merchant Seamen of Newport, 1803–1865: a Case Study in Foreign Commerce", *The Journal of Negro History*, 57:2 (April 1972) 156–168.
Quoy-Bodin Jean-Luc, "Le militaire en Maçonnerie (XVIIIème–XIXème siècles)", *Histoire, économie et société*, 2:4 (1983) 549–576. https://www.persee.fr/doc/hes_0752-5702_1983_num_2_4_1342
Raab Collection, "In the Earliest Mutiny Case We Know of Against a Jewish Captain and Ship Owner, President James Madison Stays a Sentence of Execution Against a Sailor Sentenced to Death" (2017). https://www.raabcollection.com/presidential-autographs/madison-levy?utm_source=Autographs&utm_campaign=7881a3c950-August_10_2017&utm_medium=email&utm_term=0_8ac565fac9-7881a3c950-82916181
Rapport, Michael, *Nationality and Citizenship in Revolutionary France: The Treatment of Foreigners, 1789–1799* (Oxford: Clarendon Press, 2000).
Revere, John, *A Biographical Memoir of the Life of John Revere, M.D., Professor of the Theory and Practice of Medicine in the University of New York* (New York: Joseph H. Jennings, 1847).
Roberts, Priscilla H. and Richard S. Roberts, *Thomas Barclay (1728–1793): Consul in France, Diplomat in Barbary* (Bethlehem: Lehigh UP, 2008).
Robertson, John "Journal" (unpublished), National Maritime Museum, Greenwich, JOD/202.
Rosenberg, Charles E., "Siting Epidemic Disease: 3 Centuries of American History", *The Journal of Infectious Diseases*, 197, Issue Supplement (Feb, 2008) S4–S6. https://doi.org/10.1086/524985
Rouleau, Brian, *With Sails Whitening Every Sea: Mariners and the Making of an American Maritime Empire* (Ithaca: Cornell UP, 2014).
Runyan, Timothy J., *Ships, Seafaring and Society: Essays in Maritime History* (Detroit: Wayne State UP, 1987).
Sahlins, Peter, *Unnaturally French: Foreign Citizens in the Old Regime and After* (Ithaca: Cornell UP, 2004).
Sears, Christine E., "'Most Obedient and Loving Subjects:' Impressed Seamen and the Rhetoric of Citizenship", paper submitted for the conference "1812 in the Americas", sponsored and organised by the Réseau pour le développement européen de l'histoire de la jeune Amérique et l'Université de Bretagne Occidentale, Brest, France, 7–9 June 2012.

Skinner, Ralph Nelson, "American common seamen prisoners of war in Britain during the American Revolution", thesis submitted in partial fulfillment of the requirements for the degree of Master of Arts, Department of History, Simon Fraser University (September 1975). https://summit.sfu.ca/item/3413

Stackpole, Edouard A., *Whales & Destiny: The Rivalry between America, France, and Britain for Control of the Southern Whale Fishery, 1785–1825* (Amherst: University of Massachusetts Press, 1972).

Stephen, James, *War in Disguise: the Frauds of the Neutral Flags* (London: 1806).

Stewart, Alexander, *The Life of Alexander Stewart, Prisoner of Napoleon and Preacher of the Gospel* (London: George Allen & Unwin, 1948).

Story, William, *A Journal Kept in France, During a Captivity of More Than Nine Years…* (Sunderland, George Garbutt, 1815).

Thomin, Mike, "Among Ships of Thieves on Waves of Change", *Coriolis: The Interdisciplinary Journal of Maritime Studies*, 8:1 (2018). https://ijms.nmdl.org/article/view/18598

Todd, Charles Burr, *In Olde Massachusetts: Sketches of Old Times and Places During the Early Days of the Commonwealth* (New York: Grafton Press, 1907).

Toillon, Eveline, *Les Prisonniers de la Citadelle: Poisons, cachots, et détenus (1679–1947)* (Besançon: Editions Cêtre, 2004).

Torres, Rodrigo de Oliveira, "Handling the ship: rights and duties of masters, mates, seamen and owners of ships in nineteenth-century merchant marine", *International Journal of Maritime History*, 26:587 (2014). http://ijh.sagepub.com/content/26/3/587.citation

Uhl, Robert, "Masters of the Merchant Marine", *American Heritage*, 34:3 (1983).

United States, Department of State, *Report of the Secretary of State Relative to the Papers on File in the Department of State Concerning the Unpaid Claims of Citizens of the United States Against France…* (Washington, D.C.: GPO, 1886).

Van Hille, Jean-Marc, ed., *Dictionnaire des Marins Francs-Maçons, gens de mer et professions connexes aux XVIIe, XIXe et XXe siècles* (Paris: SPM, 2011).

van Royen, Paul C., Jaap Bruijn and Jan Lucassed, eds, *Research in Maritime History No. 13: "Those Emblems of Hell": European Sailors and the Maritime Labour Market, 1570–1870* (St. John's, Newfoundland: International Maritime Economic History Association, 1997).

Vickers, Daniel, with Vince Walsh, *Young Men and the Sea: Yankee Seafarers in the Age of Sail* (New Haven: Yale UP, 2005).

Villiers, Patrick, *La France sur Mer* (Paris: Fayard, 2015).

Villiers, Patrick, *Des vaisseaux et des hommes: La marine de Louis XV et Louis XVI* (Paris: Fayard, 2021).

Vovelle, Michel, ed., *Paris et la Révolution* (Paris: Editions de la Sorbonne, 2021).

Ward, Christopher, "The Commerce of East Florida During the Embargo, 1806–1812: The Role of Amelia Island", *The Florida Historical Quarterly*, 68:2 (October 1989) 160–179.

Watt, J., E.J. Freeman and W.F. Bynum, eds, *Starving Sailors: The influence of nutrition upon naval and maritime history* (London: National Maritime Museum, 1981).

Whipple, Hank, "Sailing Under False Colors: an Historic *Ruse de Guerre*", *Coriolis: the Interdisciplinary Journal of Maritime Studies*, 5:2 (2015). https://ijms.nmdl.org/article/view/15891

Whitcomb, Edward A., "Napoleon's Prefects", *The American Historical Review*, 79:4 (October 1974) 1089–1118.
Winsor, Justin, ed., *Memorial History of Boston, including Suffolk County, Massachusetts, 1630–1880* (Boston: Osgood, 1881).
Wold, Atle L., *Privateering and Diplomacy, 1793–1807: Great Britain, Denmark-Norway and the Question of Neutral Ports* (London: Palgrave Macmillan, 2020).
Wright, William, *A Narrative of the Situation and Treatment of the English…* (London: J.D. Dewick, 1803).
Young, Jeremy, "Les marins noirs dans la Royal Navy au XVIIIe siècle", *Bulletin de la Société d'Histoire de la Guadeloupe*, 177 (May–August 2017) 1–15. https://id.erudit.org/iderudit/1042764ar

INDEX

Abercrombie, 156–8
An act concerning consuls and vice-consuls 1792, 99–101
Adam, William, 136
Adams, Henry, 34
Adams, John, 78–9, 118
Admiralty, 24, 39, 127, 138, 139, 203
Adolphe, 179
African-American seamen, 7–8, 18, 44, 66, 73, 145, 155–6, 166–8, 180, 181–2, 183, 185, 207–8, 210, 231
    research sources, 239–45
Alexander, 136
Alger, John Goldworth, 45
Algiers, 117–19, 163–4
Allen, Captain Henry, 121
Allen, Joseph, 159–60, 164
Allen, Michael, 159–60
Allen, Samuel, 180–1
"*Almanach impérial,*" 95–6
Almy, Thomas C., 154
Alonso, William, 212
American diplomats, 77, 97–124
    ability to speak French, 105
    burden of relief for distressed seamen, 100–4, 123–4
    conflict with others, 107–9, 120, 188, 189, 195–6
    consular agents, 100, 101–4, 107, 171, 214–15
    Consular Service, creation of, 97–103
    Convention Defining and Establishing the Functions and Privileges of Consuls and Vice Consuls, 98, 99
    corruption, 212
    diplomatic messengers, 199–201
    flaws in the Consular Service, 212
    French trust, lack of, 131, 132
    friendships and partnerships, 109
    improper activities, 107
    lack of clarity on consular and diplomatic services, 98–9
    lack of remuneration for consuls, 100
    as opportunists and speculators, 106
    and seamens' documentation, lack of, 135–7
American prisoners of war, 1–2, 4–5, 6, 33, 44–5, 48, 49, 51, 52, 56, 57–8, 59, 60, 67, 80–1, 88, 91, 95, 108–9, 113
    becoming a captive, 46–9
    betraying fellow prisoners, 166–8, 174
    in British prisons, 216, 217
    brutality towards prisoners, 165
    burden of aid to, 100–4, 123–4
    census, 141–2, 189, 191
    chaplains, 68–70
    charitable aid to, 70, 71–2
    civilians, 54–6
    class prejudice, 57–8
    coercion to serve on French ships, 47–8
    deaths, 12–13, 65–7, 68, 172, 174, 181–2, 183, 187, 227–9
    distribution of nationalities, 49
    escapes, 156–7, 158, 160, 167–8, 175–6, 179, 180–1, 184, 187, 224–6
    families of, 69, 70, 71
    harsh treatment, 48–9
    individuality, 211–12
    maintenance of, 48–9
    marches, 49–53, 183, 207
    prisoners helping other prisoners, 68–70
    punishments, 59–60, 62–3, 67, 68, 69, 176
    religious worship, 68–9, 70–1, 72–3
    responsibility for, 95–6
    surgeons, 69–70, 71
    treasonous activities, 184–7
    violence, 23, 59, 69
    see also prison depots

American Revolution, 125–6
  soldiers' pay issue, 115–16
American Seaman's Friend Society, 18
American ships, 1
  "capture" of own vessels, 198
  capture of, 30, 33, 39–43, 48, 103, 107, 110, 118, 136, 139, 166, 179, 181–4, 185, 194
Amiens, 53
  Peace of, 56, 82, 112
  Treaty of, 30, 54
Amsterdam, 103, 131, 155, 163, 192
Ann, 136
Ann Maria, 153
Anthill, 186
Antonia Maria, 173
Antwerp, 103, 133, 187, 190, 191, 195
Appleton, John, 47–8, 101, 105
Argus, 121
Ariel, 51
Armstrong, John, 72, 105, 108, 111, 116, 131–2, 135, 139, 210, 217
  and the 1807 release, 189–91, 193–4
  1809 release failure, 198–202
  animosity towards Skipwith and others, 189, 195–6
  assistance to prisoners of war, 188–9, 212
  career, 113–15
  census of prisoners, 141–2, 189, 191
  and Nathan Haley, 198–201
  and naturalized Americans, 196–8
  reputation, 212
Arras, 50, 53, 56–7, 58, 61, 64, 65, 66, 67, 135, 137, 160, 162, 163, 166, 167, 178, 180, 191, 197
  closure, 177
  petition to the United States President, 193
Audin, Margaret, 45, 88
Aumont, Michel, 38
The Aurora General Advertiser, 109
Austin, John, 181–2
Auxonne, 50, 53, 58, 69, 134, 177
Aymes, Jean-René, 45

Baartman, Saartje, 194
Bainbridge, Captain William, 163, 193
Baker, Captain Bakir, or Barker, 152–3
Baker, John Martin, 122
Baltimore, 145, 192
Baltimore, 160, 162

Bamber, John, 133
Barclay, Thomas, 98–9
Barlow, Joel, 105–6, 109, 111, 113, 114, 196, 199, 201–2, 204, 210
  in Algiers, 118–19
  assistance to prisoners of war, 132–3, 159, 163, 188, 205–6
  death, 119, 202, 209
  enthusiasm for privateering, 203, 204–6
  French nationality, 117
  land speculation, 115–17
  poetry, 115
Barlow, Ruth, 119, 120, 122–3
Barlow, Thomas, 119, 120
Barnet, Isaac Cox, 101–2, 104, 105, 107–8, 109, 111, 120, 122, 131, 132, 158, 198, 201, 209, 210
  assistance to prisoners of war, 197
  promotion to Paris, 214
  suspension by Armstrong, 195–6
Barney, Joshua, 199
Bartlett, Edward, 170, 172
Bassett, William, 180–1
Bayonne Decree, 32, 33, 36, 40–1, 114, 144
Bean, Benjamin, 21
Belle Poule, 156
Bennet, John, 203
Bergen, 187
Berlin Decree, 31, 33, 34, 36, 103, 114, 129, 141
Berthier, General Louis-Alexandre, Prince of Neuchatel, 79, 83–4, 87, 88, 140
Besançon, 53, 69
Bitche, 53, 58, 59–60, 68, 69, 134, 142, 160, 167, 184, 191
Biter, 51
Black Prince, 198
Blossom, 171, 172
boarding houses, 15–16, 17–18
Bois-le-Duc, 53
Bolster, W. Jeffrey, 239–40
Bon Marcel, 166, 167
Bonnel, Ulane, 38
Bonny, William, 157–8
Bordeaux, 102, 103, 104, 107, 108, 157
Boston, 135, 136, 197
Boston, 19
Boulogne-sur-Mer, 131
Bourne, Sylvanus, 131, 155, 192
Bowers, Jonathan, 135
Bowes, William, 136–7

Breda, 192
Brest, 49–50, 103, 104, 185, 198, 204, 206, 207, 216
Brestois, 19, 133
Brewster, Job Ellis, 170, 173, 217
Briançon, 53, 167–8
Brice, Robert, 157
Briggs, Bolen, 166
Britain
    blockade of ports, 26, 31, 33, 34, 37–8, 40–1, 121, 141, 144, 168–9
    maritime law, 30
    United States terminates trade, 34
British prisoners of war, 6, 45, 49, 51–2, 53, 54, 57, 59, 68–72
    and American Seaman's Protection Certificates, 130–4
    escapes, 135, 137, 167–8, 175–6
    inclusion in lists for release, 209–10
    parole prisoners, 61–2, 175, 194
    pretending to be Americans, 134–5
    release of, 216
    treasonous activities, 178–9
    see also American prisoners of war; prison depots
Briton, 157
Brunsman, Denver, 125, 126, 159, 212
Brutus, 20–1, 179
Bucaille, 166
Bunker, Christopher, 195
Bunker, Henry, 195
Bunker, Peleg, 51, 195
Bunker Hill, 204
Bureau of Military Justice, 91
Burke, Edmund, 112
Bussell, Peter, 66

Cadore Letter, 34, 114
Caen, 158
Caisse des Invalides, 142
Calais, 46, 101, 103, 131, 215
Cambrai, 50, 53, 58, 61, 65–6, 69, 134, 146, 158, 166, 177, 178, 180, 181, 207
Cameron, Daniel, 51, 52
Campbell, Captain, 153
Capricieux, 180–1, 186
Caputo, Sarah, 126
cargoes, 21, 30, 33, 34, 35–7, 39, 40–1, 42, 43, 48, 156, 166, 210
Carpenter, Benjamin, 197
Carpenter, Joseph, 133–4
Carpenter, Mary, 197
Carpentier, F., 126

Carver, Peter, 178
Case, Captain Alan, 152
Cathalan, Etienne, 100, 101, 103, 105, 109, 171, 172–3
Cathcart, James, 119
Caulaincourt, Armand Augustin Louis de, 95
Cavanagh, J., 52, 73
Challenger, 145, 146, 147
Champagny, Jean-Baptiste de Nompère de, Duke of Cadore, 33–4, 79, 92–3, 201
chaplains, 68–70
Charabot, Antoine, 172
Charabot, Joseph, 172
Charles, 154, 155
Charleston, 194
Château de Brest, 46
Château de Dieppe, 46
Chatham, 181–2, 213, 216
Cherbourg, 46–7, 50, 103, 163, 179, 196
Choate, Jean, 125
cholera, 22
citizenship, 2, 4, 6–7, 112, 125–48, 212
    alteration of identities, 144–7, 169–70
    British-made documents, 139–41
    damaged French trust in American diplomats, 131, 132
    fraudulent use of documents, 137–8
    loss of documents, 135–7
    nationality test, 138–9
    naturalized Americans, 196–8
    and navigation laws, 128–9
    proving a seaman was not working for the enemy, 142–8
    proving to the French that a seaman was American not British, 130–42, 171
    replacement documents, 138
    Seaman's Protection Certificate, 3, 4, 112, 126, 127–8, 129, 130–5, 146, 147
civilians, 54–6
Clarke, General Henri-Jacques-Guillaume, Duke of Feltre, 84–5, 88, 96, 130, 132, 139, 147, 157, 166, 168, 206, 209
    and the 1807 release, 190, 191, 196
    1809 release failure, 201
Clarke, John, 20, 68
Clubb, Stephen, 44, 46, 51–2, 64, 65, 163, 193–4, 197–8, 231
Cockrane, William, 180

Coevorden, 53
Coffin, Captain Gorham, 48, 152
Coffyn, François, 100, 112, 195, 196
Committee for Public Safety, 87, 90, 126
Committee for Relief, 162, 193, 243
   Report from the Committee for the Relief of the British Prisoners in France (1812), 71, 155, 162, 167, 183, 231–2
Comtesse d'Orsène, 180
Constant, Benjamin, 122
Constantinople, 90
Constellation, USS, 20, 163
Consular Service *see* American diplomats
Cook, John, 52
Cook, Richard, 54
Cope, George Adam, 146–7
Copenhagen, 185
Coureur, 185
Cowell, William, 198
Crawford, William H., 20, 105, 106, 108, 109, 111, 185–6
   and American prisoners of war, 123, 188
   as Minister Plenipotentiary, 120–3, 214–16
   opinion of consuls, 122
crew lists, 142–4, 153
crimps, 16, 18
Crippen, Thomas, 158, 164
Crowhurst, Patrick, 36, 38
Cutting, Nathaniel, 104, 105, 106

Dancy, J. Ross, 125
Dartmoor Prison, 4, 5, 6, 173, 184, 213, 216, 217
Dauntless, 181
Dean, Abraham, 157–8
Deane, Silas, 97, 98
Debacq, Noël Jean, 88–90, 144
Decrès, Denis, Count (then Duke) Decrès, 79, 80, 139, 157, 159, 168, 199, 208–9, 210
   and the 1807 release, 189–91
Delaware, 110
Deptford, 145
Dey of Algiers, 117–19
Dieppe, 50, 144, 181, 198
Diligent, 136
Dillon, Lieutenant William Henry, 194–5
Diot, Jean, 100, 101, 105, 107, 112, 196, 199, 203, 207, 208, 210, 214, 217
Disabled Seaman's Act 1742, 143

discipline, 19–20, 25, 26
disease and health, 22–3, 25–6, 47, 52–3, 66–7, 69–70, 169, 170, 172, 180–1
Dixon, Henry, 131
Dodd, Ambrose, 184
Dolphin, 118
Donaldson, Joseph, 118, 119
Doolittle, Isaac, 199
Doric, Captain John, 200
Dossonville, Jean Baptiste, 81
Dryad, 156
Dubois, Benjamin, 107
Duché, Elodie, 45–6
Dunkirk, 100, 195, 196, 198
Durand, James, 25
Dye, Ira, 3, 121

Echo, 181
élargissement see release of prisoners
Eliza, 136, 192
Embargo Act 1807, 32, 144, 192
Embuscade, 181
Enterprise, 139, 160–1
Erving, George, 185
escapes, 135, 137, 156–7, 158, 160, 167–8, 175–6, 184, 224–6
   and privateering, 179, 180–1, 187
Espadon, 152
Ethalion, 138
Etoile no. 2, 180, 183–4
Euryalus, 183–4
The Evening Post, 163–4
Exertion, 179
exports *see* imports and exports

Fairie, 52
false flags, 35, 36, 39–40
Faren, Hugh, 63–4
Felton, Francis, 137, 165, 217
Fenwick, Joseph, 107, 108
Flora, 21, 134
Folger, Christopher, 195
Forbes, John, 133
Forest, Thomas, 154
Fouché, Joseph, Duke of Otranto, 81–2, 83, 130, 197
Fourca, Louis, 179, 180
Fowler, Joseph, 185–6
France
   financial aid to America, 77–8
   French prisoners of war, 67–8
   maritime law, 30–5, 33–5
   neutrality, 214, 217

280   INDEX

privateering law, 38–41
structure of government, 85
White Terror, 217
François, 177
Franklin, Benjamin, 97, 98, 111, 196
Fraser, Edward, 65
Freemasonry, 16–17, 18, 81, 111, 197
French Marine, 31, 80, 176, 199
    crew lists, 142–4
Friançon, Louis, 179
Friedenberg, Zachary B., 26
Fulton, Robert, 113, 119, 199
Fund for the Relief of Guernsey Prisoners
    in France, 70
Furet, 186

Gabrielson, Mark J., 45–6
Gates, Horatio, 113
Gendarmerie, 77
General Entry Books for American
    Prisoners of War, British prison
    depots, 3
General Gates, 102, 156–8
General Lincoln, 48, 152
*Geneva Convention on the Treatment of
    Prisoners of War*, 165
Ghent, 217
Gibbs, Edward, 181
Gibson, Alexander, 154
Gilje, Paul A., 3
Giot, Pierre
Givet, 53, 58, 61, 66, 69, 136, 159, 177, 178
Goodman, George, 131–3, 134, 196
Goulhot, Philippe Jean-Baptiste Nicolas,
    85–8, 89–90, 130, 133, 140, 144, 147,
    157, 160, 178, 188, 197, 205, 209
    and the 1807 release, 190–1
    on release of George D. Wilson, 167–8
Green, Henry, 145, 160–3, 164, 240
Grenoble, 168
Griffiths, Arthur, 45
Guidal, General Joseph, 172

Hale, John, 19
Haley, George, 20–1
Haley, Nathan, 21, 198–201, 204, 206–7,
    210
Hamburg, 99, 133
Happy Return, 200–1
Hardi, 198
Hare, 198
Harman, John, 157
Harmonie, 139
Harrison, Hugh, 139

Hartford Wits, 115
Hayes, Daniel, 194
Hazard, 185
Hearn, 19
Helicon, 152
Hero, 185
Holland Trader, 33
Homans, Benjamin, 15, 159, 164
Homans, John Wood, 159
Hopewell, 186
hospitals, 47, 66–7, 70, 163, 181
Houel, Charles Louis, 88, 90–1, 144, 205
Houmeau, Didier, 45
Hudson, Thomas, 175
Huffington, Captain, 192
Hulbert, Archer B., 116–17
Humphreys, David, 117, 118
Hussar, 47, 71, 137, 138
Hyades, 197

Imlay, Gilbert, 117, 199
imports and exports, 128
impressment, 4, 5–6, 23–7, 52, 71, 108–9,
    112, 125–6, 165, 212
    escapes from, 169–71
    impressed Americans and the Toulon
        Conspiracy, 168–74
    and nationality, 144–7
    release from, 139–40
Indomptable, 181
Insurgent, 161, 162
Intrépide, 36
Izette, 73

Jackson, Thomas, 102, 157
Jamaica, 145
Jarvis, Leonard, 47, 196
Jea, John, 44, 73, 207–8, 210, 230
Jean, 52
Jefferson, Thomas, 98, 111, 118, 122,
    199–200
Jersey, 185
Jersey, 12–13
Johnson, Emory R., 100
Johnson, James, 155–6
Jones, John Paul, 17, 105
Jones, William, 157
Joseph, 137
Juno, 186

Kaplan, Lawrence S., 202
Knight, William, 145
Kufstein, 93–4

La Hougue, 183
La Rochelle, 103
Lady Washington, 139
Lafayette, Marquis de, 86, 122
Laforêt, Antoine de, 95
Lanautte, Alexandre Maurice Blanc de, Comte d'Hauterive, 95, 95n61
Land, Isaac, 125
Langley, Harold D., 11, 16
Lark, 163
Lasalle, Captain Denis-Guillaume, 166
Le Goff, T.J.A., 177
Le Guellaff, Florence, 38
Le Havre, 101, 103, 104, 140, 203
Le Réhabilitateur ou l'Ami des opprimés, 90
Lee, Arthur, 97, 98
Lee, William, 15, 58, 103, 104–5, 108, 109, 114, 120, 122, 209
Lemisch, Jesse, 11
Lespagnol, André, 38
Letters of Marque, 39, 177, 204
Lewis, Asa, 153
Lewis, Benjamin, 198
Lewis, Michael, 45, 55, 57, 167
Lexhorn, John, 155
Leyden, 156
lice, 22, 66, 170–1
Linnell, Joshua, 137–8, 184
Liverpool, 16–17
Livingston, Edward, 112–13
Livingston, John R., 104, 105, 113
Livingston, Robert R., 105, 108, 109, 140
 and the Louisiana Purchase, 112, 188
 as Minister Plenipotentiary, 111–13, 188
Livorno, 19, 99
Lloyd's Patriotic Fund, 70
Longwy, 50, 53, 58, 66, 133, 137
Lorient, 101, 103, 105, 198, 208
Louis XVI, 78, 83, 86, 88
Louisiana Purchase 1803, 112, 202
Loup Marin, 134–5, 180

Madison, James, 34, 101–2, 131, 196, 204
Maky, Thomas, 179, 182
Maraudeur, 181
Maret, Hugues-Bernard, Duke of Bassano, 93–4, 119–20, 185–6, 203, 206
Maria, 118, 163
Mariner, Joshua, 145
maritime law, 29
 avoidance of regulations, 36–7
 Britain, 30, 33
 broken voyages and re-exporting, 36–7
 cargoes, 35–7
 and citizenship, 128–9
 false flags, 35, 36, 39–40
 France, 30–5
 privateering law, 38–41
 registration papers for ships and cargoes, 34–6, 43
 United States, 31, 32, 33–4
Maritime United Society, 70
Mark, Peter, 179, 180
marriage, 23, 69, 197
Mars, 173
Marseilles, 100, 103, 168–9, 171, 172–3
Martin, Thomas, 182–3, 183–4
Mary & Eliza, 163–4
Marzagalli, Silvia, 37
Massachusetts, 152, 222–3
May, William, 137
McChord, John, 145
McClure, James, 196, 197–8
McLeod, Colin, 121
mental health, 22–3, 26
Mentor, 54
merchant seamen
 abandonment by captains/masters, 20–1, 100
 burden of relief for, 100–4
 captains, authority and power of, 19–20
 on captured vessels, 42–3
 descriptions of, 12
 desertions, 102
 disease and health, 22–3
 distressed/stranded seamen, 99–100, 101–2, 103, 109–10, 188
 in the early republic, 11–28
 employment opportunities, 14–16, 18–19, 37
 enslavement of, 117–19
 needs of, 98, 99–101
 separation from naval sailors, 11, 12
 shipboard life, 21–2, 25–6, 28
 social attitudes to, 13–14, 18
 unskilled, 15
 vulnerability, 23
 wages, 14–15, 16, 20, 24, 28, 37, 48
 wild behaviour on shore, 102
 see also American prisoners of war; citizenship; nationality
Meteor, 157
Metz, 66–7
Meyer, Christopher, 102
Mezières, 191
Milan Decree, 32, 33, 34, 36, 103, 114, 129
Minerva, 131, 166

Ministère de la Guerre (Ministry of War), 77, 79, 83–91, 95–6, 132, 144, 157, 188, 197, 201, 205
  Pensions division, 85, 87, 90
  reforms and upheavals, 89–90
Ministère de la Marine et des Colonies (Ministry of Marine and Colonies), 77, 79, 80–1, 95, 144, 154, 157, 188, 211
Ministère de la Police générale (Ministry of Police General), 77, 81–3, 83, 95–6
Ministère des Relations Extérieurs (Ministry of External Relations), 77, 92–6, 147, 188, 191, 201
Ministers Plenipotentiary, 1, 20, 47, 78, 95, 96, 99, 105, 111–24, 134, 151, 185–6, 188
  creation of a hierarchy, 123–4
  see also Armstrong, John; Barlow, Joel; Crawford, William H.; Livingston, Robert R.
Ministry of Justice, 56, 77, 79
Ministry of the Interior, 77, 95–6
Minotaur, 71, 154–6, 158
Minute, 184–5
Mitchell, Caster, 27
Moniteur Universel, 93
Monroe, James, 6, 78, 118, 132, 196, 215
Mont Dauphin, 53
Moreau-Zanelli, Jocelyne, 116–17
Morieux, Renaud, 46, 47, 50, 143, 174
Morlaix, 100, 107, 136, 152, 153, 173, 196, 207–8, 215
Morris, Gouverneur, 105, 112
Morris, Robert, 182
Mountflorence, James, 108, 110
Mulvey, Farrell, 71
Murat, Inès, 202

Nancy, 53
Nantes, 103, 154, 157, 196
Napoleon, 1, 5, 30–1, 32, 33, 33–4, 54, 132, 140, 159, 177, 188, 197, 202
  and the 1807 release, 190–1
  1809 release failure, 201
  and the 1813 release, 208–9, 210
  exile, 202
  interest in America, 202
  minister appointments, 79
  and the proposed 1812 release, 205–6
Narcissus, 25

nationality, 2, 29, 34–5, 38, 41–2, 77, 125, 212
  and flags, 143
  and impressment, 144–7
  nationality test, 138–9
  proving that a seaman was American not British, 130–42
  verification, 126
Naval Act 1794, 12
Navigation Act 1651, 30, 128
Navigation Act 1660, 30, 128
Nehill (Neal), John, 137, 162–3, 164, 193
Neptune, 33
Neutrality Act 1794, 185
New York, 12–13, 145, 198, 215
newspapers, 3, 55, 108–9, 133, 202, 230
Nichols, John, 131, 134, 196
Niger, 139
Non-Importation Act 1806, 31
Non-Intercourse Act 1809, 32, 33
Norris, Joseph, 135
Northumberland, 162
Northwest Ordinance 1787, 116

O'Brien, Captain Donat Henchy, 68, 134
Ocean, 136
Ohio Company, 116
Oxnard, Thomas, 206–7, 210

Pacaud, Mr, 142, 189, 191
Paine, Thomas, 112, 199
Palfrey, William, 105
Paris, 86, 103–4, 106, 108, 110, 114, 122, 195
Parker, Daniel, 106, 111, 112, 113, 114, 116, 117, 123
passports, 77, 82, 98, 120, 212
  see also Seaman's Protection Certificate
Patrick, William, 183
Patriote, 160
Patterson, William, 196
Peace, 54
Pelican, 121
Perkins, Thomas, 192
Perl-Rosenthal, Nathan, 126, 127, 212
Persévérant, 180
Phénix, 154
Philadelphia, 145, 146, 147, 159
Philadelphia, USS, 162
Phoebe, 133
Pille, Louis-Alexandre, 88

pirates, 27–8, 29, 39, 42–3, 129
Pitcairn, Joseph, 133
plague, 169, 170
Playfair, William, 116, 117
Plumper, 182–3, 184
pneumonia, 22
police, 77, 81–3, 95–6
Police Bulletin, 194
Polly, 173, 179
Portchester Prison, 173
Porter, Joshua, 137–8, 184
Port-Saint-Louis, 169
Portsmouth (England), 68, 184, 216
Pourvoyeur, 181
Preble, Henry, 200, 203, 204–5, 206, 210, 230
Prefecture of the Police of the Seine, 82–3
Preira, Antoine-Joseph (Balidar), 181
priests, 87, 90, 91
Princesse de Bologne, 166
prison depots, 53–60
    allowances, 64–5
    conditions, 46–7, 167, 211
    escapes, 63, 67, 68
    food shortages, 64–5, 163
    forced labour, 63–4
    government of, 59
    living conditions, 60–73
    musters, 62–3
    prisoners' letters, 62
    schools, 69, 71
prison ships and hulks, 13, 61, 63, 68, 165, 173, 181, 184, 216, 239
prisoners of war *see* American prisoners of war; British prisoners of war
privateering, 2, 19, 27–8, 37, 78, 101, 107, 136, 166, 212–13, 215
    Algerine privateers, 118
    American privateers, 6, 203–4, 217
    bad prizes, 152–3
    "capture" of own vessels, 198
    crews and recruitment, 151, 177–80, 184–7, 204–10
    cycle of seamen's captures, 181–4
    French privateering law, 38–41, 177
    Letters of Marque, 39, 177, 204
    pay and prize money, 179–80, 187
    reality for crews of captured vessels, 42–3
Prize Council, 41, 42, 48, 49, 107, 152
Prosperity, 160
Puerto Pasajes, 194

Purcell, John, 140–1, 188
Putney, Martha S., 239, 242, 244

Quasi-War, 38, 79, 110

Radius, 185
Rambouillet Decree, 33, 114, 144
Rand, John, 136
ransoms, 27, 117–18, 119, 163
Rediker, Marcus, 11
registration papers (for ships), 34–6, 43
Réglement Sur les Armemens en course, 39
Regulus, 158
release of prisoners, 82, 93, 110–11, 112, 114, 120, 126, 140, 144
    1807 release, 189–98, 218–19
    1809 release failure, 198–202
    1813 release, 202–10, 219–22
    after escaping, 157–8
    British prisoners of war, 216
    captures from the *General Gates* by the *Abercrombie*, 156–8
    as a cause of distress to seamen, 215–17
    compassion cases, 158–60, 164
    cycle of captures, 181–4
    exchanges, 61, 62, 73, 94, 95, 112, 151, 152, 211
    fighting/serving with the French, 166, 175–87
    fighting/serving with the French seen as treason, 184–7
    impressed Americans and the Toulon Conspiracy, 168–74
    individual releases, 223
    lack of ships back to America, 214–15, 217
    from the *Massachusetts and Saratoga*, 222–3
    negotiated releases, 188–210
    passengers, 153–4, 159–60
    prisoner in Algiers, 163–4
    prisoners on the *Minotaur*, 154–6
    ransoms, 27, 117–18, 119, 163
    release of Americans from British prisons, 215
    sailors of the United States Navy, 160–3
    trading information for freedom, 165–74
    types of, 151

Relief and Protection of American Seamen (1796 legislation), 112–13
Relief of Distressed Seamen in the Ports of Europe (report), 103
Rennes, 53
research sources, 2–4, 45–6, 230–45
   African-American seamen, 239–45
   Archives départmentales (AD), 236–7
   Archives diplomatiques (Arch. dip.), 235
   Archives nationales (Arch. nat.), 235
   British sources, 238–9
   French sources, 232–7
   future work, 212–13
   Service Historique de la Défense (SHD), 233–5
   United States sources, 237
Rhin, 173
Rhode Island, 145, 157
Richardson, William, 170, 172, 173, 173–4, 179, 180, 182
Riley, John, 135
Ripner, William, 198, 199
Rively, Thomas, 179, 180
Robertson, John, 57
Rocher, Joseph, 131, 134, 196
Rodeur, 186
Roi de Naples, 181
Rolla, 36
Roscoff, 50, 152
Rose, 133
Rotch, William, 195
Rouanet, David, 45, 50, 178
Rouen, 88, 126
Royal Navy, 5–6, 11, 13–14, 19–20, 31, 121, 129, 135, 184, 186–7, 213, 215
   captured ships, 182–3
   crew lists, 142–4
   escorting convoys, 37, 38
   floggings, 165
   impressment, 4, 5–6, 23–7, 52, 71, 108–9, 112, 125, 139–40, 144–7, 165
   sea patrols, 37–8
   shipboard life, 28
   Transport Board, 211
Russell, Bedford, 134–5
Russell, John, 145
Russell, Jonathan, 100–4, 103–4, 178, 199, 201, 203, 217

Saint Anne, 154
Saint Malo, 50, 177, 182
Saint Servan, 105, 107
Sally, 179
San Joseph, 173–4, 179, 180, 182
Santa Maria, 153
Saratoga, 152, 223
Sarrelibre, 53, 58, 59, 60, 66, 160, 181, 183, 184, 191
Sauvage, 197
Savage, William, 127
Savary, Anne Jean Marie René, Duke of Rovigo, 81, 96, 132
Schalck de la Faverie, Alfred, 202
Scioto Company, 116
scurvy, 26
Seaman's Protection Certificate, 3, 4, 112, 126, 127–8, 129, 146, 147, 151, 162, 167, 169, 184, 191, 193, 212, 240–1, 242–3
   forging of, 130–1
   given to British prisoners of war, 130–4, 135
   loss of, 135–7
   replacement documents, 138
   use by imposters, 138
Seaver, Benjamin Franklin, 20–1, 199
Secret Police, 81
Sedan, 53, 59
Service Historique de la Défense, 2
sexually transmitted diseases, 22
Shannon, 26, 71, 145, 161, 162, 240
Shaw, William, 194, 195
Sir William Douglas, 194
Skeen, Edward, 113–14
Skipwith, Fulwar, 72, 103, 104, 105, 106, 107, 109, 123, 126, 130, 184, 188, 217
   animosity towards Armstrong, 189
   assistance to prisoners of war, 160–3, 163, 178, 189, 194
   census of prisoners, 141–2, 189, 191
   and distressed seamen, 110, 133, 138
   proposal for nationality test, 138–9
slavery, 27–8, 117–19, 194–5
smallpox, 22, 92, 173
Smith, George F., 163–4
Smith, John, 101
Smith, William, 184–5, 186
Sorcière, 133
Sparrow, Elizabeth, 172
Sparrow, Vickary, 198
spies, 81, 82, 97, 130, 172, 199, 235
Stag, 134
Stewart, Thomas, 179, 180
Stoffers, J., 21

INDEX 285

Stralsund, 184, 185
Strawbridge, James, 159, 164
Success, 185
Swan, James, 117, 199

Talleyrand-Périgord, Charles Maurice de, 79, 92, 94, 95, 109, 110, 199, 215
Teazer, 182–3
terminology, 7–8
Thomas, Richard, 171
Tom, 182
Tonnante, 169–70, 170
Torris, Jean François, 112, 198–9
Toulon Conspiracy, 168–74
Tour Solidor, Saint-Servan, 46
trade, 13, 30
  restrictions, 31–2
  United States terminates trade with Britain, 34
treason, 178–9, 184–7
Treaty of Amity and Commerce Between the United States and France (1778), 78, 98
Treaty of Amity, Commerce and Navigation (Jay Treaty) (1794), 78, 129
Tripoli, 162, 193
True-Blooded Yankee, 204, 206–7, 209, 216, 230
tuberculosis, 22, 159
Tucker, Samuel, 145
Two Brothers, 136
Tyler, Royall, 27
typhus, 26, 66, 170–1

Undaunted, 169, 170, 171–2, 173, 174, 184
Union, 201
United States
  Consular Service, creation of, 97–103
  Declaration of Independence, 111
  declares war on Britain, 1
  Department of State, 146, 147, 159
  maritime law, 31, 32, 33–4
  neutrality, 1, 19, 31, 33–6, 41–2, 126, 212
  response to impressment, 125–6
  state cohesion, lack of, 13
  terminates trade with Britain, 34
United States Congress, 13, 99, 113, 116, 118, 127
United States Navy, 12, 13–14, 14–15, 20, 203

Vail, Aaron, 101, 105, 107, 109, 121–2, 123, 207, 208, 215, 217
Vaillant, 194
Valenciennes, 50, 53, 58, 61, 63–4, 66, 132, 136, 140, 155, 162, 163, 177, 180, 183, 191
Van, John, 136
Vauban, 53, 59, 60, 167
Vedra, 133
Verdun, 44–5, 50, 53, 54, 55–6, 57, 58, 64, 69, 71, 130, 131, 133, 134, 137, 178, 191, 194–5
Vigilant, 201
Villet, Charles, 130
Villiers, Patrick, 38
Vincennes, 63
violence, 23, 59, 69, 86
Volontaire, 171

wages, 14–15, 16, 20, 24, 28, 37, 48
Wallabout Bay, 13
War of 1812, 2, 5, 6, 34, 94, 120, 135, 184, 185, 189, 201–3, 213, 214, 216, 217
Ward, John, 181
Warden, David Bailie, 23, 103, 105, 108, 114, 119–20, 122, 132, 195, 209, 214, 217
Warspite, 173
Washington, George, 113, 115
Wasp, 215–16
Waterman, Stephen, 54
Wellington, Duke of, 122, 214
whalers, 195
William & Emma, 194
Williams, John, 145
Williams, Thomas, 178
Wilson, George D., 166–8, 174
Wiltshire, John, 135, 178, 216
Wirion, General Louis, 56, 71, 194–5
Wolfe, Reverend Robert, 69–70, 178
Wolverine, 173
Woodward, Charles, 154, 155
Worms, René, 38
Wright, Hannah, 106

Yarico, 203
yellow fever, 22
Young, William, 136

Zimmerman, James Fulton, 125

Printed in the United States
by Baker & Taylor Publisher Services